My Boyfriend
IS A
BEAR

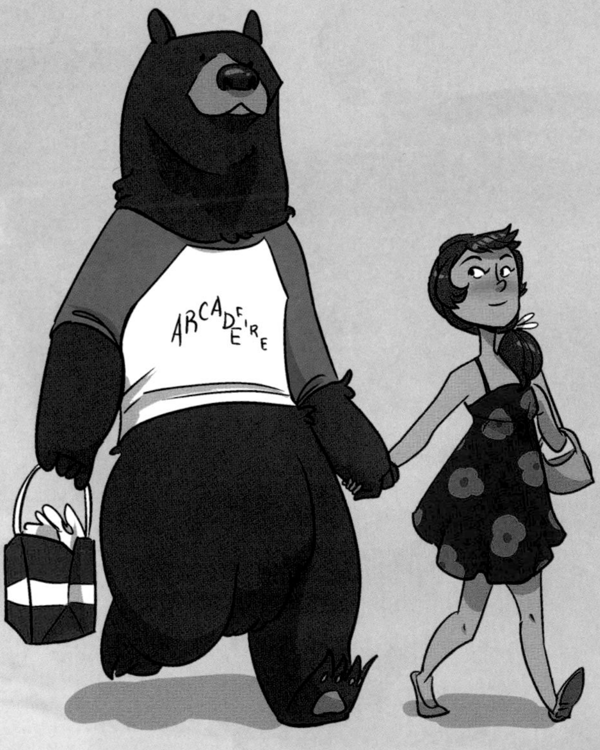
ARCADE FIRE

My Boyfriend IS A BEAR

written by
PAMELA RIBON

illustrated and colored by
CAT FARRIS

♥

lettered by
SAIDA TEMOFONTE

color assists by
**CAITLIN LIKE, GABRIEL FISCHER,
RON CHAN, ALLYSON WILLSEY & JON SIRUNO**

ONI PRESS

AN ONI PRESS PUBLICATION

GRAPHIC
RIB

designed by **Kate Z. Stone**
edited by **Ari Yarwood** and **Charlie Chu**

♥

Published by Oni Press, Inc.

Joe Nozemack founder & chief financial officer
James Lucas Jones publisher
Charlie Chu v.p. of creative & business development
Brad Rooks director of operations
Rachel Reed marketing manager
Melissa Meszaros publicity manager
Troy Look director of design & production
Hilary Thompson senior graphic designer
Kate Z. Stone junior graphic designer
Angie Knowles digital prepress lead
Ari Yarwood executive editor
Robin Herrera senior editor
Desiree Wilson associate editor
Alissa Sallah administrative assistant
Jung Lee logistics associate

onipress.com
facebook.com/onipress
twitter.com/onipress
onipress.tumblr.com
instagram.com/onipress

pamie.com / @pamelaribon
cattifer.com / @Cattifer

First Edition: April 2018
ISBN 978-1-62010-487-3
eISBN 978-1-62010-488-0
Library of Congress Control Number: 2017952716

For Jason.
You ripped open that "It's It"
and that was it for me.
***Grah*.**

PAMELA RIBON

♥

For Ron.
Thanks for bearing with me.

CAT FARRIS

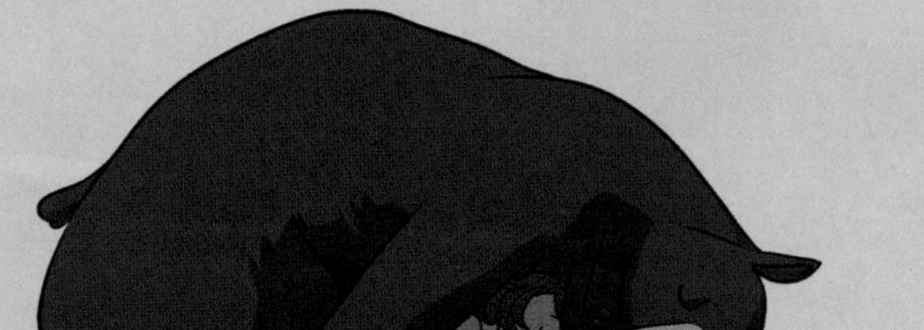

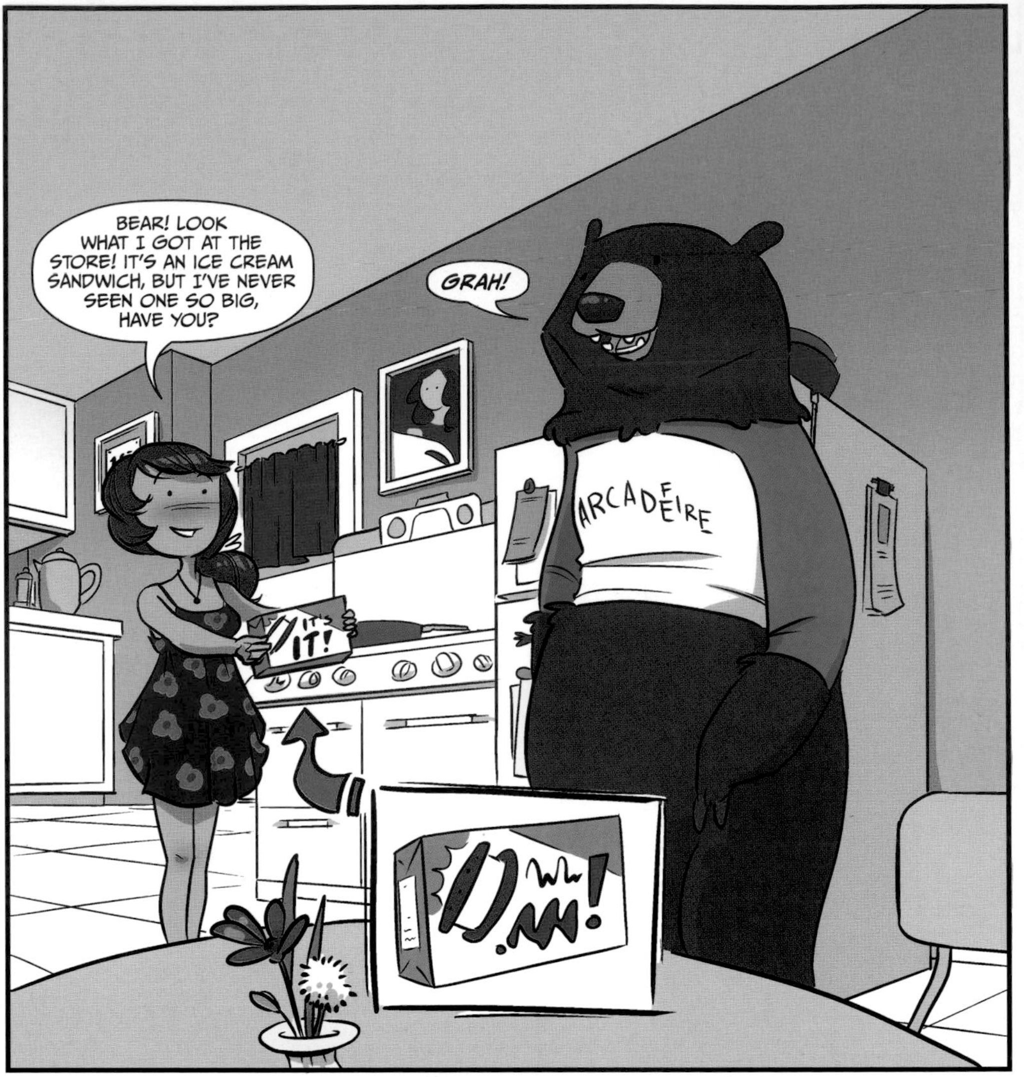
BEAR! LOOK WHAT I GOT AT THE STORE! IT'S AN ICE CREAM SANDWICH, BUT I'VE NEVER SEEN ONE SO BIG, HAVE YOU?
GRAH!
ARCADE FIRE
IT'S IT!

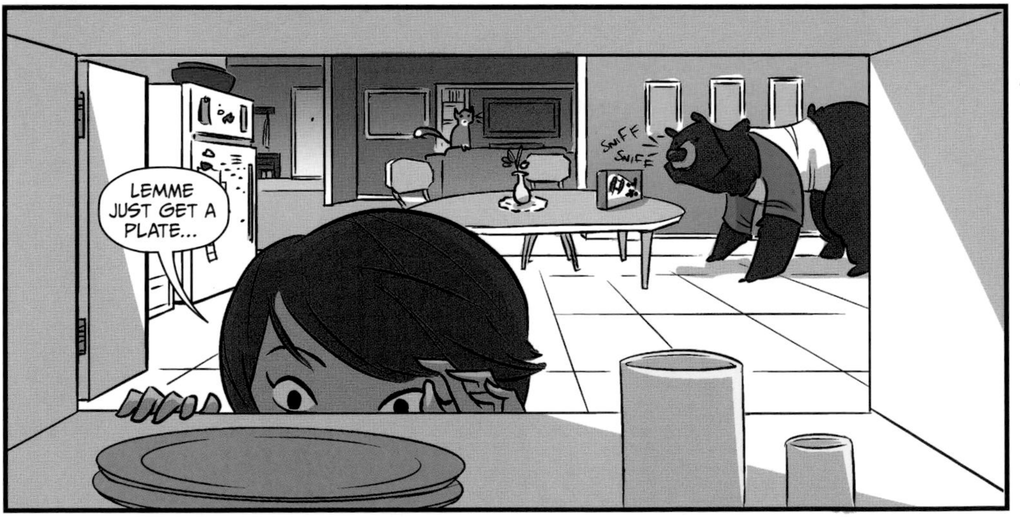
LEMME JUST GET A PLATE...
SNIFF SNIFF

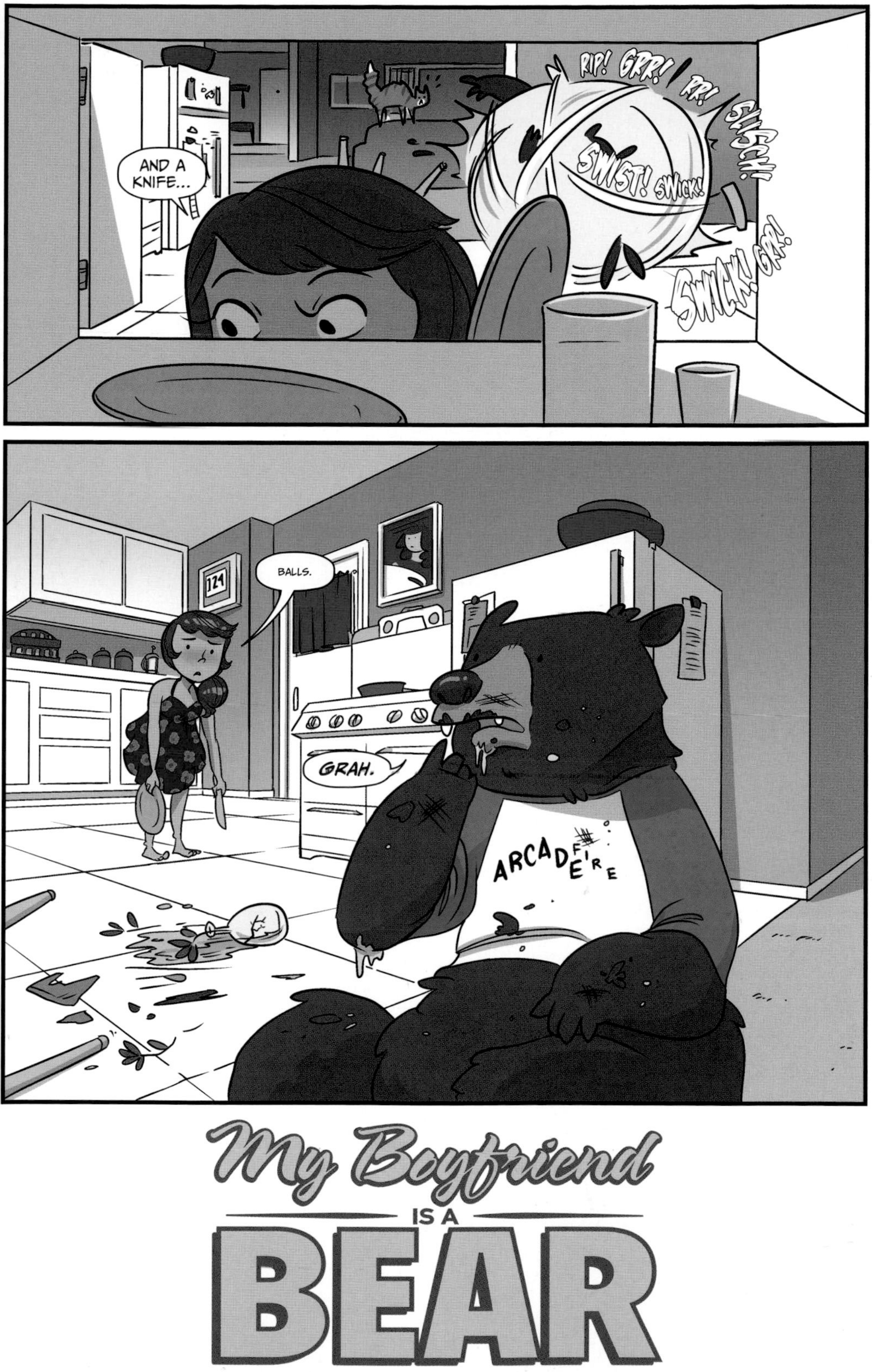
AND A KNIFE...
RIP! GRR! RR!
SLISCH!
SWIST! SWICK!
SWICK! GRR!
BALLS.
GRAH.

My Boyfriend IS A BEAR

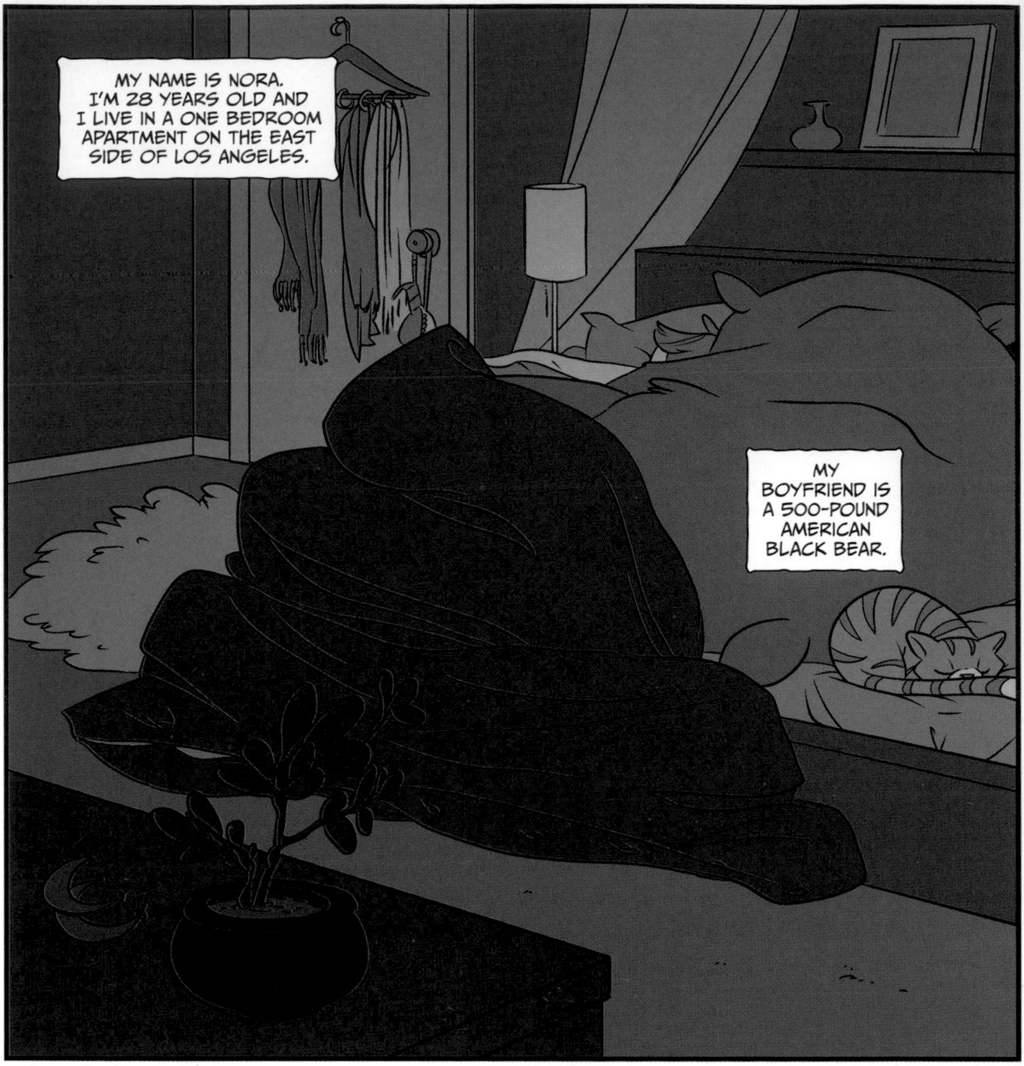
MY NAME IS NORA. I'M 28 YEARS OLD AND I LIVE IN A ONE BEDROOM APARTMENT ON THE EAST SIDE OF LOS ANGELES.
MY BOYFRIEND IS A 500-POUND AMERICAN BLACK BEAR.

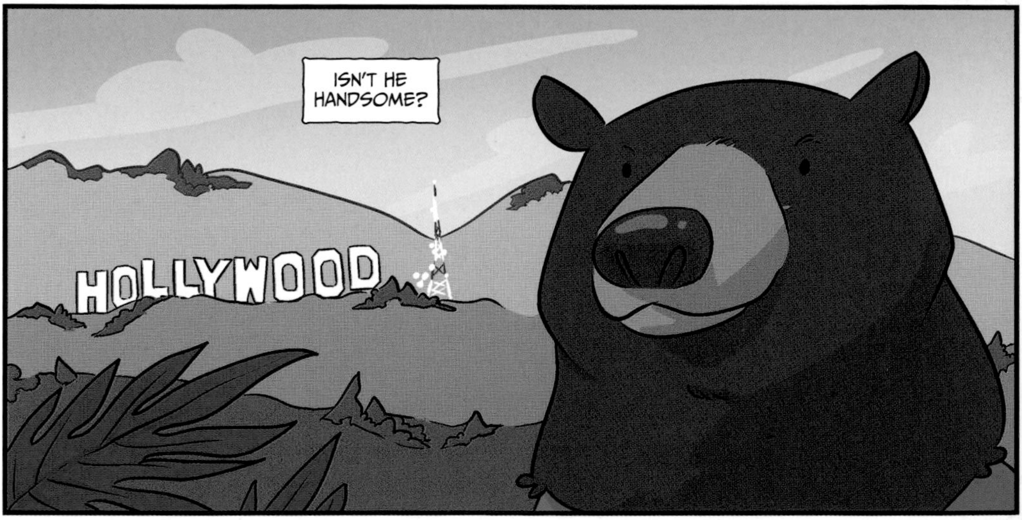
ISN'T HE HANDSOME?
HOLLYWOOD

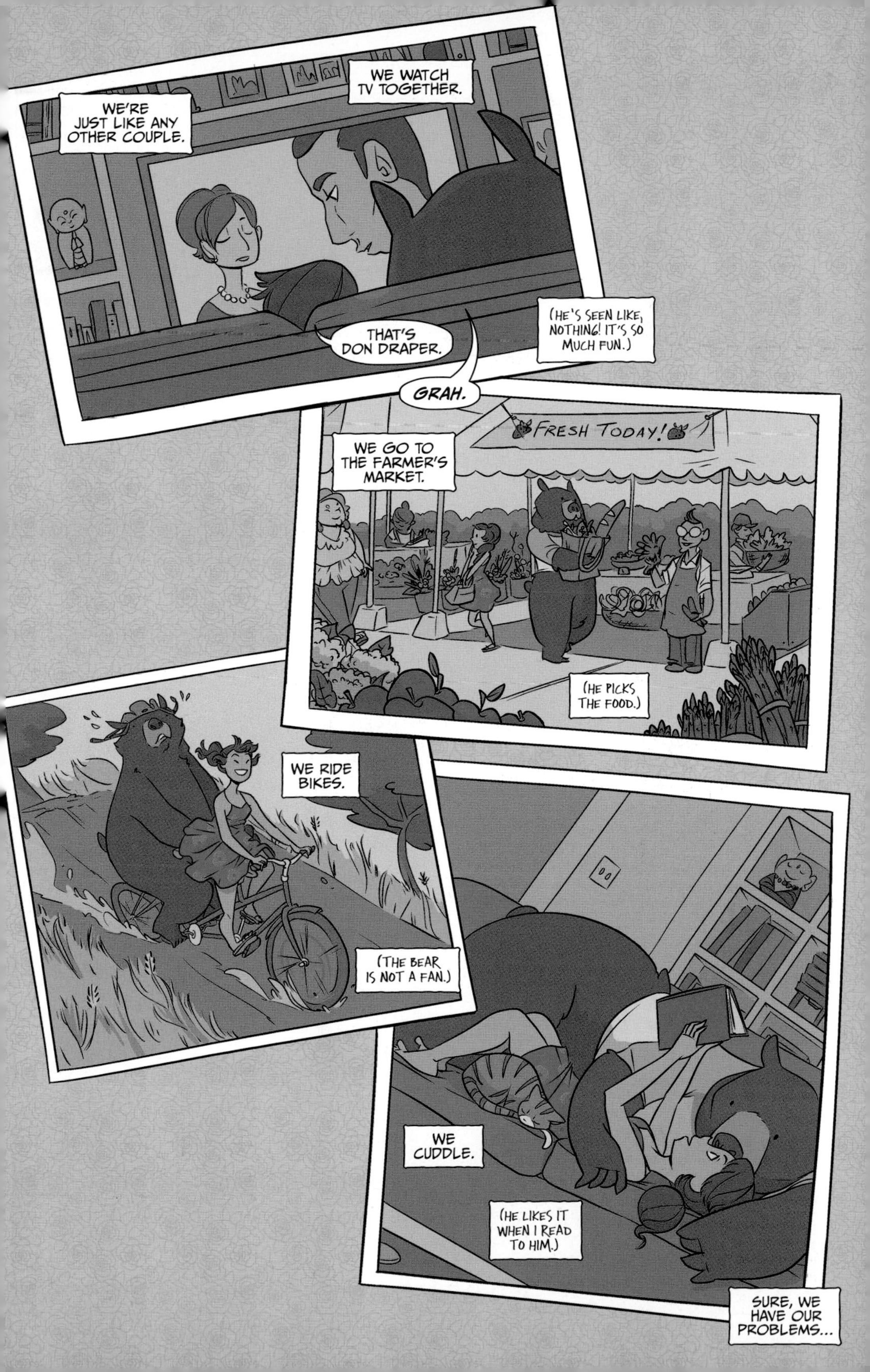
WE'RE JUST LIKE ANY OTHER COUPLE.
WE WATCH TV TOGETHER.
THAT'S DON DRAPER.
GRAH.
(HE'S SEEN LIKE, NOTHING! IT'S SO MUCH FUN.)
WE GO TO THE FARMER'S MARKET.
FRESH TODAY!
(HE PICKS THE FOOD.)
WE RIDE BIKES.
(THE BEAR IS NOT A FAN.)
WE CUDDLE.
(HE LIKES IT WHEN I READ TO HIM.)
SURE, WE HAVE OUR PROBLEMS...

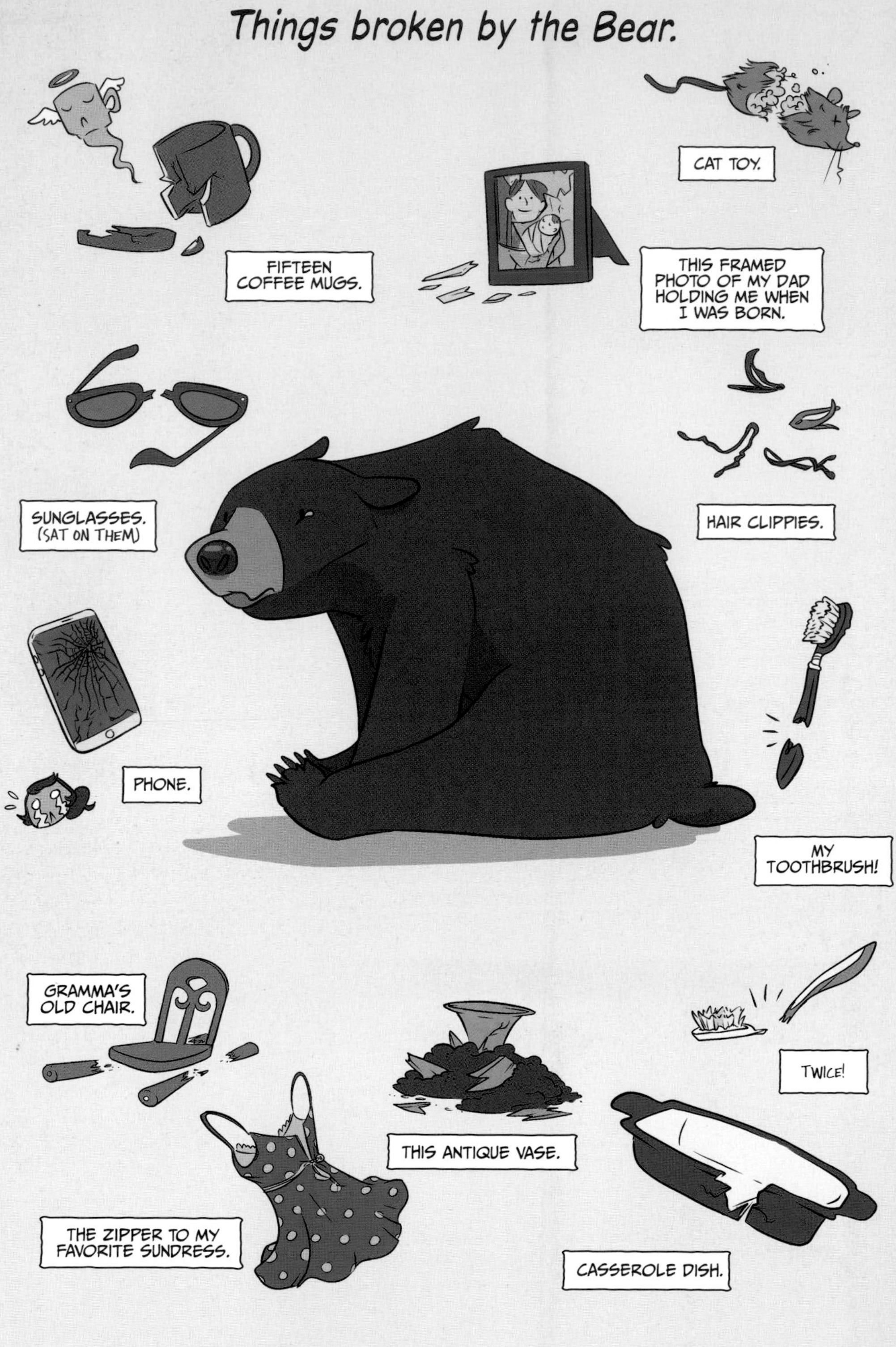
Things broken by the Bear.
FIFTEEN COFFEE MUGS.
THIS FRAMED PHOTO OF MY DAD HOLDING ME WHEN I WAS BORN.
CAT TOY.
SUNGLASSES. (SAT ON THEM)
HAIR CLIPPIES.
PHONE.
MY TOOTHBRUSH!
GRAMMA'S OLD CHAIR.
THIS ANTIQUE VASE.
TWICE!
THE ZIPPER TO MY FAVORITE SUNDRESS.
CASSEROLE DISH.

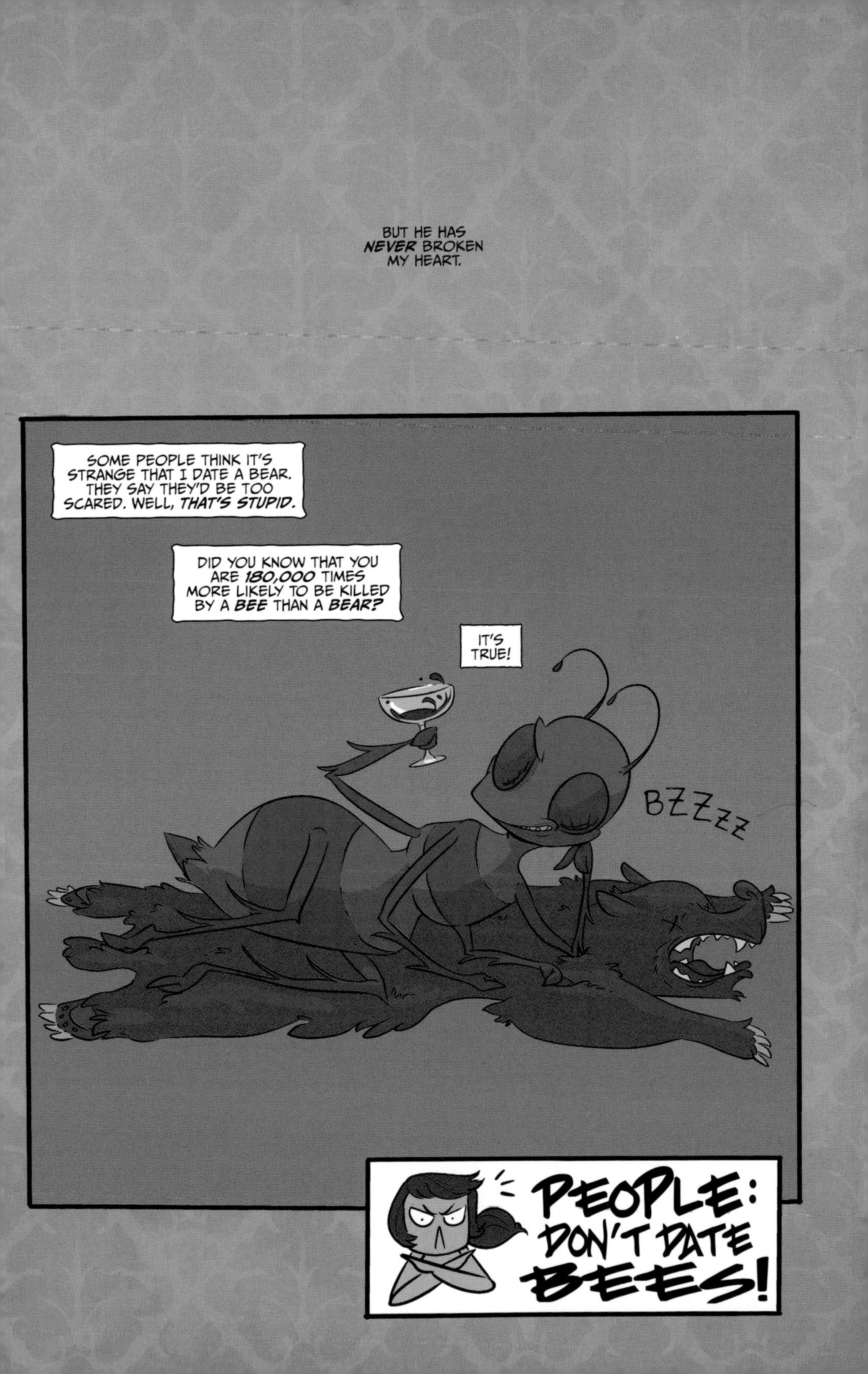
BUT HE HAS NEVER BROKEN MY HEART.
SOME PEOPLE THINK IT'S STRANGE THAT I DATE A BEAR. THEY SAY THEY'D BE TOO SCARED. WELL, THAT'S STUPID.
DID YOU KNOW THAT YOU ARE 180,000 TIMES MORE LIKELY TO BE KILLED BY A BEE THAN A BEAR?
IT'S TRUE!
BZZzz
PEOPLE: DON'T DATE BEES!

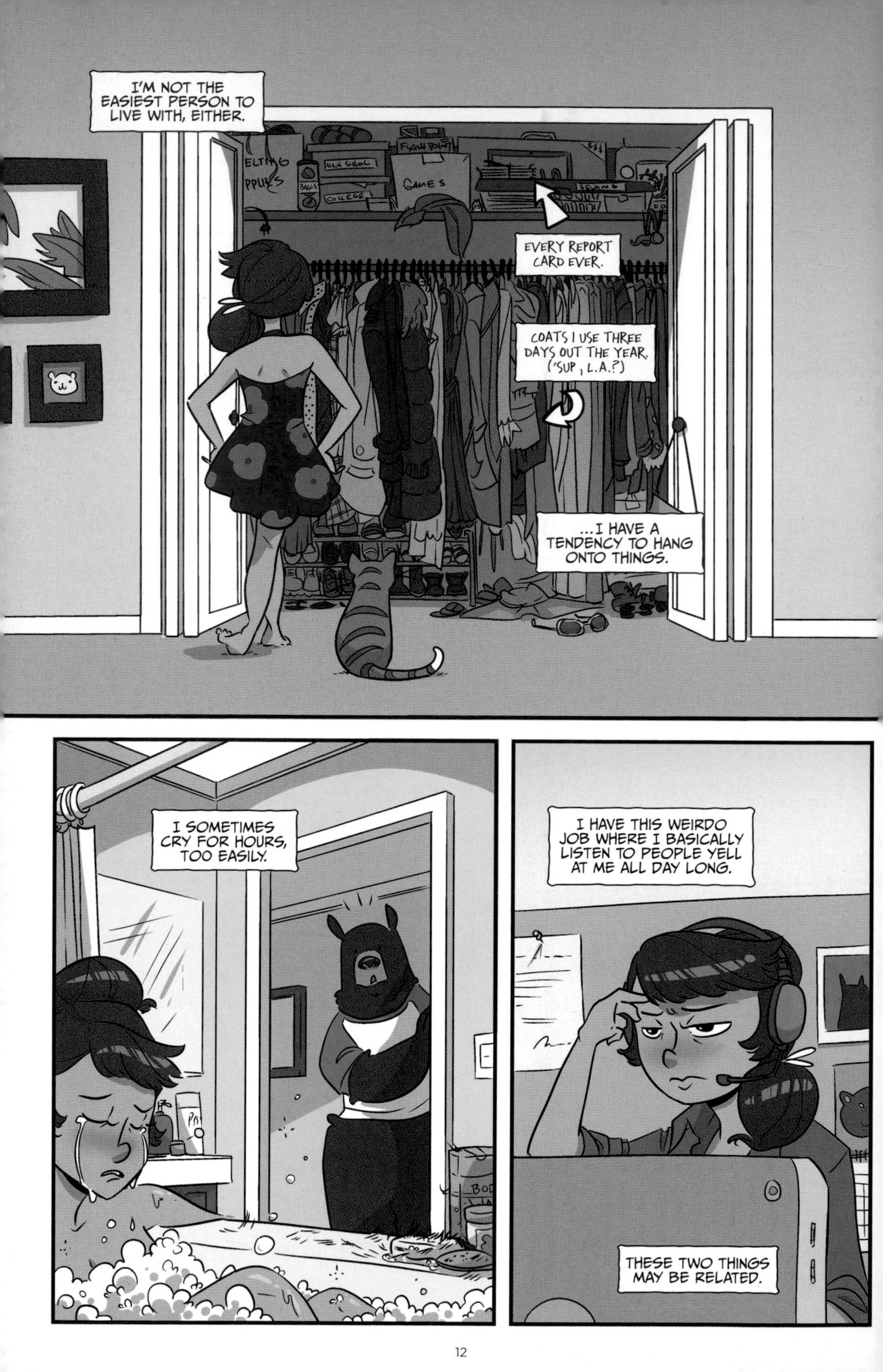
I'M NOT THE EASIEST PERSON TO LIVE WITH, EITHER.
GAMES
EVERY REPORT CARD EVER.
COATS I USE THREE DAYS OUT THE YEAR. ('SUP, L.A.?)
...I HAVE A TENDENCY TO HANG ONTO THINGS.
I SOMETIMES CRY FOR HOURS, TOO EASILY.
I HAVE THIS WEIRDO JOB WHERE I BASICALLY LISTEN TO PEOPLE YELL AT ME ALL DAY LONG.
THESE TWO THINGS MAY BE RELATED.

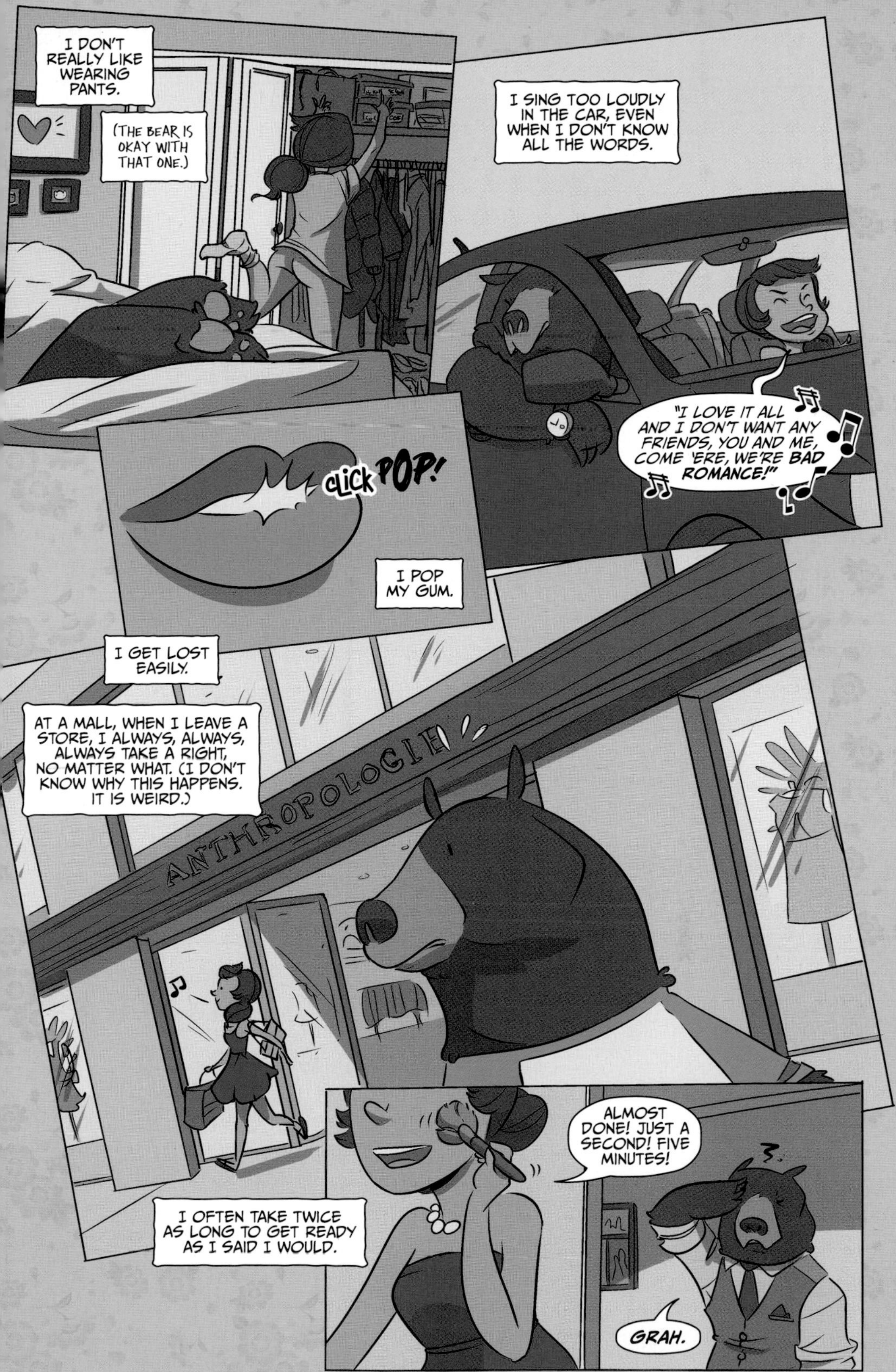
I DON'T REALLY LIKE WEARING PANTS.
(THE BEAR IS OKAY WITH THAT ONE.)
I SING TOO LOUDLY IN THE CAR, EVEN WHEN I DON'T KNOW ALL THE WORDS.
"I LOVE IT ALL AND I DON'T WANT ANY FRIENDS, YOU AND ME, COME 'ERE, WE'RE BAD ROMANCE!"
CLICK POP!
I POP MY GUM.
I GET LOST EASILY.
AT A MALL, WHEN I LEAVE A STORE, I ALWAYS, ALWAYS, ALWAYS TAKE A RIGHT, NO MATTER WHAT. (I DON'T KNOW WHY THIS HAPPENS. IT IS WEIRD.)
ANTHROPOLOGIE
I OFTEN TAKE TWICE AS LONG TO GET READY AS I SAID I WOULD.
ALMOST DONE! JUST A SECOND! FIVE MINUTES!
GRAH.

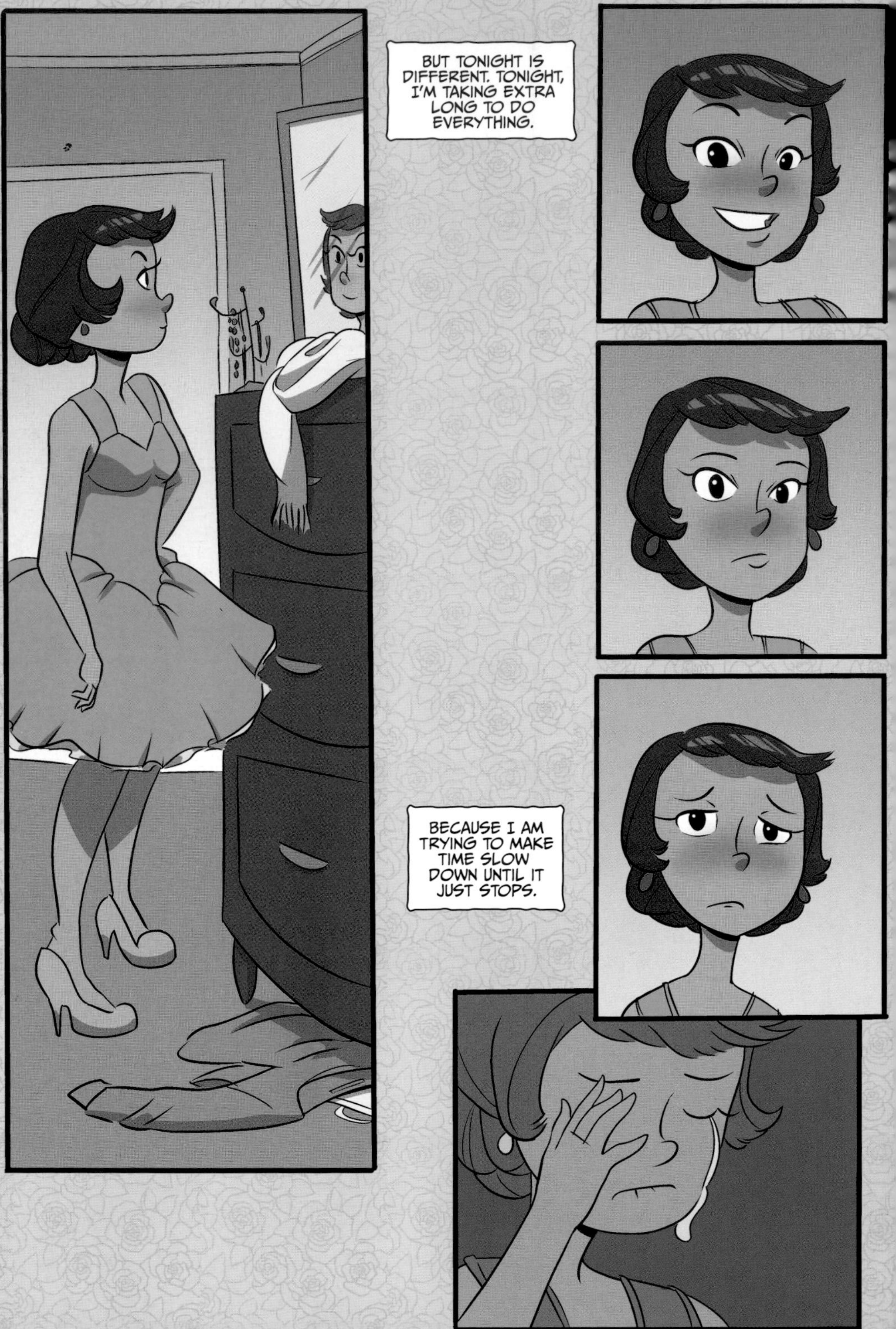
BUT TONIGHT IS DIFFERENT. TONIGHT, I'M TAKING EXTRA LONG TO DO EVERYTHING.
BECAUSE I AM TRYING TO MAKE TIME SLOW DOWN UNTIL IT JUST STOPS.

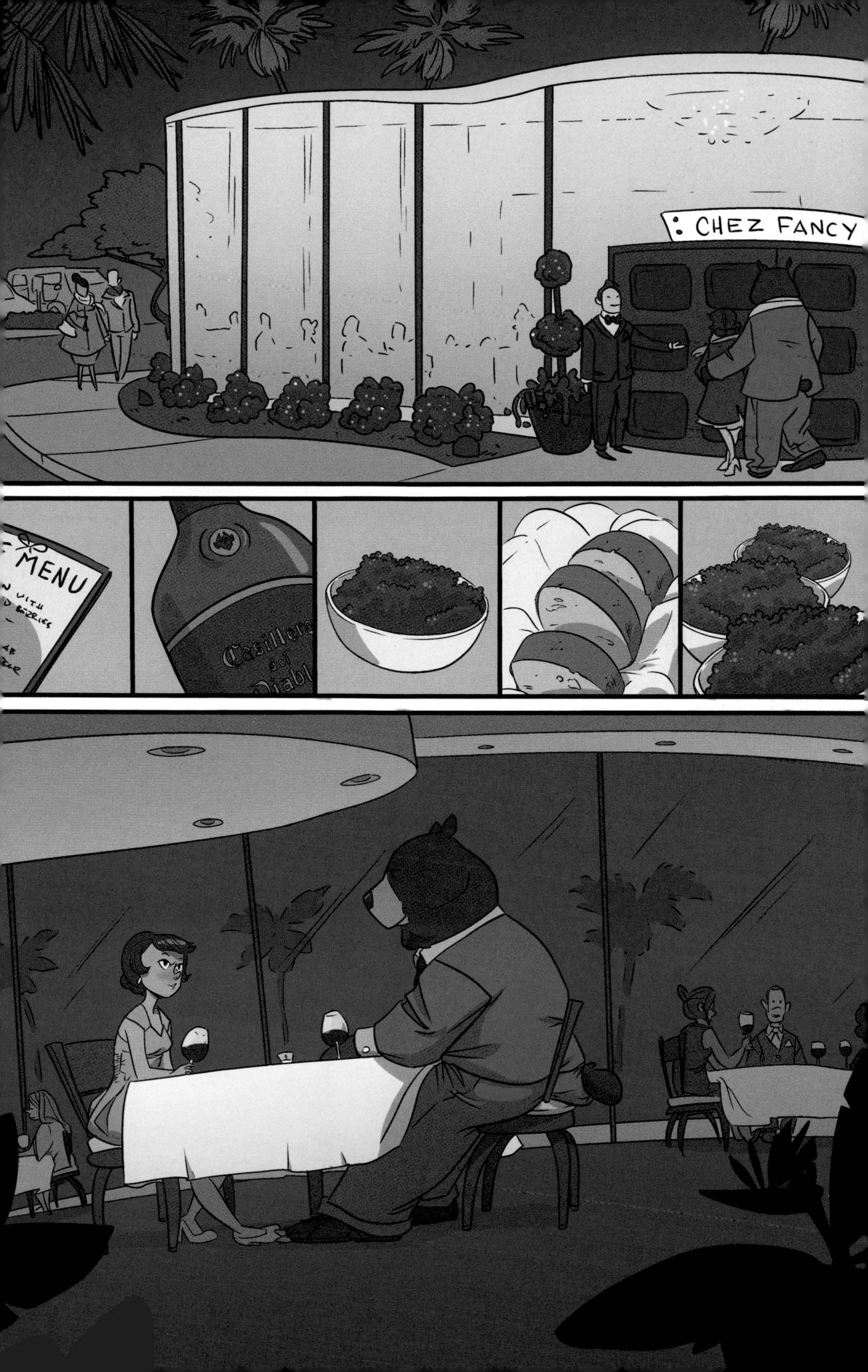
CHEZ FANCY
MENU
Casillero
del

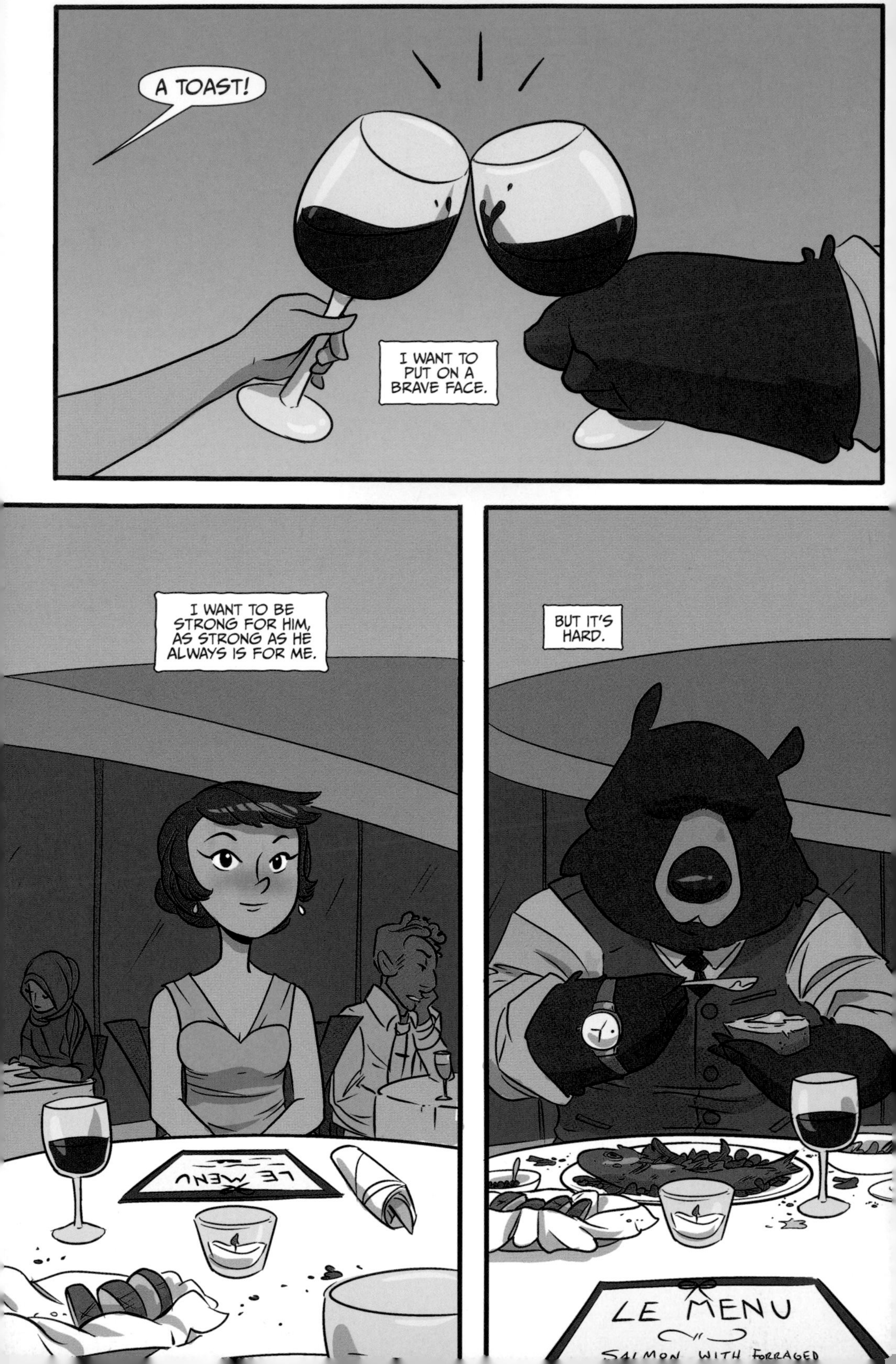
A TOAST!
I WANT TO PUT ON A BRAVE FACE.
I WANT TO BE STRONG FOR HIM, AS STRONG AS HE ALWAYS IS FOR ME.
BUT IT'S HARD.
LE MENU
SALMON WITH FORRAGED

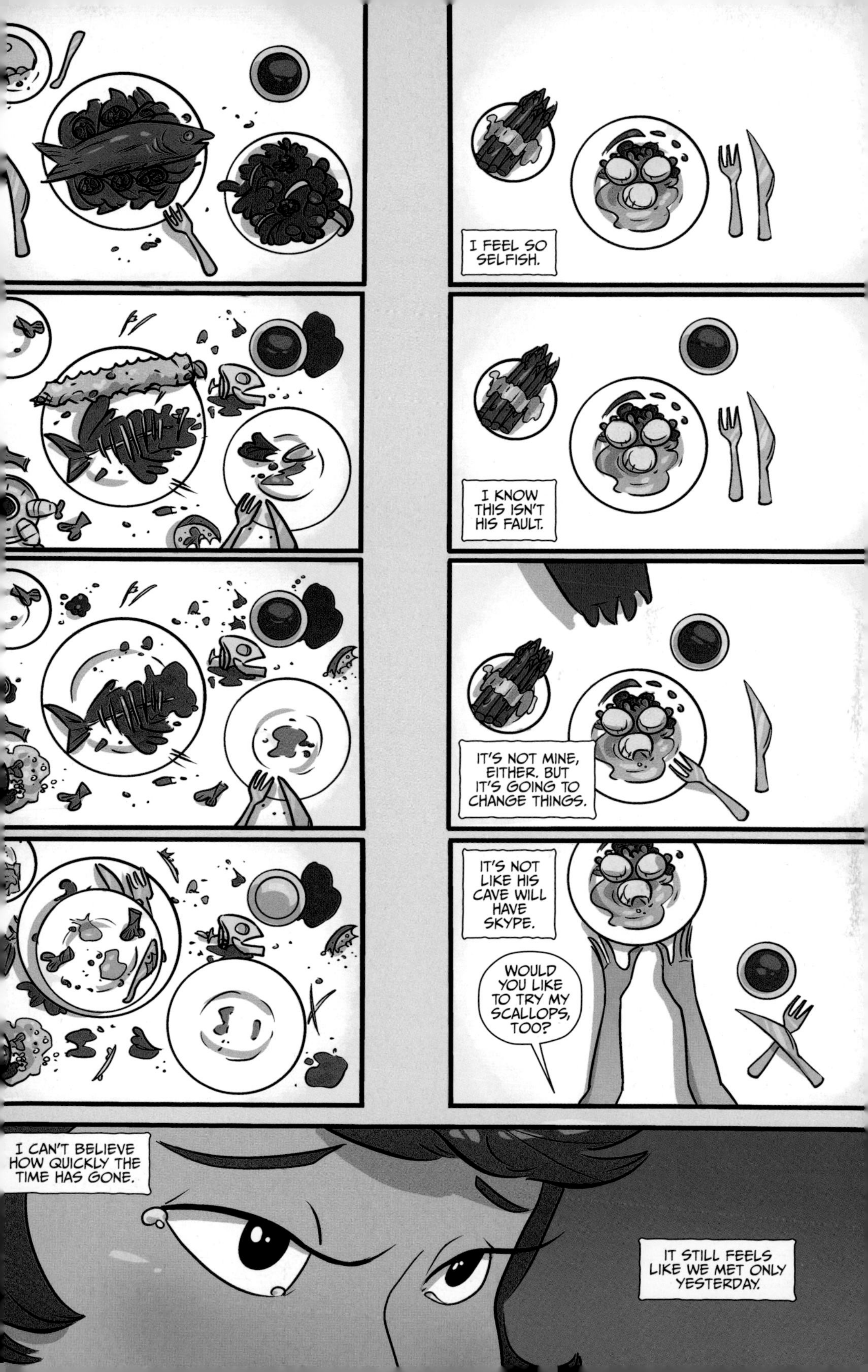
I FEEL SO SELFISH.
I KNOW THIS ISN'T HIS FAULT.
IT'S NOT MINE, EITHER. BUT IT'S GOING TO CHANGE THINGS.
IT'S NOT LIKE HIS CAVE WILL HAVE SKYPE.
WOULD YOU LIKE TO TRY MY SCALLOPS, TOO?
I CAN'T BELIEVE HOW QUICKLY THE TIME HAS GONE.
IT STILL FEELS LIKE WE MET ONLY YESTERDAY.

I WAS CAMPING. IT WAS APRIL. I REMEMBER IT WAS COLDER THAN I'D PREPARED FOR.
THIS WAS WHEN I WAS STILL DATING BEN.
ABOUT SIX MONTHS AGO...

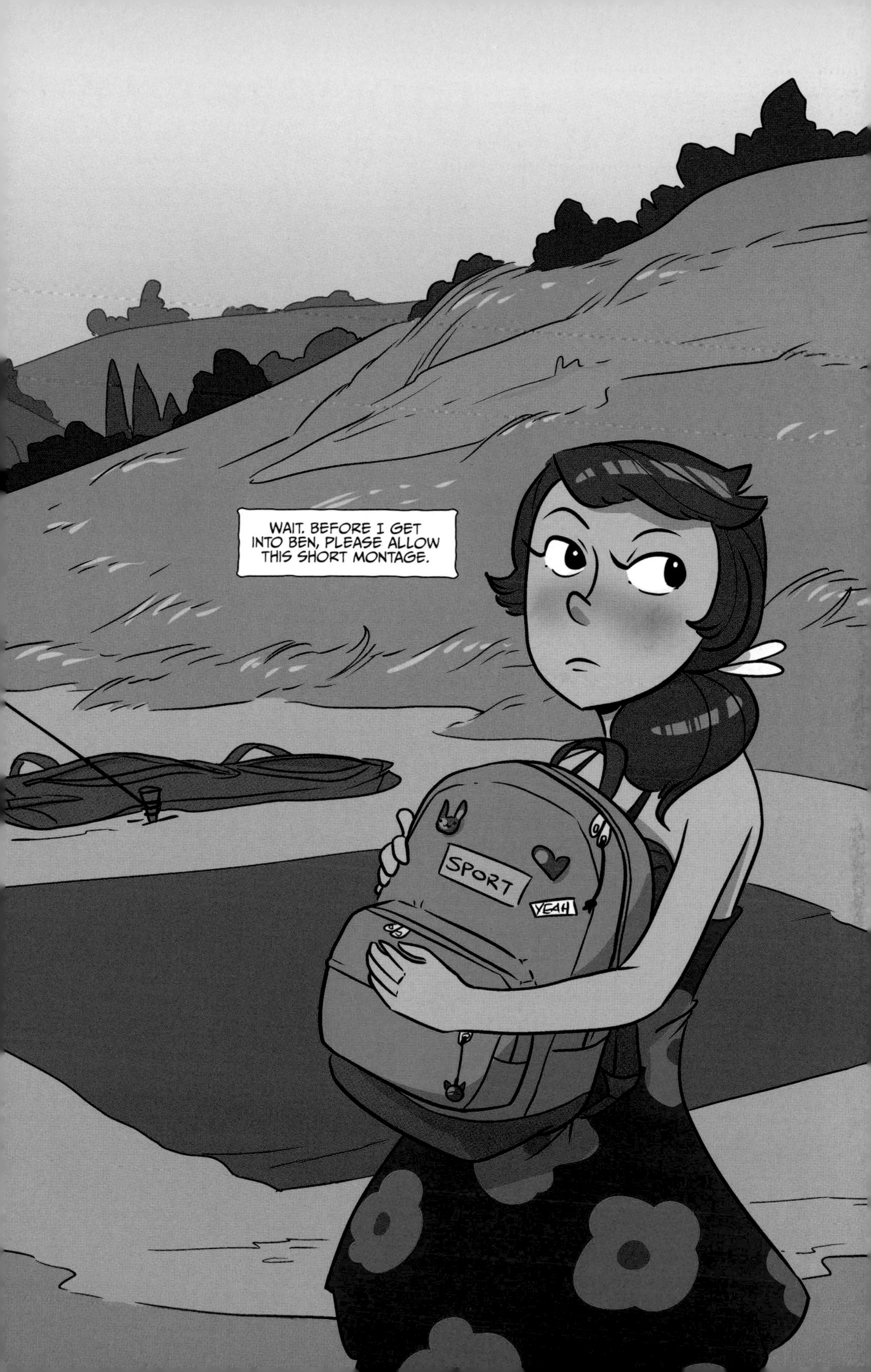
WAIT. BEFORE I GET INTO BEN, PLEASE ALLOW THIS SHORT MONTAGE.
SPORT
YEAH

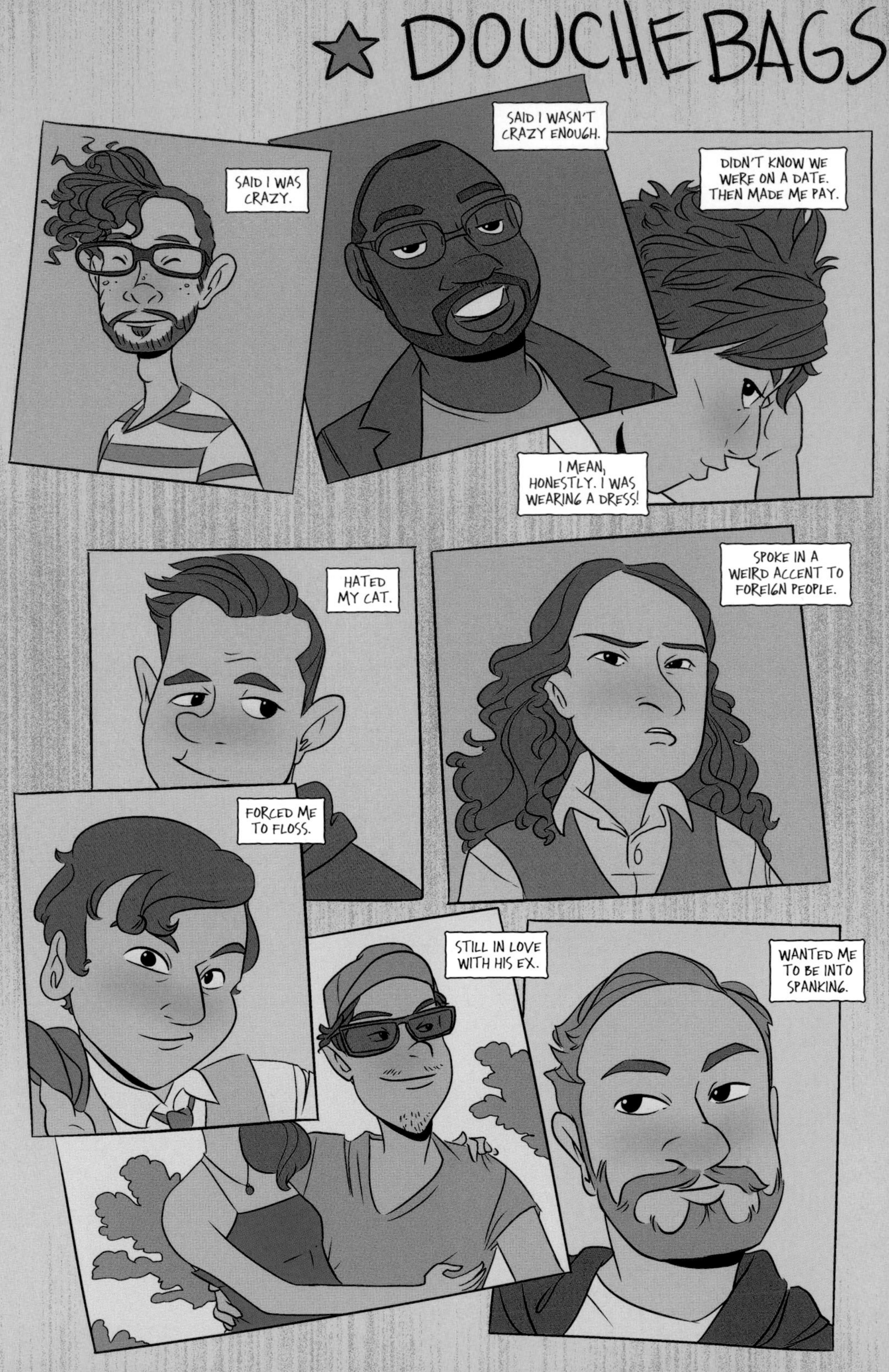
DOUCHEBAGS
SAID I WAS CRAZY.
SAID I WASN'T CRAZY ENOUGH.
DIDN'T KNOW WE WERE ON A DATE. THEN MADE ME PAY.
I MEAN, HONESTLY. I WAS WEARING A DRESS!
HATED MY CAT.
SPOKE IN A WEIRD ACCENT TO FOREIGN PEOPLE.
FORCED ME TO FLOSS.
STILL IN LOVE WITH HIS EX.
WANTED ME TO BE INTO SPANKING.

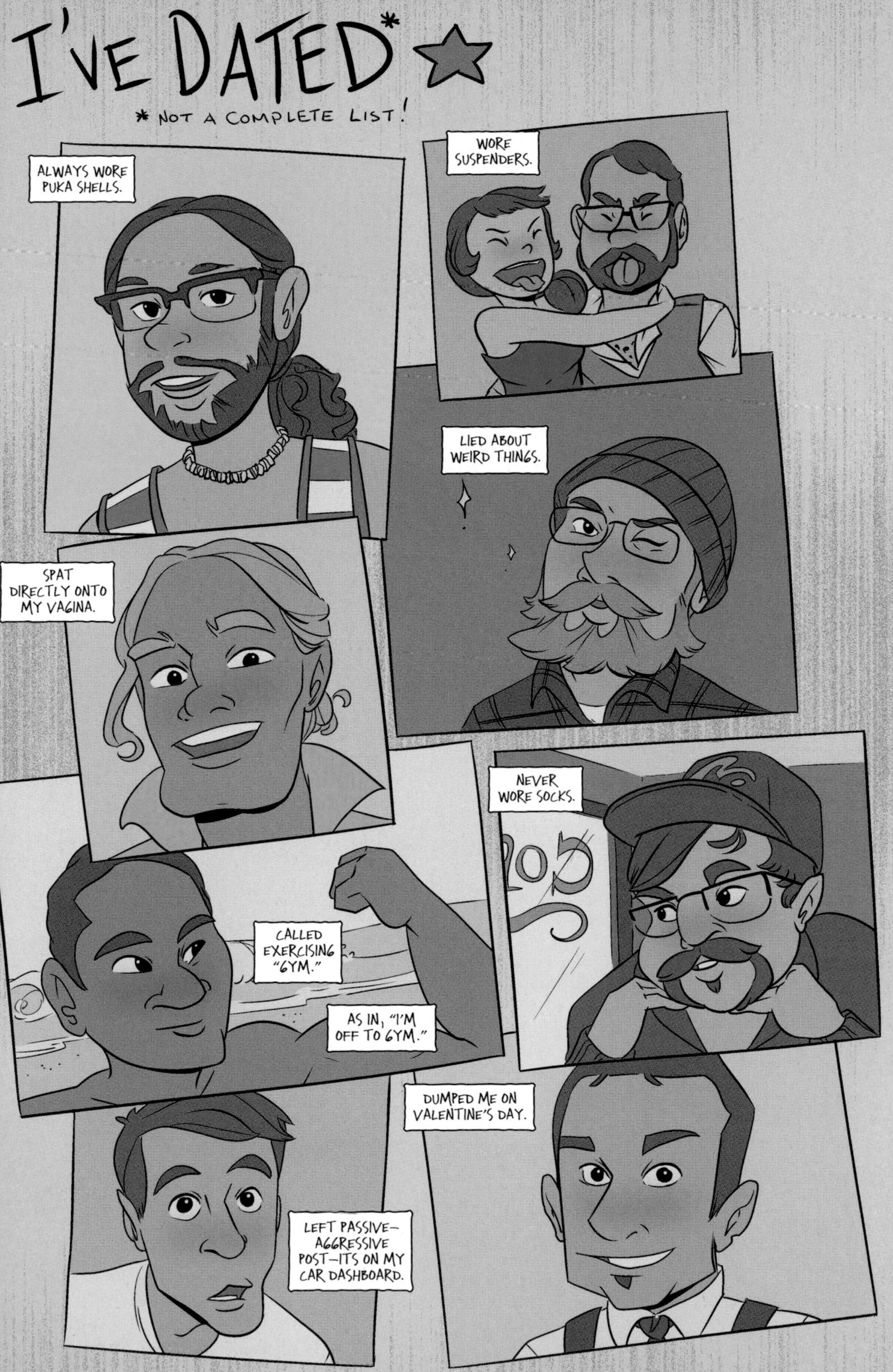
I'VE DATED*
* NOT A COMPLETE LIST!
ALWAYS WORE PUKA SHELLS.
WORE SUSPENDERS.
LIED ABOUT WEIRD THINGS.
SPAT DIRECTLY ONTO MY VAGINA.
NEVER WORE SOCKS.
CALLED EXERCISING "GYM."
AS IN, "I'M OFF TO GYM."
DUMPED ME ON VALENTINE'S DAY.
LEFT PASSIVE-AGGRESSIVE POST-ITS ON MY CAR DASHBOARD.

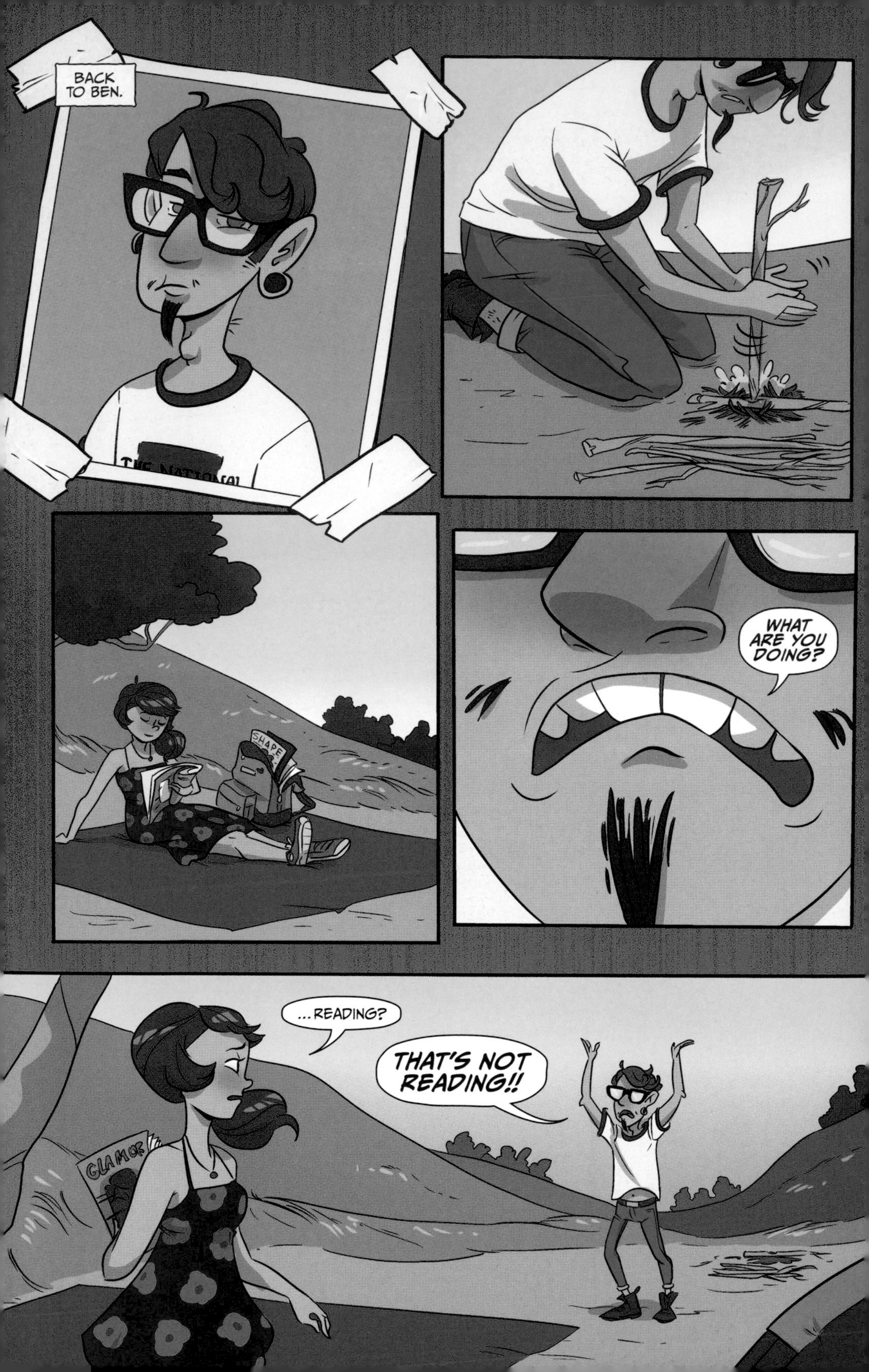
BACK TO BEN.
THE NATIONAL
SHAPE
WHAT ARE YOU DOING?
...READING?
THAT'S NOT READING!!
GLAMOR

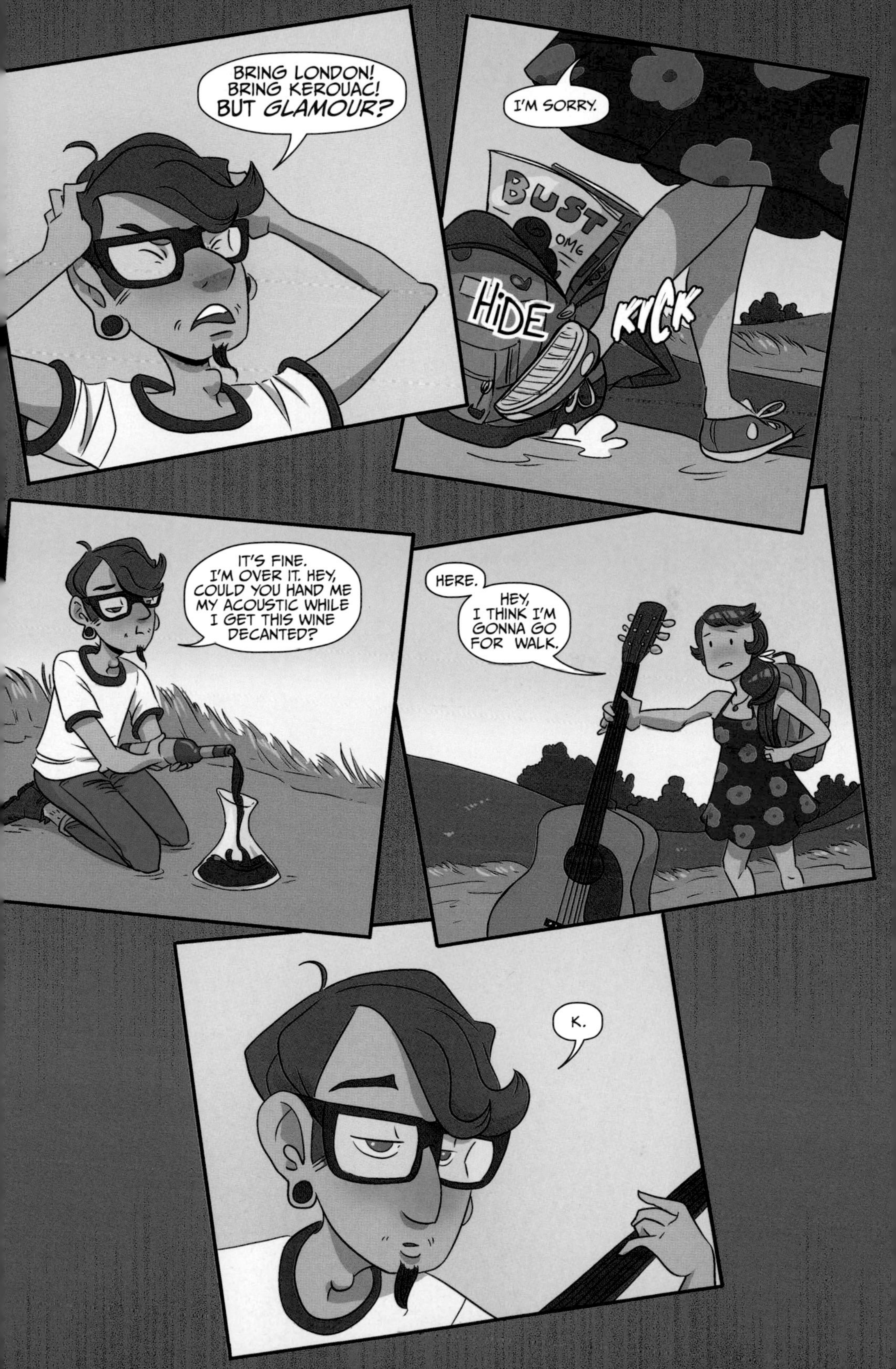
BRING LONDON! BRING KEROUAC! BUT GLAMOUR?
I'M SORRY.
BUST
OMG
HIDE
KICK
IT'S FINE. I'M OVER IT. HEY, COULD YOU HAND ME MY ACOUSTIC WHILE I GET THIS WINE DECANTED?
HERE.
HEY, I THINK I'M GONNA GO FOR WALK.
K.

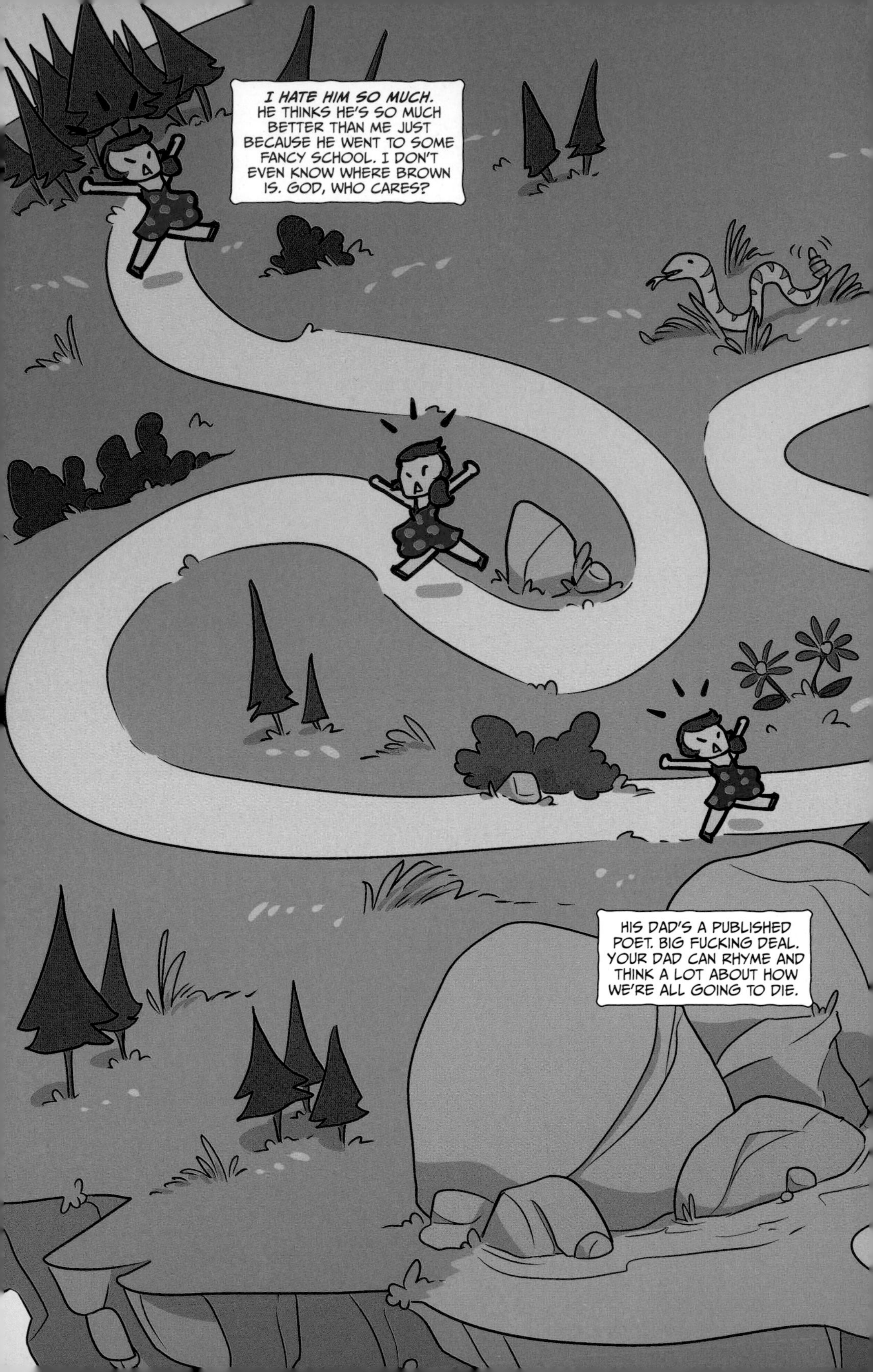
I HATE HIM SO MUCH. HE THINKS HE'S SO MUCH BETTER THAN ME JUST BECAUSE HE WENT TO SOME FANCY SCHOOL. I DON'T EVEN KNOW WHERE BROWN IS. GOD, WHO CARES?
HIS DAD'S A PUBLISHED POET. BIG FUCKING DEAL. YOUR DAD CAN RHYME AND THINK A LOT ABOUT HOW WE'RE ALL GOING TO DIE.

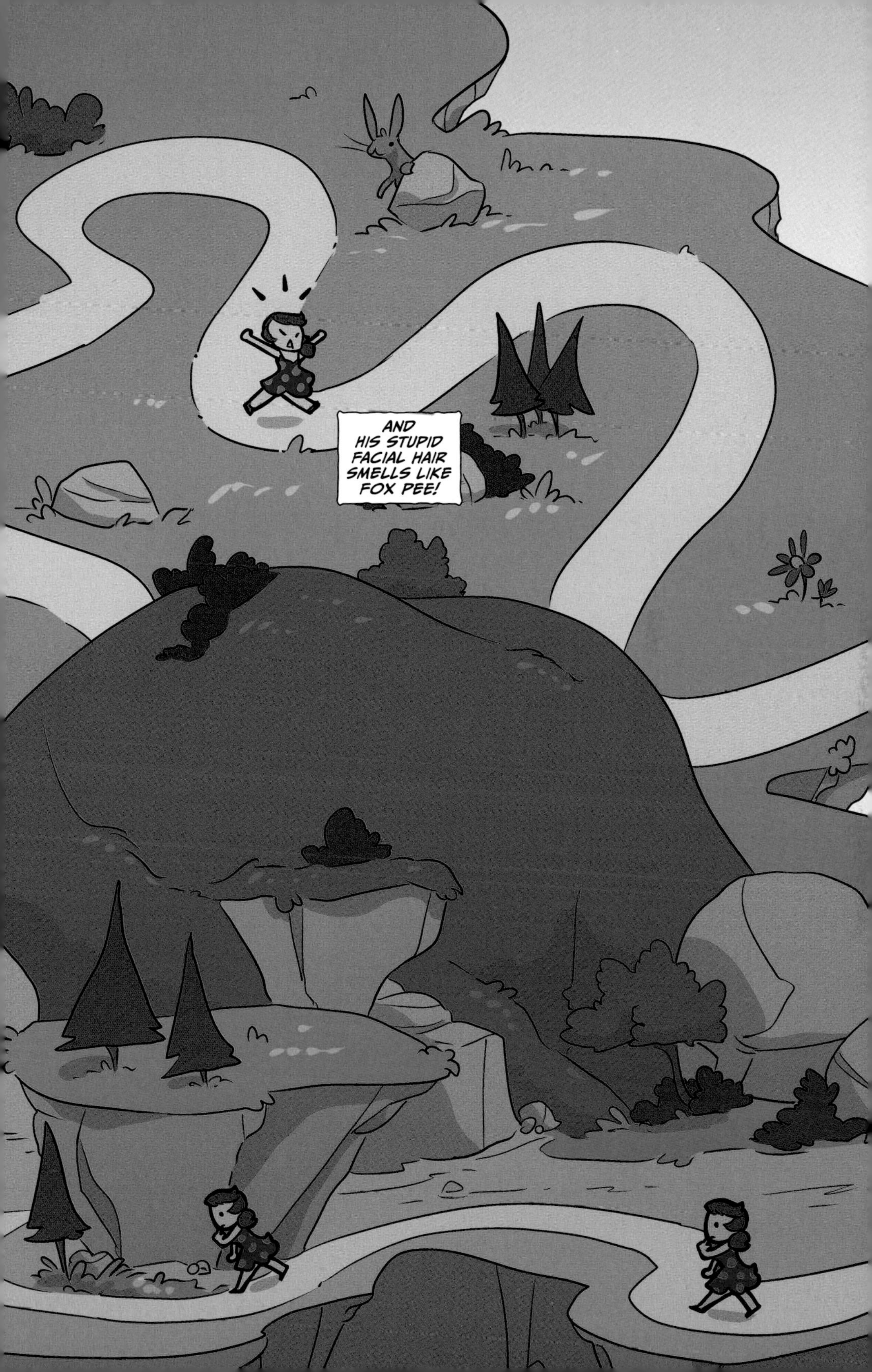
AND HIS STUPID FACIAL HAIR SMELLS LIKE FOX PEE!

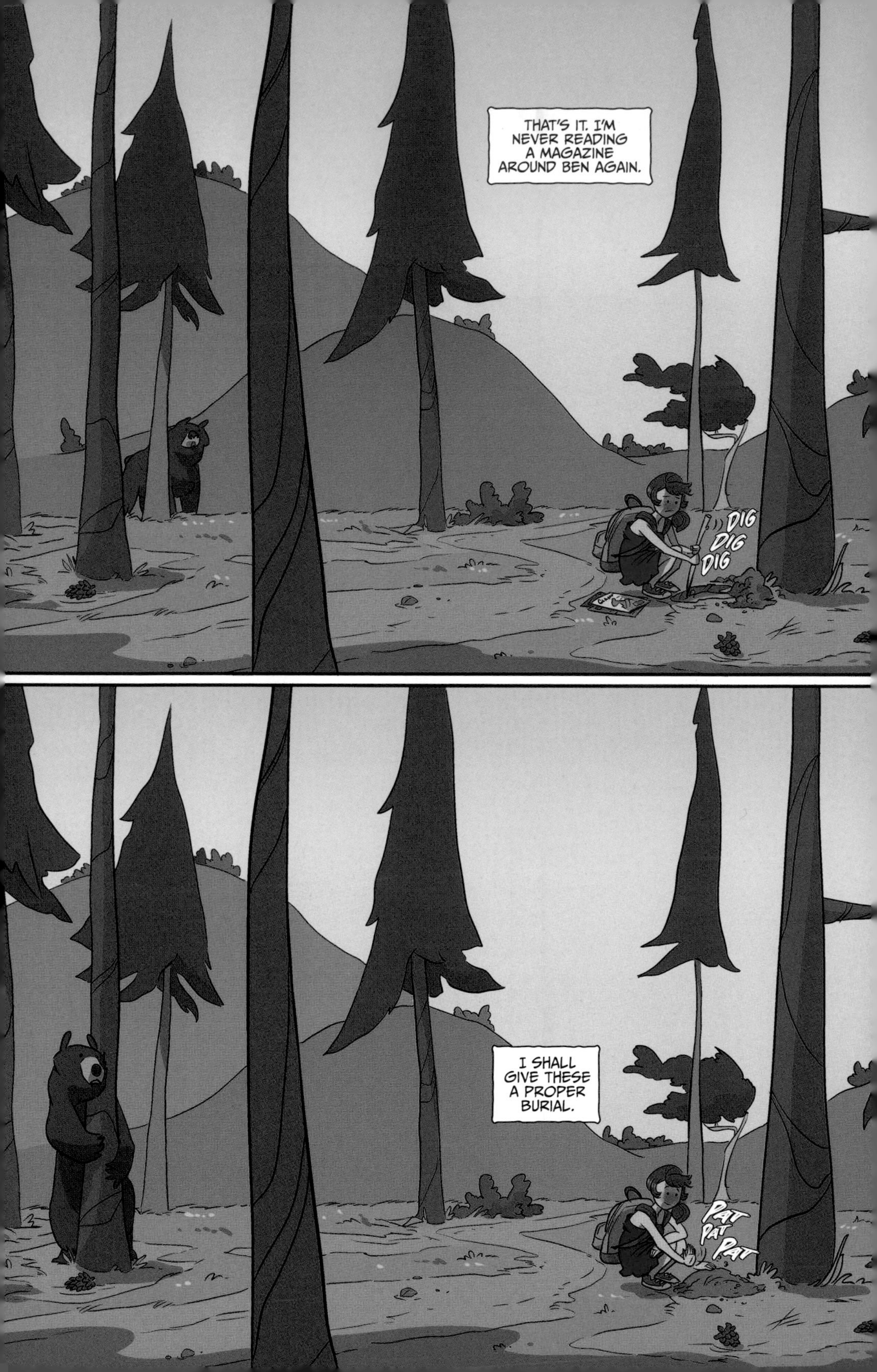
THAT'S IT. I'M NEVER READING A MAGAZINE AROUND BEN AGAIN.
DIG DIG DIG
I SHALL GIVE THESE A PROPER BURIAL.
PAT PAT PAT

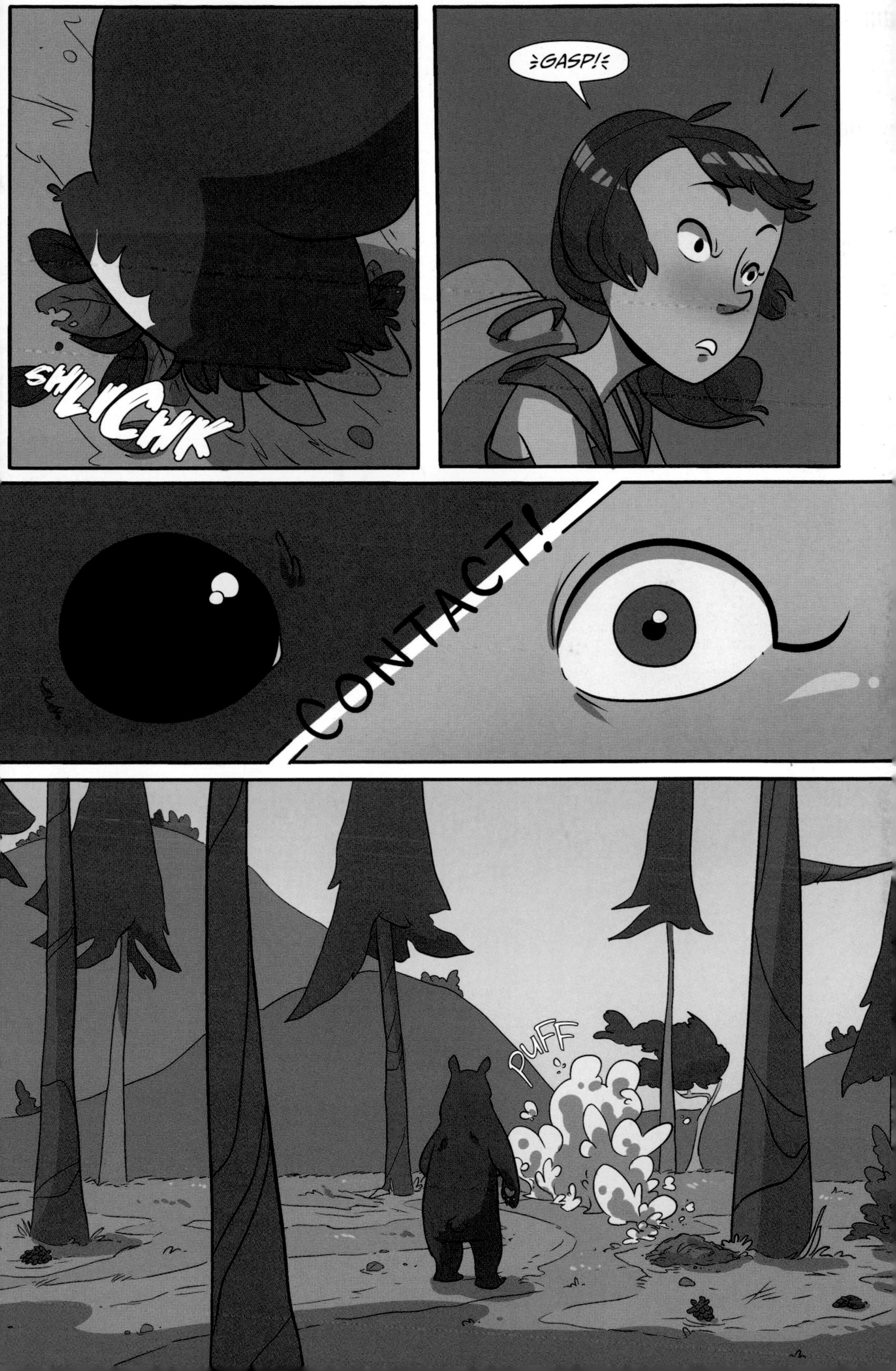
SHLICHK
GASP!
CONTACT!
PUFF

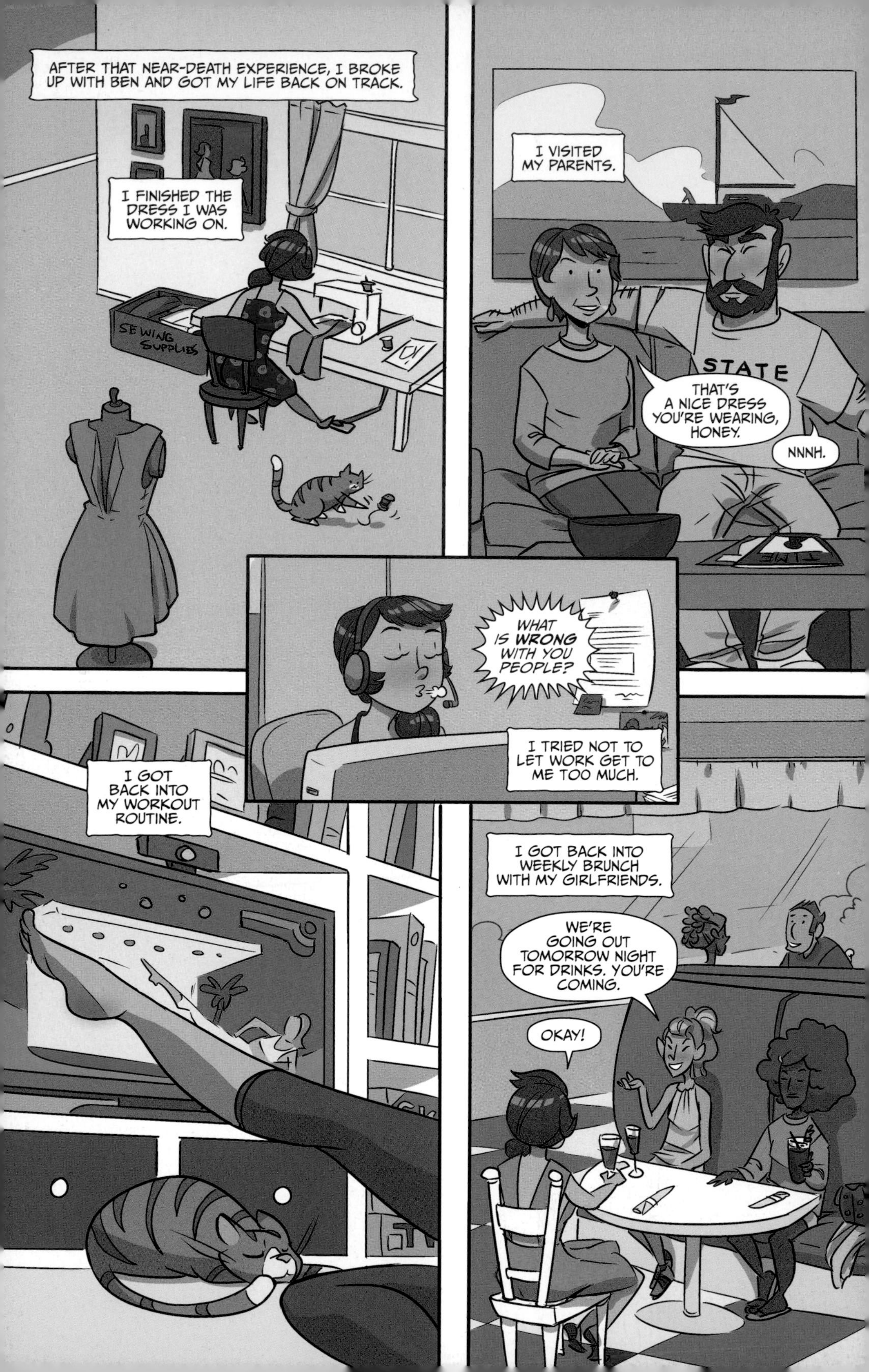
AFTER THAT NEAR-DEATH EXPERIENCE, I BROKE UP WITH BEN AND GOT MY LIFE BACK ON TRACK.
I FINISHED THE DRESS I WAS WORKING ON.
SEWING SUPPLIES
I VISITED MY PARENTS.
STATE
THAT'S A NICE DRESS YOU'RE WEARING, HONEY.
NNNH.
WHAT IS **WRONG** WITH YOU PEOPLE?
I TRIED NOT TO LET WORK GET TO ME TOO MUCH.
I GOT BACK INTO MY WORKOUT ROUTINE.
I GOT BACK INTO WEEKLY BRUNCH WITH MY GIRLFRIENDS.
WE'RE GOING OUT TOMORROW NIGHT FOR DRINKS. YOU'RE COMING.
OKAY!

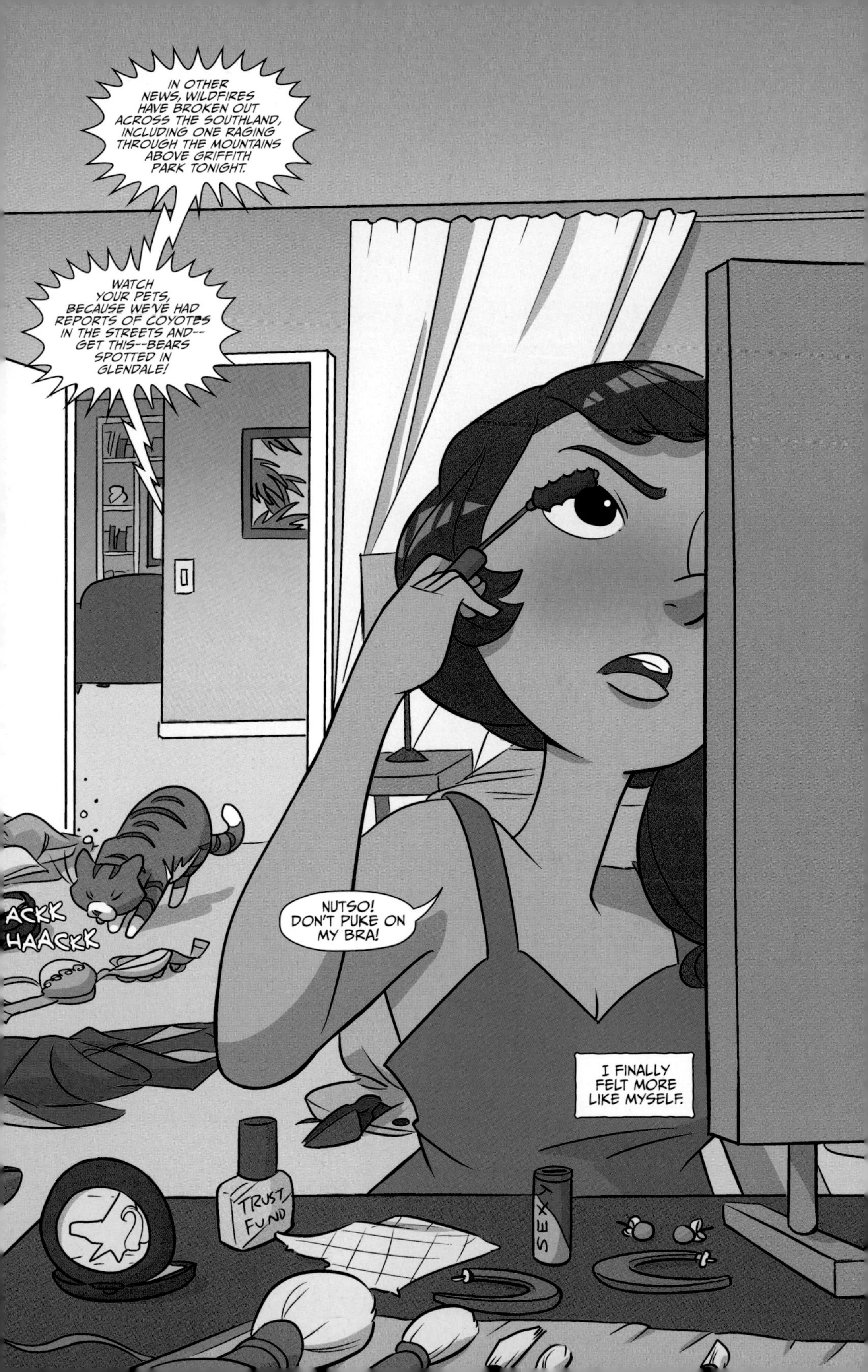
IN OTHER NEWS, WILDFIRES HAVE BROKEN OUT ACROSS THE SOUTHLAND, INCLUDING ONE RAGING THROUGH THE MOUNTAINS ABOVE GRIFFITH PARK TONIGHT.
WATCH YOUR PETS, BECAUSE WE'VE HAD REPORTS OF COYOTES IN THE STREETS AND-- GET THIS--BEARS SPOTTED IN GLENDALE!
ACKK HAACKK
NUTSO! DON'T PUKE ON MY BRA!
I FINALLY FELT MORE LIKE MYSELF.
TRUST FUND
SEXY

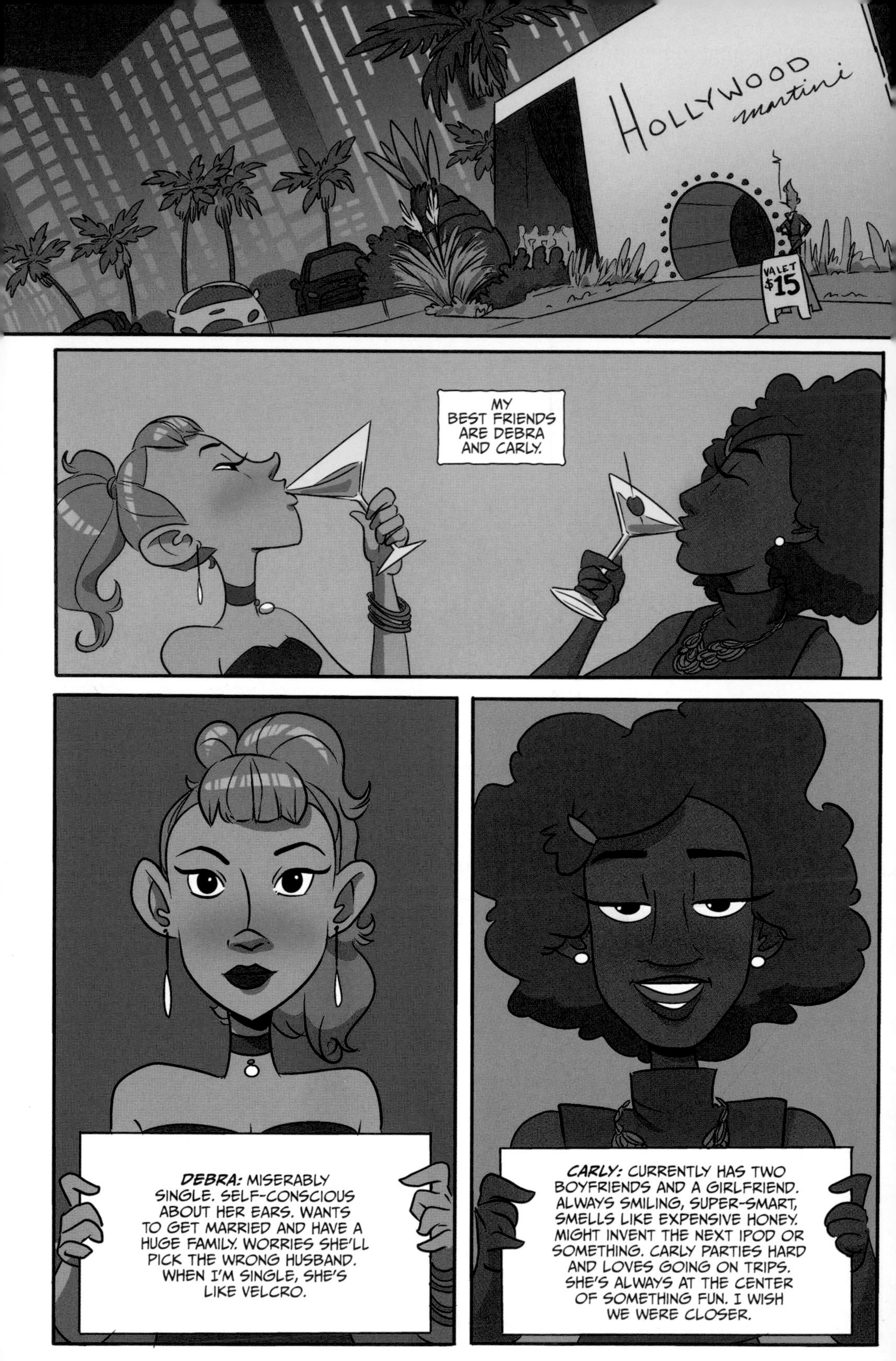
HOLLYWOOD
martini
VALET
$15
MY BEST FRIENDS ARE DEBRA AND CARLY.
DEBRA: MISERABLY SINGLE. SELF-CONSCIOUS ABOUT HER EARS. WANTS TO GET MARRIED AND HAVE A HUGE FAMILY. WORRIES SHE'LL PICK THE WRONG HUSBAND. WHEN I'M SINGLE, SHE'S LIKE VELCRO.
CARLY: CURRENTLY HAS TWO BOYFRIENDS AND A GIRLFRIEND. ALWAYS SMILING, SUPER-SMART, SMELLS LIKE EXPENSIVE HONEY. MIGHT INVENT THE NEXT IPOD OR SOMETHING. CARLY PARTIES HARD AND LOVES GOING ON TRIPS. SHE'S ALWAYS AT THE CENTER OF SOMETHING FUN. I WISH WE WERE CLOSER.

WE TOASTED TO THE END OF BEN.

CLINK

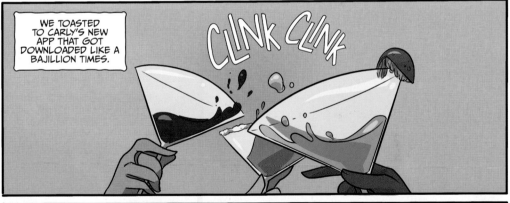

WE TOASTED TO DEBRA'S FIVE-POUND WEIGHT LOSS AFTER A TWO-WEEK BOOT CAMP.

CLINK

WE TOASTED TO CARLY'S NEW APP THAT GOT DOWNLOADED LIKE A BAJILLION TIMES.

CLINK CLINK

WE TOASTED UNTIL WE GOT A LITTLE TOASTED.

MARTINIS TASTE GOOD.

CLINK CLINK CLINK

I LOOK GOOD.

I FEEL GOOD.

I LOVE MY FRIENDS. OH, HOW I HAVE MISSED THEM SO.

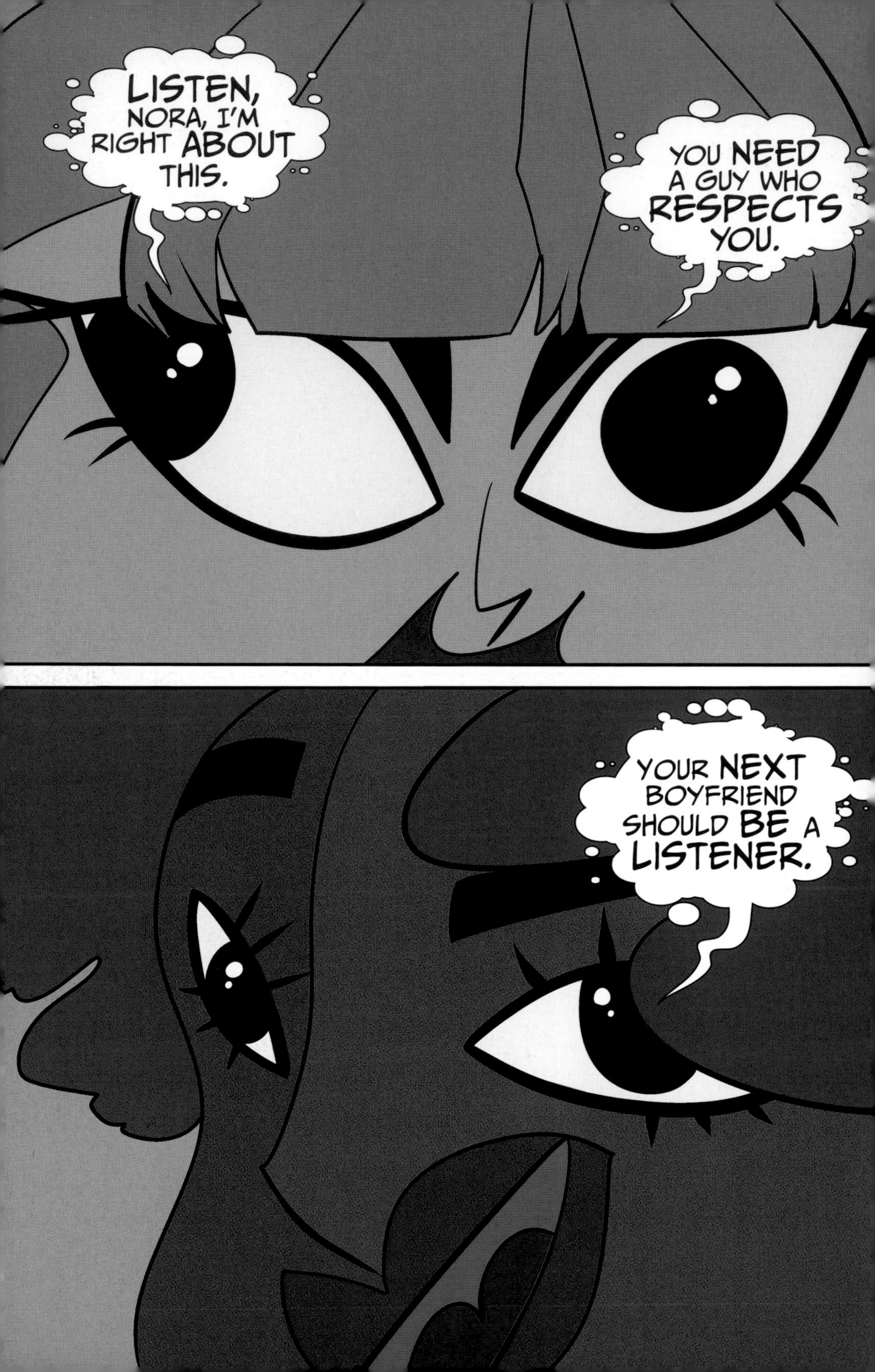
LISTEN, NORA, I'M RIGHT ABOUT THIS.
YOU NEED A GUY WHO RESPECTS YOU.
YOUR NEXT BOYFRIEND SHOULD BE A LISTENER.

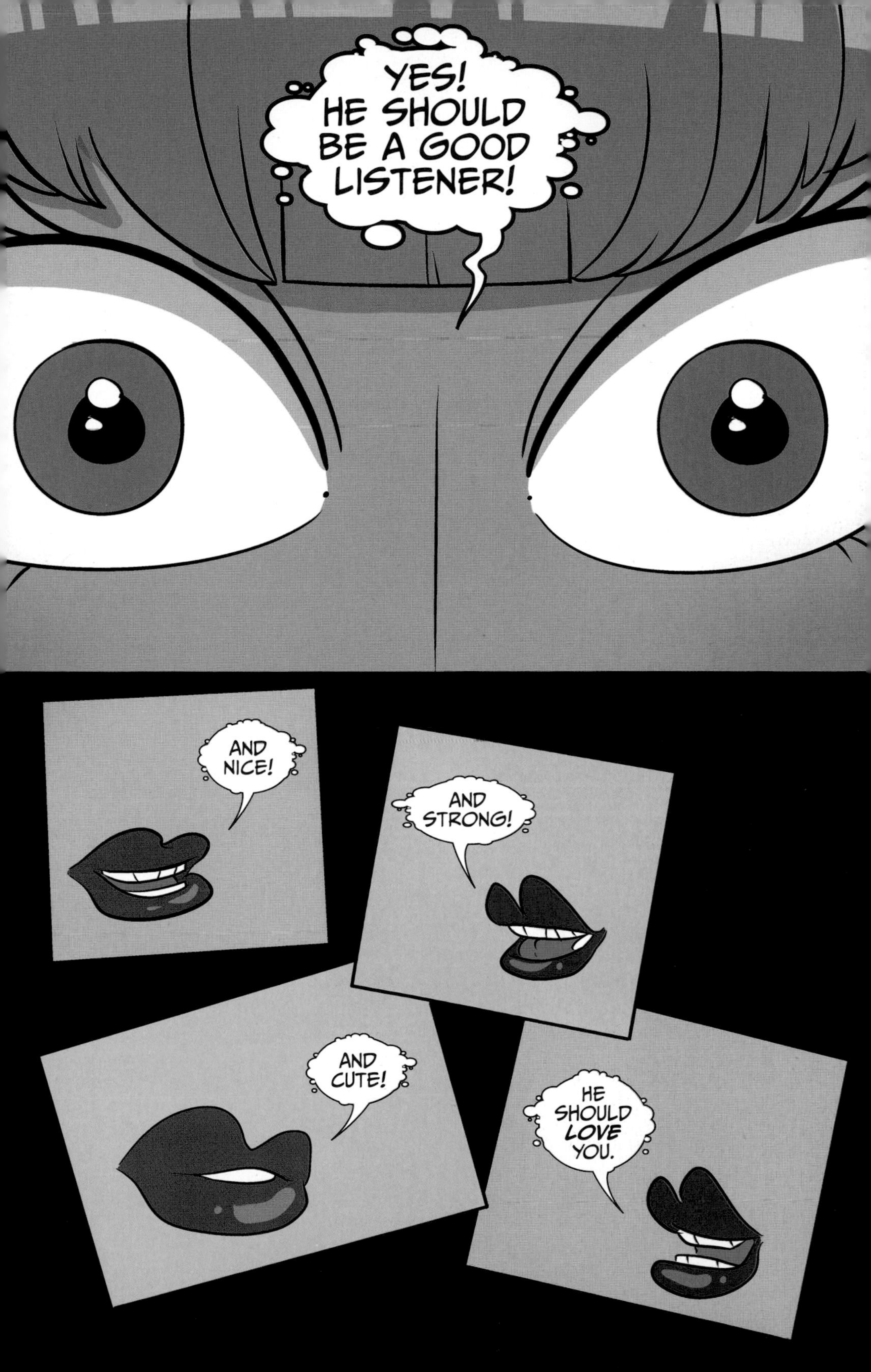
YES! HE SHOULD BE A GOOD LISTENER!
AND NICE!
AND STRONG!
AND CUTE!
HE SHOULD **LOVE** YOU.

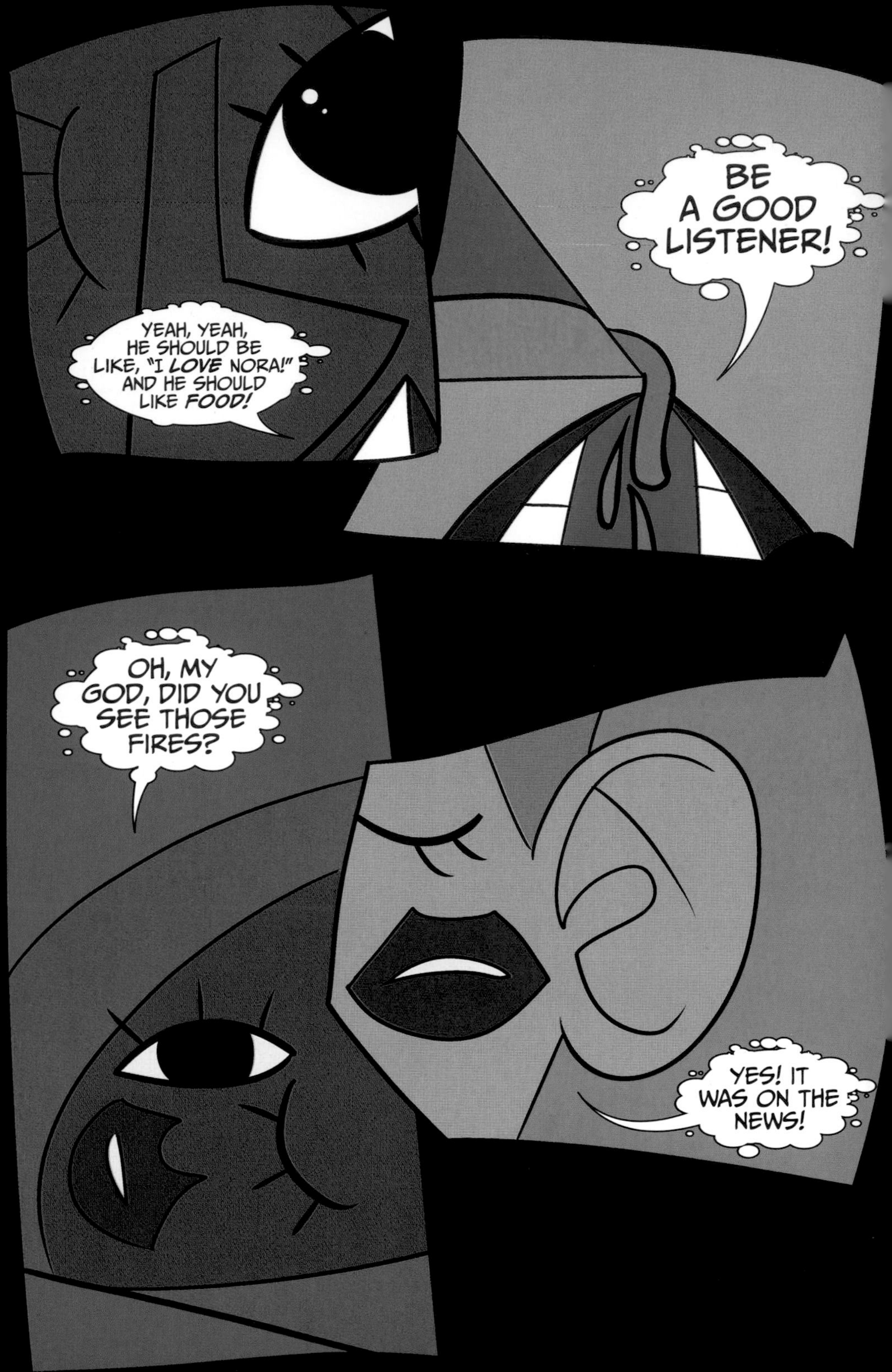
YEAH, YEAH, HE SHOULD BE LIKE, "I LOVE NORA!" AND HE SHOULD LIKE FOOD!
BE A GOOD LISTENER!
OH, MY GOD, DID YOU SEE THOSE FIRES?
YES! IT WAS ON THE NEWS!

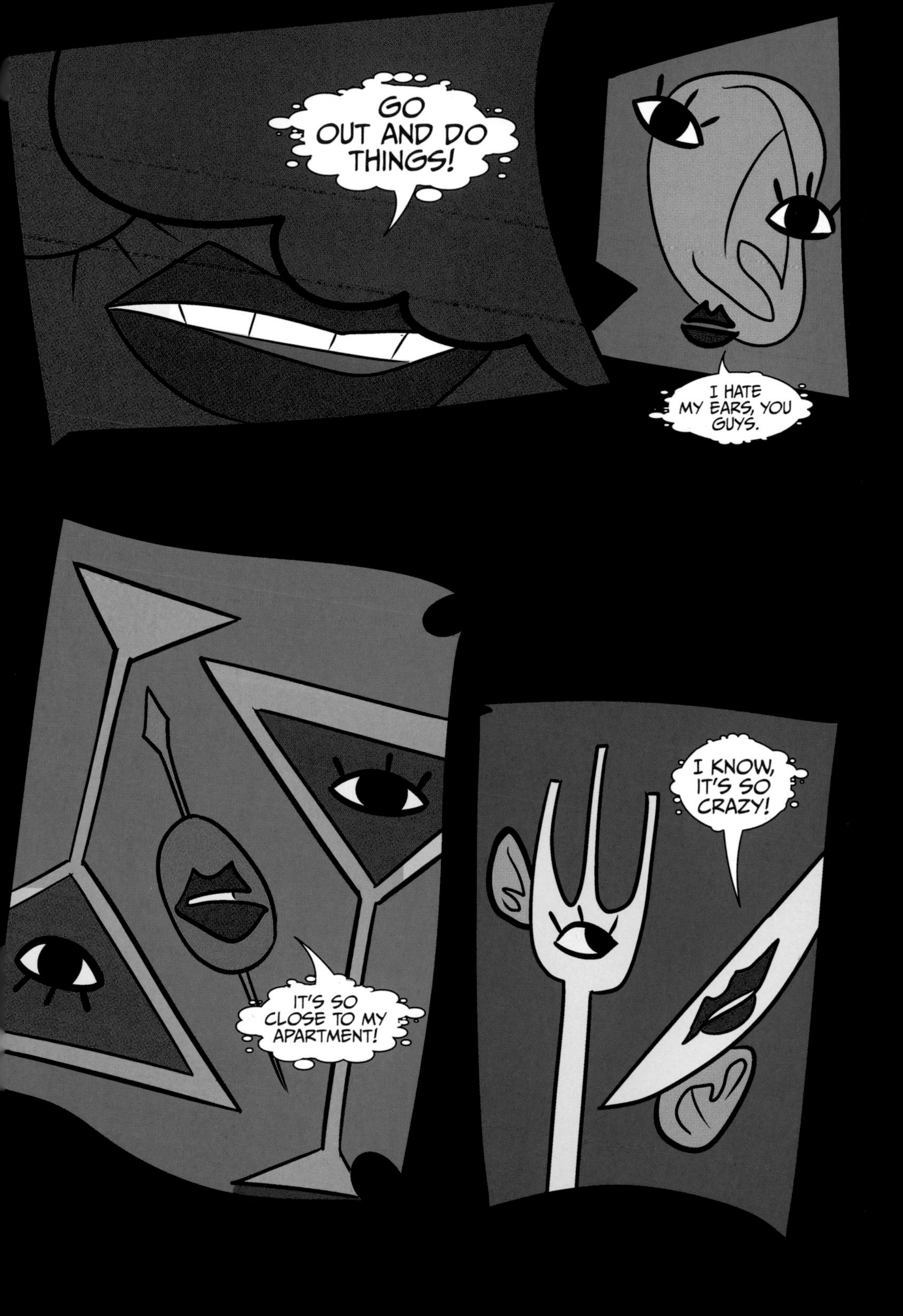
GO OUT AND DO THINGS!
I HATE MY EARS, YOU GUYS.
IT'S SO CLOSE TO MY APARTMENT!
I KNOW, IT'S SO CRAZY!

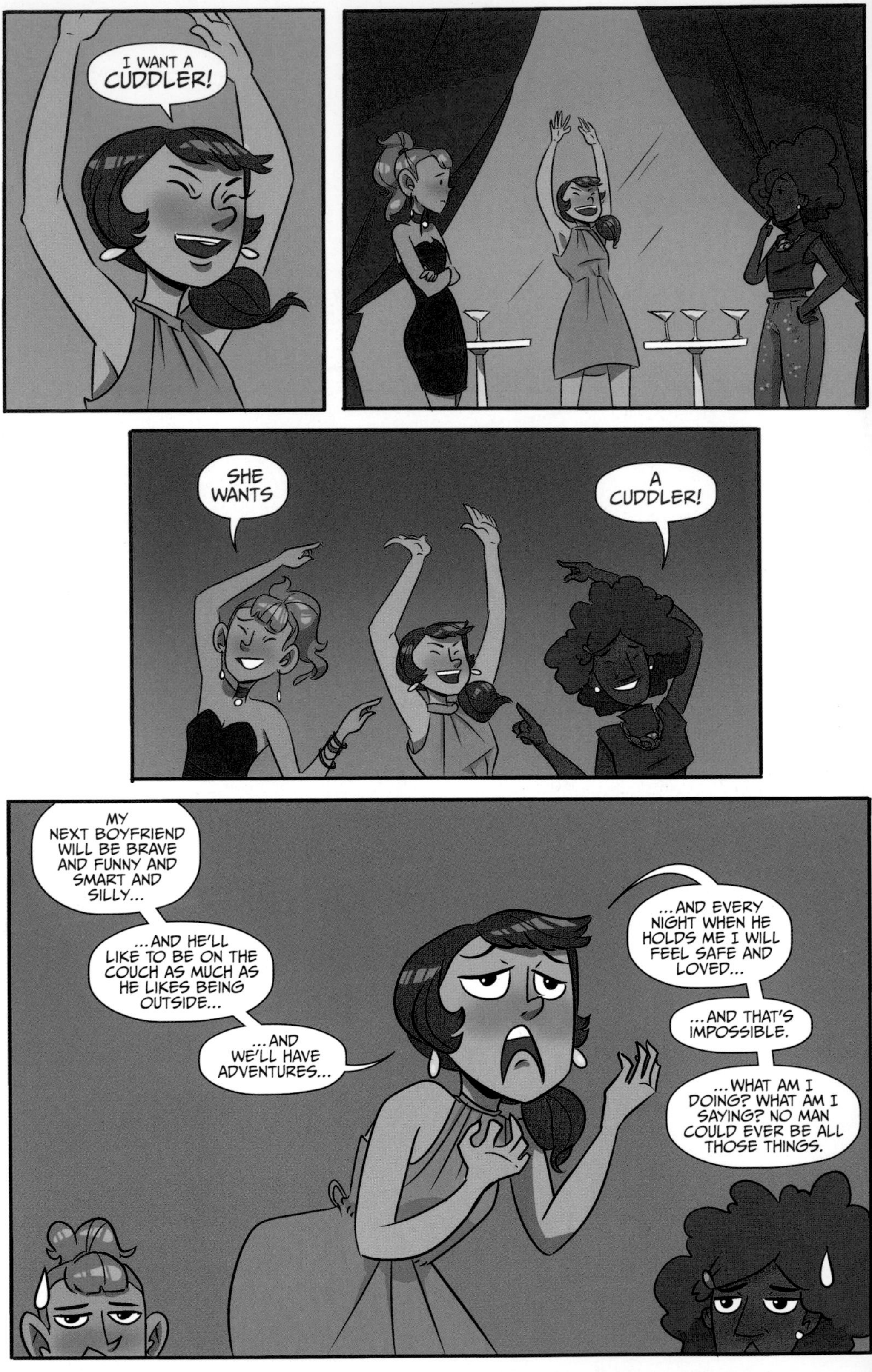
I WANT A CUDDLER!
SHE WANTS
A CUDDLER!
MY NEXT BOYFRIEND WILL BE BRAVE AND FUNNY AND SMART AND SILLY...
...AND HE'LL LIKE TO BE ON THE COUCH AS MUCH AS HE LIKES BEING OUTSIDE...
...AND WE'LL HAVE ADVENTURES...
...AND EVERY NIGHT WHEN HE HOLDS ME I WILL FEEL SAFE AND LOVED...
...AND THAT'S IMPOSSIBLE.
...WHAT AM I DOING? WHAT AM I SAYING? NO MAN COULD EVER BE ALL THOSE THINGS.

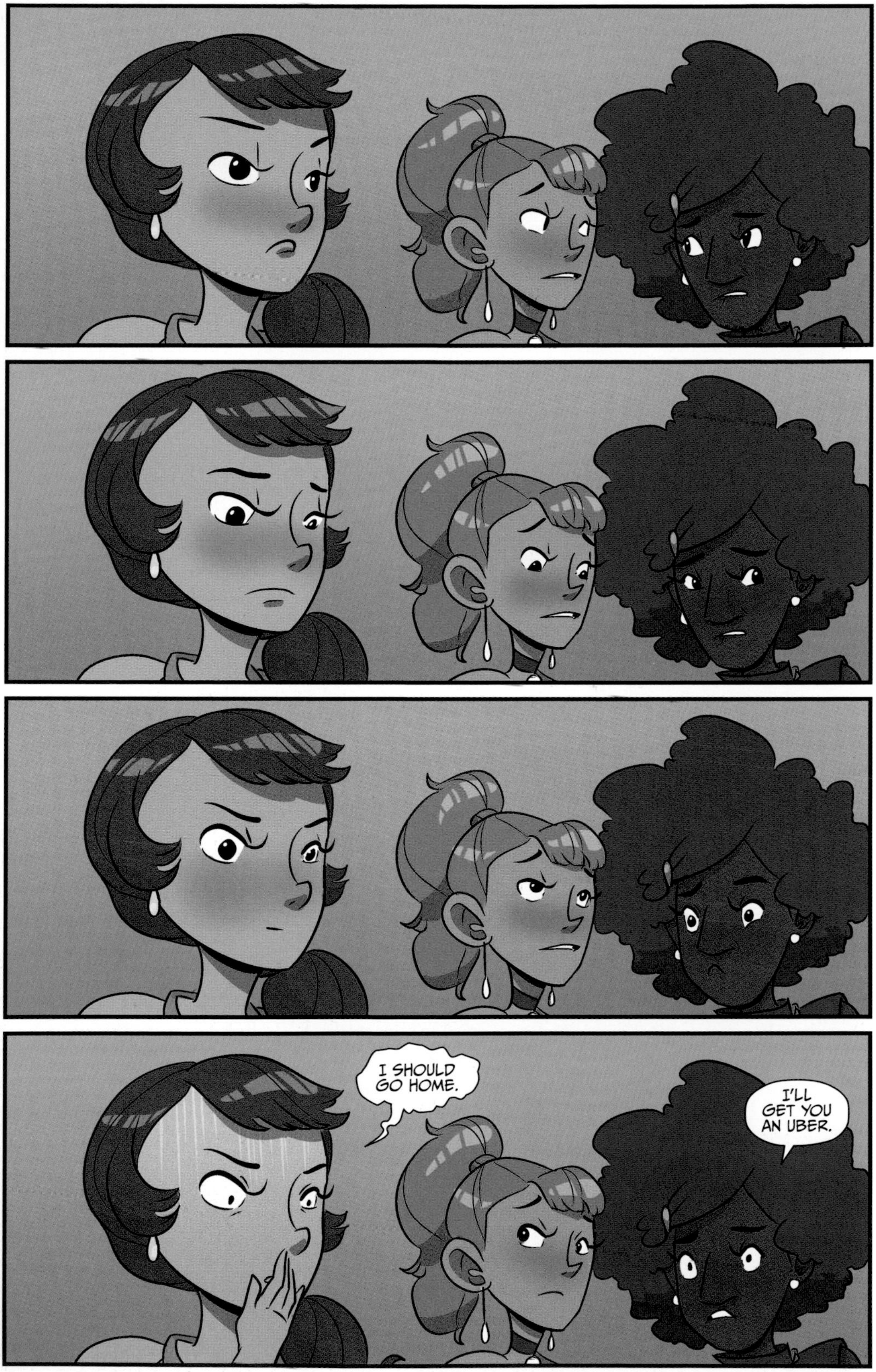
I SHOULD GO HOME.
I'LL GET YOU AN UBER.

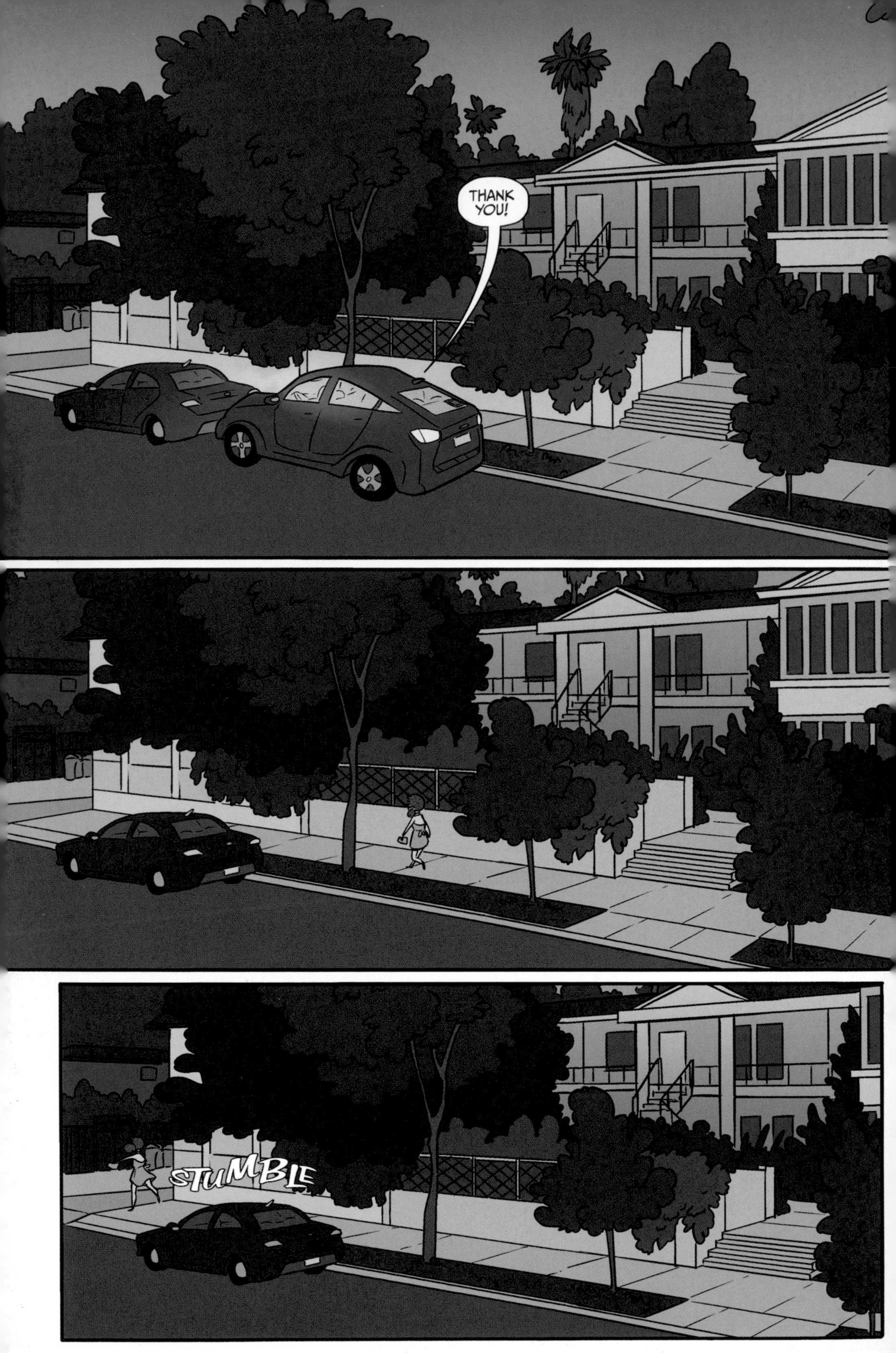
THANK YOU!
STUMBLE

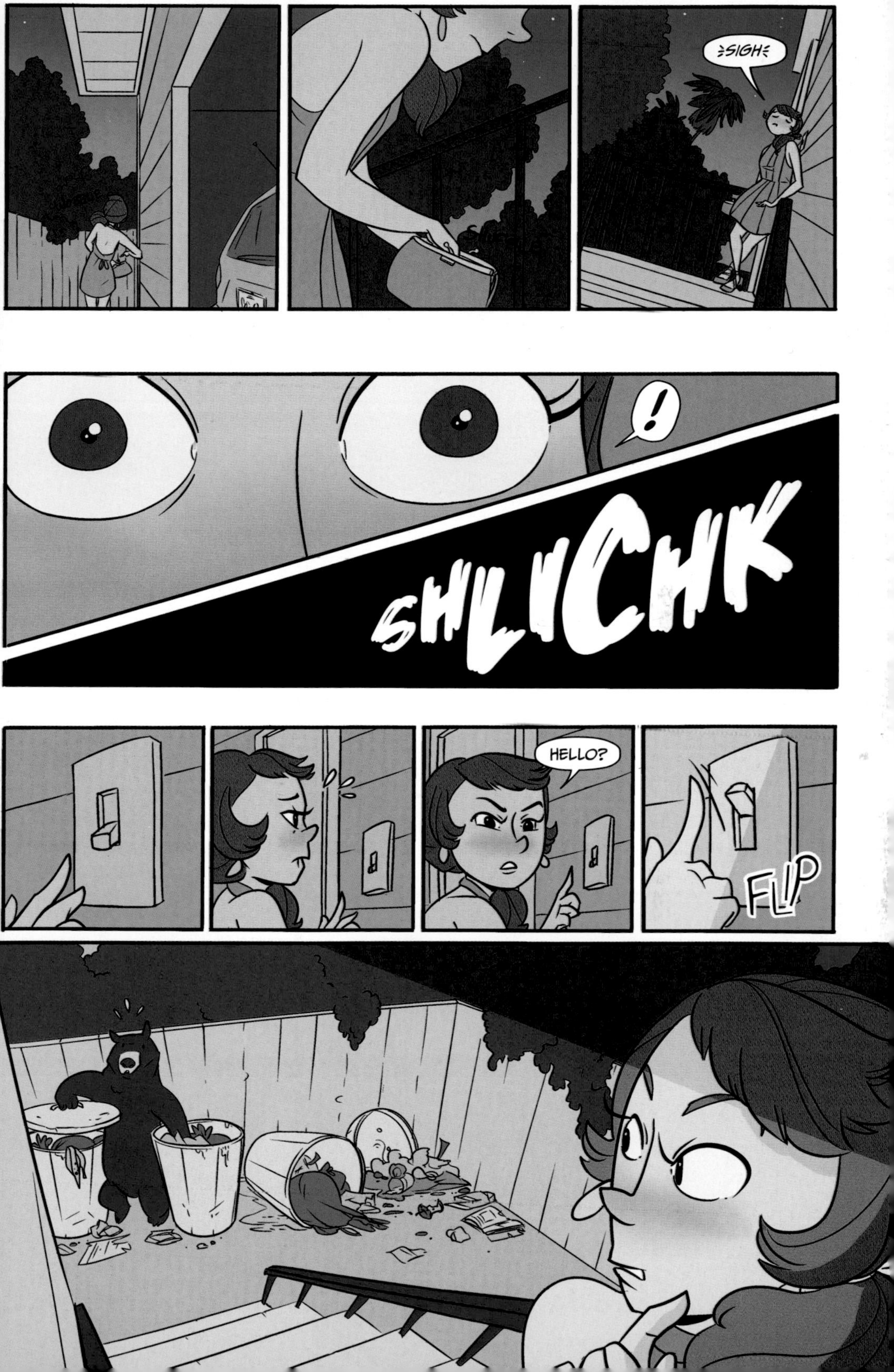
SIGH
!
SHLICHK
HELLO?
FLIP

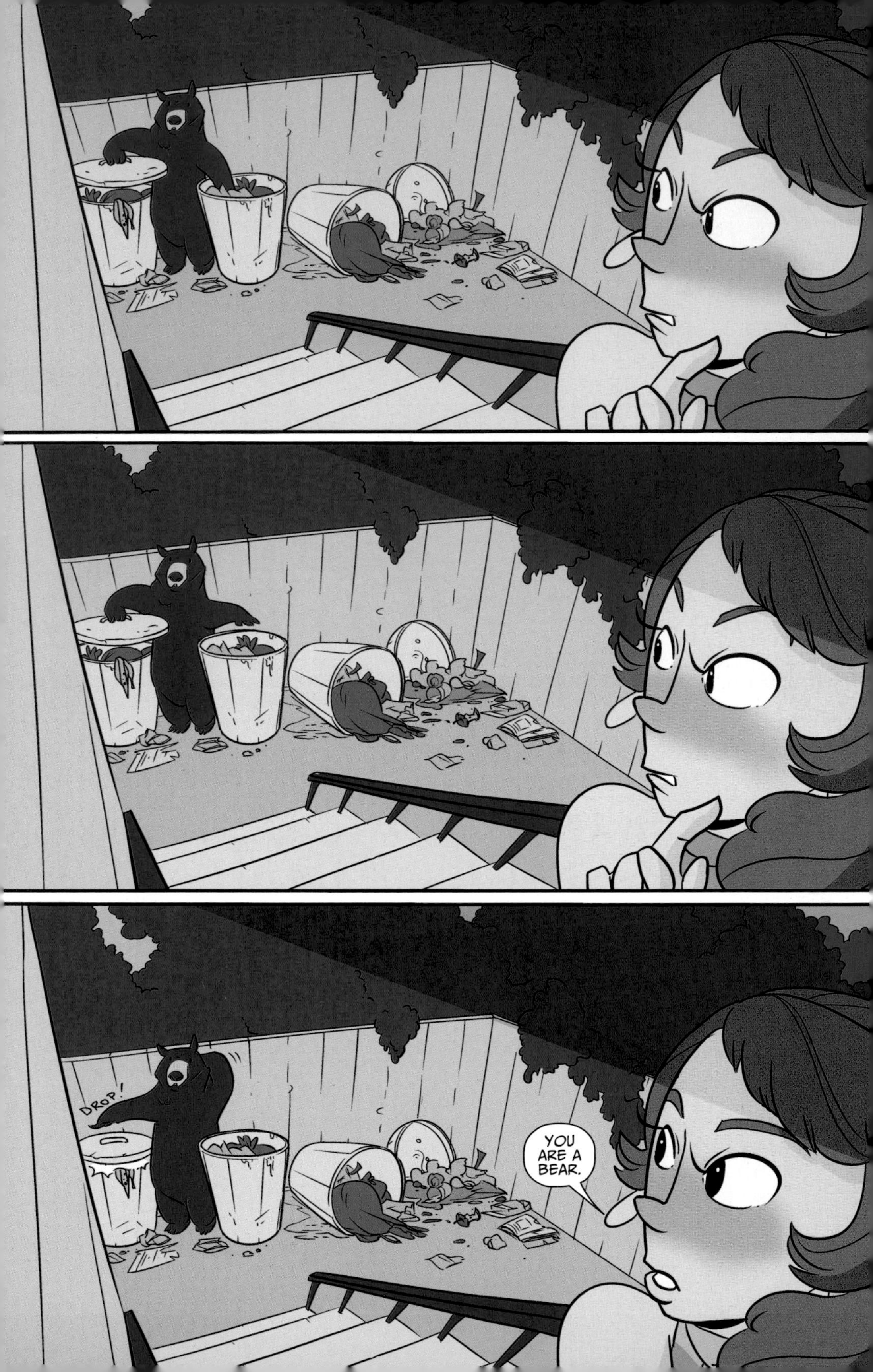
DROP!
YOU ARE A BEAR.

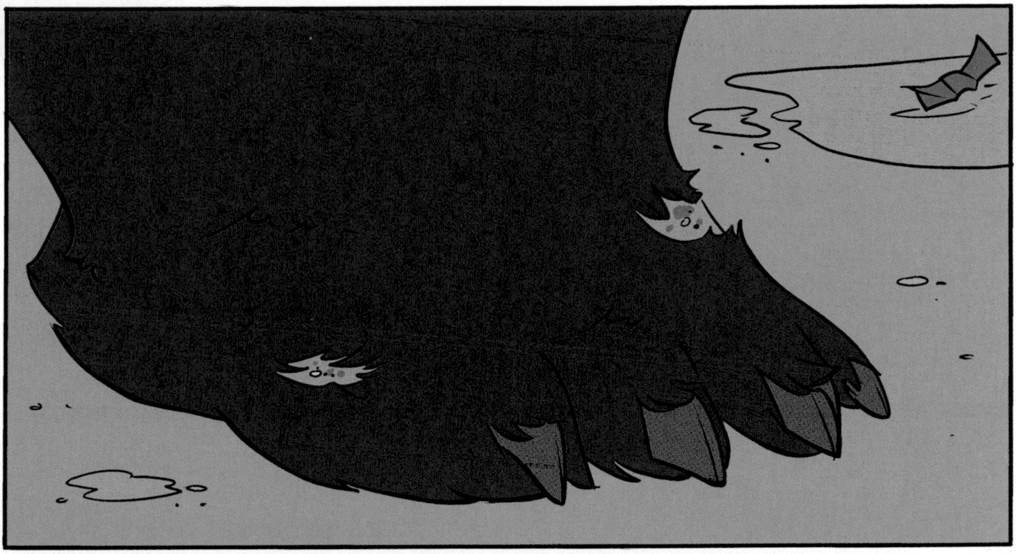

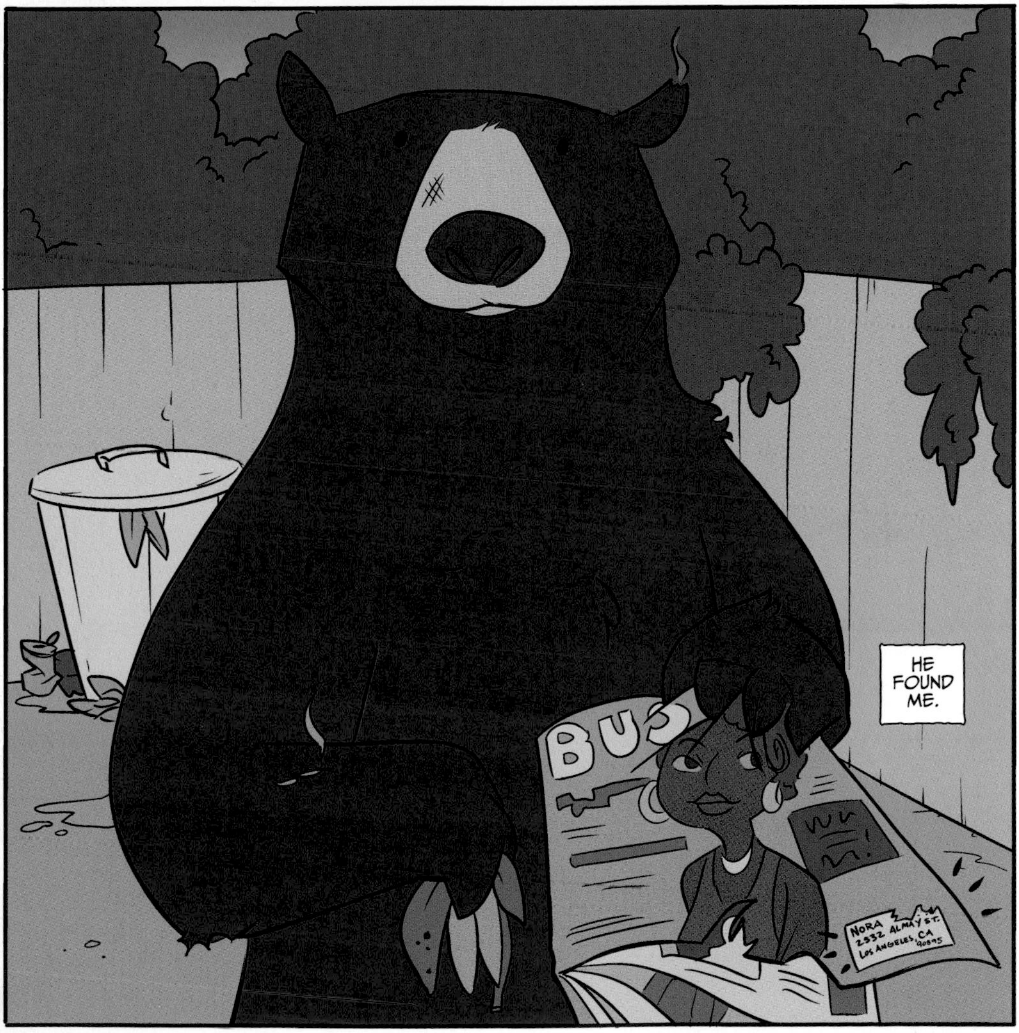
HE FOUND ME.
BUS
NORA
2332 ALMAY ST.
LOS ANGELES, CA
90895

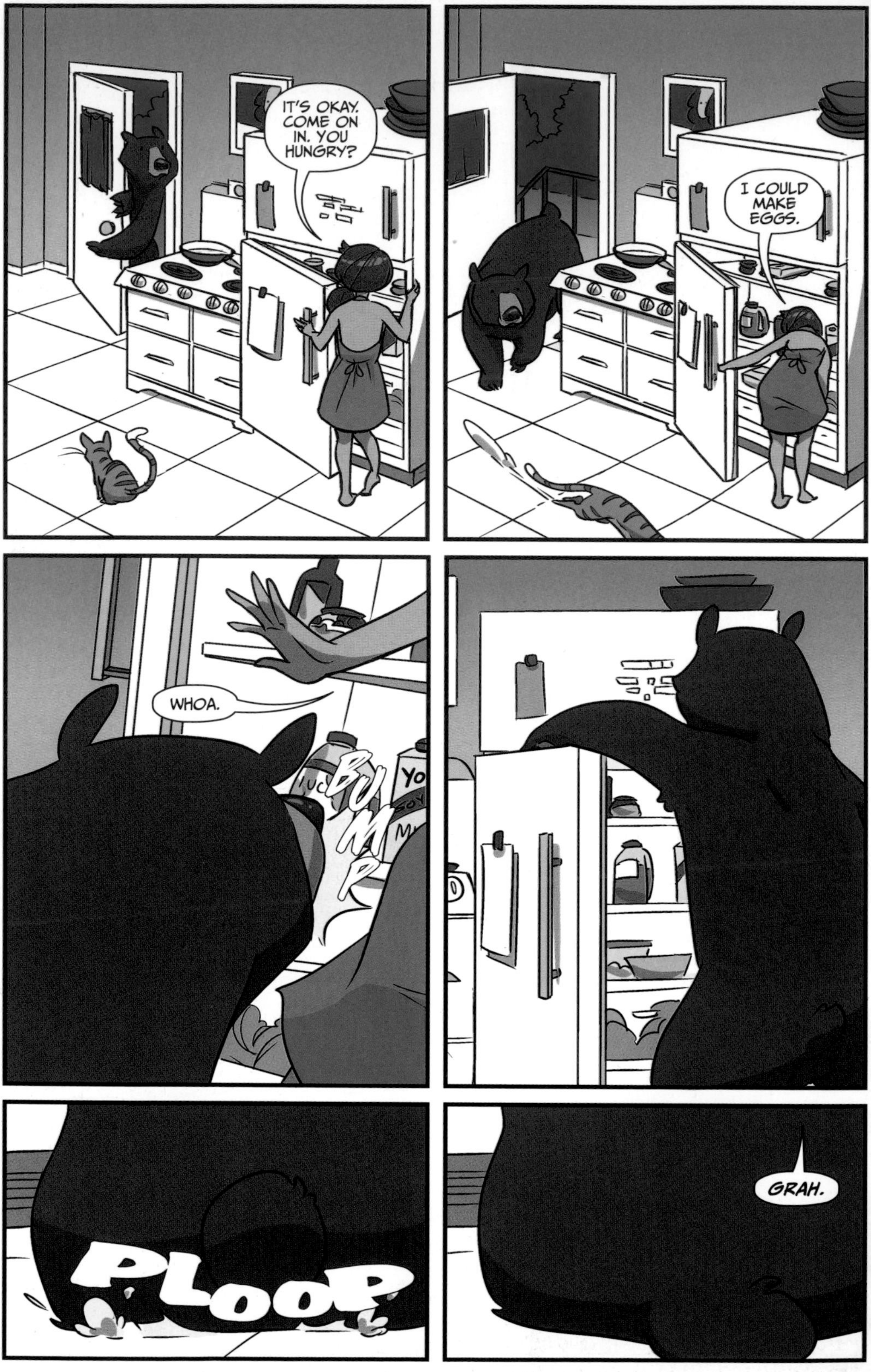
IT'S OKAY. COME ON IN. YOU HUNGRY?
I COULD MAKE EGGS.
WHOA.
BUMP
PLOOP
GRAH.

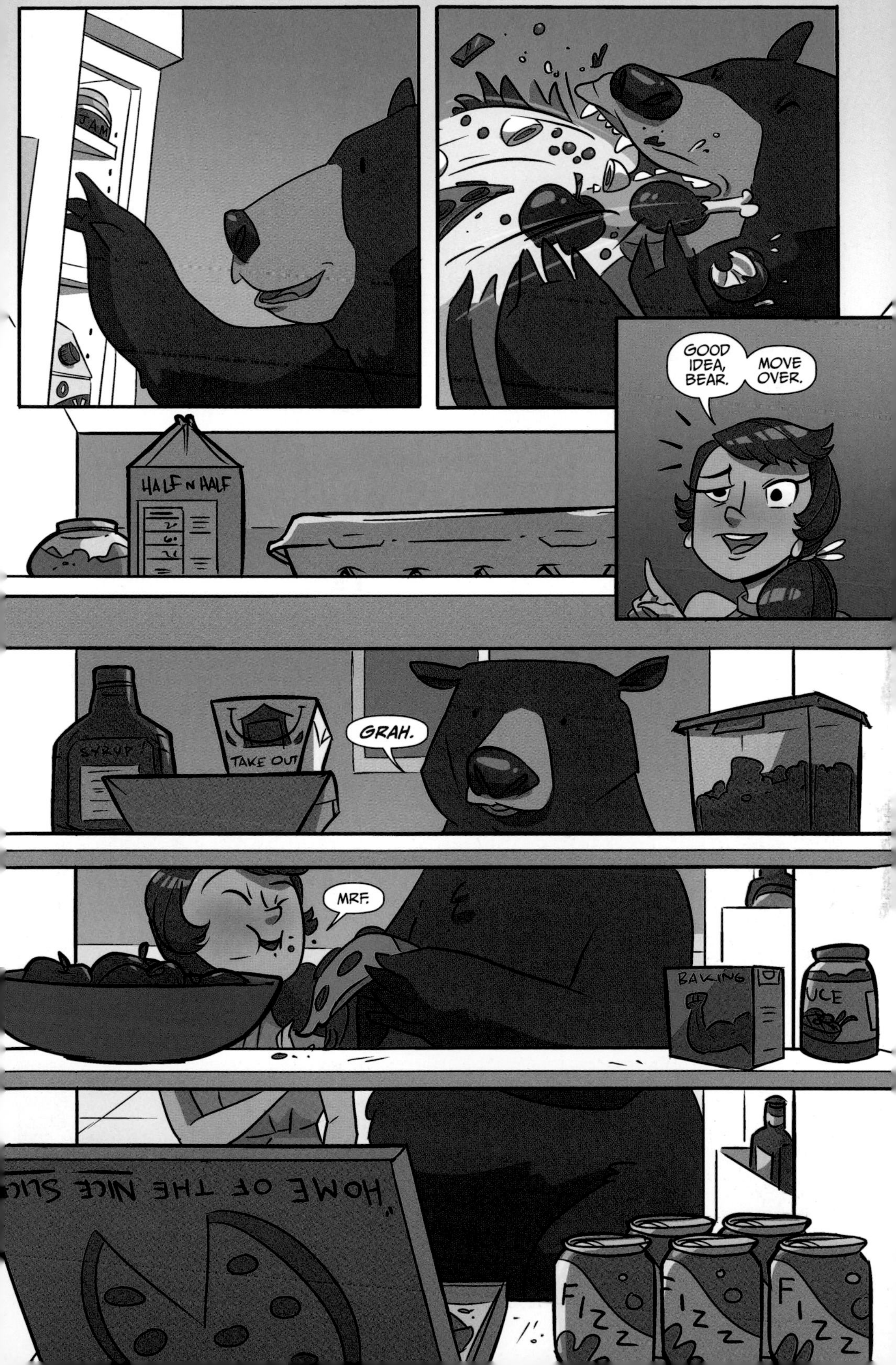
JAM
GOOD IDEA, BEAR.
MOVE OVER.
HALF N HALF
SYRUP
TAKE OUT
GRAH.
MRF.
BAKING
UCE
HOME OF THE NICE SLIC
FIZZ
FIZZ
FIZZ

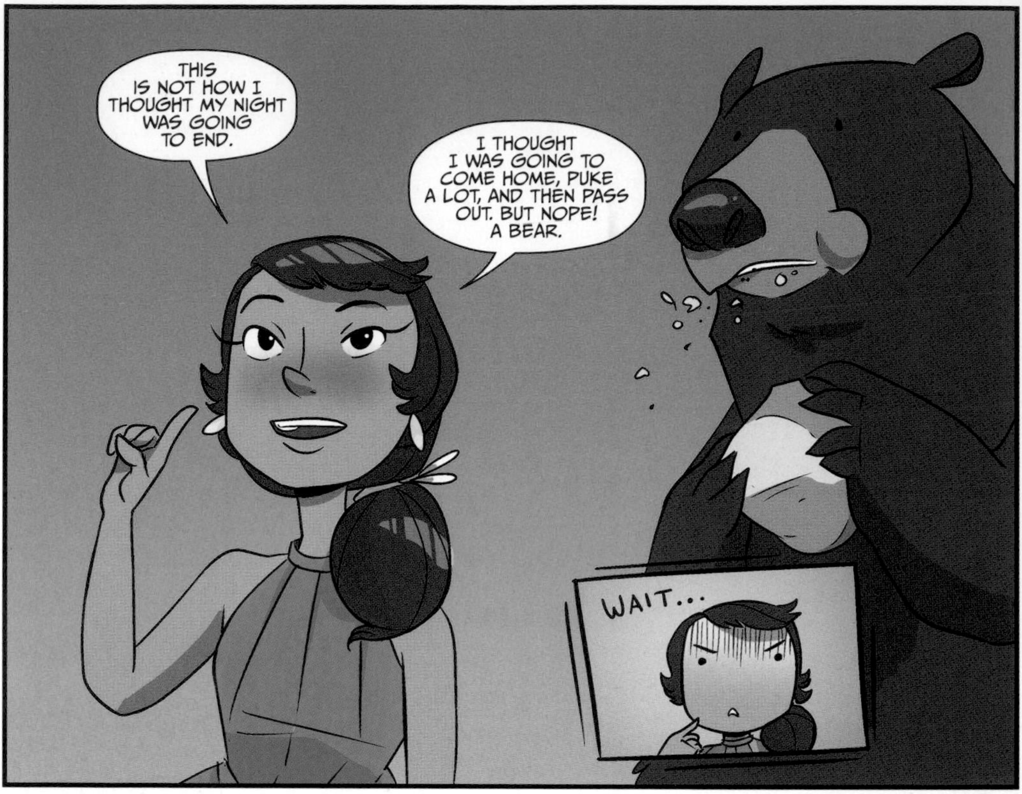
THIS IS NOT HOW I THOUGHT MY NIGHT WAS GOING TO END.
I THOUGHT I WAS GOING TO COME HOME, PUKE A LOT, AND THEN PASS OUT. BUT NOPE! A BEAR.
WAIT...

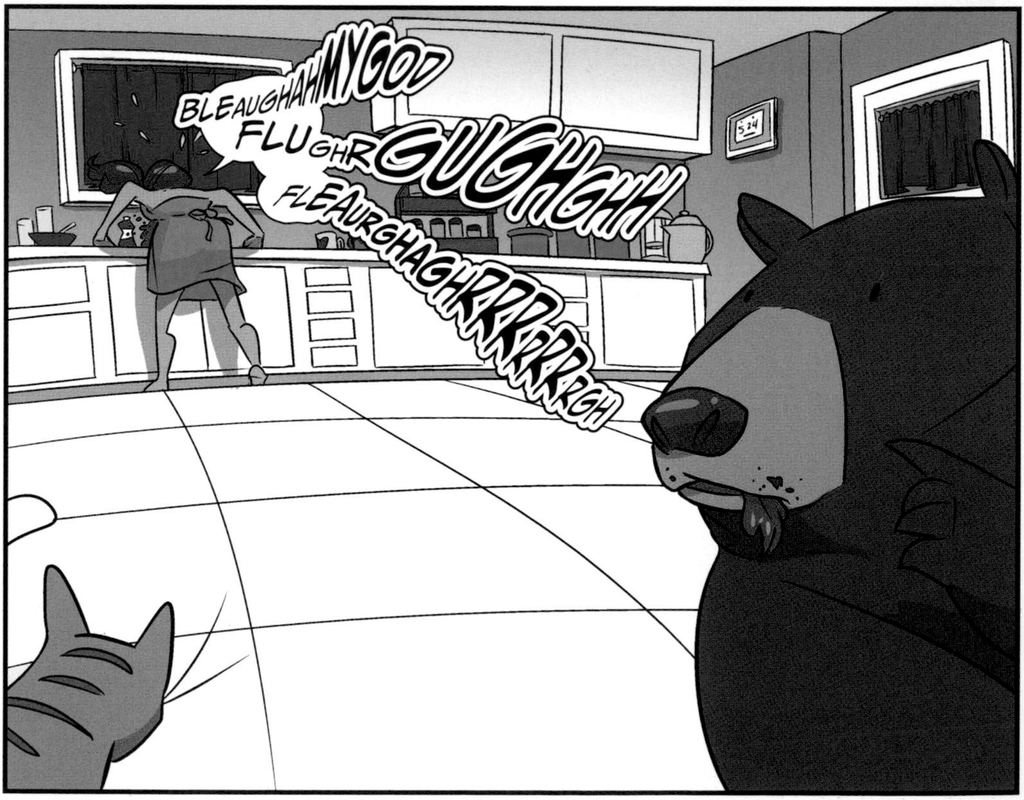
BLEAUGHAHMYGOD
FLUGHRGUGHGHH
FLEAURGHAGHRRRRRRRRRGH

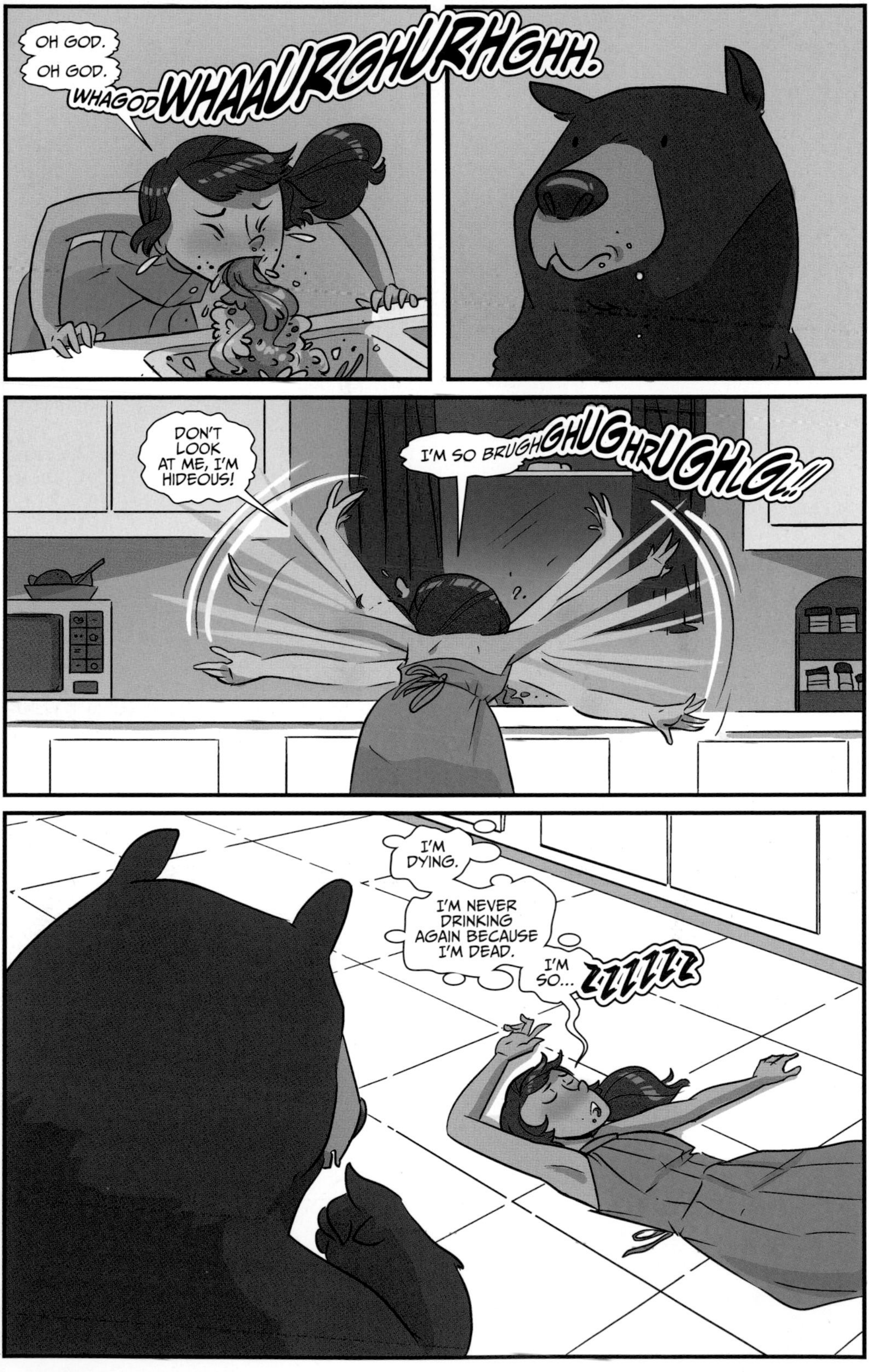
OH GOD.
OH GOD.
WHAGOD WHAAURGHURHGHH.
DON'T LOOK AT ME, I'M HIDEOUS!
I'M SO BRUGHGHUGHRUGHLG..!!
I'M DYING.
I'M NEVER DRINKING AGAIN BECAUSE I'M DEAD.
I'M SO...
ZZZZZZ

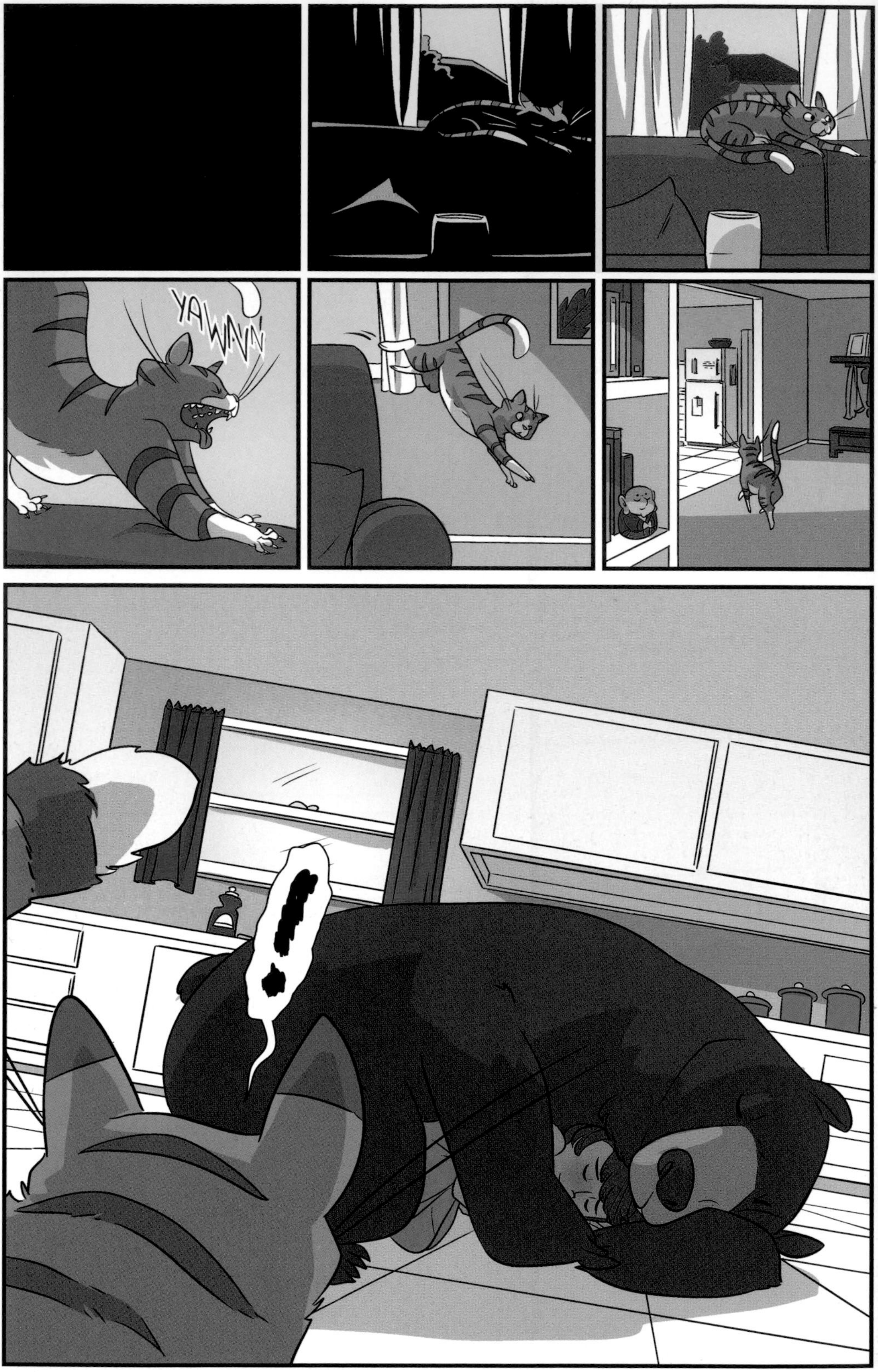
YAWN'N'
!

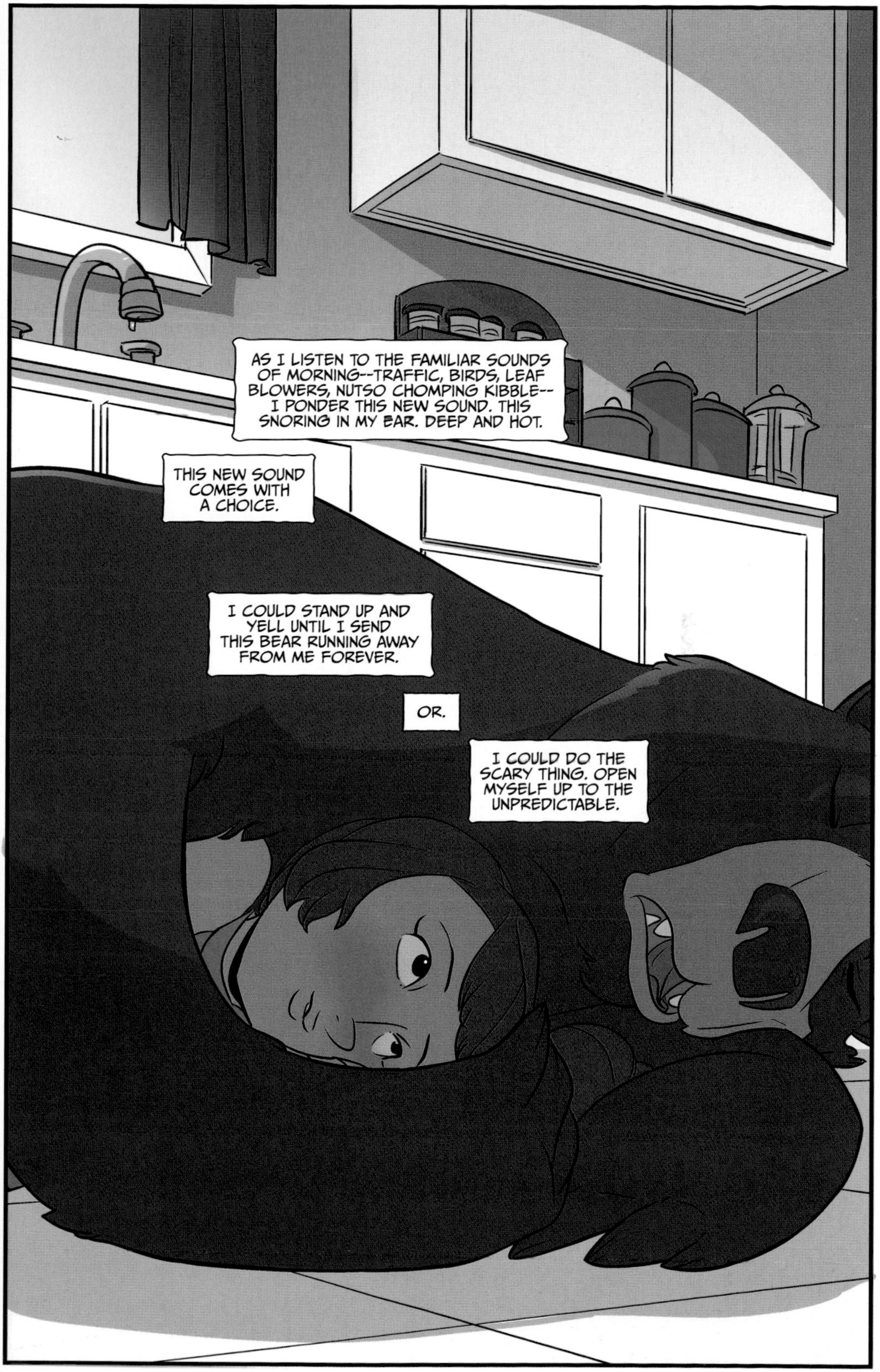
AS I LISTEN TO THE FAMILIAR SOUNDS OF MORNING--TRAFFIC, BIRDS, LEAF BLOWERS, NUTSO CHOMPING KIBBLE-- I PONDER THIS NEW SOUND. THIS SNORING IN MY EAR. DEEP AND HOT.
THIS NEW SOUND COMES WITH A CHOICE.
I COULD STAND UP AND YELL UNTIL I SEND THIS BEAR RUNNING AWAY FROM ME FOREVER.
OR.
I COULD DO THE SCARY THING. OPEN MYSELF UP TO THE UNPREDICTABLE.

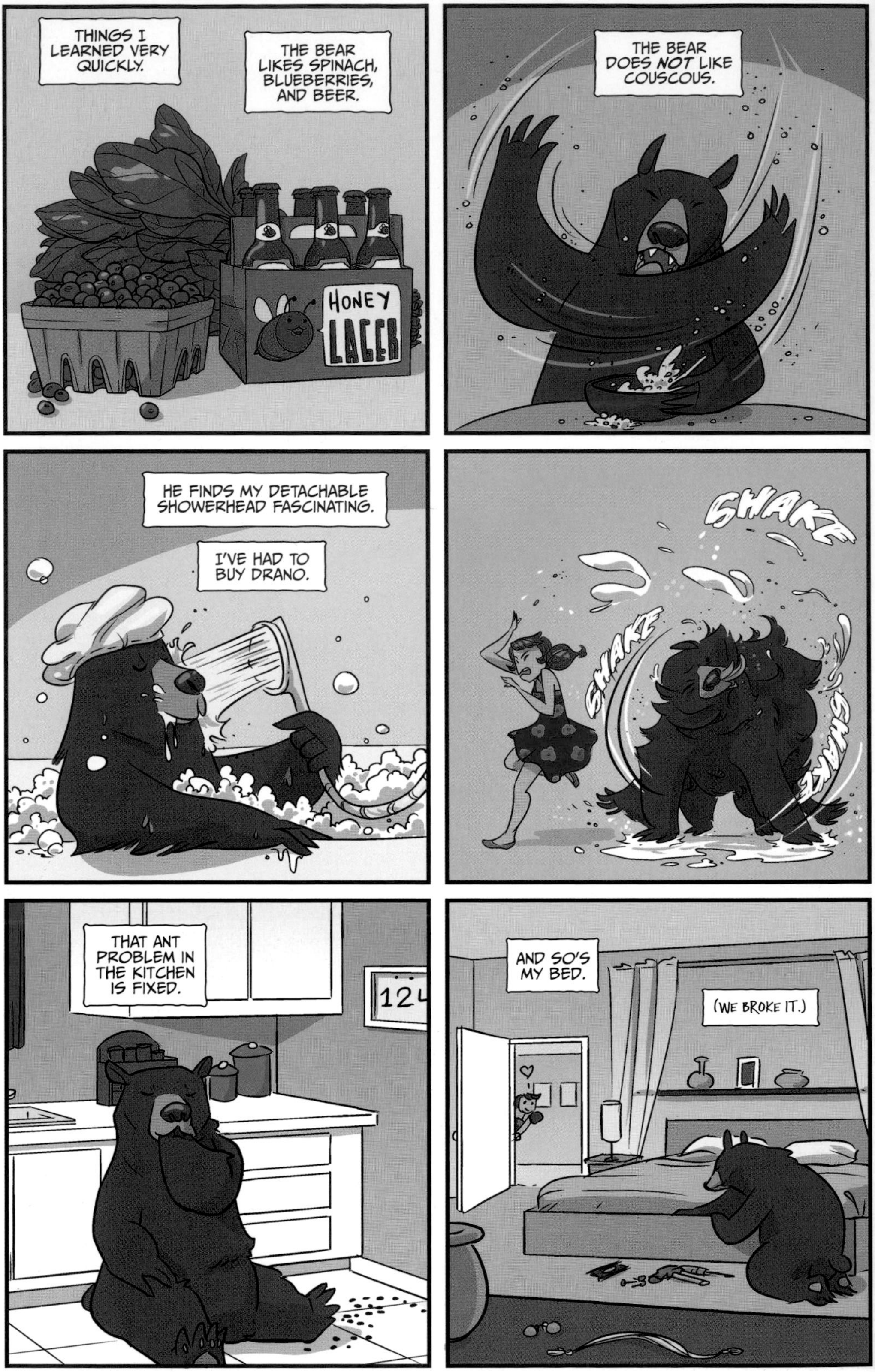
THINGS I LEARNED VERY QUICKLY.
THE BEAR LIKES SPINACH, BLUEBERRIES, AND BEER.
HONEY LAGER
THE BEAR DOES NOT LIKE COUSCOUS.
HE FINDS MY DETACHABLE SHOWERHEAD FASCINATING.
I'VE HAD TO BUY DRANO.
SHAKE
SHAKE
SHAKE
THAT ANT PROBLEM IN THE KITCHEN IS FIXED.
AND SO'S MY BED.
(WE BROKE IT.)

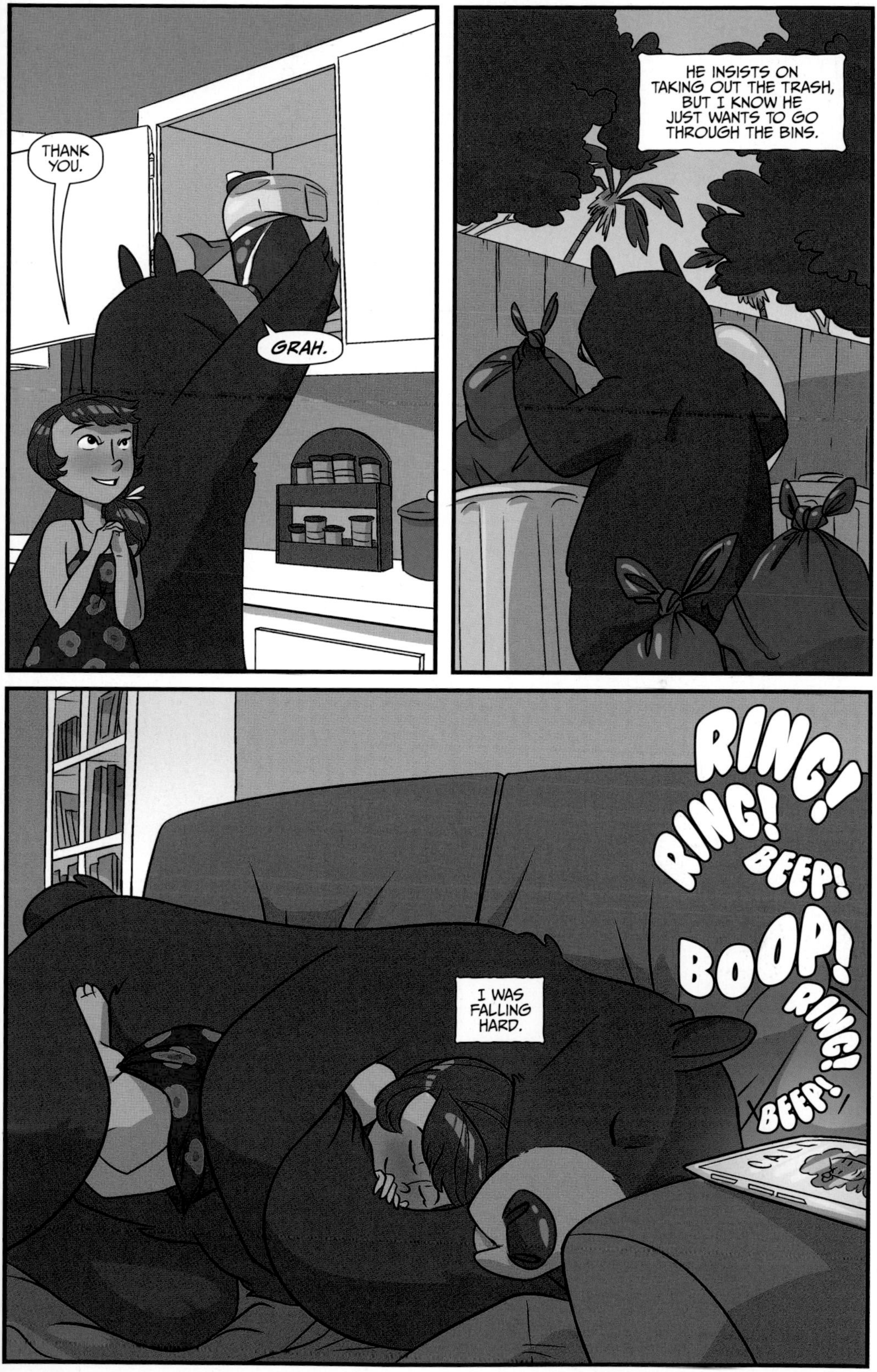
THANK YOU.
GRAH.
HE INSISTS ON TAKING OUT THE TRASH, BUT I KNOW HE JUST WANTS TO GO THROUGH THE BINS.
RING!
RING!
BEEP!
BOOP!
RING!
BEEP!
I WAS FALLING HARD.

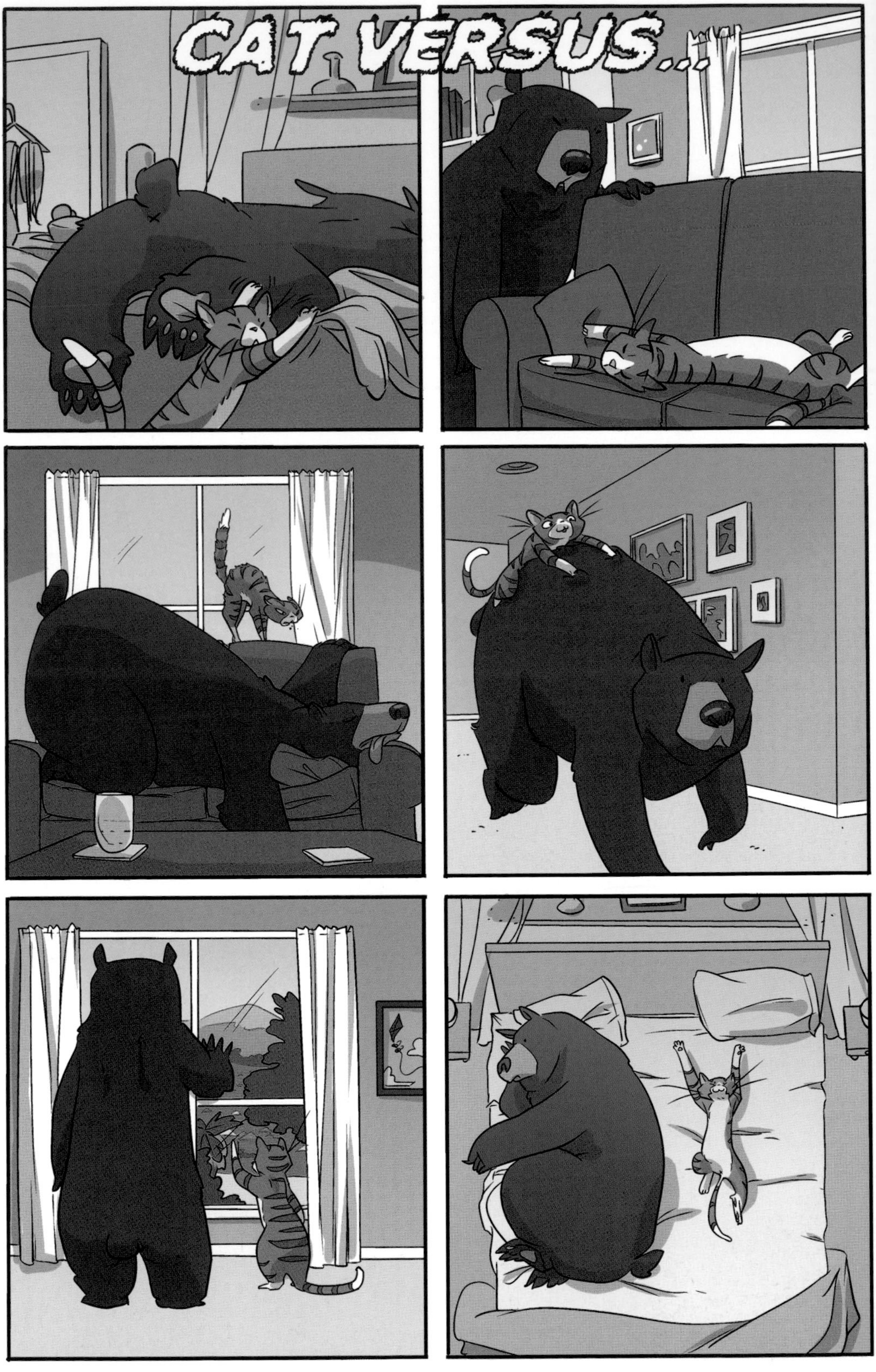
CAT VERSUS...

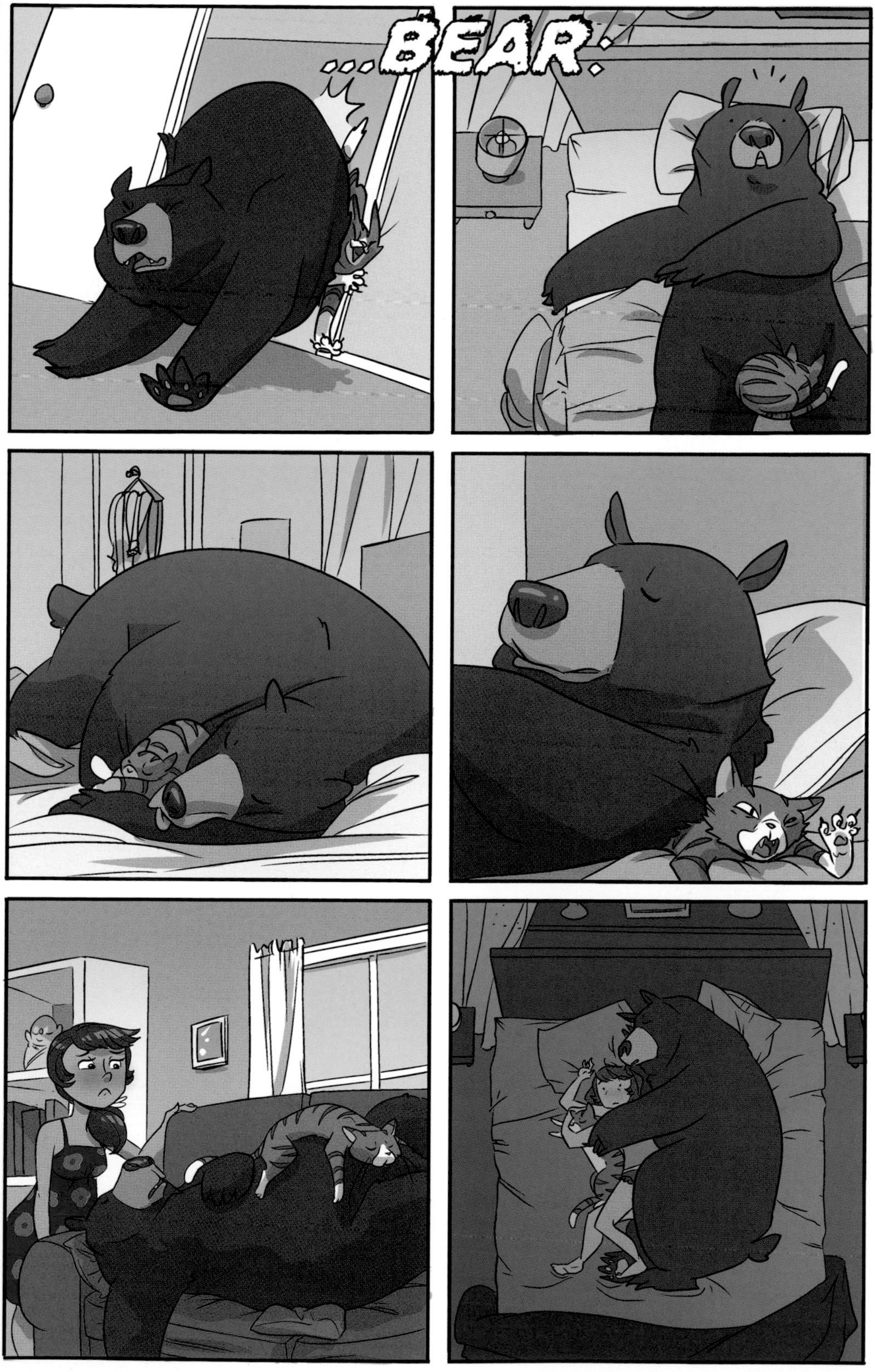
...BEAR!

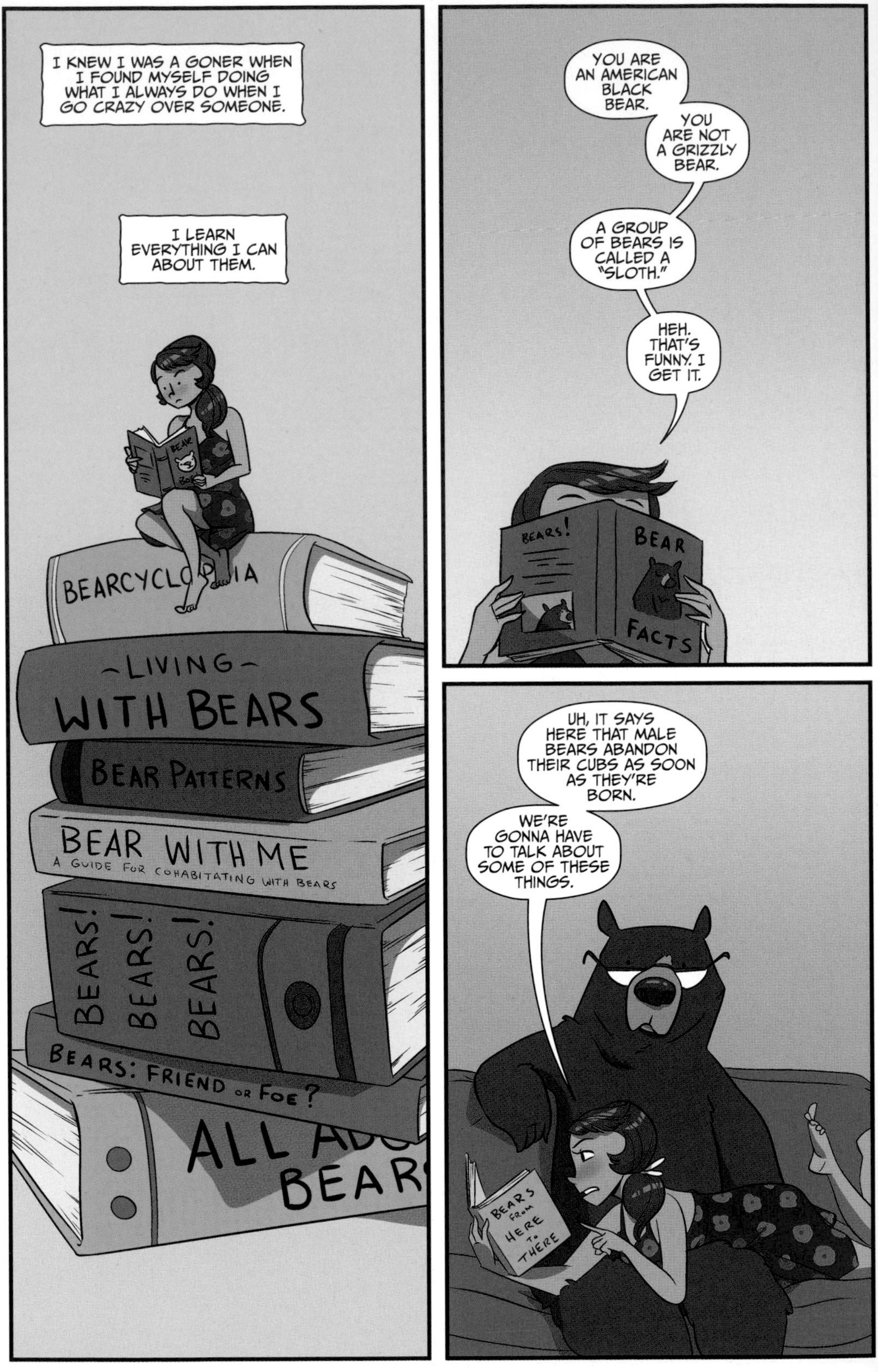
I KNEW I WAS A GONER WHEN I FOUND MYSELF DOING WHAT I ALWAYS DO WHEN I GO CRAZY OVER SOMEONE.
I LEARN EVERYTHING I CAN ABOUT THEM.
BEARCYCLOP IA
-LIVING- WITH BEARS
BEAR PATTERNS
BEAR WITH ME
A GUIDE FOR COHABITATING WITH BEARS
BEARS! BEARS! BEARS!
BEARS: FRIEND OR FOE?
YOU ARE AN AMERICAN BLACK BEAR.
YOU ARE NOT A GRIZZLY BEAR.
A GROUP OF BEARS IS CALLED A "SLOTH."
HEH. THAT'S FUNNY. I GET IT.
BEARS!
BEAR FACTS
UH, IT SAYS HERE THAT MALE BEARS ABANDON THEIR CUBS AS SOON AS THEY'RE BORN.
WE'RE GONNA HAVE TO TALK ABOUT SOME OF THESE THINGS.
BEARS FROM HERE TO THERE

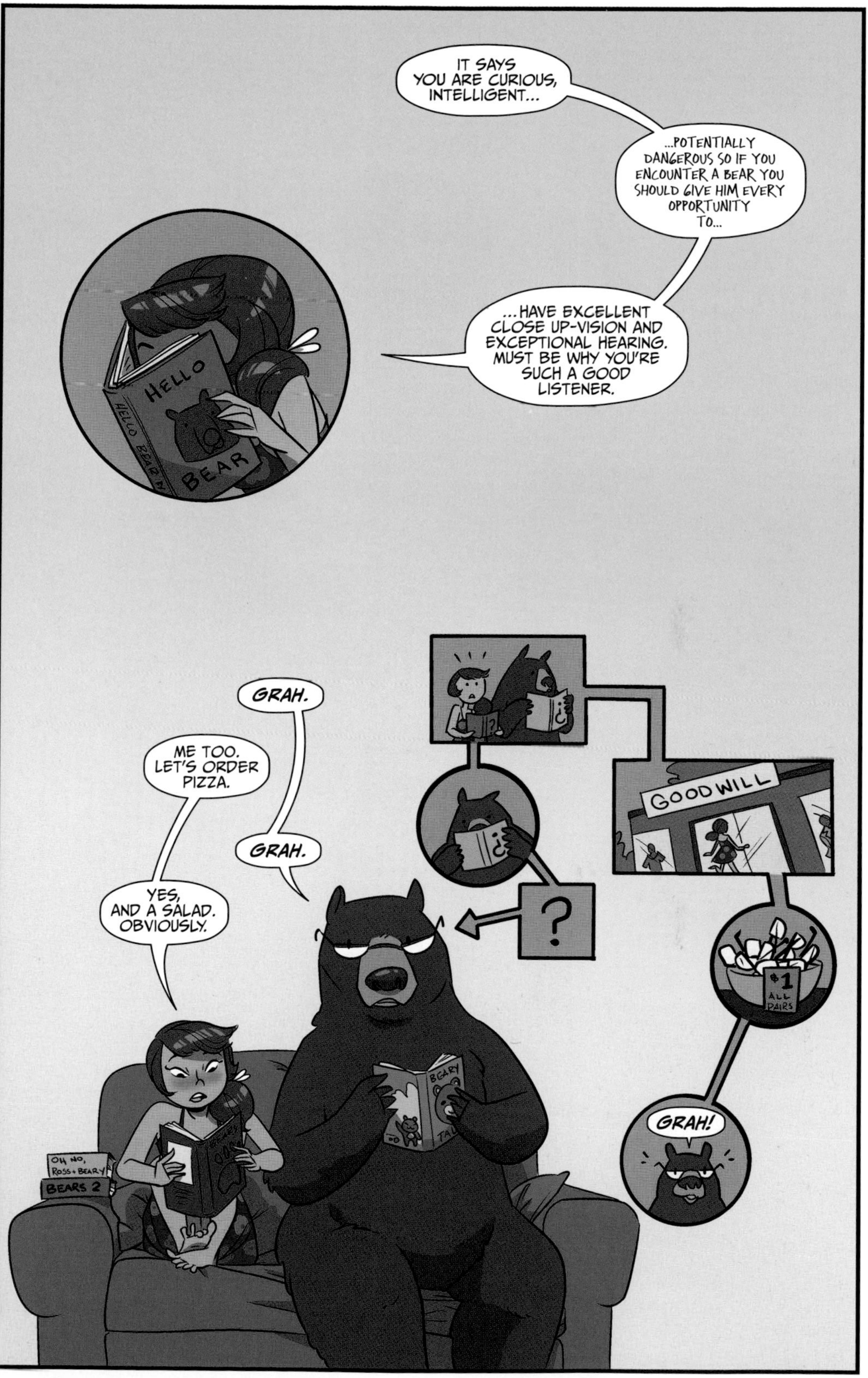
IT SAYS YOU ARE CURIOUS, INTELLIGENT...
...POTENTIALLY DANGEROUS SO IF YOU ENCOUNTER A BEAR YOU SHOULD GIVE HIM EVERY OPPORTUNITY TO...
...HAVE EXCELLENT CLOSE UP-VISION AND EXCEPTIONAL HEARING. MUST BE WHY YOU'RE SUCH A GOOD LISTENER.
HELLO BEAR
GRAH.
ME TOO. LET'S ORDER PIZZA.
GRAH.
YES, AND A SALAD. OBVIOUSLY.
GOODWILL
?
$1 ALL PAIRS
GRAH!
BEARY TAL
OH NO, ROSS + BEARY
BEARS 2

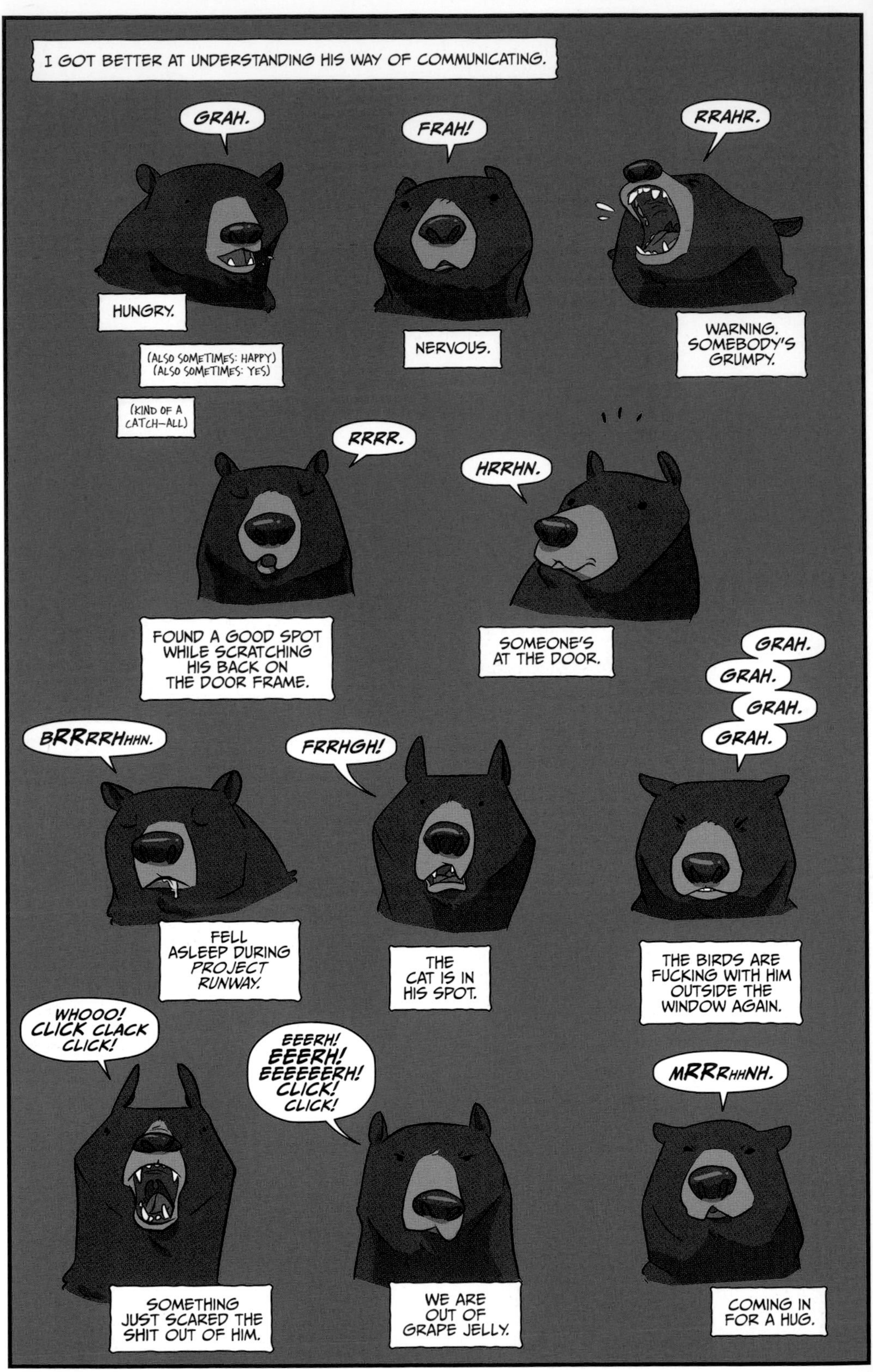
I GOT BETTER AT UNDERSTANDING HIS WAY OF COMMUNICATING.
GRAH.
HUNGRY.
(ALSO SOMETIMES: HAPPY)
(ALSO SOMETIMES: YES)
(KIND OF A CATCH-ALL)
FRAH!
NERVOUS.
RRAHR.
WARNING. SOMEBODY'S GRUMPY.
RRRR.
FOUND A GOOD SPOT WHILE SCRATCHING HIS BACK ON THE DOOR FRAME.
HRRHN.
SOMEONE'S AT THE DOOR.
BRRRRHHHN.
FELL ASLEEP DURING PROJECT RUNWAY.
FRRHGH!
THE CAT IS IN HIS SPOT.
GRAH.
GRAH.
GRAH.
GRAH.
THE BIRDS ARE FUCKING WITH HIM OUTSIDE THE WINDOW AGAIN.
WHOOO! CLICK CLACK CLICK!
SOMETHING JUST SCARED THE SHIT OUT OF HIM.
EEERH! EEERH! EEEEEERH! CLICK! CLICK!
WE ARE OUT OF GRAPE JELLY.
MRRRHHNH.
COMING IN FOR A HUG.

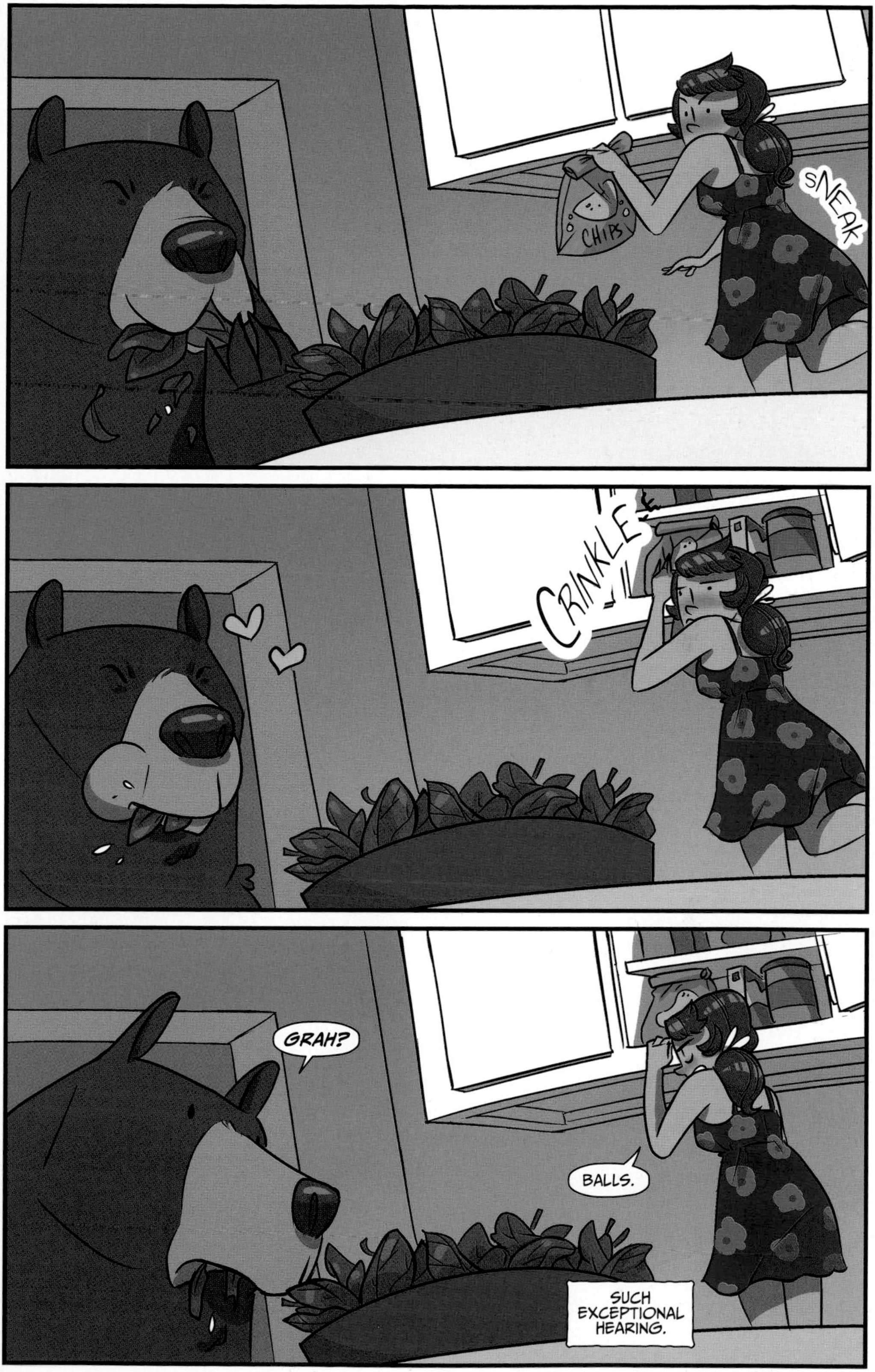
CHIPS
SNEAK
CRINKLE
GRAH?
BALLS.
SUCH EXCEPTIONAL HEARING.

WE ALSO
LEARNED A VERY
IMPORTANT LESSON...

...EVEN
THOUGH
IT'S FUN...

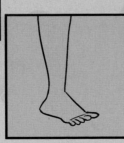

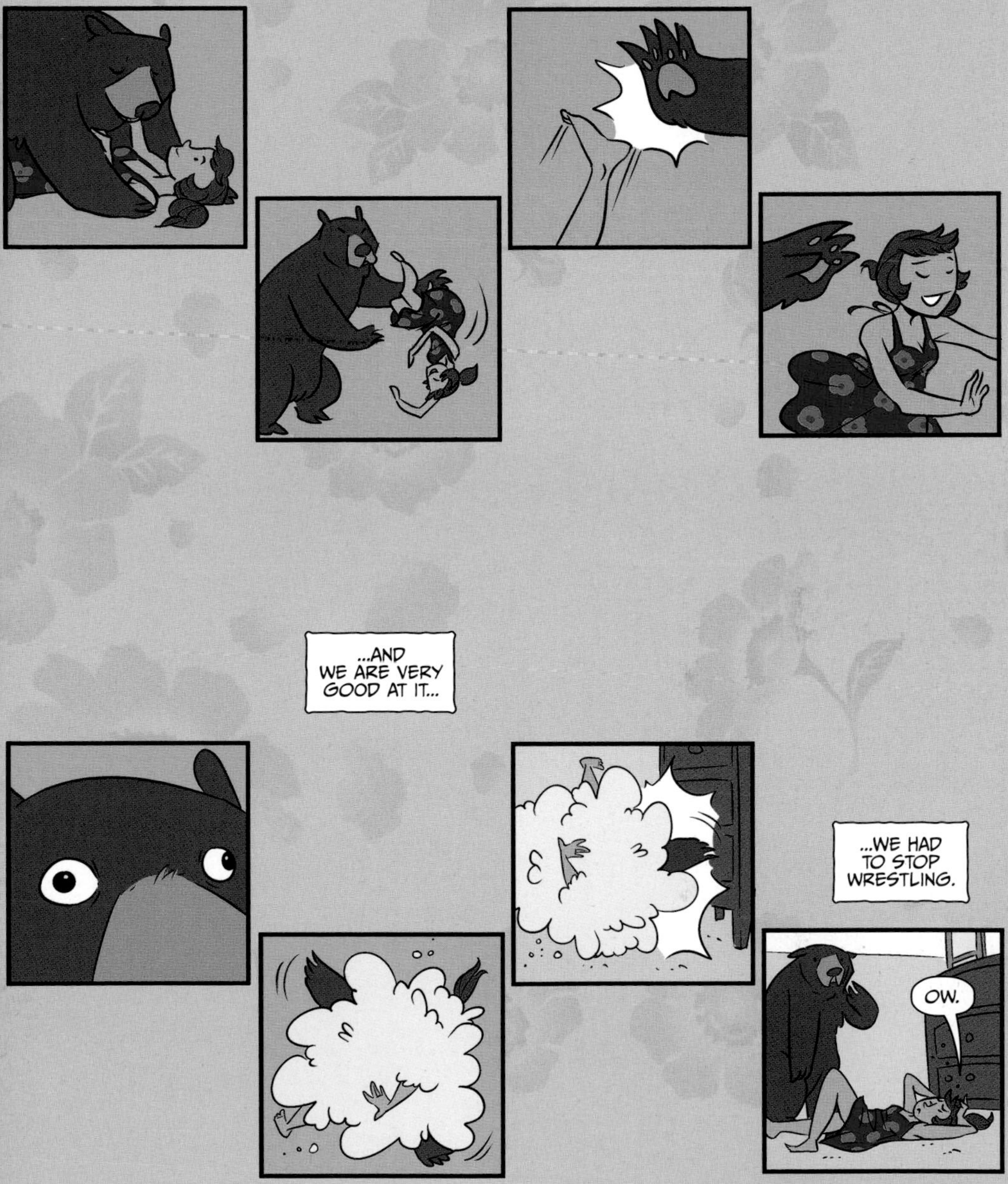
...AND WE ARE VERY GOOD AT IT...
...WE HAD TO STOP WRESTLING.
OW.

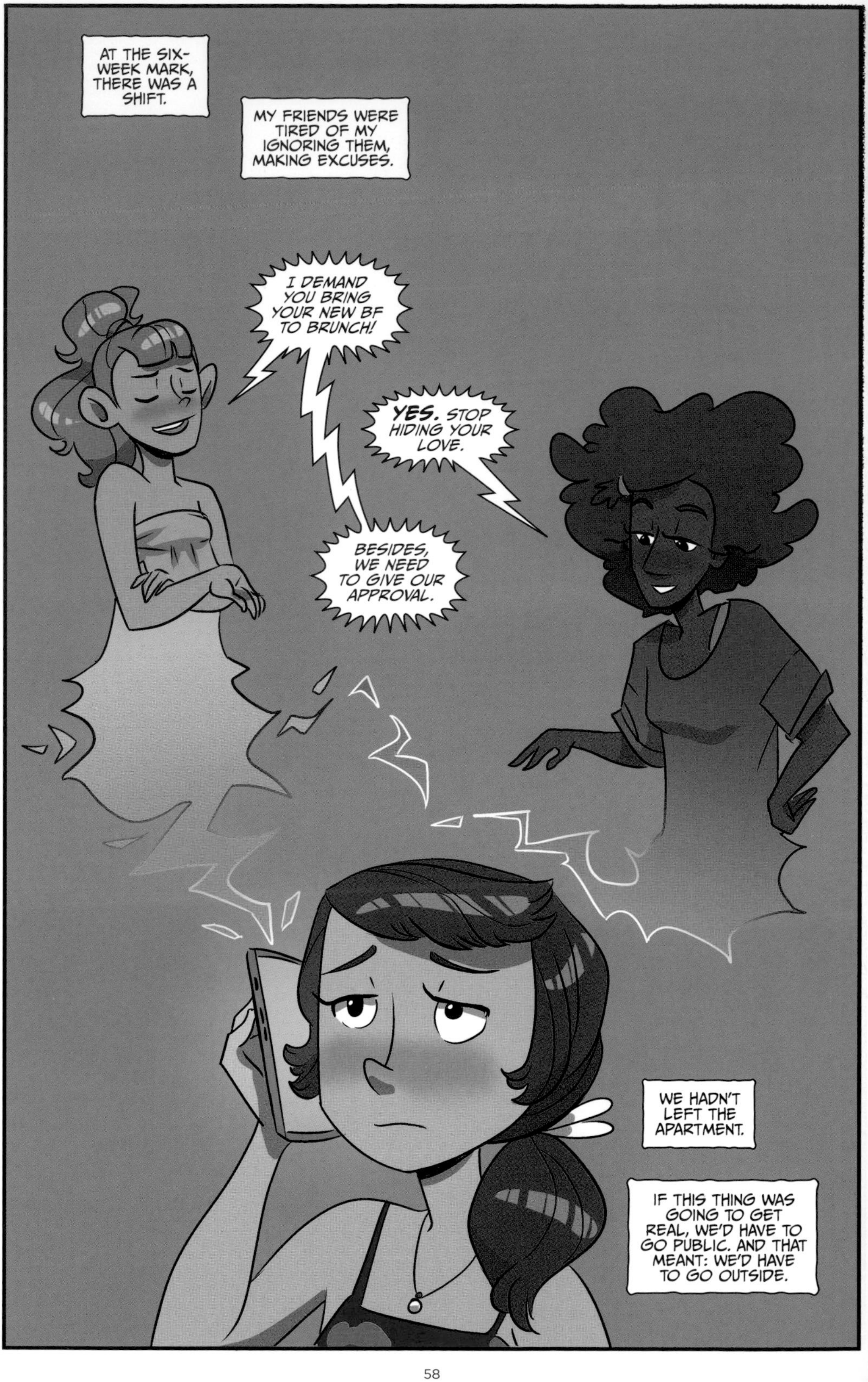

AT THE SIX-WEEK MARK, THERE WAS A SHIFT.
MY FRIENDS WERE TIRED OF MY IGNORING THEM, MAKING EXCUSES.
I DEMAND YOU BRING YOUR NEW BF TO BRUNCH!
YES. STOP HIDING YOUR LOVE.
BESIDES, WE NEED TO GIVE OUR APPROVAL.
WE HADN'T LEFT THE APARTMENT.
IF THIS THING WAS GOING TO GET REAL, WE'D HAVE TO GO PUBLIC. AND THAT MEANT: WE'D HAVE TO GO OUTSIDE.

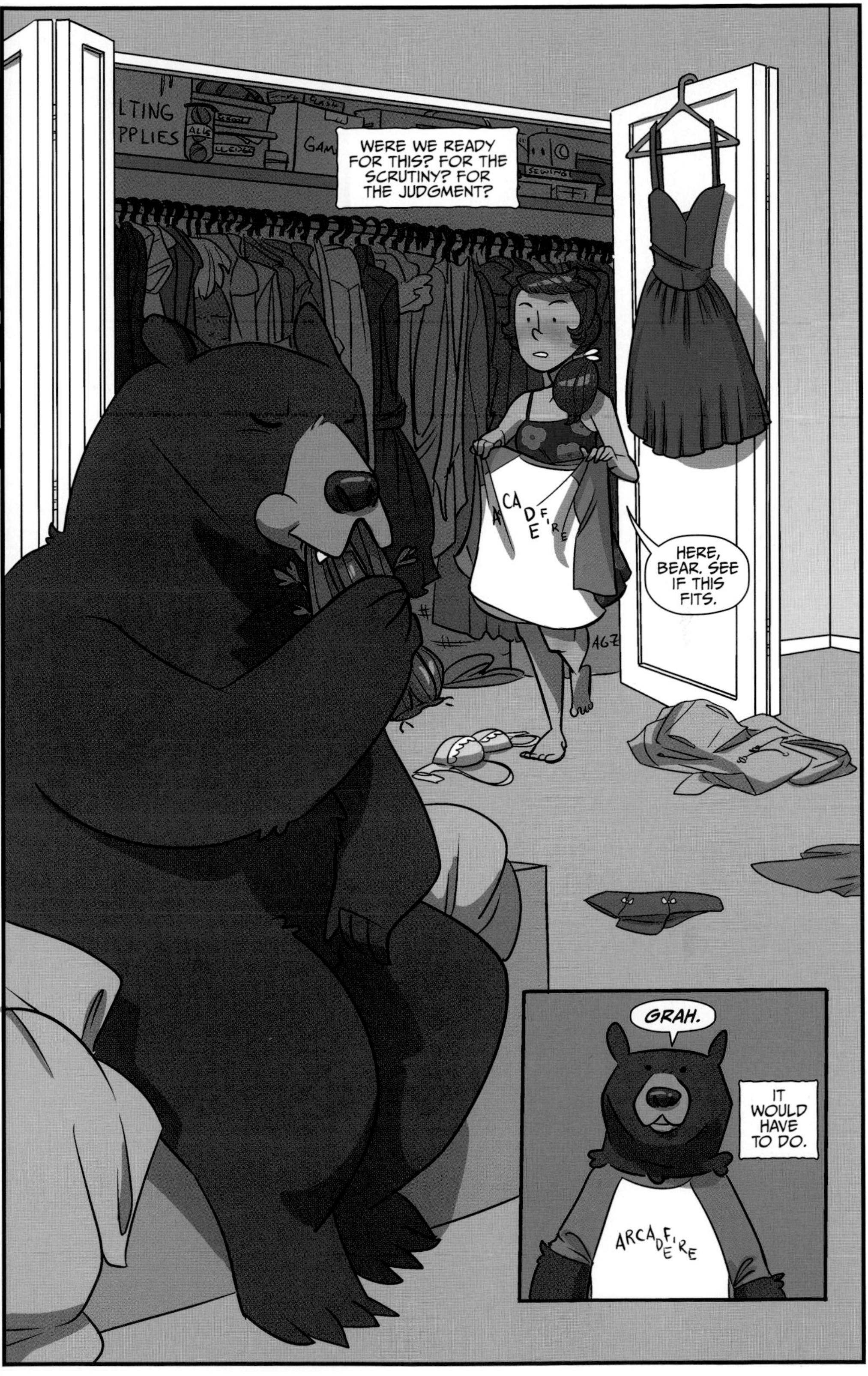
WERE WE READY FOR THIS? FOR THE SCRUTINY? FOR THE JUDGMENT?
HERE, BEAR. SEE IF THIS FITS.
GRAH.
IT WOULD HAVE TO DO.

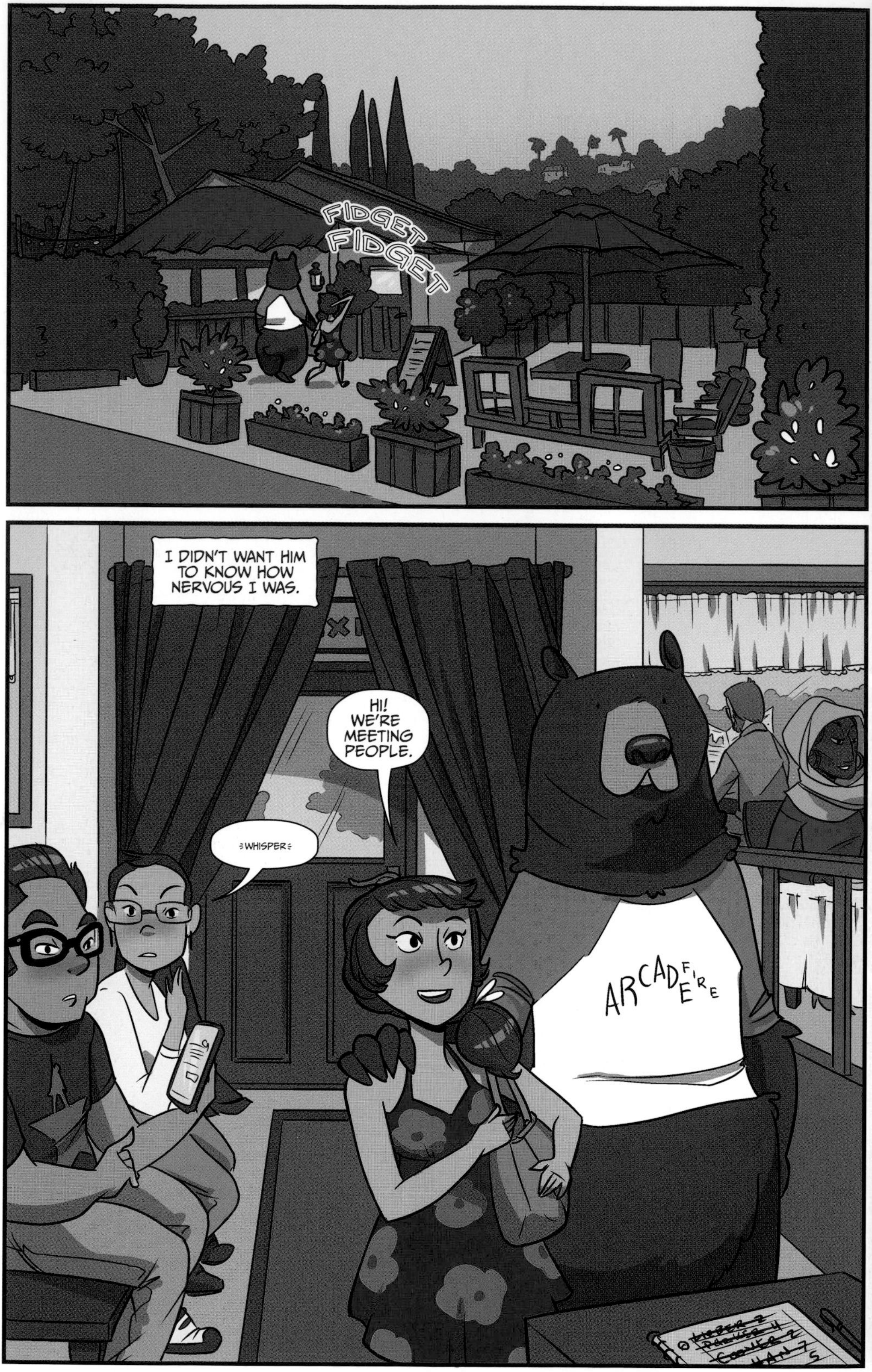
FIDGET
FIDGET
I DIDN'T WANT HIM TO KNOW HOW NERVOUS I WAS.
HI! WE'RE MEETING PEOPLE.
WHISPER
ARCADE FIRE

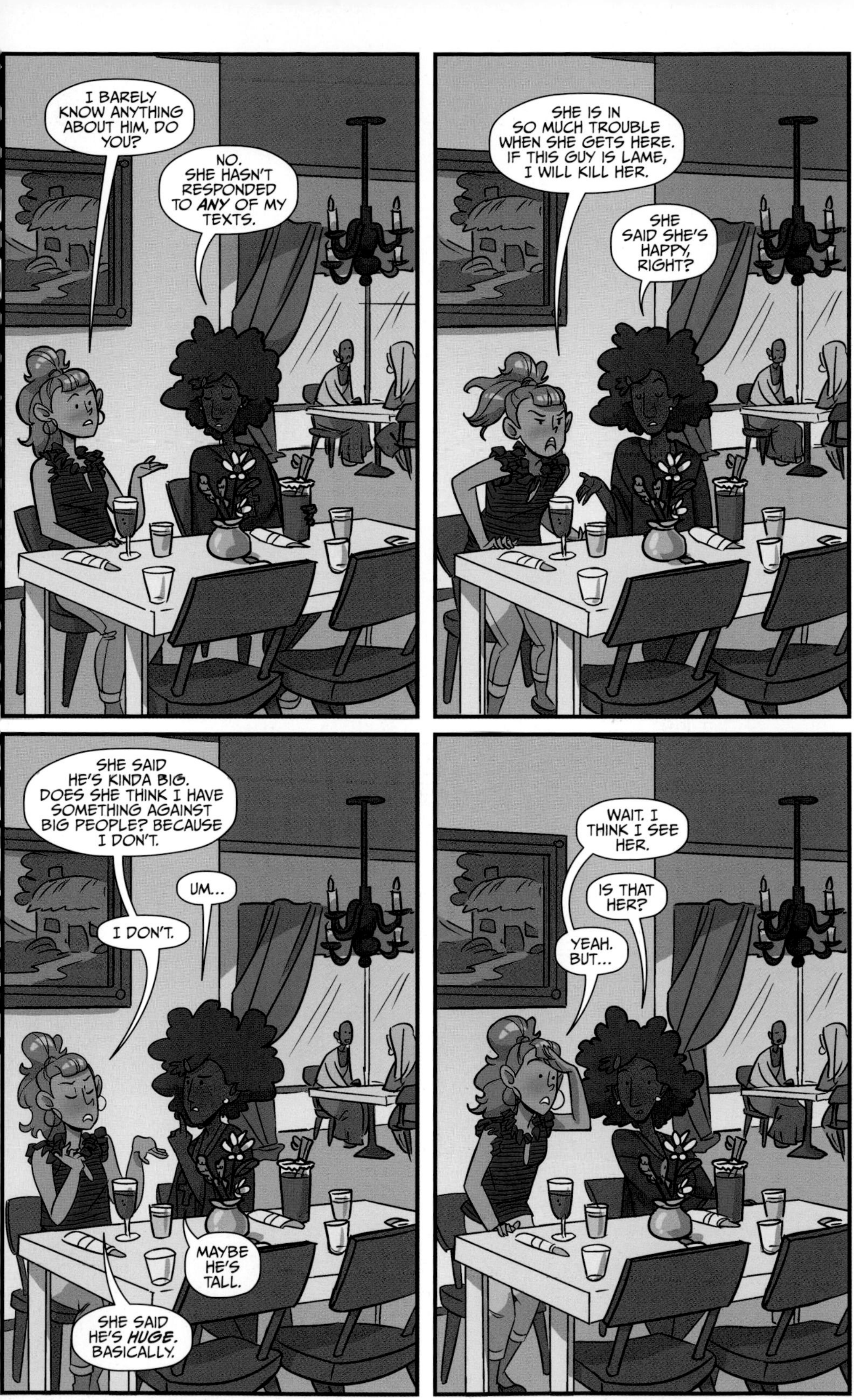

I BARELY KNOW ANYTHING ABOUT HIM, DO YOU?
NO. SHE HASN'T RESPONDED TO ANY OF MY TEXTS.
SHE IS IN SO MUCH TROUBLE WHEN SHE GETS HERE. IF THIS GUY IS LAME, I WILL KILL HER.
SHE SAID SHE'S HAPPY, RIGHT?
SHE SAID HE'S KINDA BIG. DOES SHE THINK I HAVE SOMETHING AGAINST BIG PEOPLE? BECAUSE I DON'T.
UM...
I DON'T.
MAYBE HE'S TALL.
SHE SAID HE'S HUGE. BASICALLY.
WAIT. I THINK I SEE HER.
IS THAT HER?
YEAH. BUT...

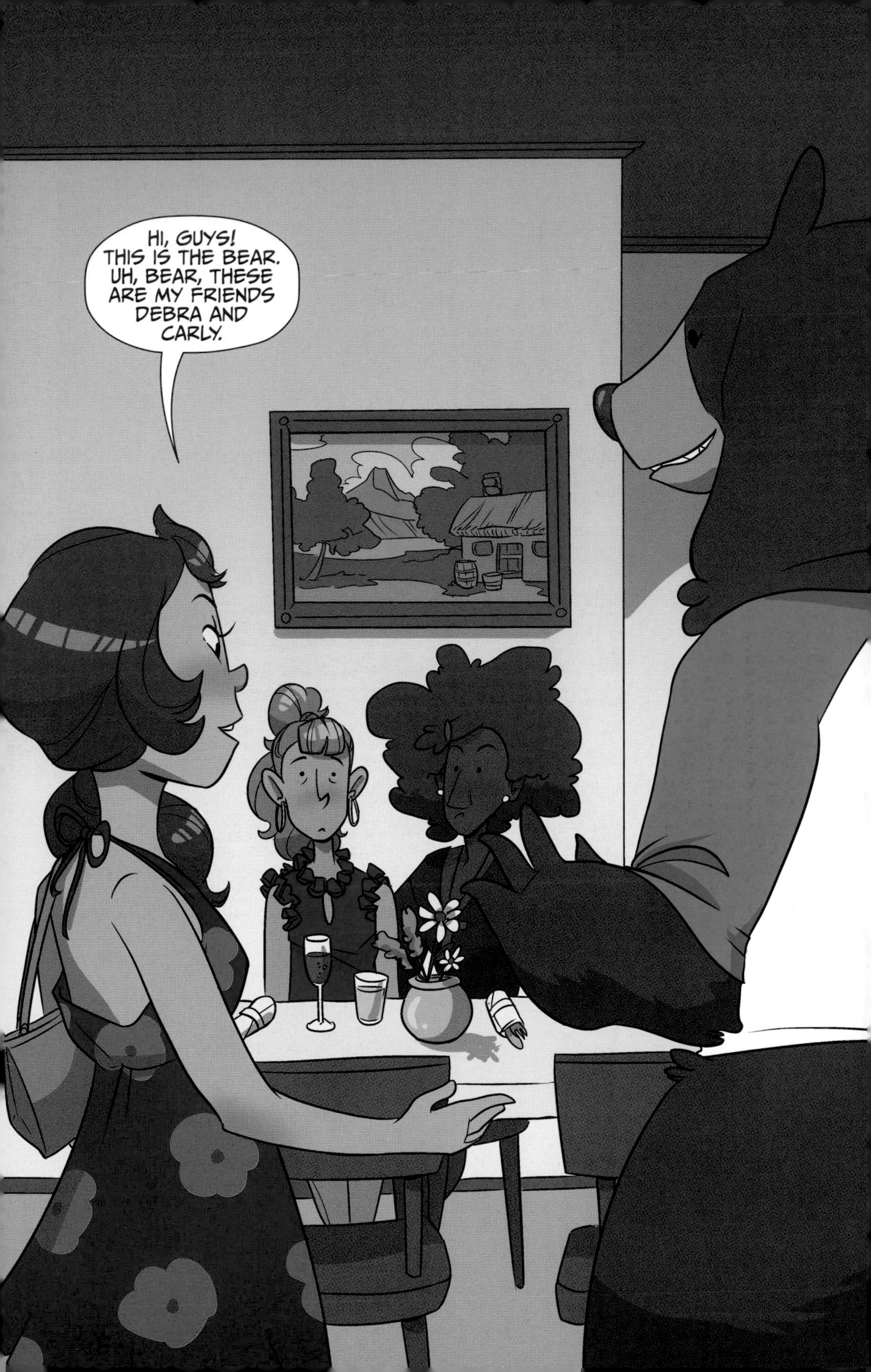
HI, GUYS! THIS IS THE BEAR. UH, BEAR, THESE ARE MY FRIENDS DEBRA AND CARLY.

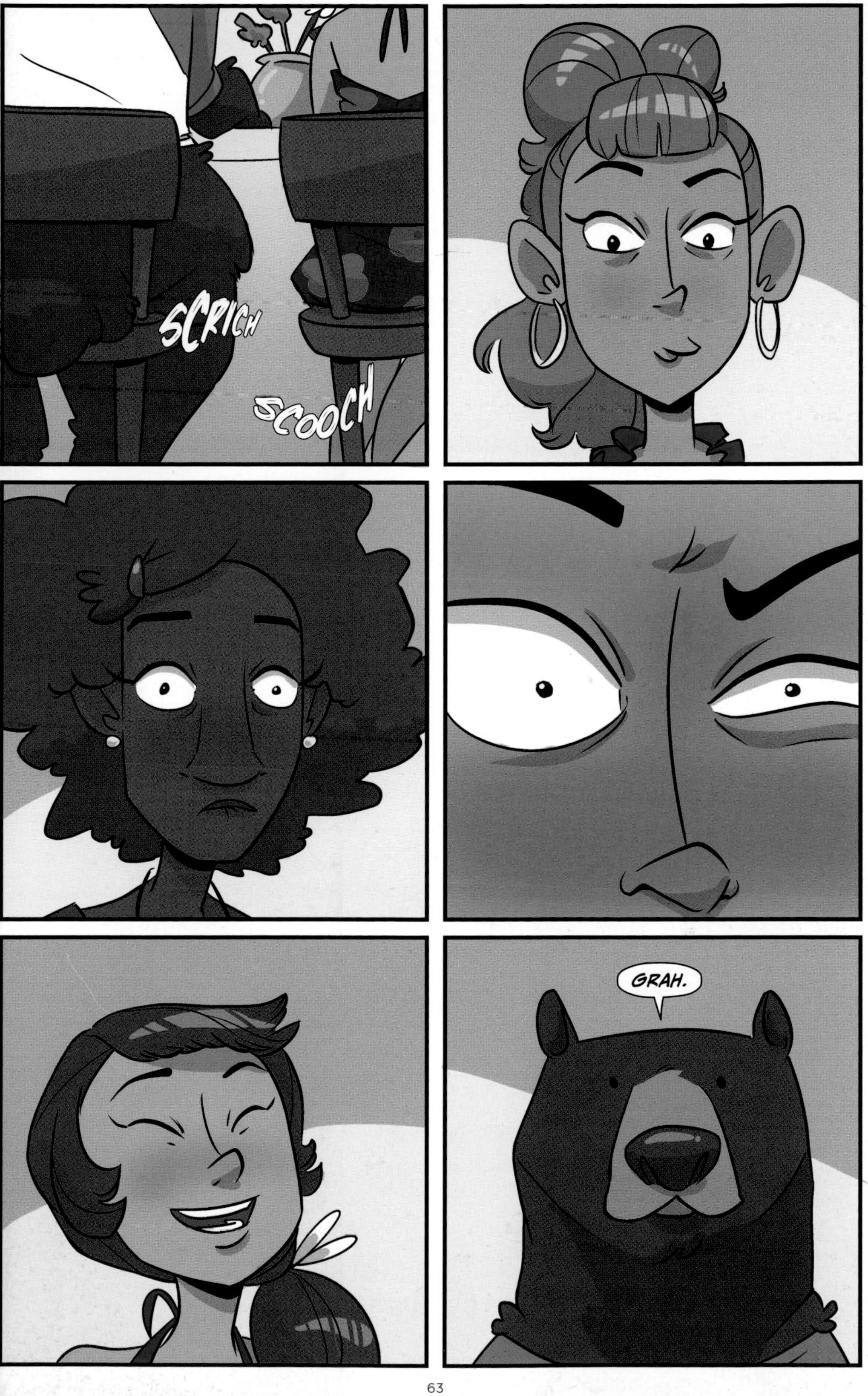
SCRICH
SCOOCH
GRAH.

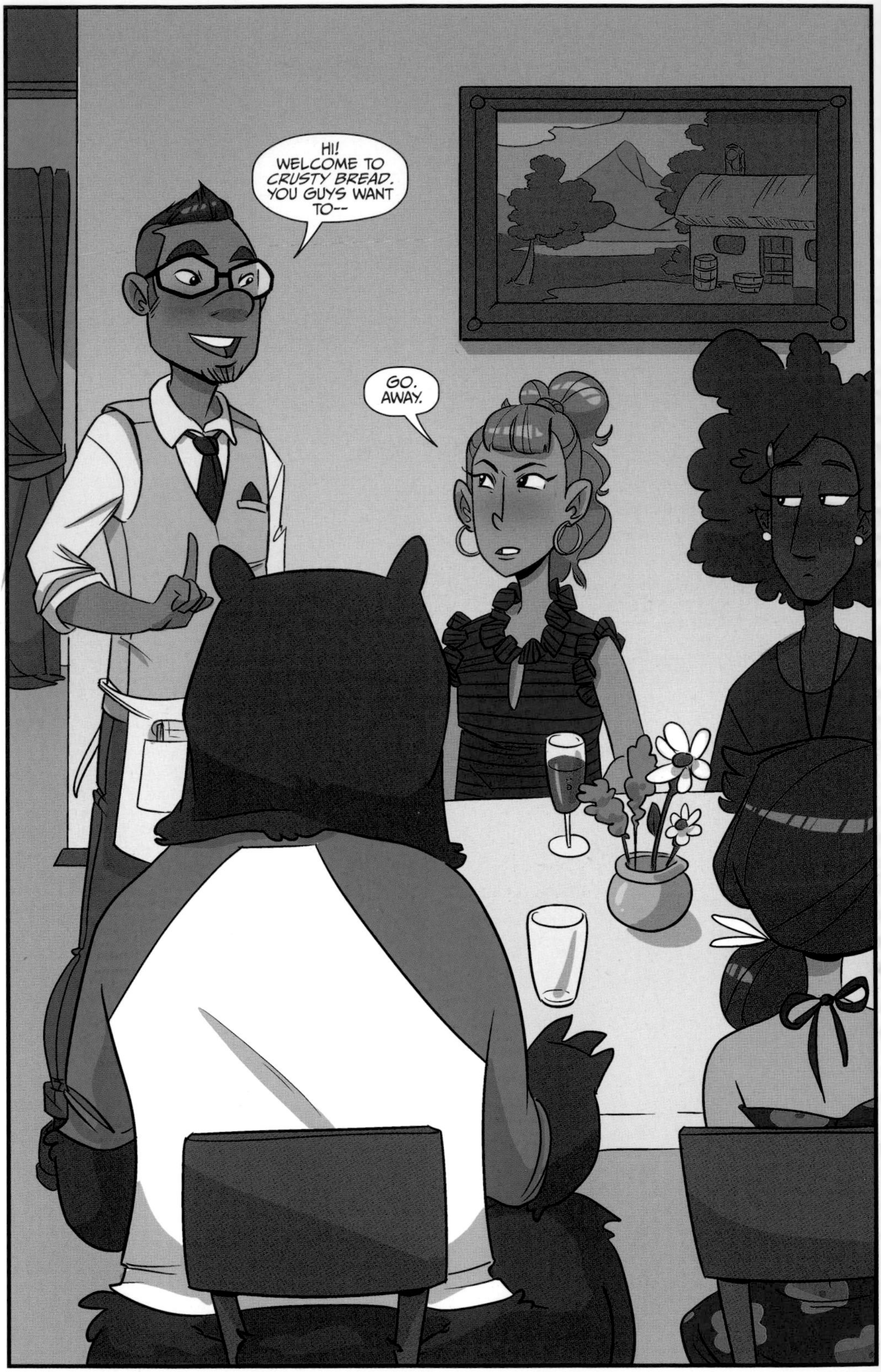
HI! WELCOME TO CRUSTY BREAD. YOU GUYS WANT TO--
GO. AWAY.

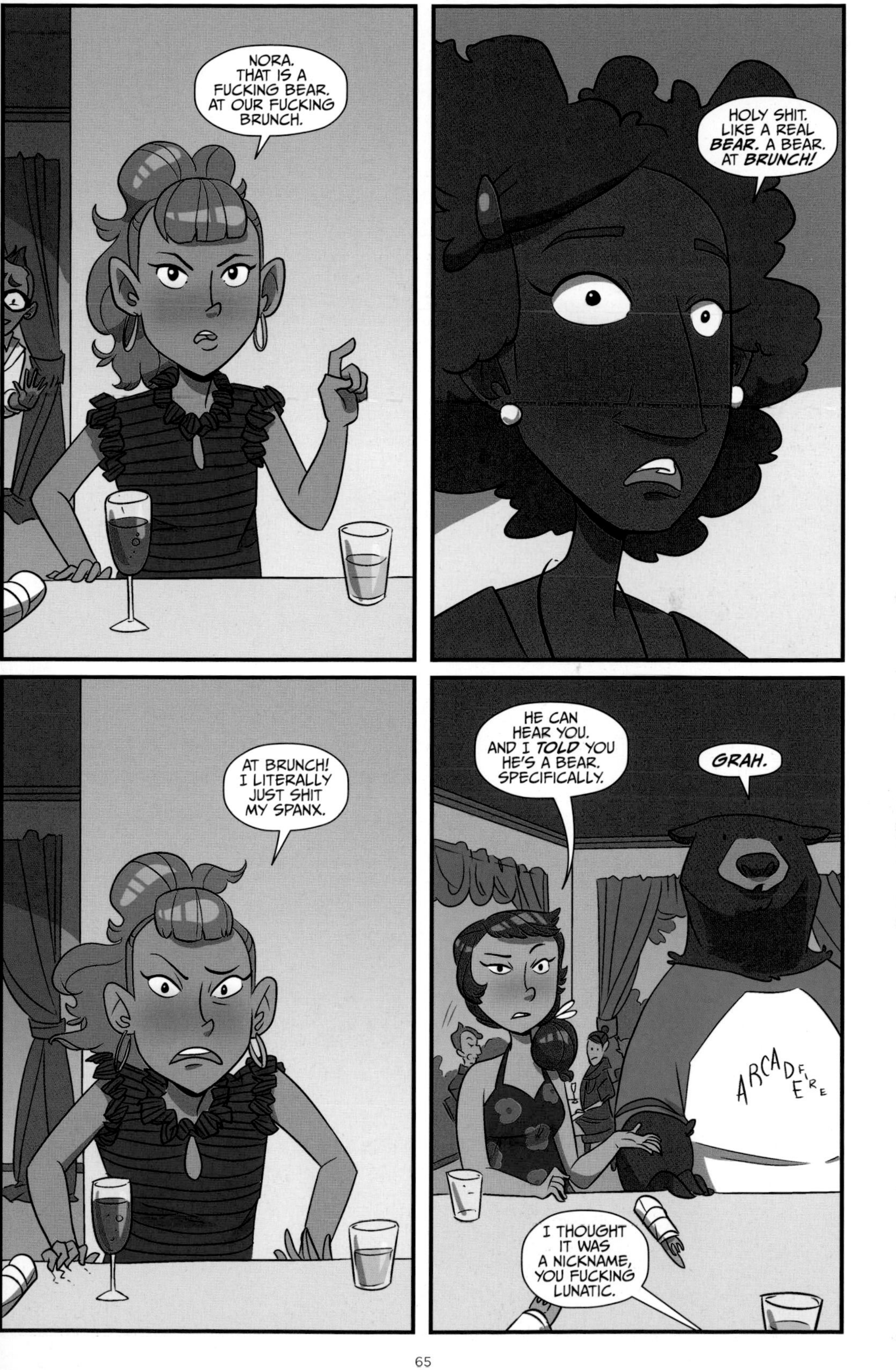
NORA. THAT IS A FUCKING BEAR. AT OUR FUCKING BRUNCH.
HOLY SHIT. LIKE A REAL **BEAR.** A BEAR. AT **BRUNCH!**
AT BRUNCH! I LITERALLY JUST SHIT MY SPANX.
HE CAN HEAR YOU. AND I ***TOLD*** YOU HE'S A BEAR. SPECIFICALLY.
GRAH.
ARCADE FIRE
I THOUGHT IT WAS A NICKNAME, YOU FUCKING LUNATIC.

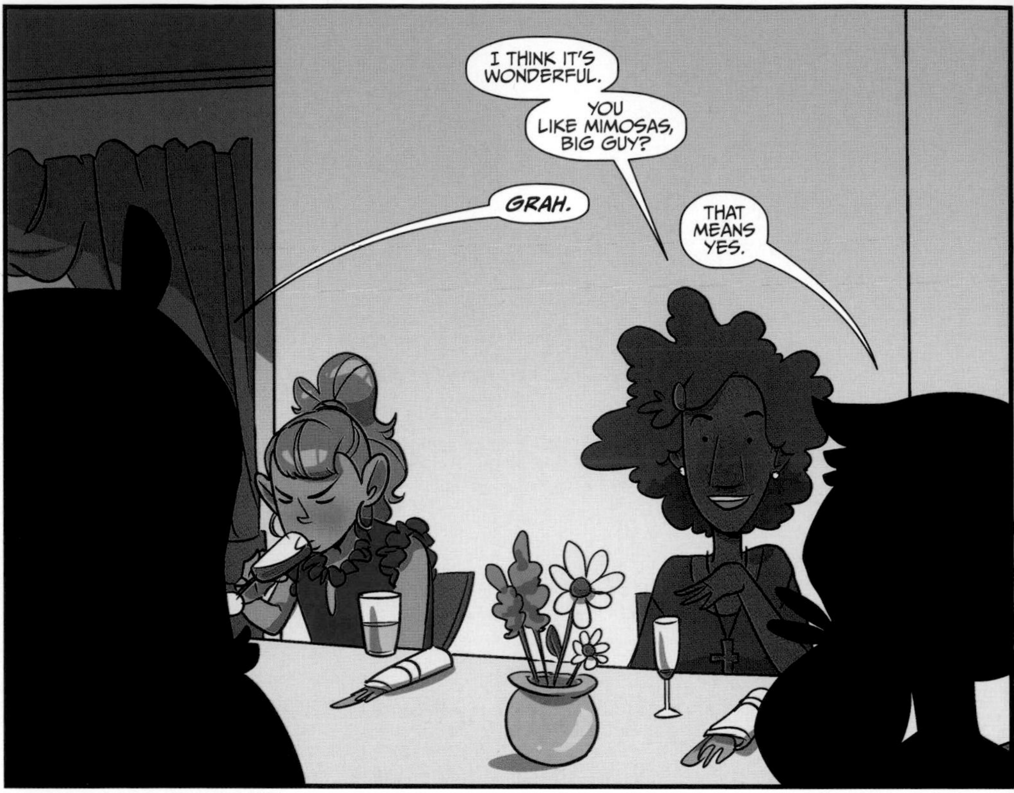
I THINK IT'S WONDERFUL.
YOU LIKE MIMOSAS, BIG GUY?
GRAH.
THAT MEANS YES.

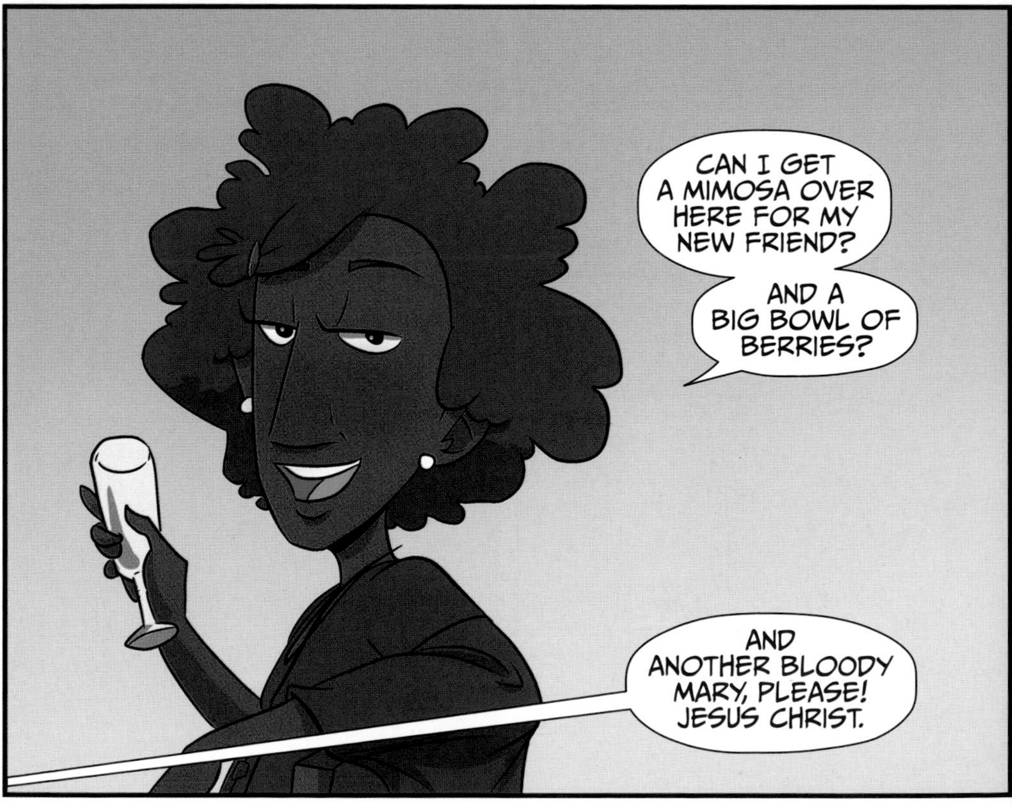
CAN I GET A MIMOSA OVER HERE FOR MY NEW FRIEND?
AND A BIG BOWL OF BERRIES?
AND ANOTHER BLOODY MARY, PLEASE! JESUS CHRIST.

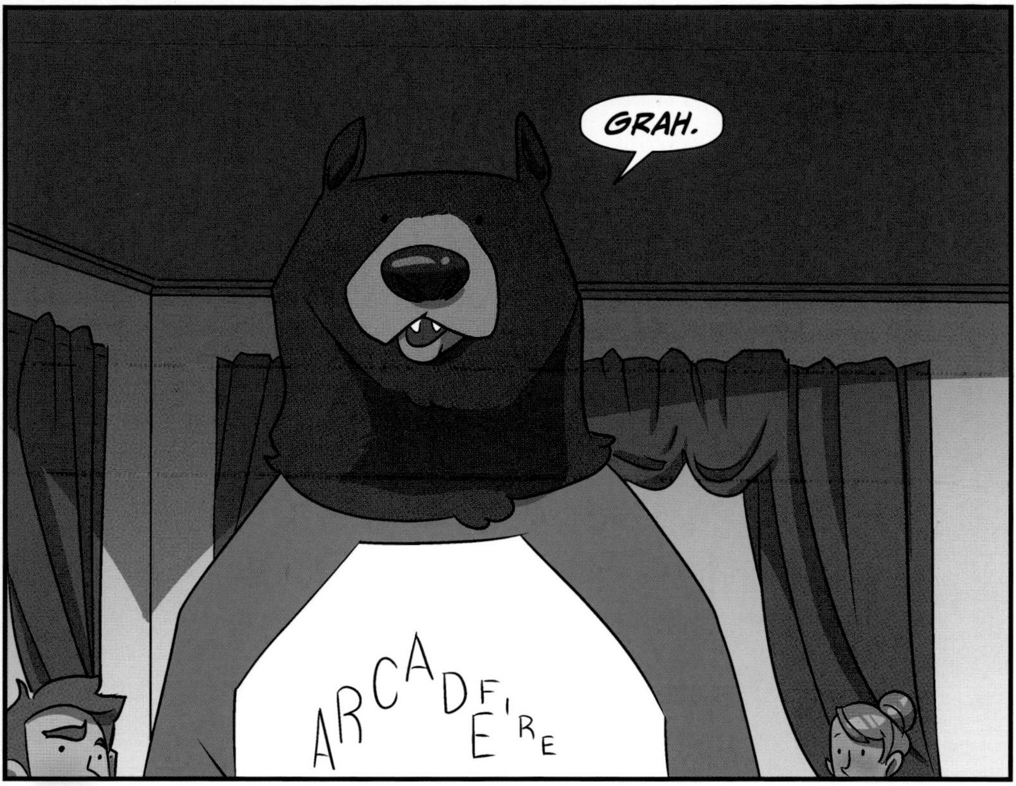
GRAH.
ARCADE FIRE

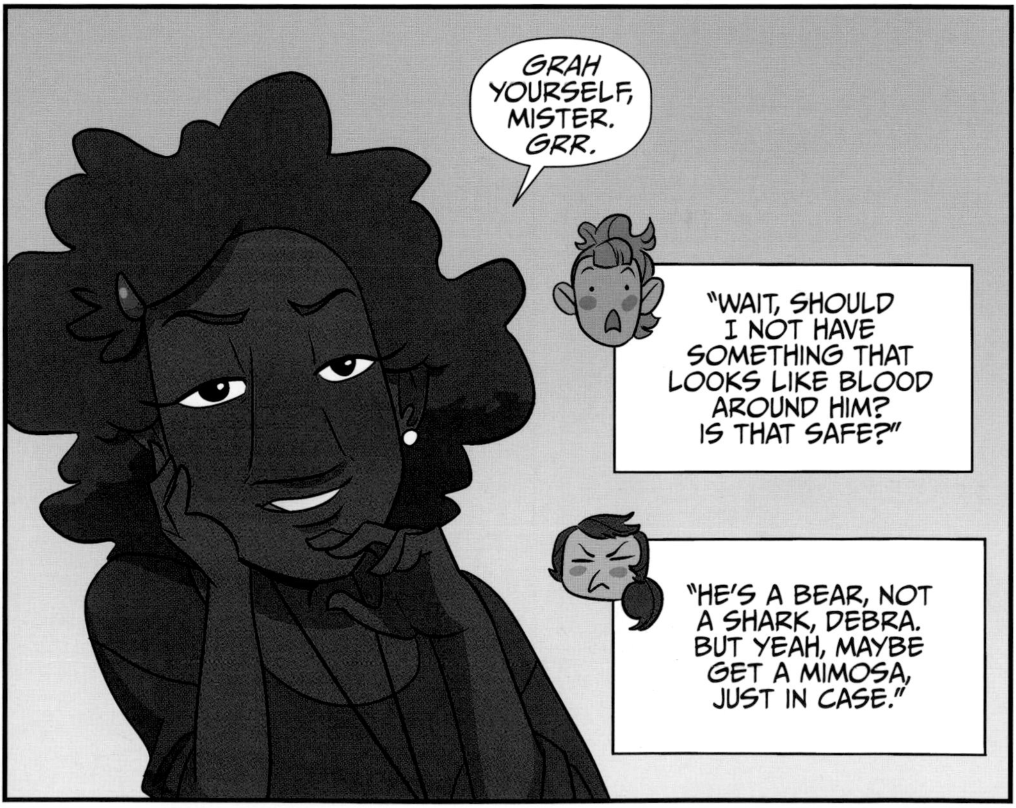
GRAH YOURSELF, MISTER. GRR.
"WAIT, SHOULD I NOT HAVE SOMETHING THAT LOOKS LIKE BLOOD AROUND HIM? IS THAT SAFE?"
"HE'S A BEAR, NOT A SHARK, DEBRA. BUT YEAH, MAYBE GET A MIMOSA, JUST IN CASE."

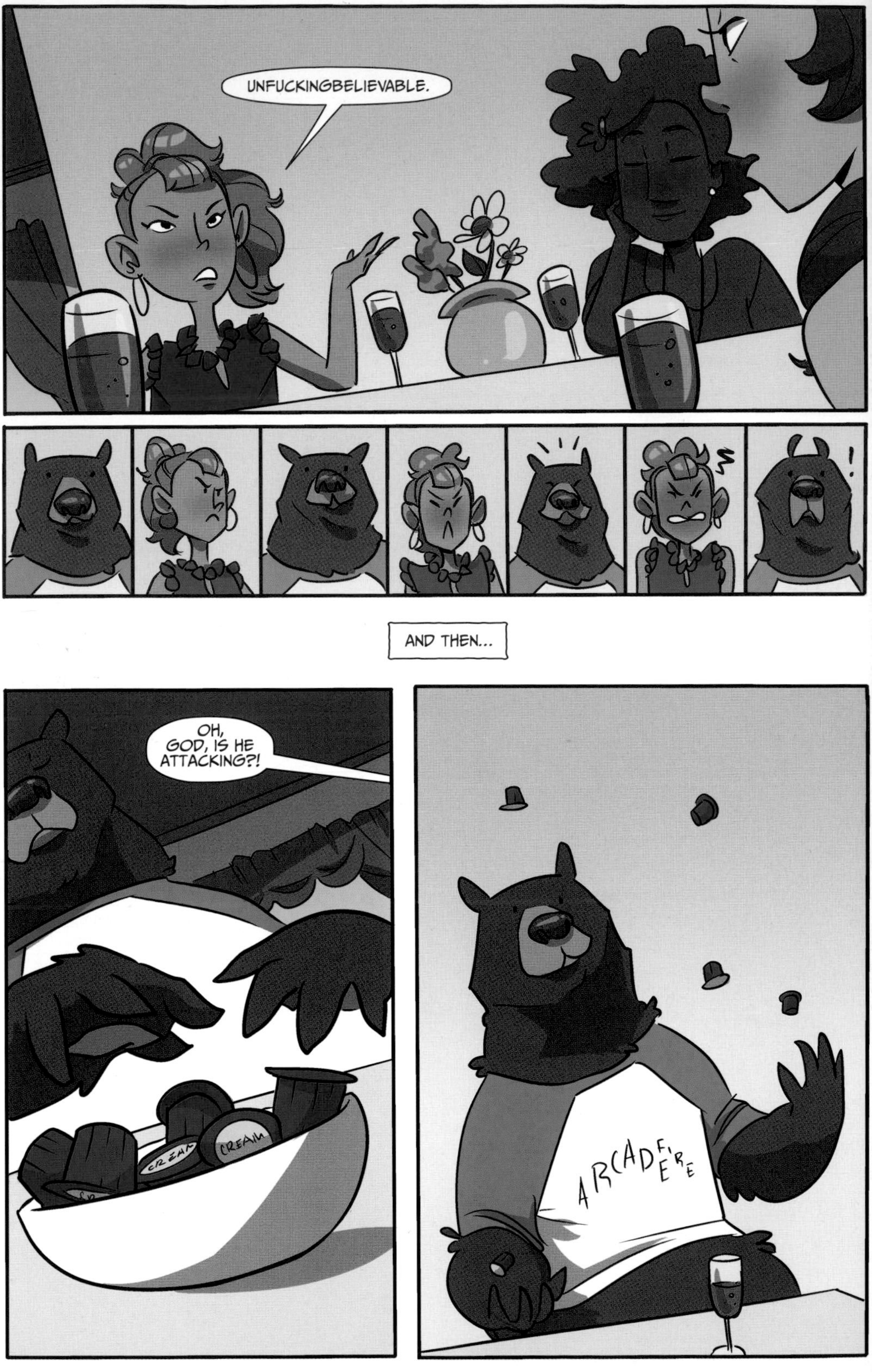
UNFUCKINGBELIEVABLE.
!
AND THEN...
OH, GOD, IS HE ATTACKING?!
CREAM
CREAM
ARCADE FIRE

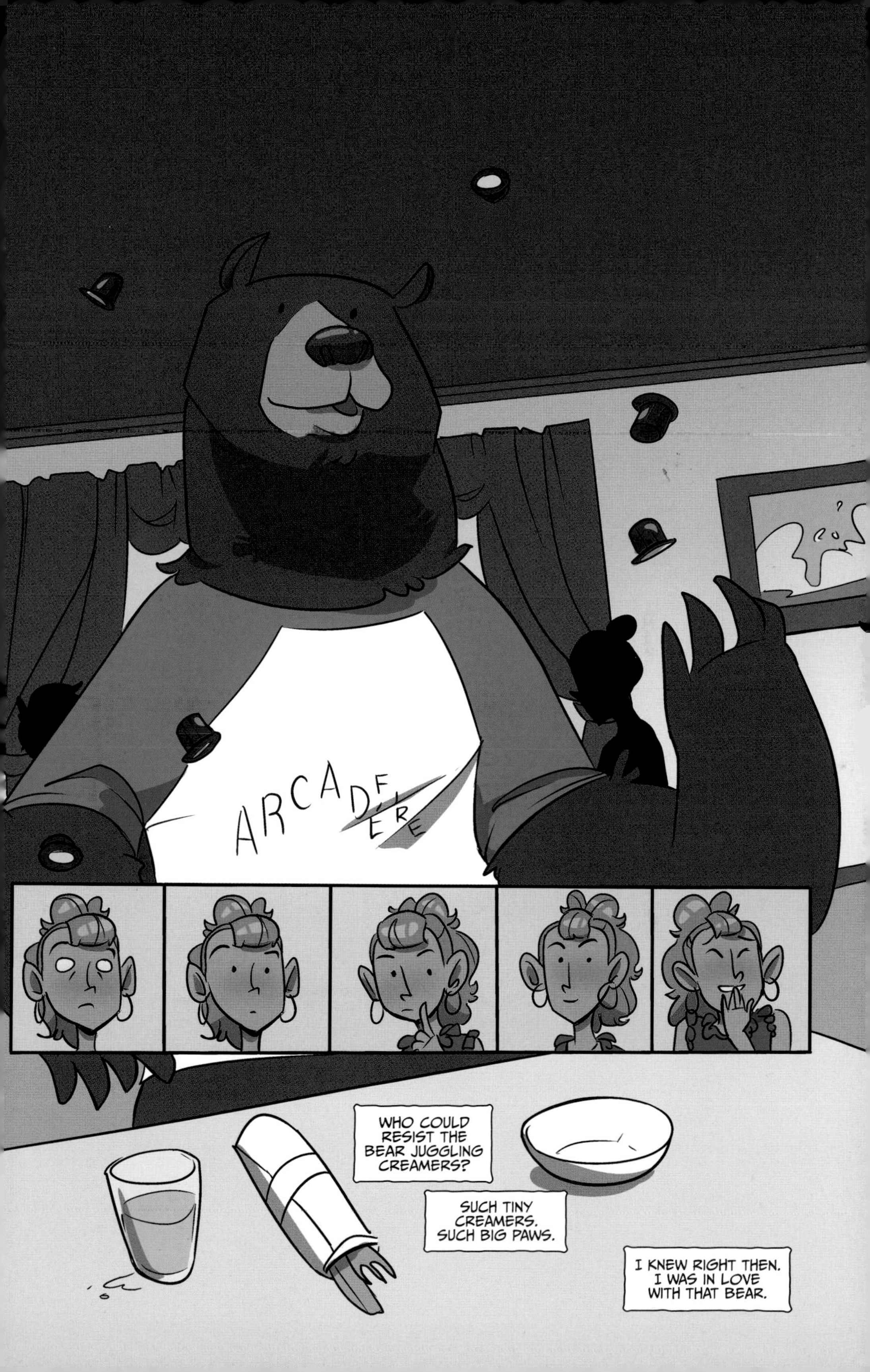
ARCADE FIRE
WHO COULD RESIST THE BEAR JUGGLING CREAMERS?
SUCH TINY CREAMERS. SUCH BIG PAWS.
I KNEW RIGHT THEN. I WAS IN LOVE WITH THAT BEAR.

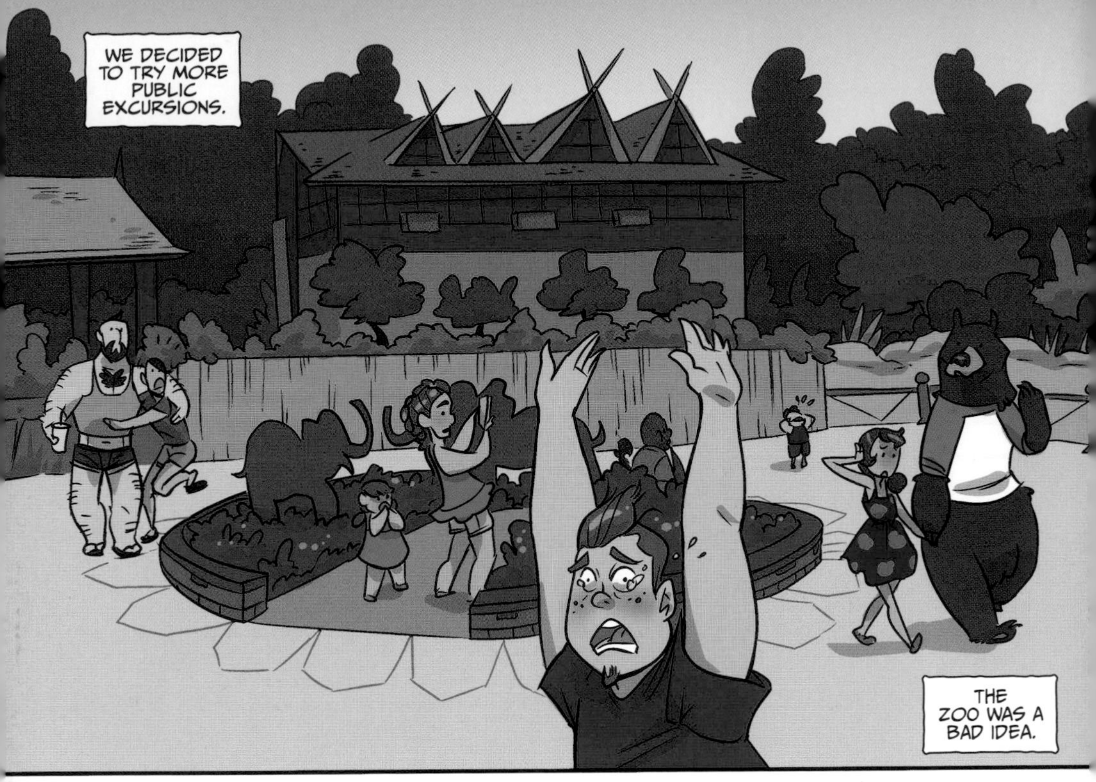
WE DECIDED TO TRY MORE PUBLIC EXCURSIONS.
THE ZOO WAS A BAD IDEA.

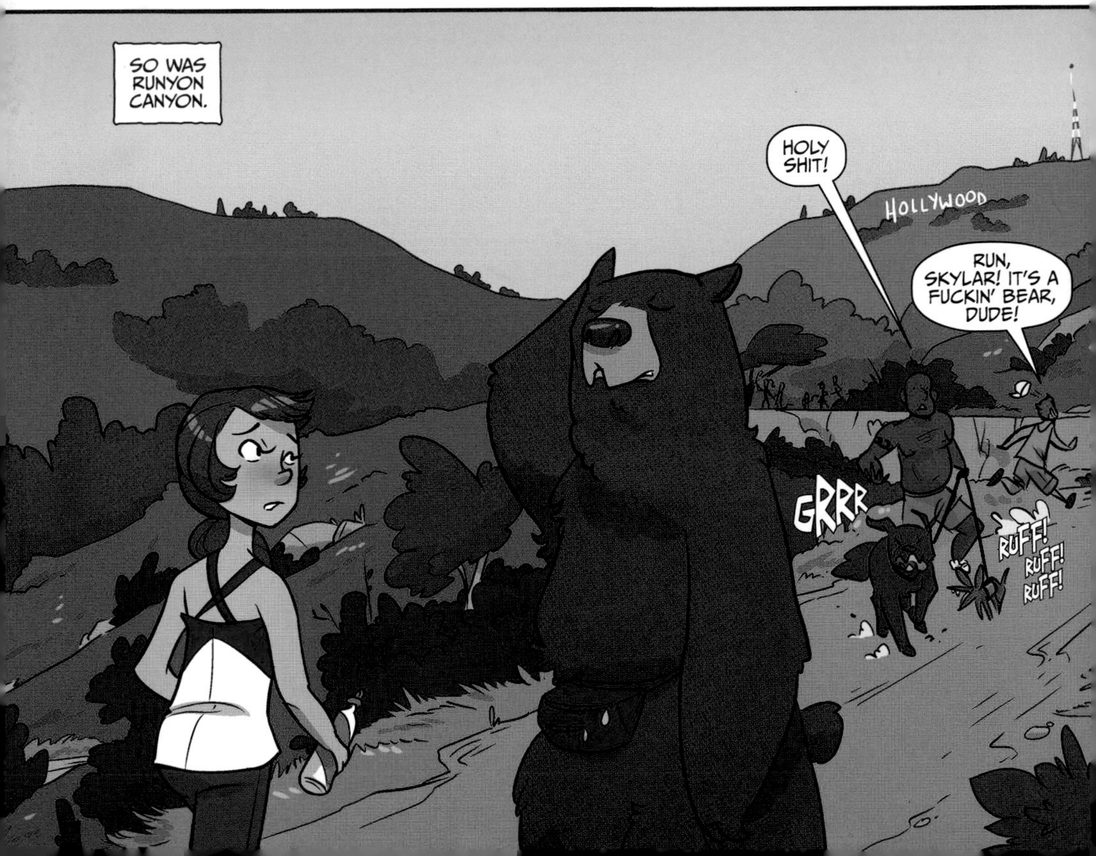
SO WAS RUNYON CANYON.
HOLLYWOOD
HOLY SHIT!
RUN, SKYLAR! IT'S A FUCKIN' BEAR, DUDE!
GRRR
RUFF! RUFF! RUFF!

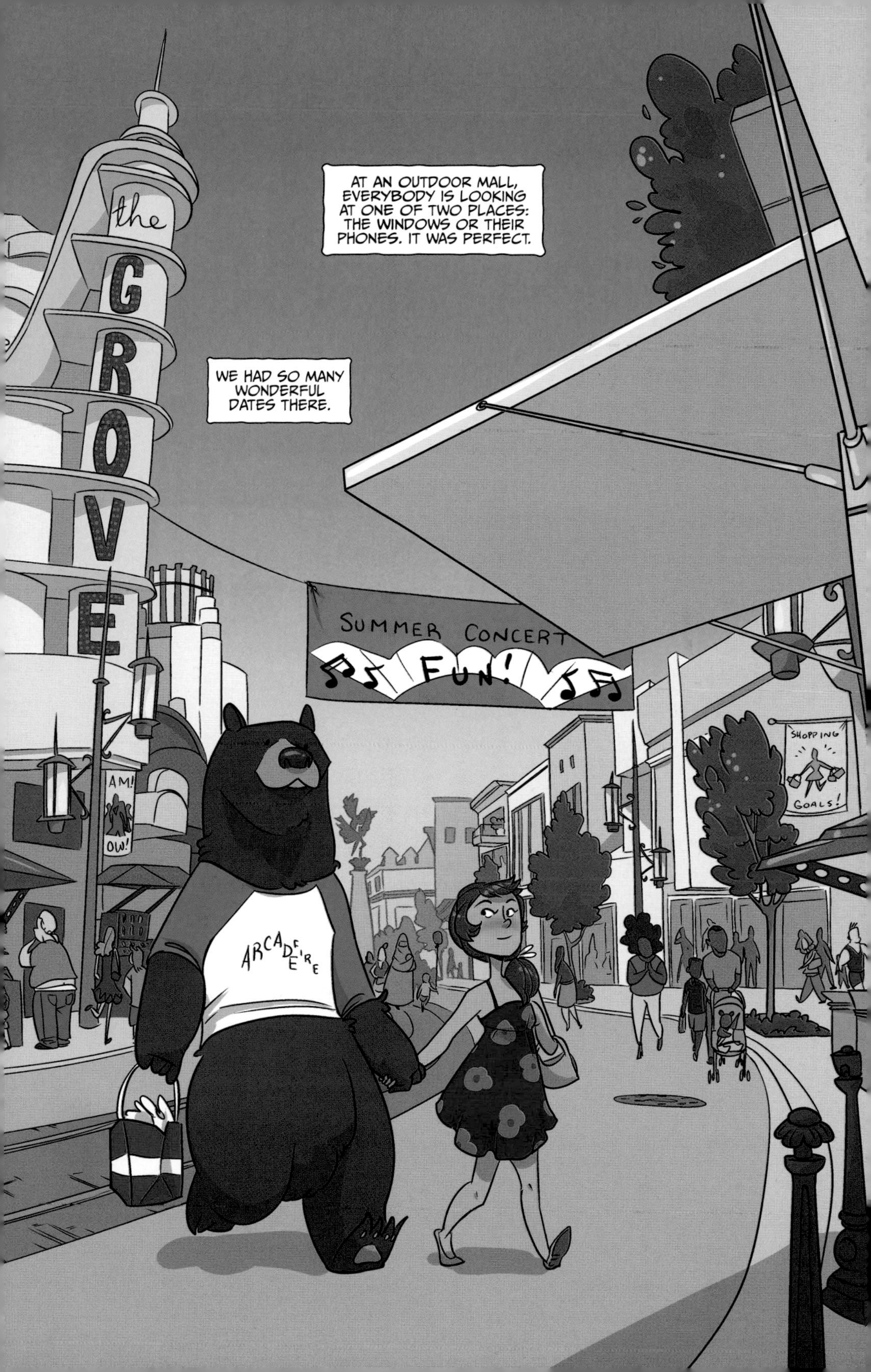
AT AN OUTDOOR MALL, EVERYBODY IS LOOKING AT ONE OF TWO PLACES: THE WINDOWS OR THEIR PHONES. IT WAS PERFECT.
WE HAD SO MANY WONDERFUL DATES THERE.
the GROVE
SUMMER CONCERT FUN!
SHOPPING GOALS!
ARCADE FIRE

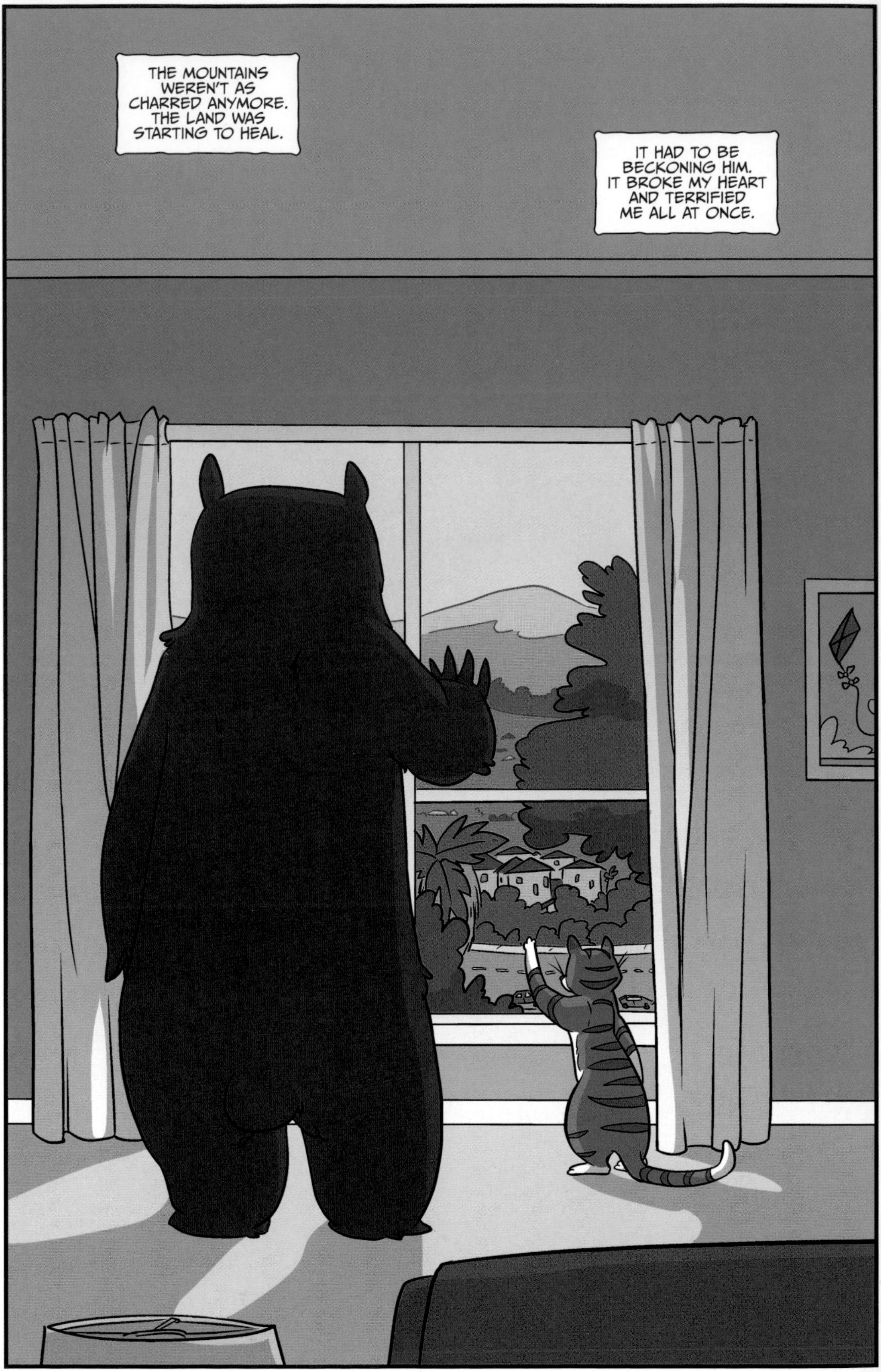
THE MOUNTAINS WEREN'T AS CHARRED ANYMORE. THE LAND WAS STARTING TO HEAL.
IT HAD TO BE BECKONING HIM. IT BROKE MY HEART AND TERRIFIED ME ALL AT ONCE.

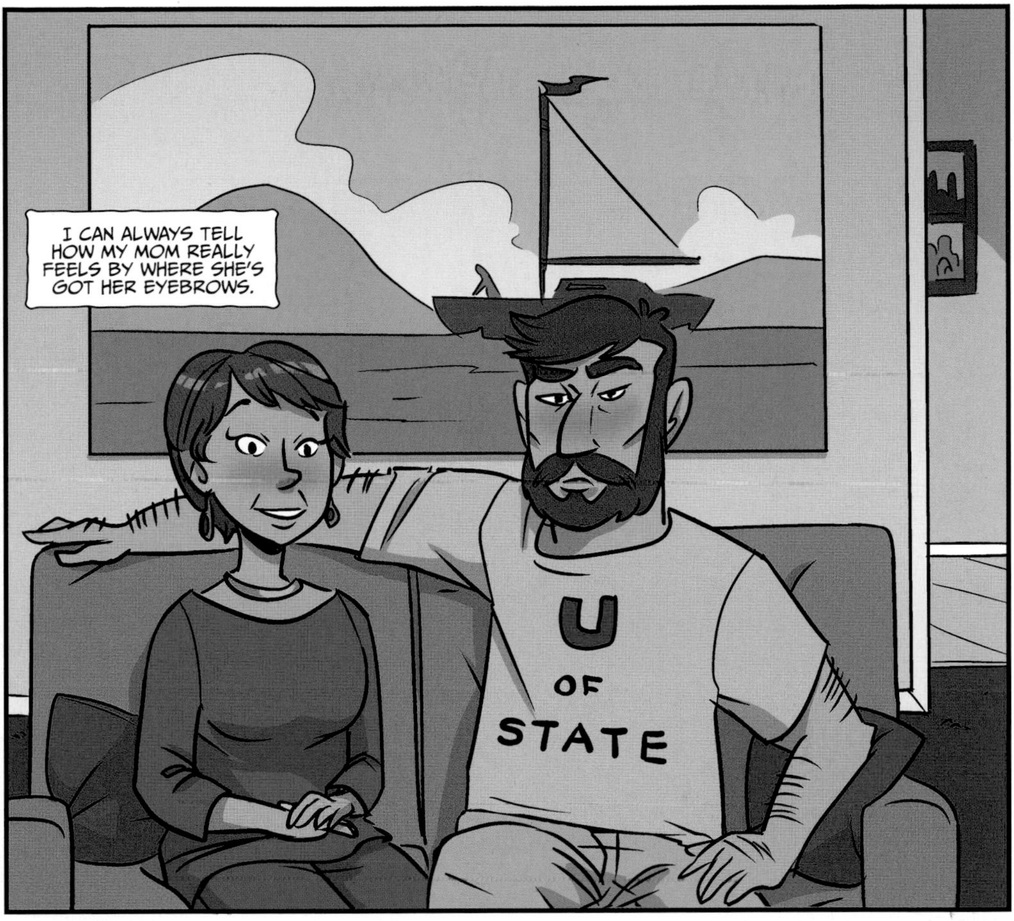
I CAN ALWAYS TELL HOW MY MOM REALLY FEELS BY WHERE SHE'S GOT HER EYEBROWS.
U OF STATE

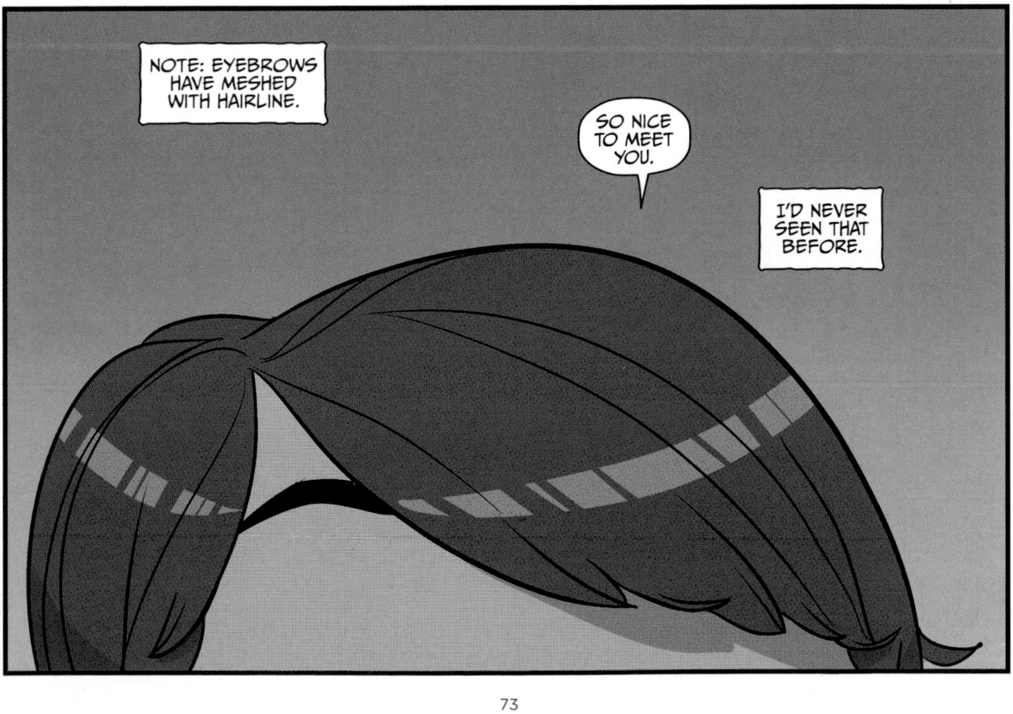
NOTE: EYEBROWS HAVE MESHED WITH HAIRLINE.
SO NICE TO MEET YOU.
I'D NEVER SEEN THAT BEFORE.

CAT VERSUS BEAR:
PROBLEMS WITH CLAWS

BEAR.

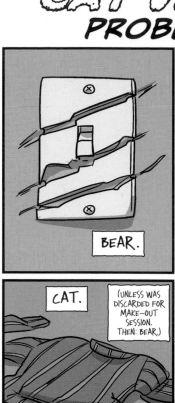
BEAR.

CAT.

BEAR.

CAT.

(UNLESS WAS DISCARDED FOR MAKE-OUT SESSION. THEN: BEAR.)

BEAR.

DIFFICULT TO DETERMINE.

BEAR.

CAT.

AW, HELL, NO! YOU GUYS!

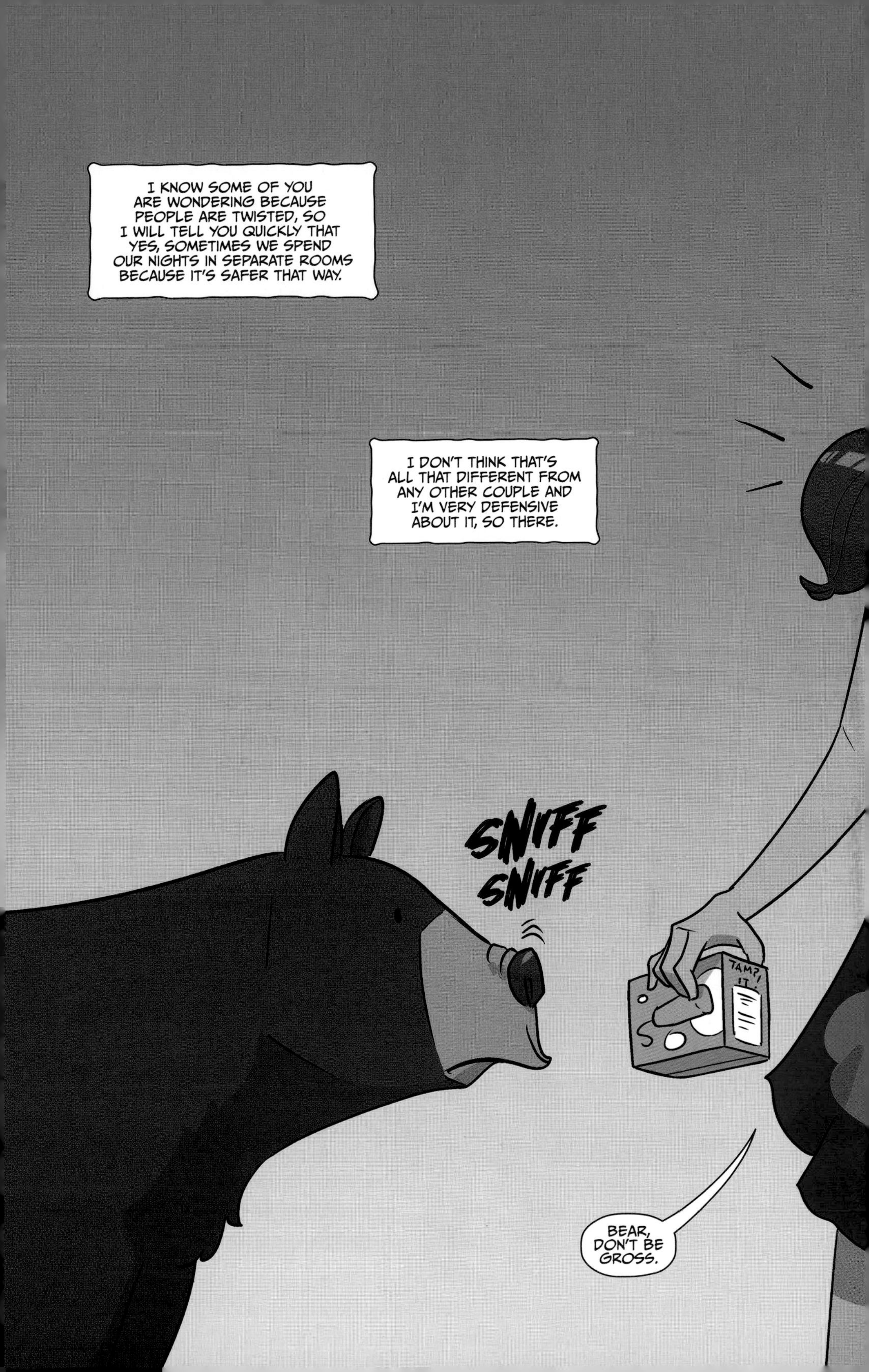
I KNOW SOME OF YOU ARE WONDERING BECAUSE PEOPLE ARE TWISTED, SO I WILL TELL YOU QUICKLY THAT YES, SOMETIMES WE SPEND OUR NIGHTS IN SEPARATE ROOMS BECAUSE IT'S SAFER THAT WAY.
I DON'T THINK THAT'S ALL THAT DIFFERENT FROM ANY OTHER COUPLE AND I'M VERY DEFENSIVE ABOUT IT, SO THERE.
SNIFF SNIFF
BEAR, DON'T BE GROSS.

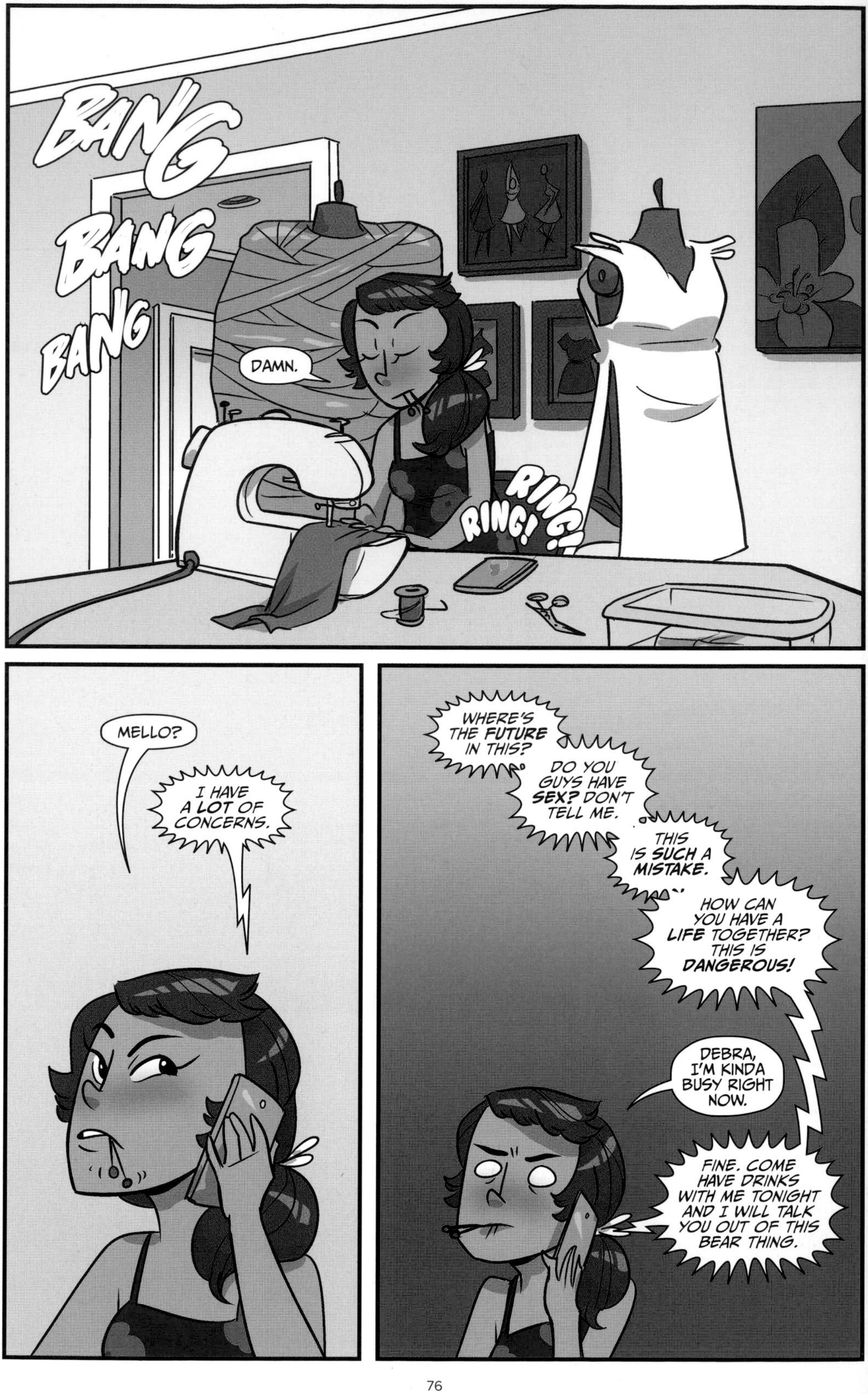
BANG
BANG
BANG
DAMN.
RING!
RING!
MELLO?
I HAVE A LOT OF CONCERNS.
WHERE'S THE FUTURE IN THIS?
DO YOU GUYS HAVE SEX? DON'T TELL ME.
THIS IS SUCH A MISTAKE.
HOW CAN YOU HAVE A LIFE TOGETHER? THIS IS DANGEROUS!
DEBRA, I'M KINDA BUSY RIGHT NOW.
FINE. COME HAVE DRINKS WITH ME TONIGHT AND I WILL TALK YOU OUT OF THIS BEAR THING.

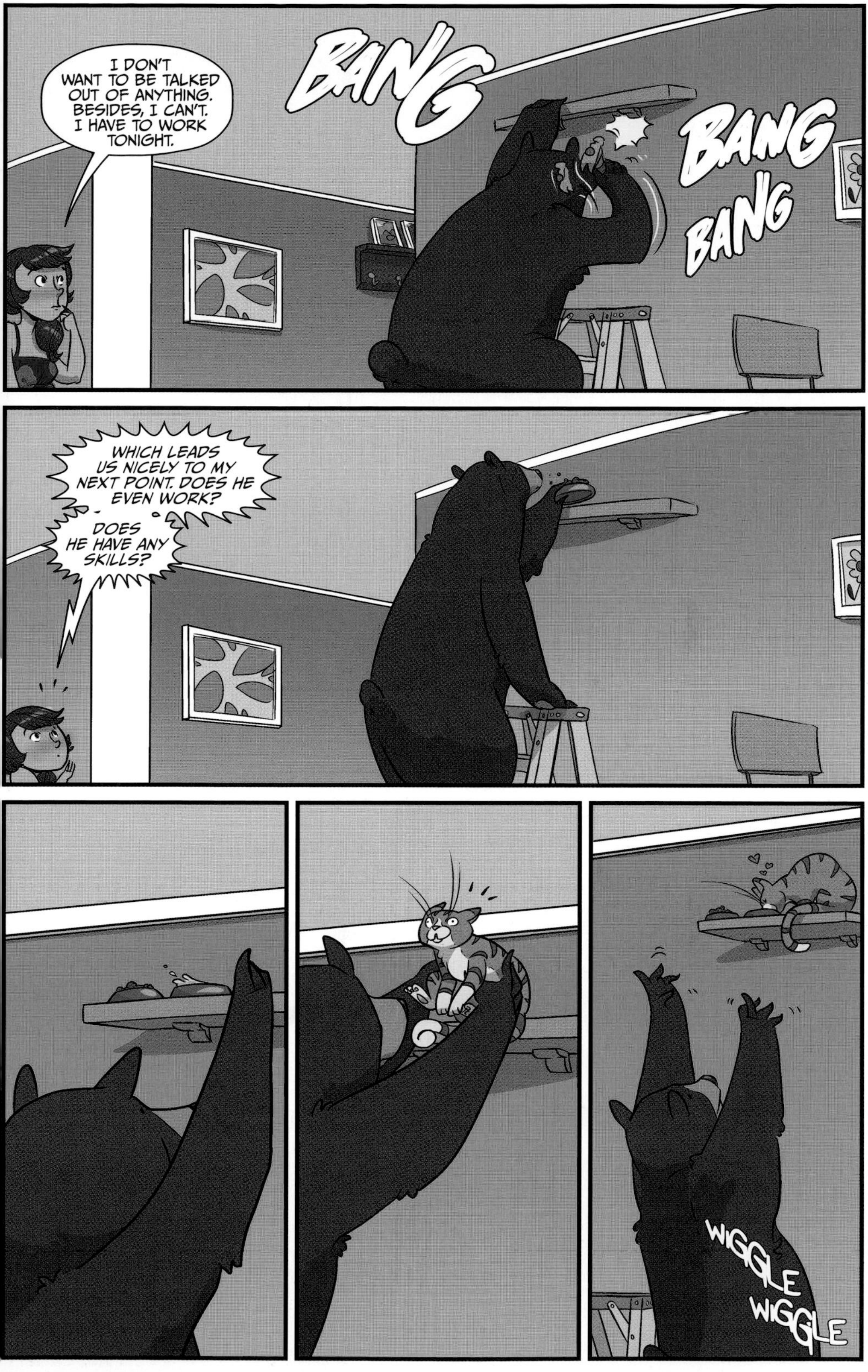
I DON'T WANT TO BE TALKED OUT OF ANYTHING. BESIDES, I CAN'T. I HAVE TO WORK TONIGHT.
BANG
BANG
BANG
BANG
WHICH LEADS US NICELY TO MY NEXT POINT. DOES HE EVEN WORK?
DOES HE HAVE ANY SKILLS?
WIGGLE
WIGGLE

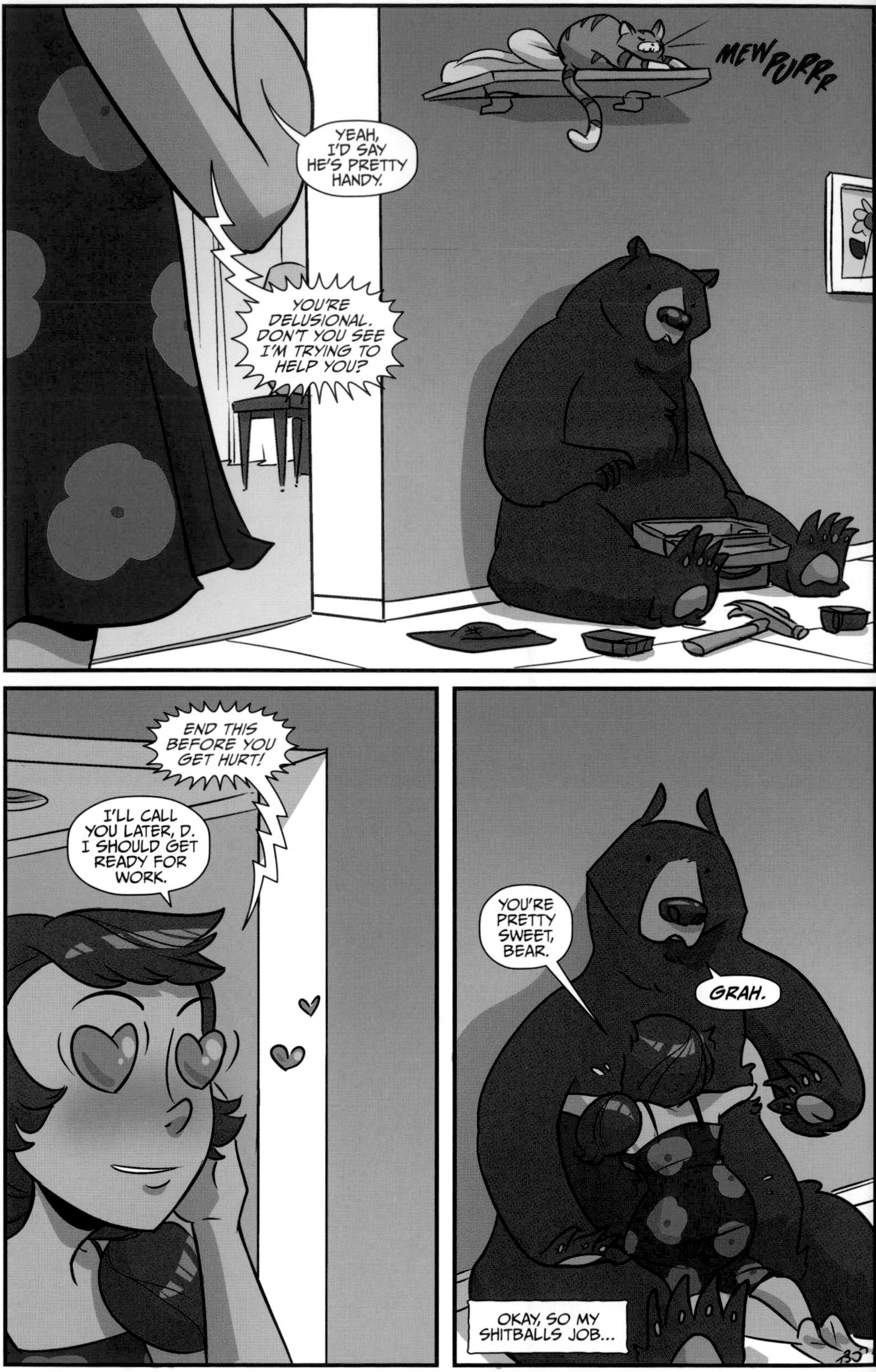
MEW PURRR
YEAH, I'D SAY HE'S PRETTY HANDY.
YOU'RE DELUSIONAL. DON'T YOU SEE I'M TRYING TO HELP YOU?
END THIS BEFORE YOU GET HURT!
I'LL CALL YOU LATER, D. I SHOULD GET READY FOR WORK.
YOU'RE PRETTY SWEET, BEAR.
GRAH.
OKAY, SO MY SHITBALLS JOB...

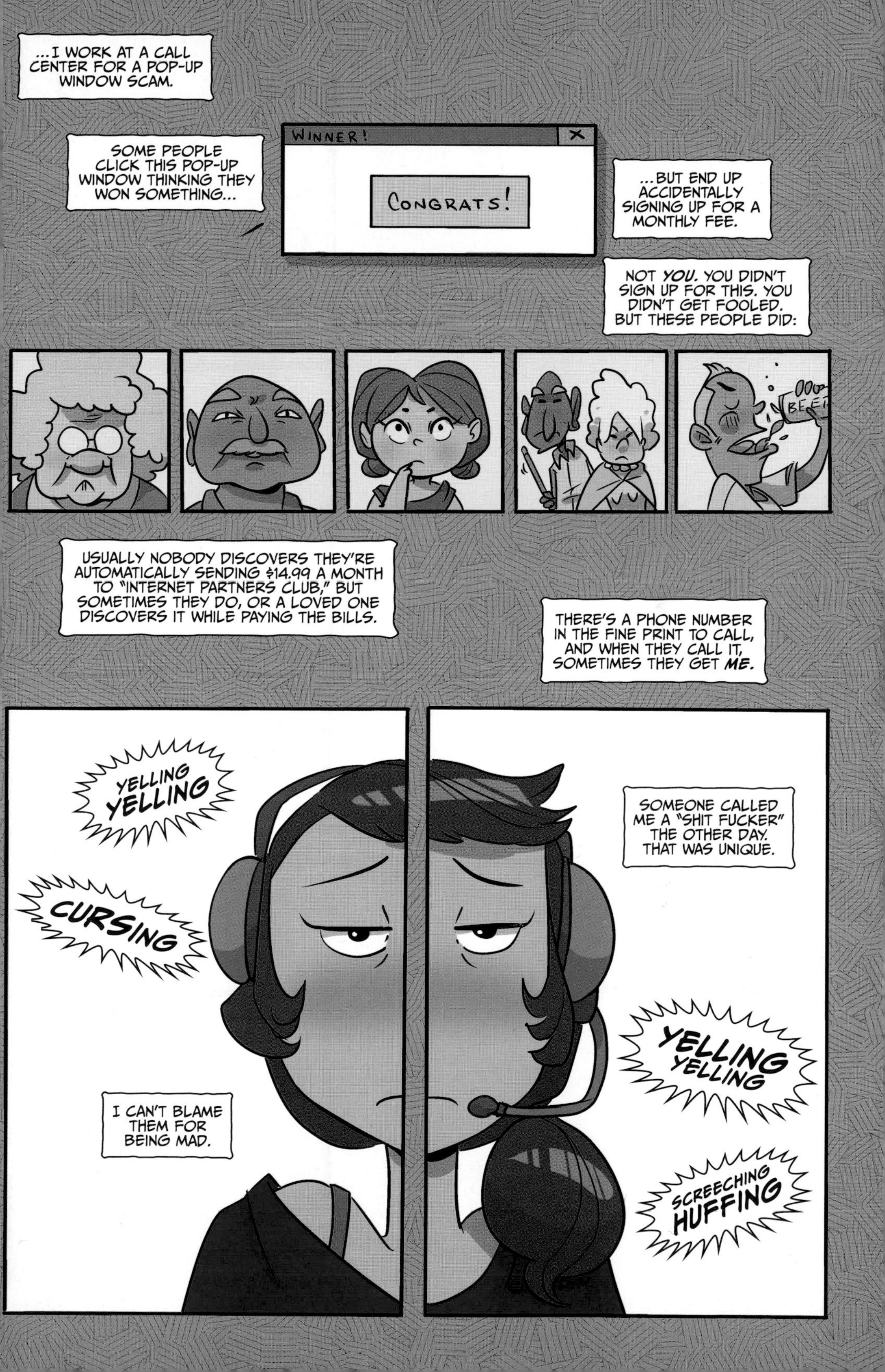
...I WORK AT A CALL CENTER FOR A POP-UP WINDOW SCAM.
SOME PEOPLE CLICK THIS POP-UP WINDOW THINKING THEY WON SOMETHING...
WINNER!
CONGRATS!
...BUT END UP ACCIDENTALLY SIGNING UP FOR A MONTHLY FEE.
NOT *YOU.* YOU DIDN'T SIGN UP FOR THIS. YOU DIDN'T GET FOOLED. BUT THESE PEOPLE DID:
USUALLY NOBODY DISCOVERS THEY'RE AUTOMATICALLY SENDING $14.99 A MONTH TO "INTERNET PARTNERS CLUB," BUT SOMETIMES THEY DO, OR A LOVED ONE DISCOVERS IT WHILE PAYING THE BILLS.
THERE'S A PHONE NUMBER IN THE FINE PRINT TO CALL, AND WHEN THEY CALL IT, SOMETIMES THEY GET *ME.*
YELLING YELLING
CURSING
I CAN'T BLAME THEM FOR BEING MAD.
SOMEONE CALLED ME A "SHIT FUCKER" THE OTHER DAY. THAT WAS UNIQUE.
YELLING YELLING
SCREECHING HUFFING

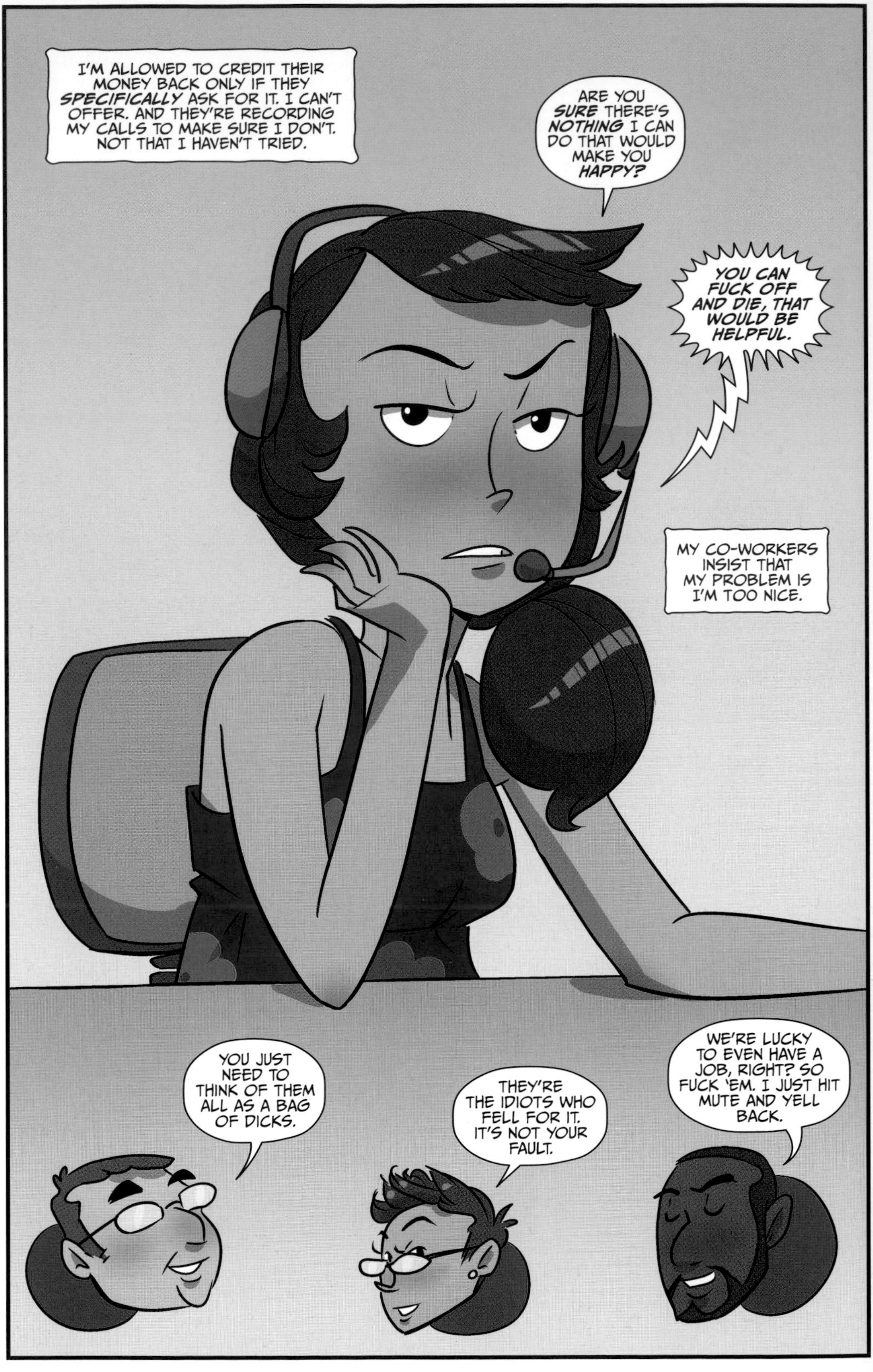
I'M ALLOWED TO CREDIT THEIR MONEY BACK ONLY IF THEY *SPECIFICALLY* ASK FOR IT. I CAN'T OFFER. AND THEY'RE RECORDING MY CALLS TO MAKE SURE I DON'T. NOT THAT I HAVEN'T TRIED.
ARE YOU *SURE* THERE'S *NOTHING* I CAN DO THAT WOULD MAKE YOU *HAPPY?*
YOU CAN FUCK OFF AND DIE, THAT WOULD BE HELPFUL.
MY CO-WORKERS INSIST THAT MY PROBLEM IS I'M TOO NICE.
YOU JUST NEED TO THINK OF THEM ALL AS A BAG OF DICKS.
THEY'RE THE IDIOTS WHO FELL FOR IT. IT'S NOT YOUR FAULT.
WE'RE LUCKY TO EVEN HAVE A JOB, RIGHT? SO FUCK 'EM. I JUST HIT MUTE AND YELL BACK.

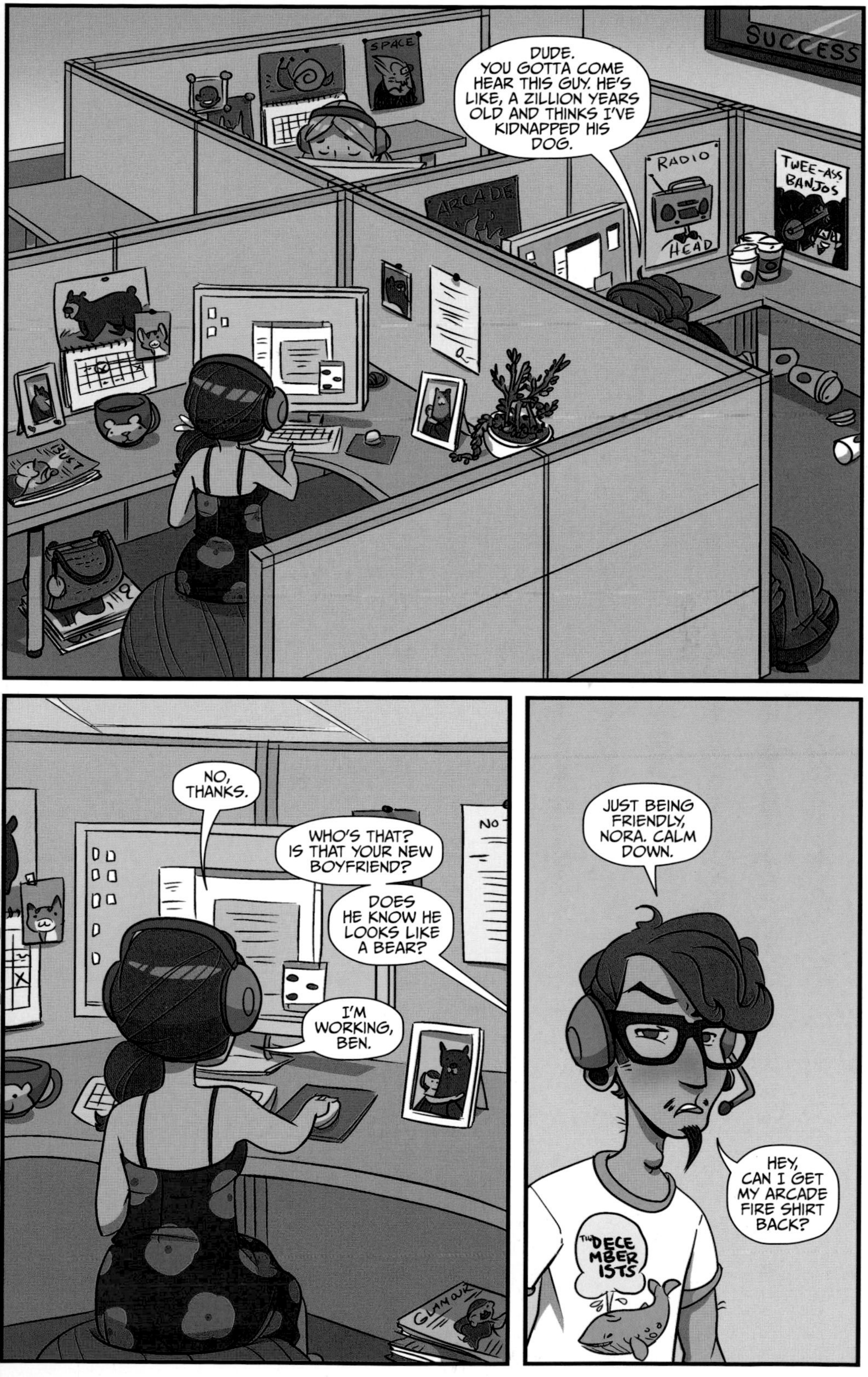
SUCCESS
SPACE
DUDE. YOU GOTTA COME HEAR THIS GUY. HE'S LIKE, A ZILLION YEARS OLD AND THINKS I'VE KIDNAPPED HIS DOG.
RADIO HEAD
TWEE-ASS BANJOS
ARCADE
BUST
NO, THANKS.
WHO'S THAT? IS THAT YOUR NEW BOYFRIEND?
DOES HE KNOW HE LOOKS LIKE A BEAR?
I'M WORKING, BEN.
GLAMOUR
JUST BEING FRIENDLY, NORA. CALM DOWN.
HEY, CAN I GET MY ARCADE FIRE SHIRT BACK?
THE DECEMBERISTS

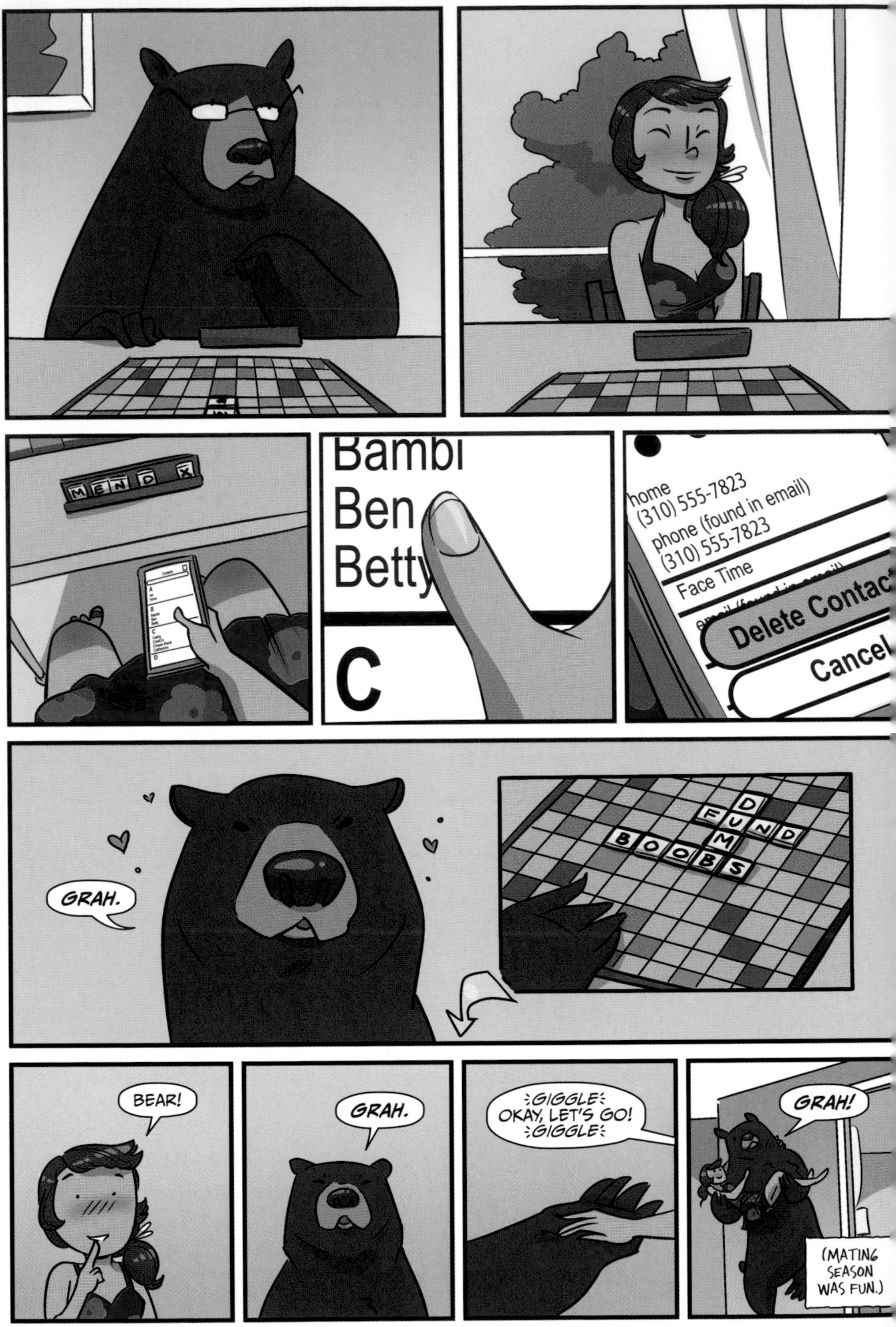

MENDX
Bambi
Ben
Betty
C
home
(310) 555-7823
phone (found in email)
(310) 555-7823
Face Time
Delete Contac
Cancel
GRAH.
D
FUND
M
BOOBS
BEAR!
GRAH.
GIGGLE
OKAY, LET'S GO!
GIGGLE
GRAH!
(MATING SEASON WAS FUN.)

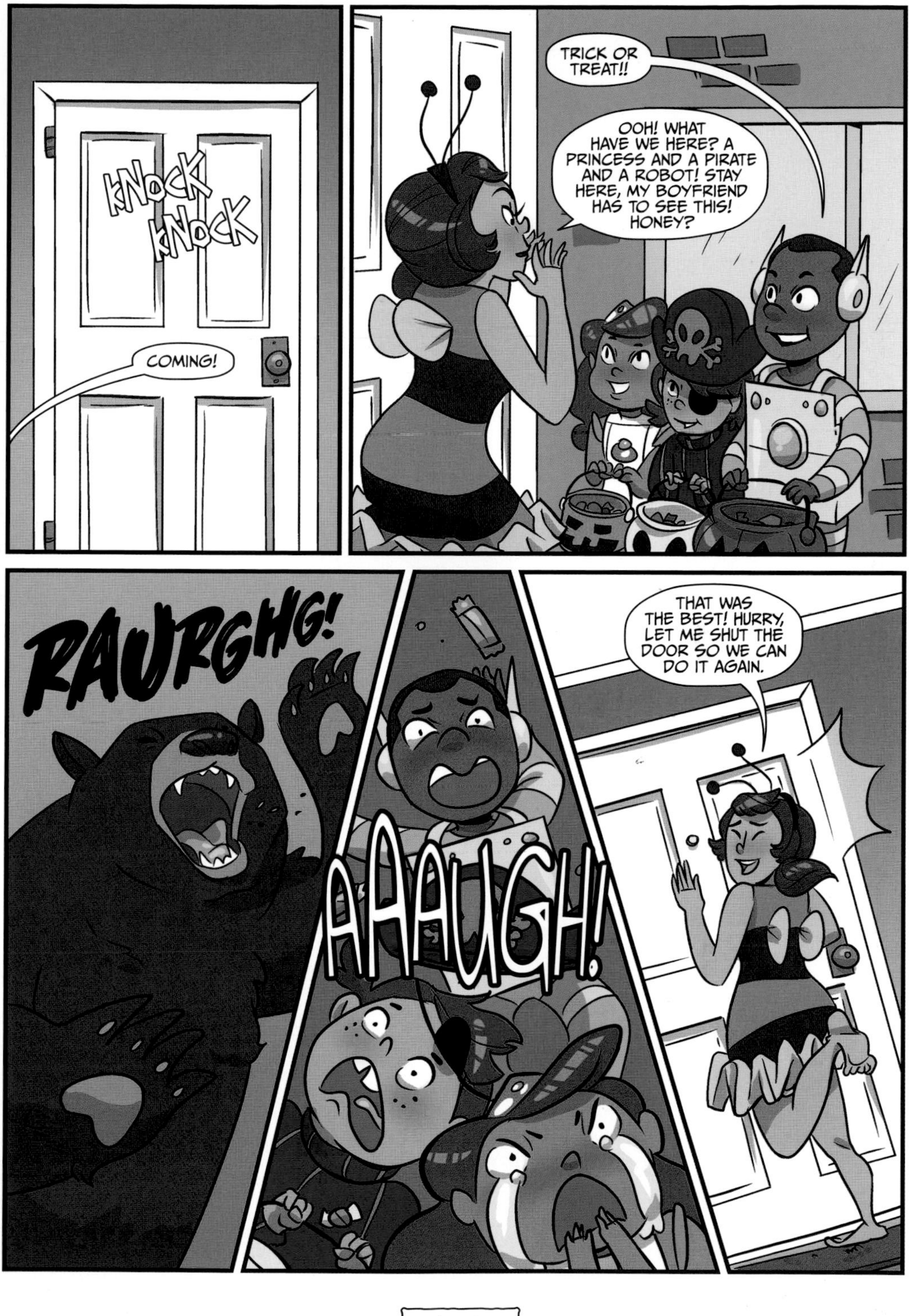
KNOCK
KNOCK
COMING!
TRICK OR TREAT!!
OOH! WHAT HAVE WE HERE? A PRINCESS AND A PIRATE AND A ROBOT! STAY HERE, MY BOYFRIEND HAS TO SEE THIS! HONEY?
RAURGHG!
AAAUGH!
THAT WAS THE BEST! HURRY, LET ME SHUT THE DOOR SO WE CAN DO IT AGAIN.

(SO WAS HALLOWEEN.)

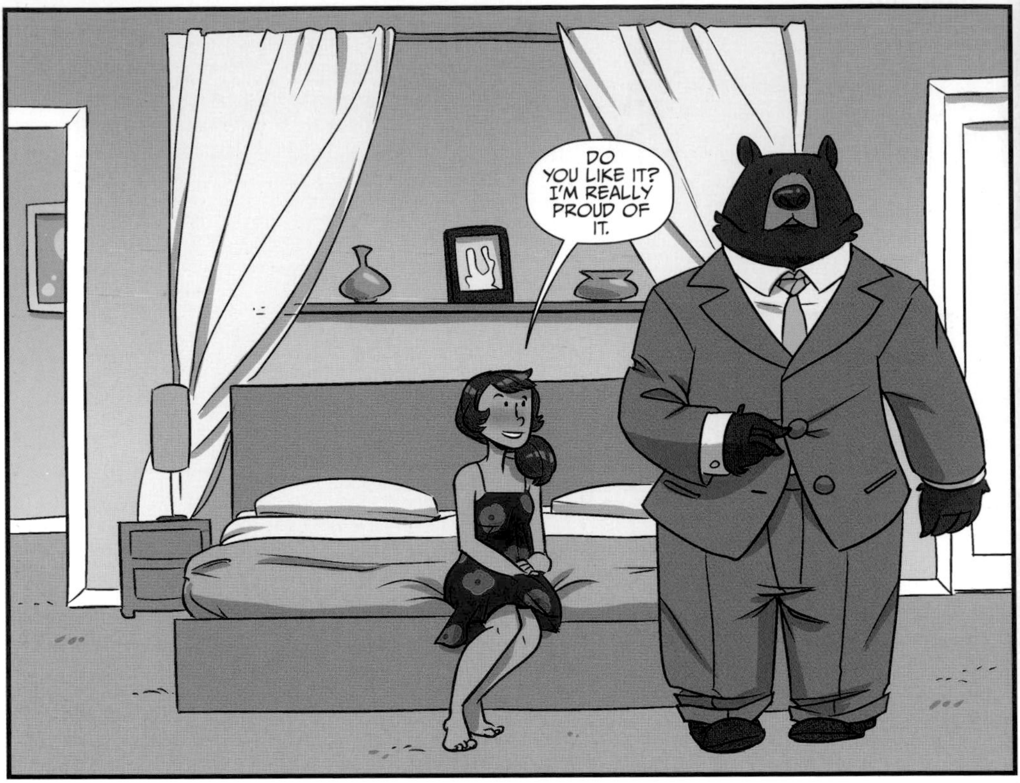
DO YOU LIKE IT? I'M REALLY PROUD OF IT.

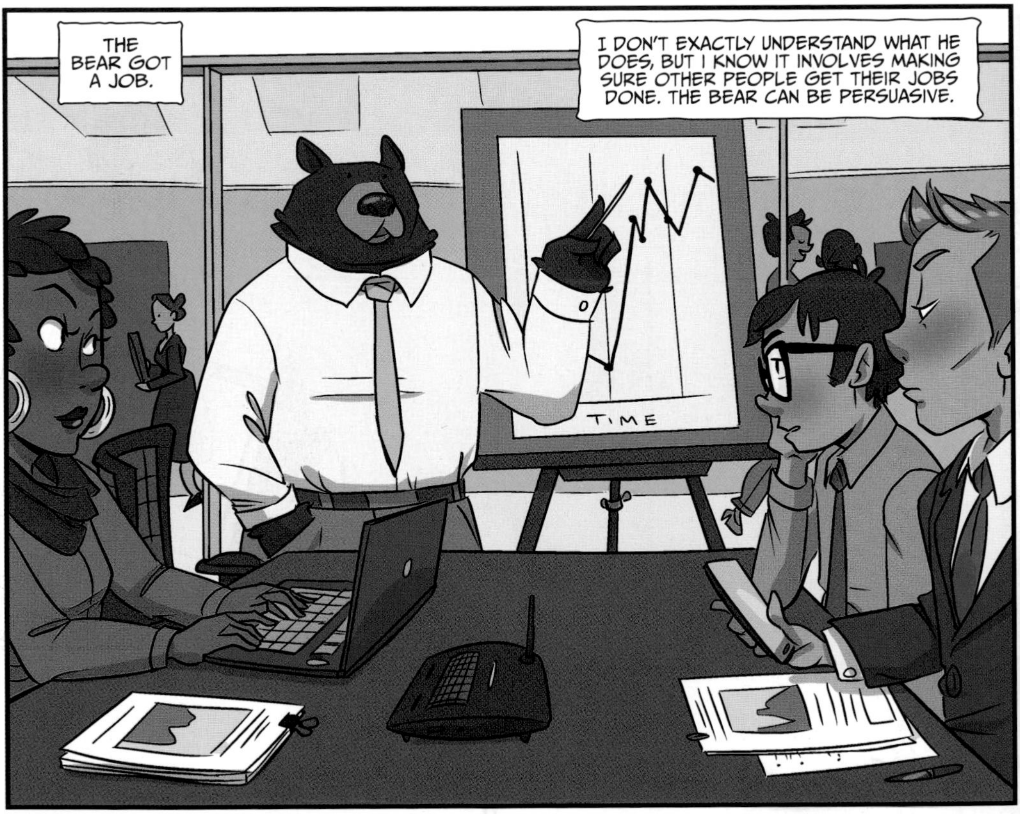
THE BEAR GOT A JOB.
I DON'T EXACTLY UNDERSTAND WHAT HE DOES, BUT I KNOW IT INVOLVES MAKING SURE OTHER PEOPLE GET THEIR JOBS DONE. THE BEAR CAN BE PERSUASIVE.
TIME

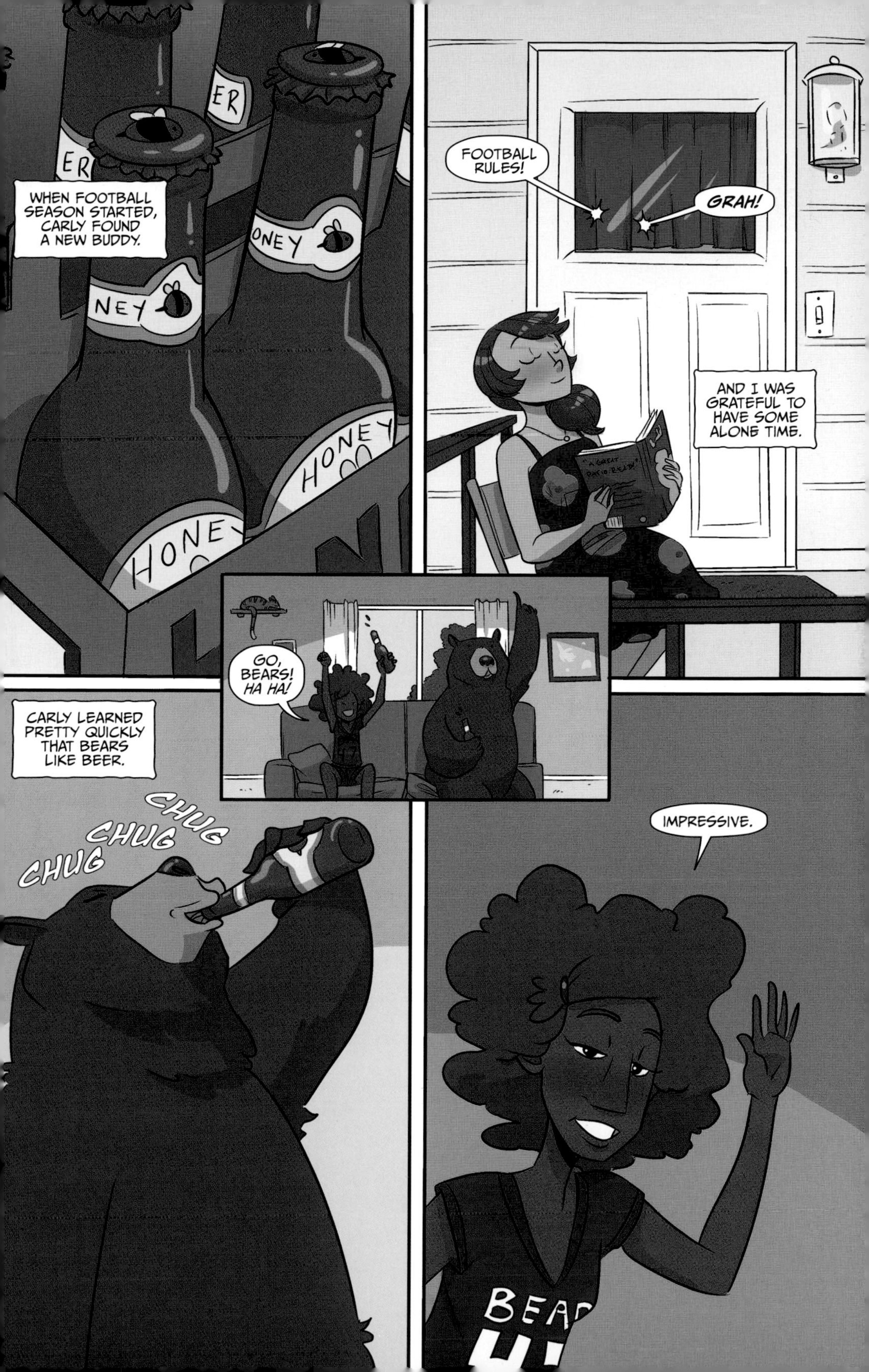
WHEN FOOTBALL SEASON STARTED, CARLY FOUND A NEW BUDDY.
HONEY
FOOTBALL RULES!
GRAH!
AND I WAS GRATEFUL TO HAVE SOME ALONE TIME.
GO, BEARS! HA HA!
CARLY LEARNED PRETTY QUICKLY THAT BEARS LIKE BEER.
CHUG CHUG CHUG
IMPRESSIVE.

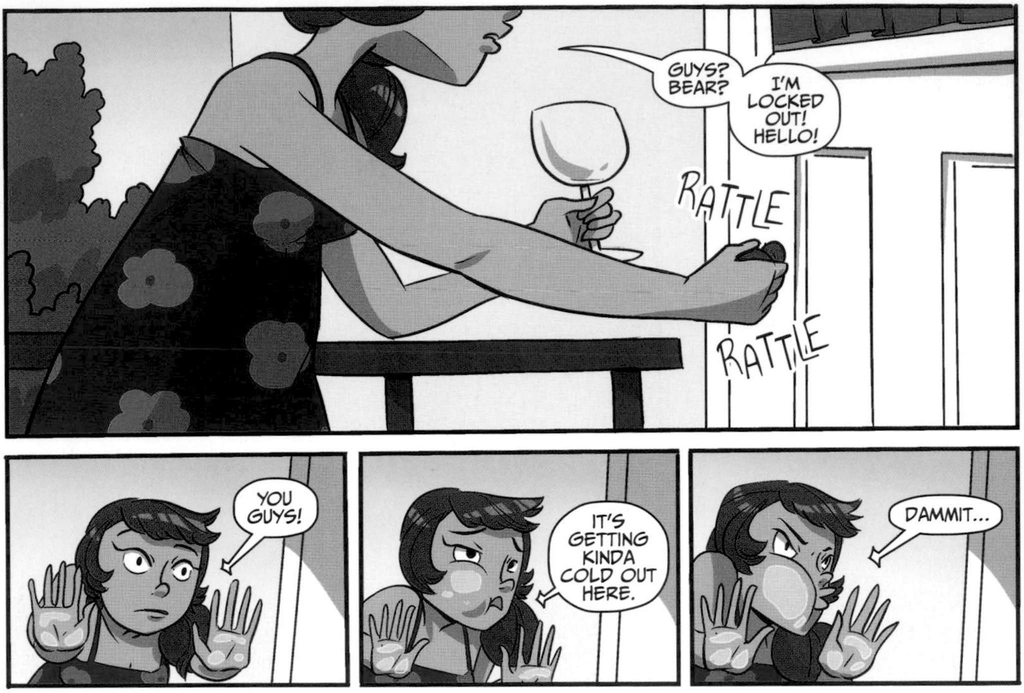
GUYS? BEAR?
I'M LOCKED OUT! HELLO!
RATTLE
RATTLE
YOU GUYS!
IT'S GETTING KINDA COLD OUT HERE.
DAMMIT...

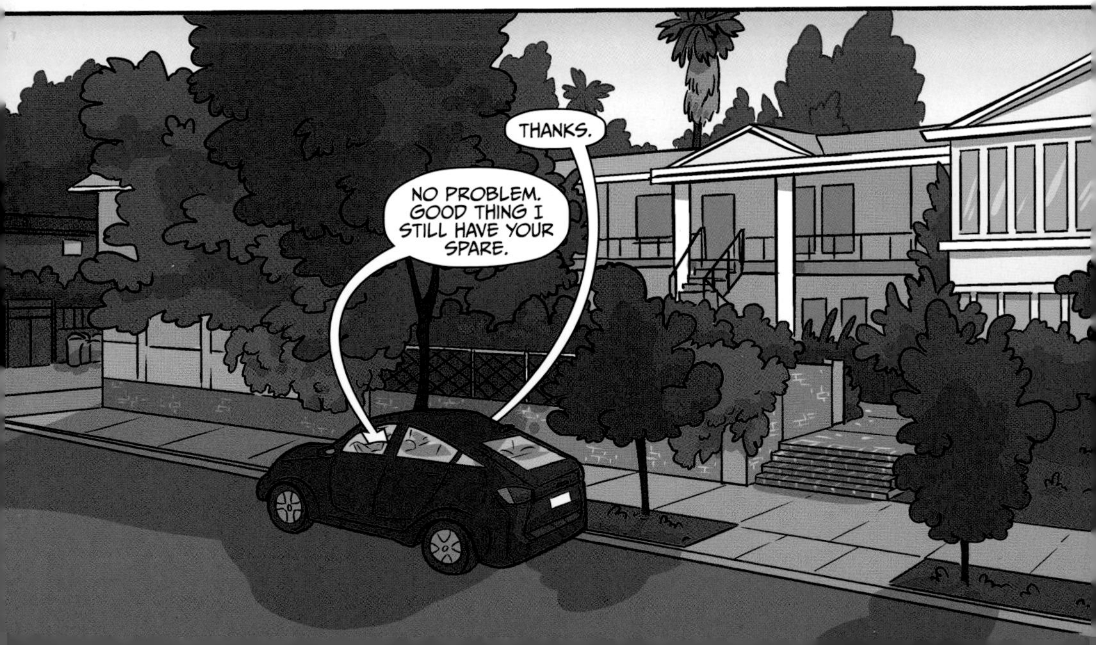
THANKS.
NO PROBLEM. GOOD THING I STILL HAVE YOUR SPARE.

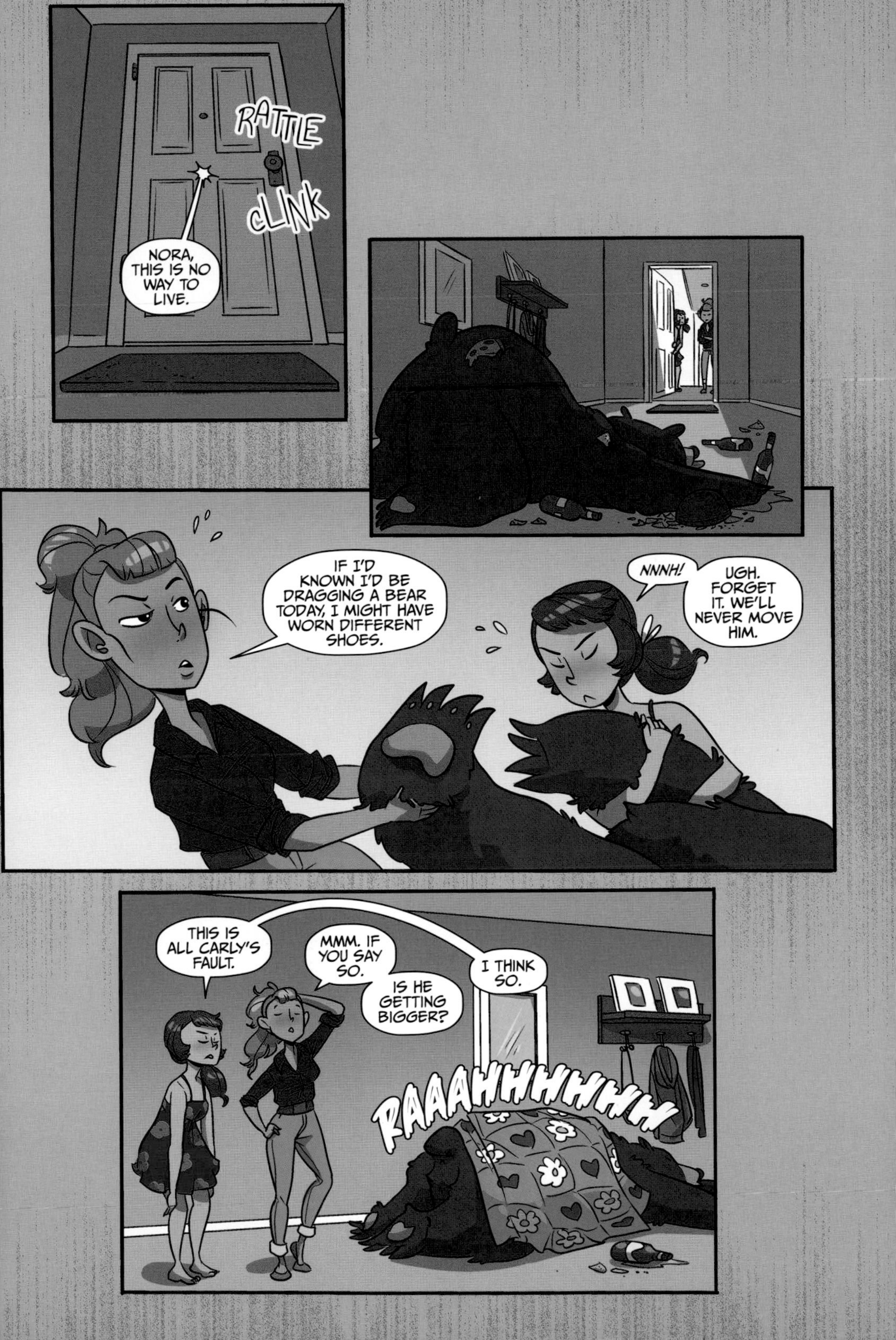
RATTLE
CLINK
NORA, THIS IS NO WAY TO LIVE.
IF I'D KNOWN I'D BE DRAGGING A BEAR TODAY, I MIGHT HAVE WORN DIFFERENT SHOES.
NNNH!
UGH. FORGET IT. WE'LL NEVER MOVE HIM.
THIS IS ALL CARLY'S FAULT.
MMM. IF YOU SAY SO.
I THINK SO.
IS HE GETTING BIGGER?
RAAAHHHHHHH

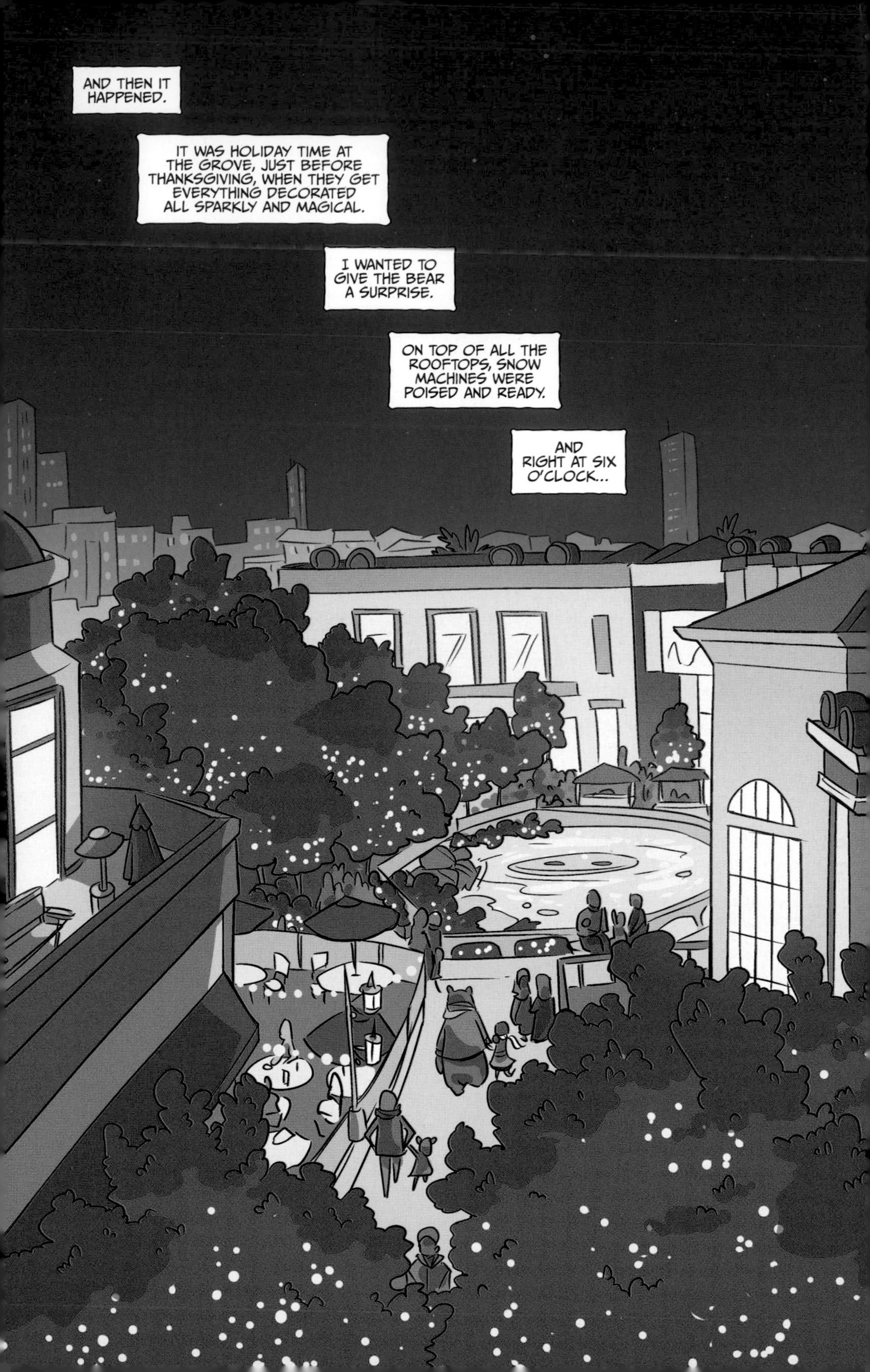
AND THEN IT HAPPENED.
IT WAS HOLIDAY TIME AT THE GROVE, JUST BEFORE THANKSGIVING, WHEN THEY GET EVERYTHING DECORATED ALL SPARKLY AND MAGICAL.
I WANTED TO GIVE THE BEAR A SURPRISE.
ON TOP OF ALL THE ROOFTOPS, SNOW MACHINES WERE POISED AND READY.
AND RIGHT AT SIX O'CLOCK...

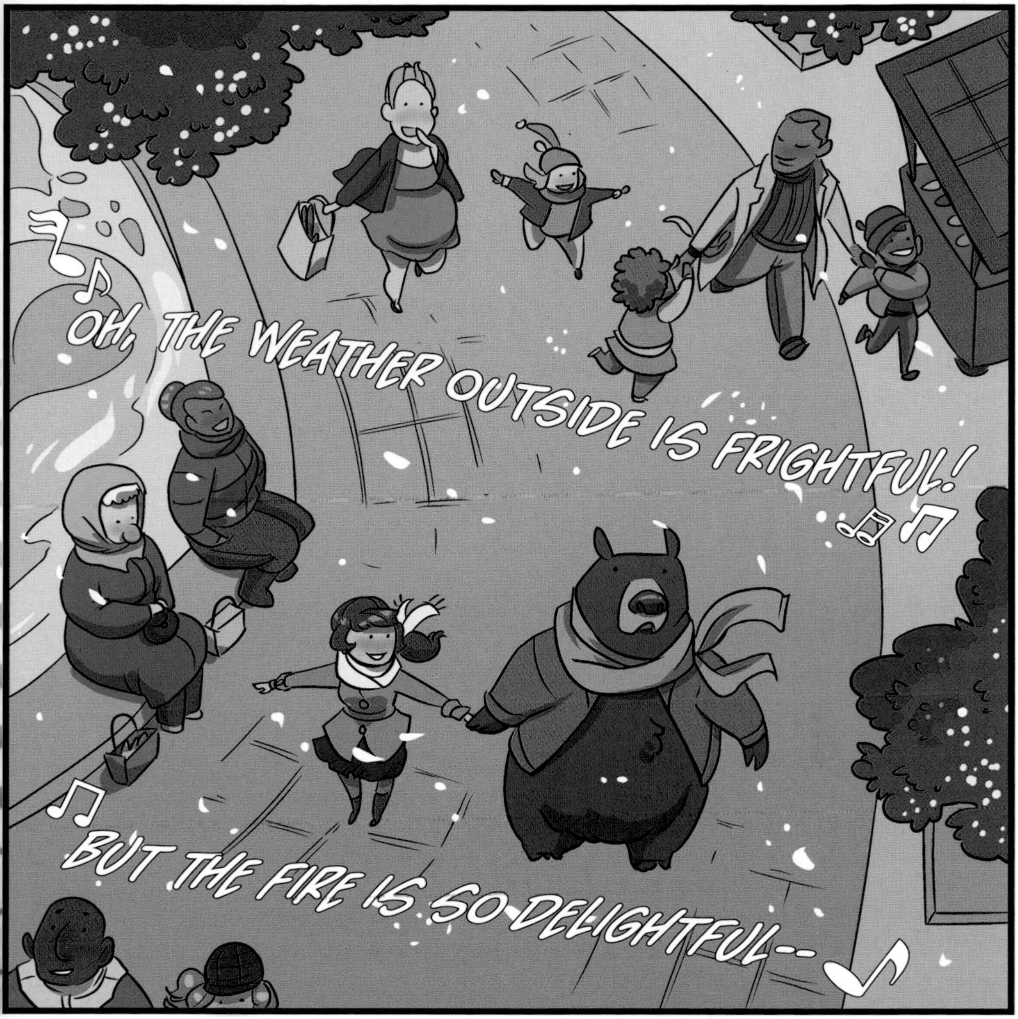
OH, THE WEATHER OUTSIDE IS FRIGHTFUL!
BUT THE FIRE IS SO DELIGHTFUL--

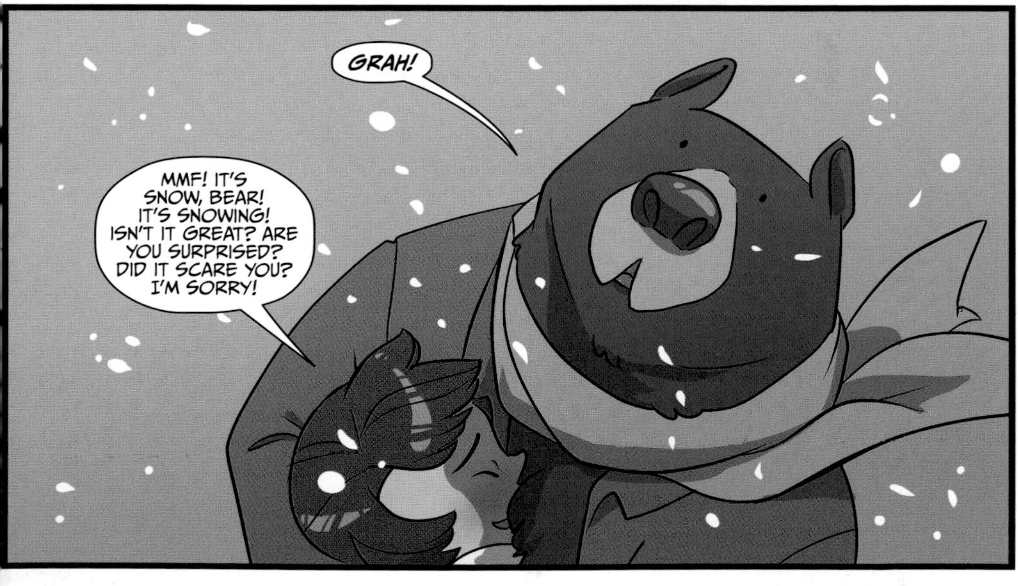
GRAH!
MMF! IT'S SNOW, BEAR! IT'S SNOWING! ISN'T IT GREAT? ARE YOU SURPRISED? DID IT SCARE YOU? I'M SORRY!

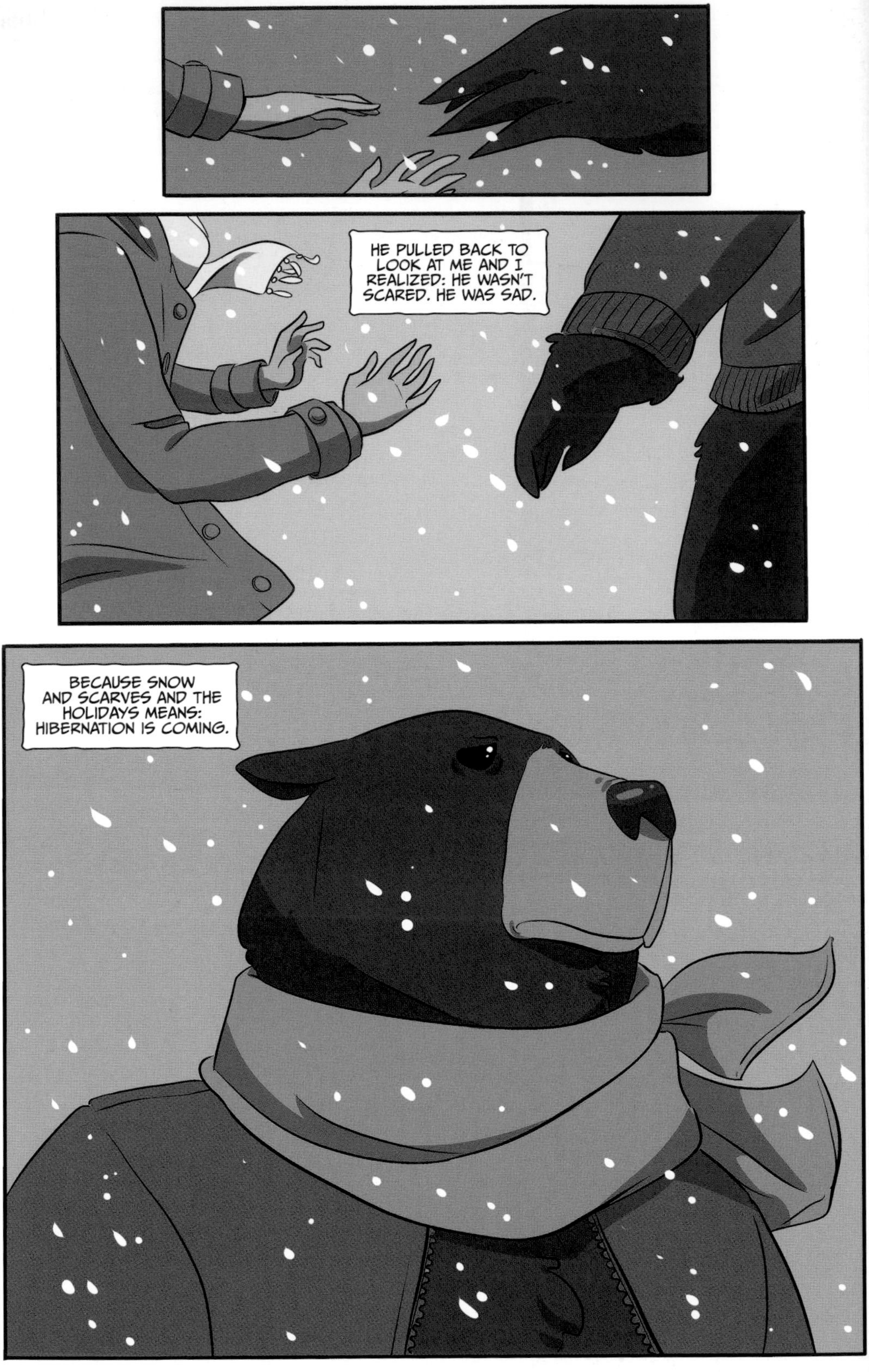
HE PULLED BACK TO LOOK AT ME AND I REALIZED: HE WASN'T SCARED. HE WAS SAD.
BECAUSE SNOW AND SCARVES AND THE HOLIDAYS MEANS: HIBERNATION IS COMING.

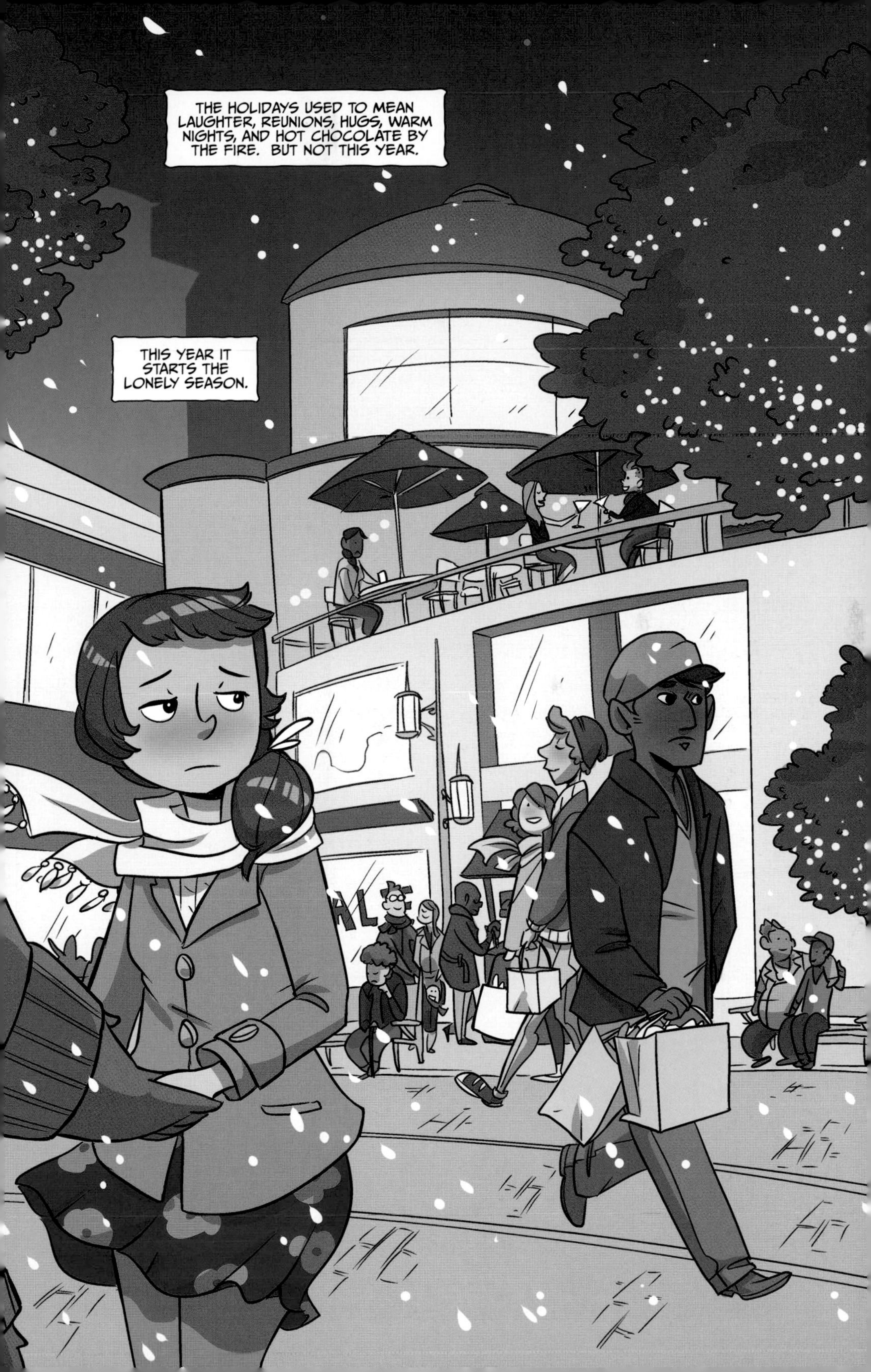
THE HOLIDAYS USED TO MEAN LAUGHTER, REUNIONS, HUGS, WARM NIGHTS, AND HOT CHOCOLATE BY THE FIRE. BUT NOT THIS YEAR.
THIS YEAR IT STARTS THE LONELY SEASON.

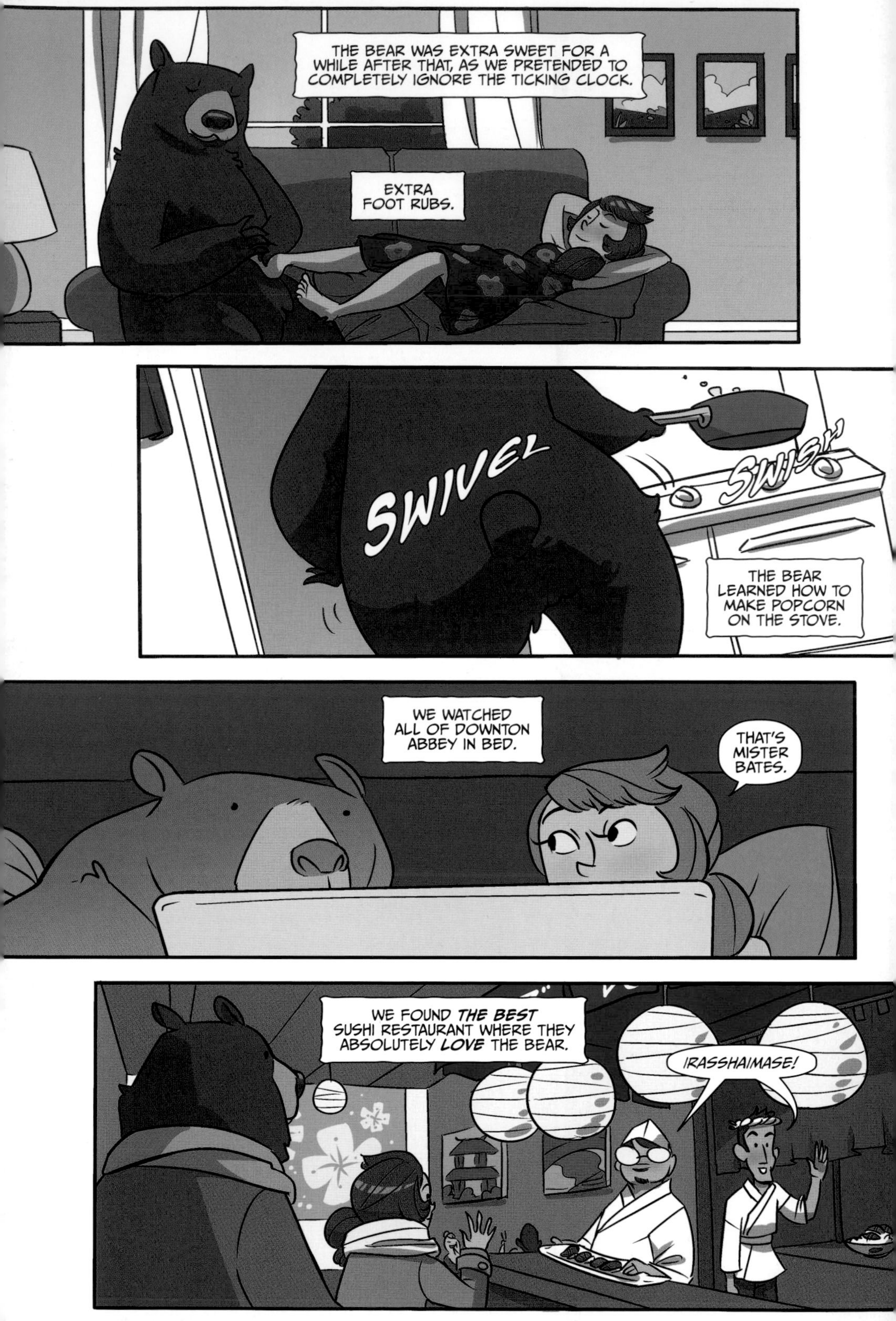
THE BEAR WAS EXTRA SWEET FOR A WHILE AFTER THAT, AS WE PRETENDED TO COMPLETELY IGNORE THE TICKING CLOCK.
EXTRA FOOT RUBS.
SWIVEL
SWISH
THE BEAR LEARNED HOW TO MAKE POPCORN ON THE STOVE.
WE WATCHED ALL OF DOWNTON ABBEY IN BED.
THAT'S MISTER BATES.
WE FOUND *THE BEST* SUSHI RESTAURANT WHERE THEY ABSOLUTELY *LOVE* THE BEAR.
IRASSHAIMASE!

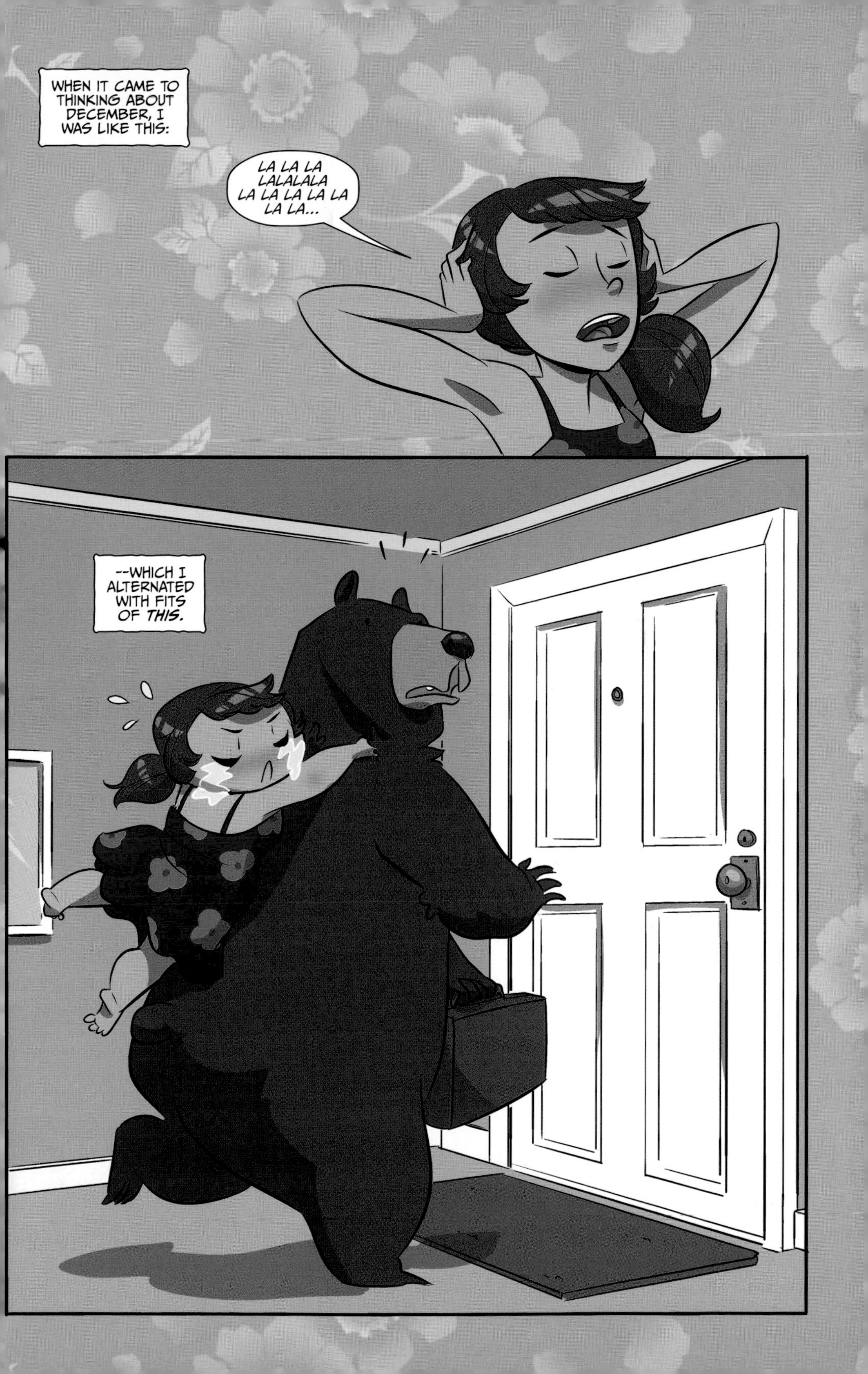
WHEN IT CAME TO THINKING ABOUT DECEMBER, I WAS LIKE THIS:
LA LA LA LALALALA LA LA LA LA LA LA LA...
--WHICH I ALTERNATED WITH FITS OF *THIS.*

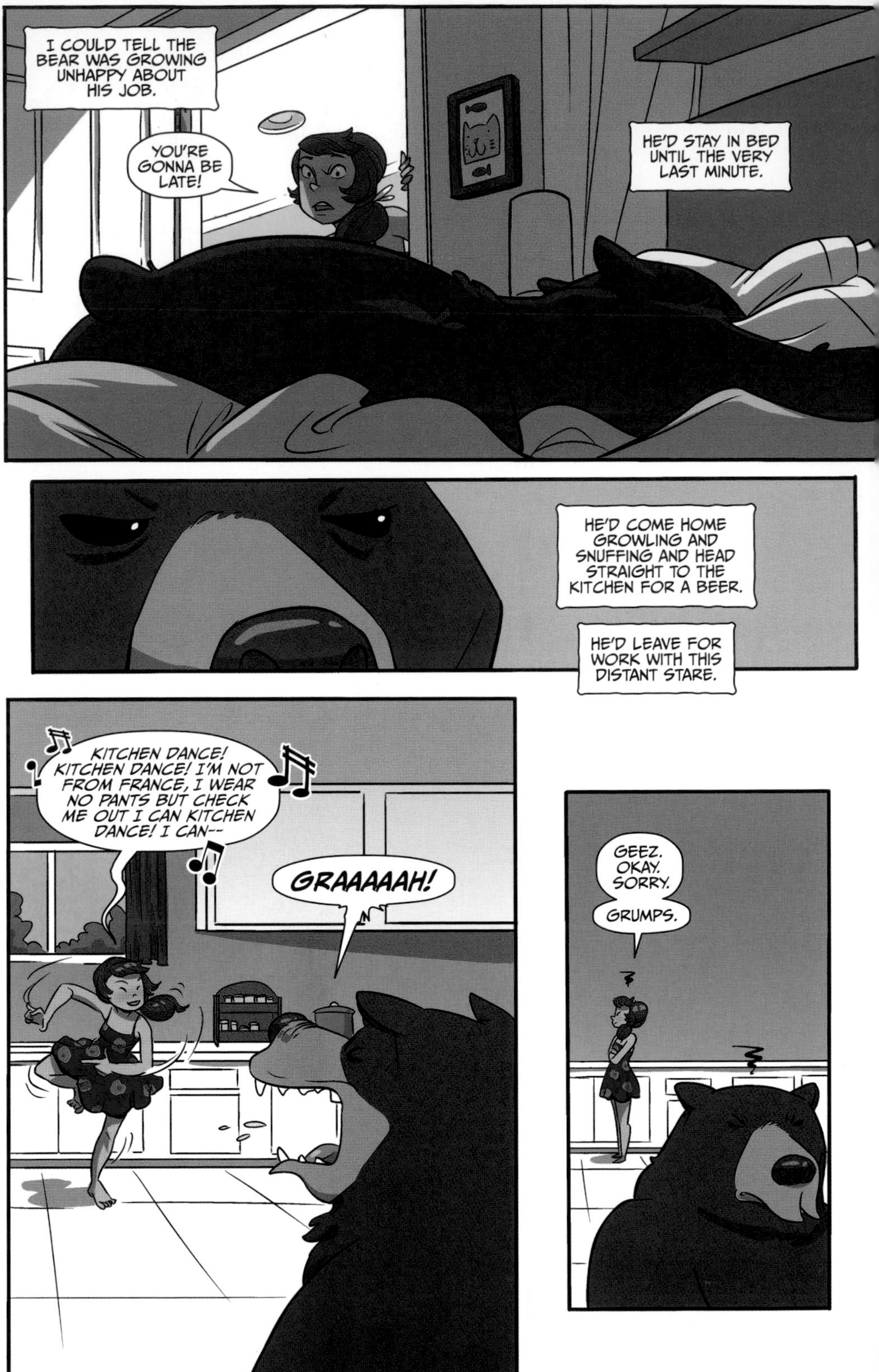

I COULD TELL THE BEAR WAS GROWING UNHAPPY ABOUT HIS JOB.
YOU'RE GONNA BE LATE!
HE'D STAY IN BED UNTIL THE VERY LAST MINUTE.
HE'D COME HOME GROWLING AND SNUFFING AND HEAD STRAIGHT TO THE KITCHEN FOR A BEER.
HE'D LEAVE FOR WORK WITH THIS DISTANT STARE.
KITCHEN DANCE! KITCHEN DANCE! I'M NOT FROM FRANCE, I WEAR NO PANTS BUT CHECK ME OUT I CAN KITCHEN DANCE! I CAN--
GRAAAAAH!
GEEZ. OKAY. SORRY.
GRUMPS.

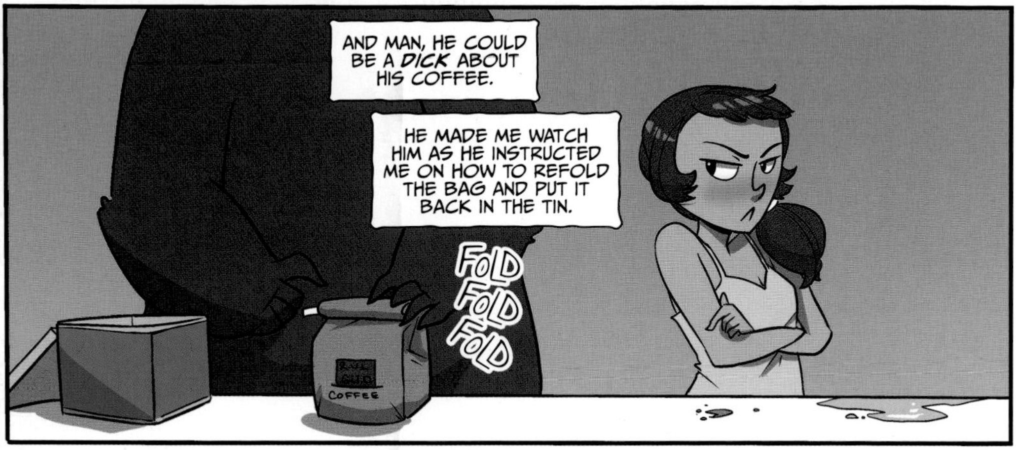
AND MAN, HE COULD BE A *DICK* ABOUT HIS COFFEE.
HE MADE ME WATCH HIM AS HE INSTRUCTED ME ON HOW TO REFOLD THE BAG AND PUT IT BACK IN THE TIN.
FOLD FOLD FOLD
COFFEE

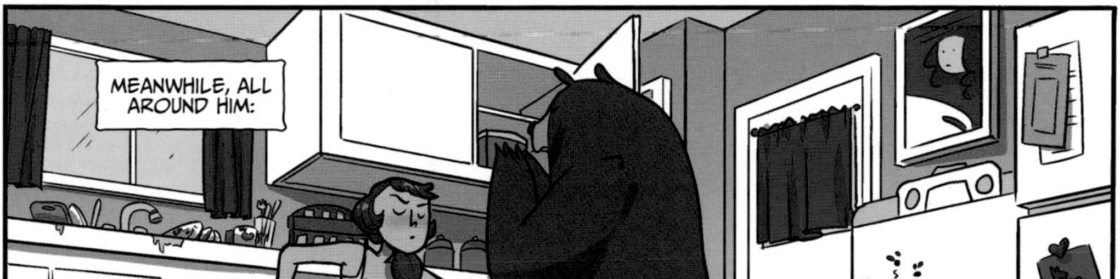
MEANWHILE, ALL AROUND HIM:
OKAY, BEAR. I'LL TRY TO BE BETTER ABOUT THAT.
...YOUR *MAJESTY.*

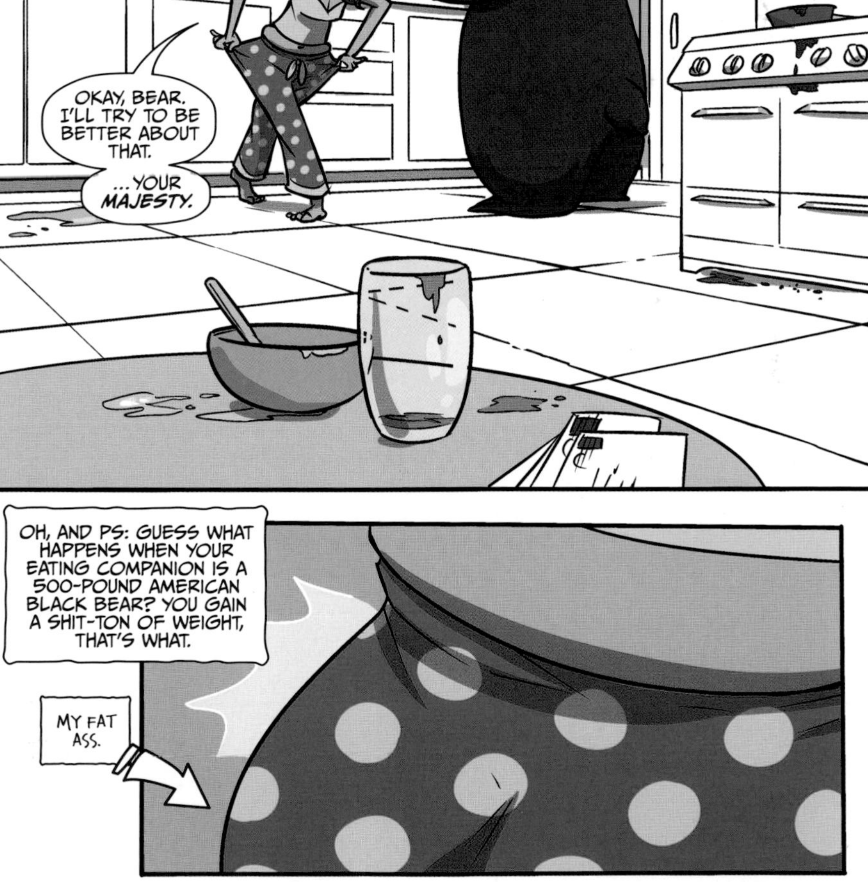
OH, AND PS: GUESS WHAT HAPPENS WHEN YOUR EATING COMPANION IS A 500-POUND AMERICAN BLACK BEAR? YOU GAIN A SHIT-TON OF WEIGHT, THAT'S WHAT.
MY FAT ASS.

MY JOB WAS BECOMING A SHIT PILE, TOO.

HEY, DID YOU SEE THERE'S A NEW SCHEDULE?

THEY CHANGED MY HOURS! HOW CAN THEY JUST *DO* THAT?

DON'T FORGET

BECAUSE THEY WANT US TO QUIT. THIS PLACE IS GOING DOWN THE SHITTER. I HEAR THEY'RE GETTING SUED. I'M NOT QUITTING. I'M MILKING THIS PLACE FOR EVERY LAST PENNY.

HEFTY BEAR

DID I TELL YOU I GOT RID OF MY TELEVISION? BEST DECISION I EVER MADE.

DECEMBER

29	30	X 1	X 2	X 3	4	5
6	7	8	9	10		C +P
13	APPT 14	15	16	17	18	19

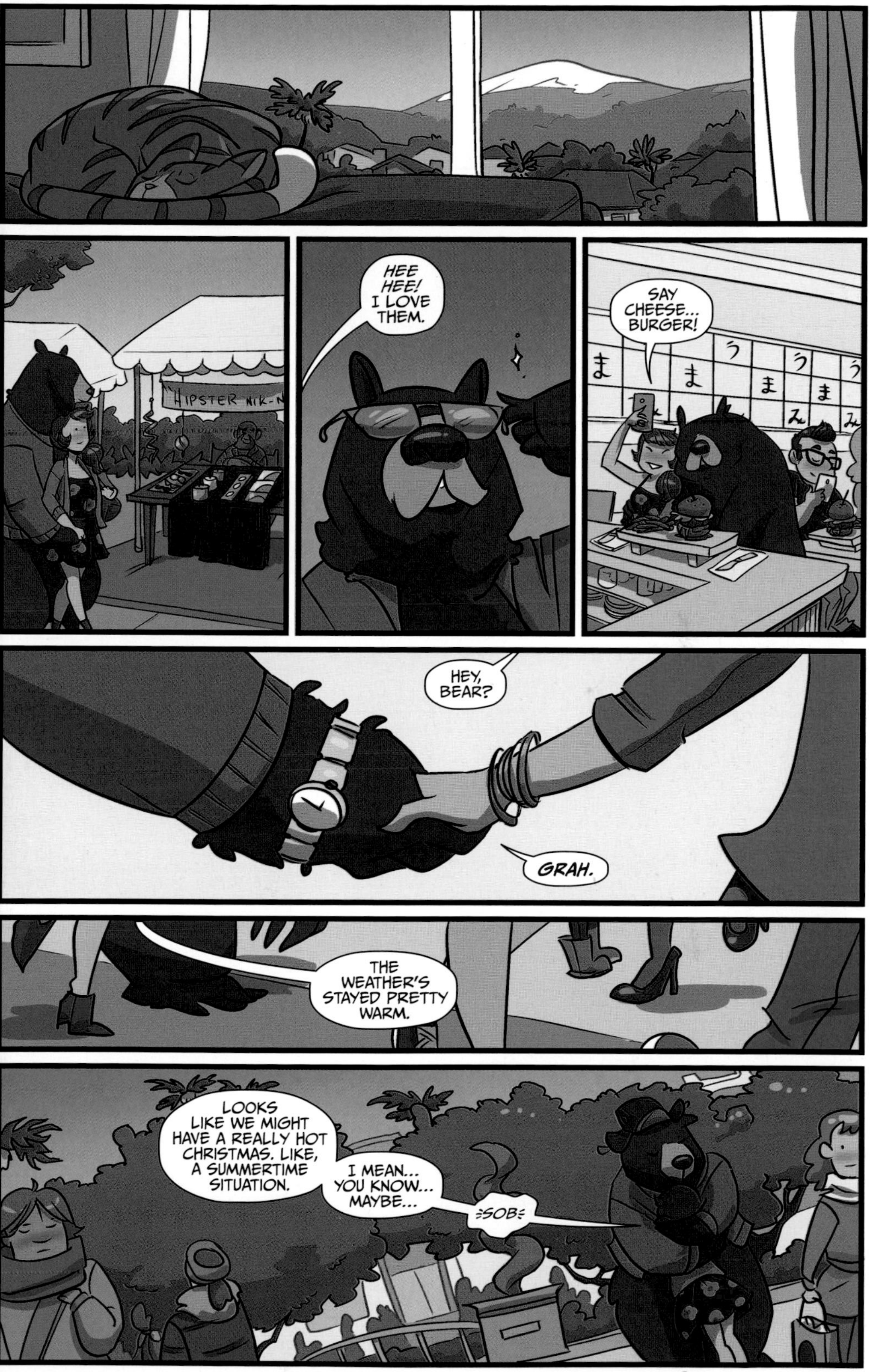
HEE HEE! I LOVE THEM.
SAY CHEESE... BURGER!
HEY, BEAR?
GRAH.
THE WEATHER'S STAYED PRETTY WARM.
LOOKS LIKE WE MIGHT HAVE A REALLY HOT CHRISTMAS. LIKE, A SUMMERTIME SITUATION.
I MEAN... YOU KNOW... MAYBE...
SOB

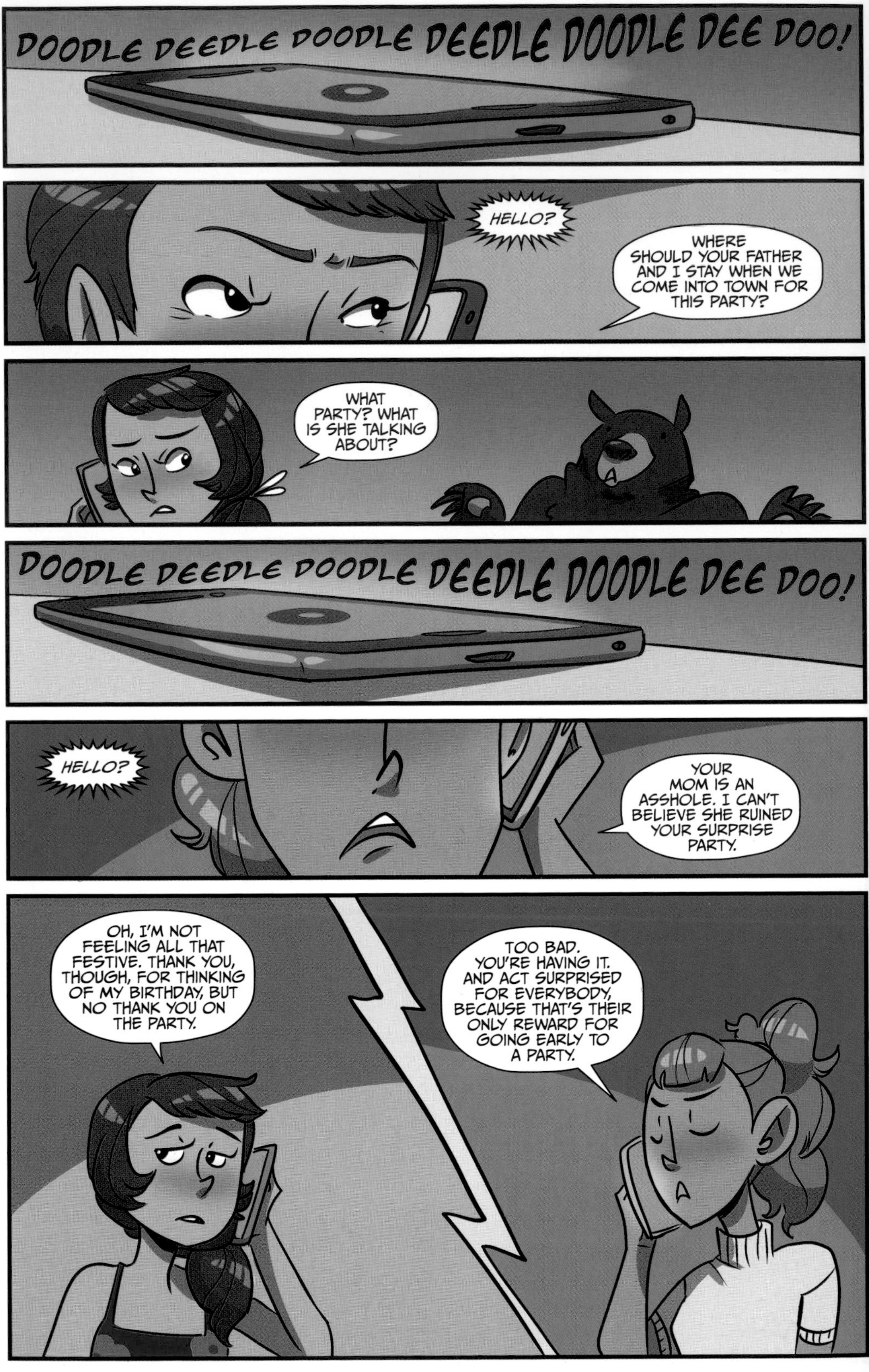
DOODLE DEEDLE DOODLE DEEDLE DOODLE DEE DOO!
HELLO?
WHERE SHOULD YOUR FATHER AND I STAY WHEN WE COME INTO TOWN FOR THIS PARTY?
WHAT PARTY? WHAT IS SHE TALKING ABOUT?
DOODLE DEEDLE DOODLE DEEDLE DOODLE DEE DOO!
HELLO?
YOUR MOM IS AN ASSHOLE. I CAN'T BELIEVE SHE RUINED YOUR SURPRISE PARTY.
OH, I'M NOT FEELING ALL THAT FESTIVE. THANK YOU, THOUGH, FOR THINKING OF MY BIRTHDAY, BUT NO THANK YOU ON THE PARTY.
TOO BAD. YOU'RE HAVING IT. AND ACT SURPRISED FOR EVERYBODY, BECAUSE THAT'S THEIR ONLY REWARD FOR GOING EARLY TO A PARTY.

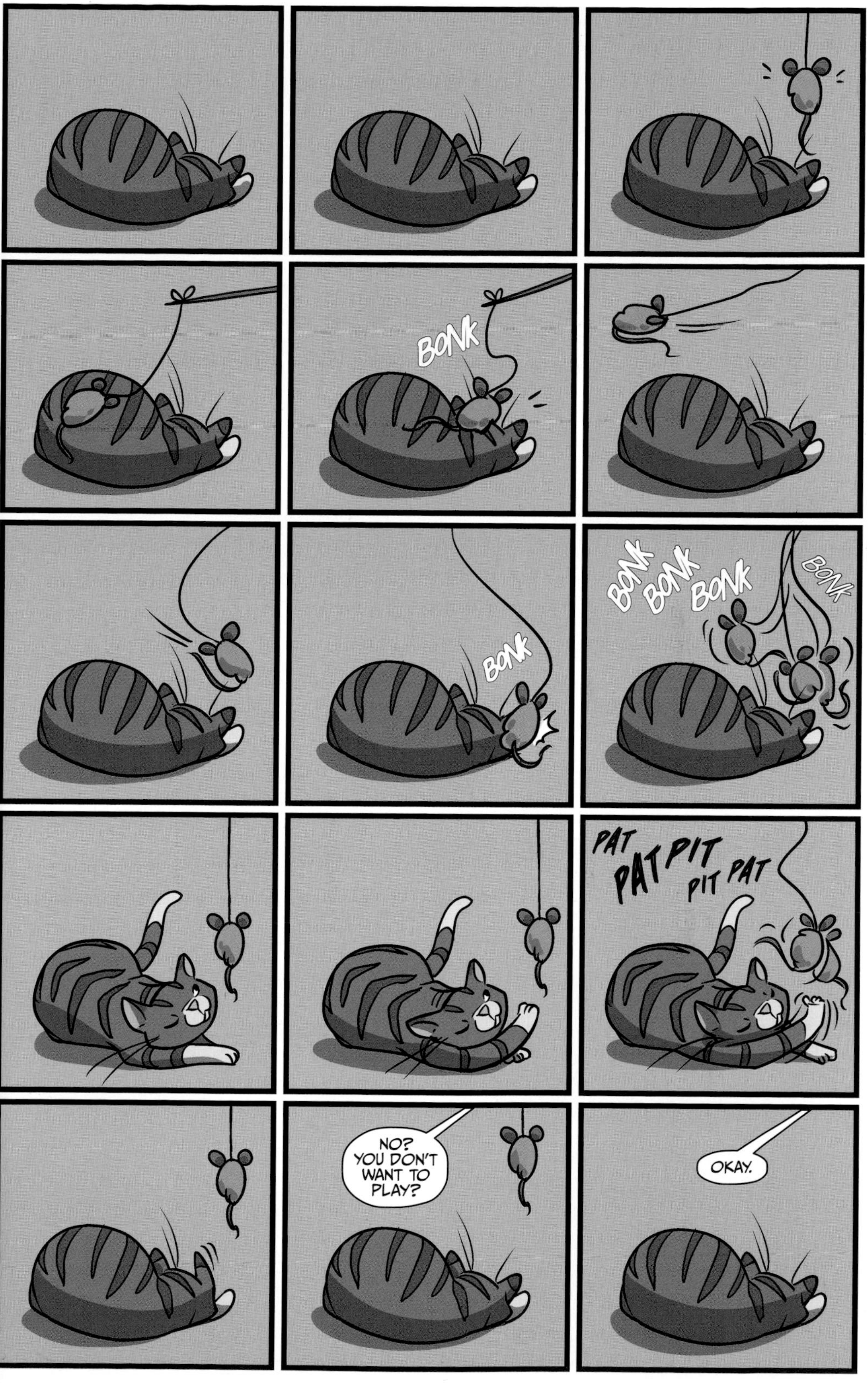
BONK
BONK
BONK
BONK
BONK
BONK
PAT
PAT PIT
PIT PAT
NO? YOU DON'T WANT TO PLAY?
OKAY.

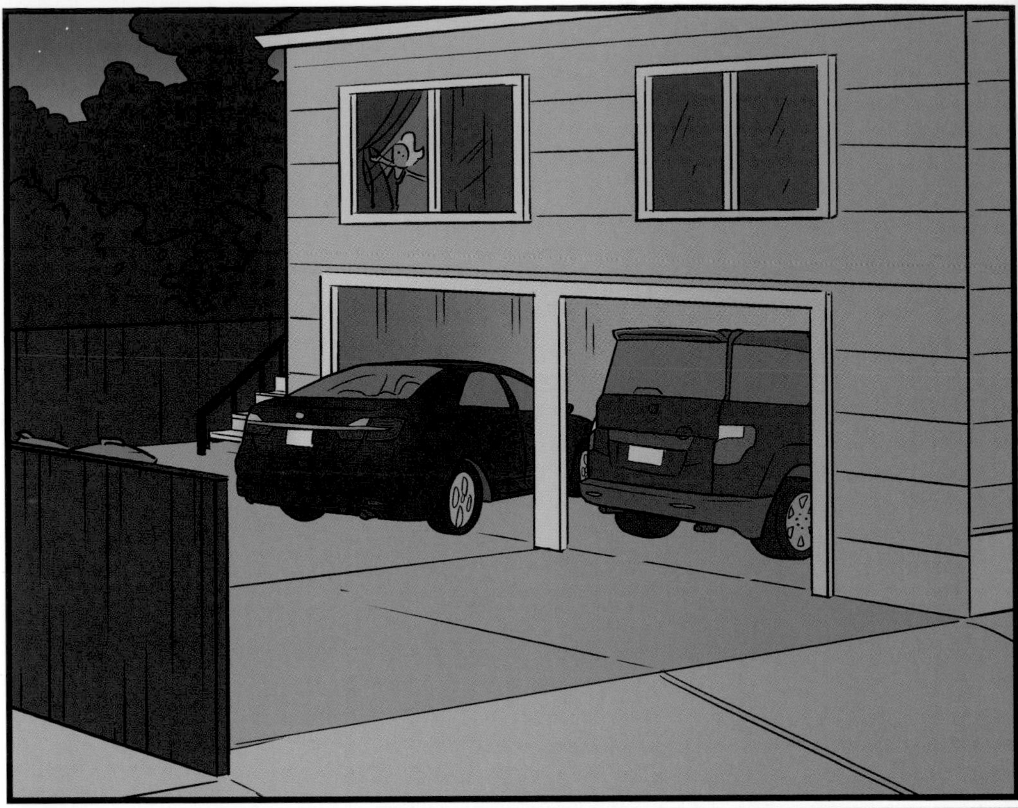

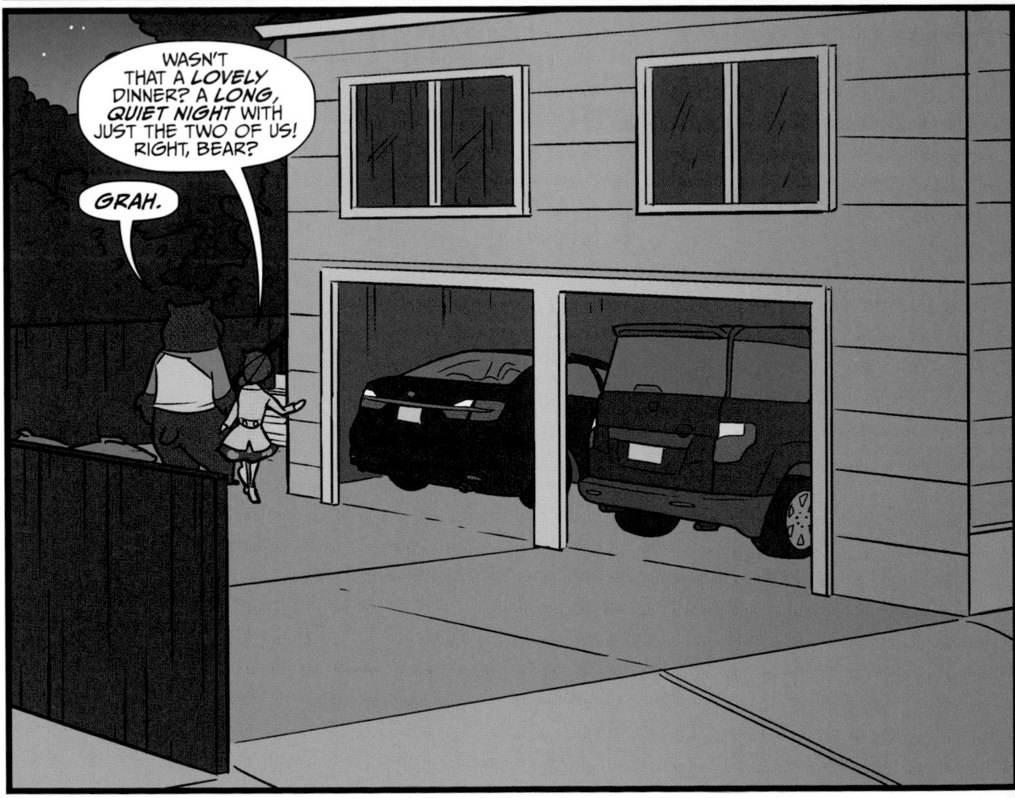
WASN'T THAT A LOVELY DINNER? A LONG, QUIET NIGHT WITH JUST THE TWO OF US! RIGHT, BEAR?
GRAH.

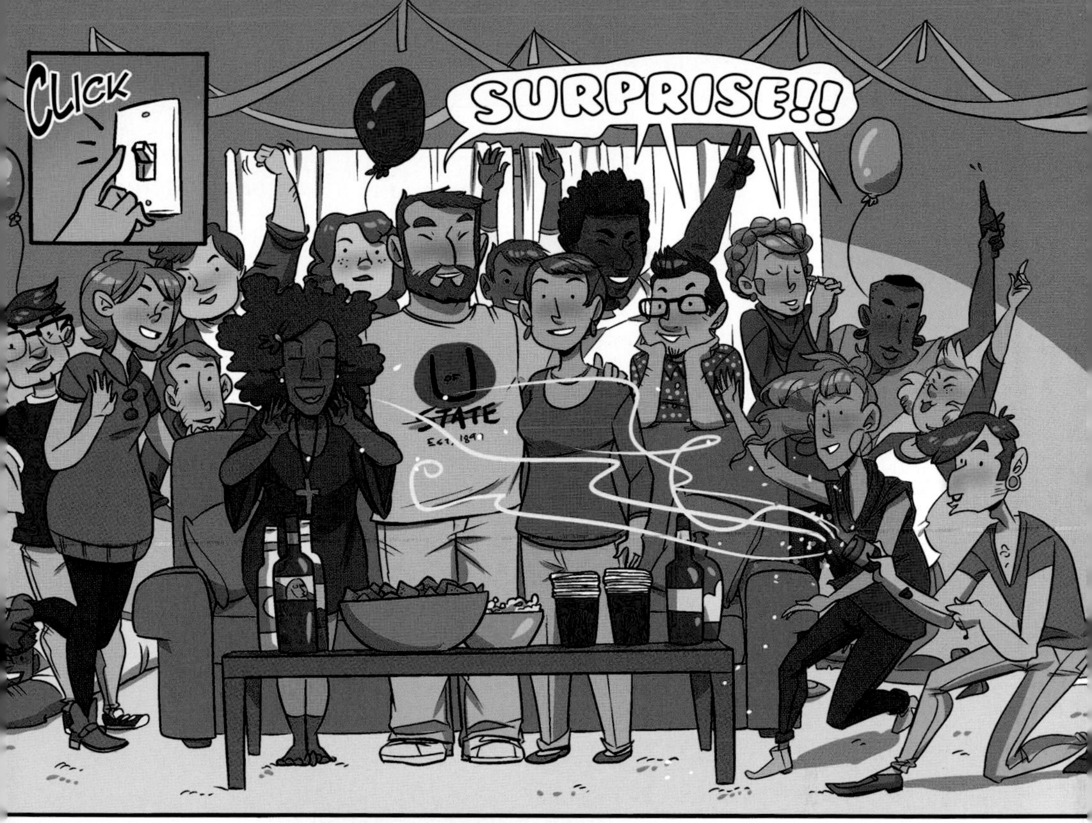
CLICK
SURPRISE!!
U OF STATE EST. 1897

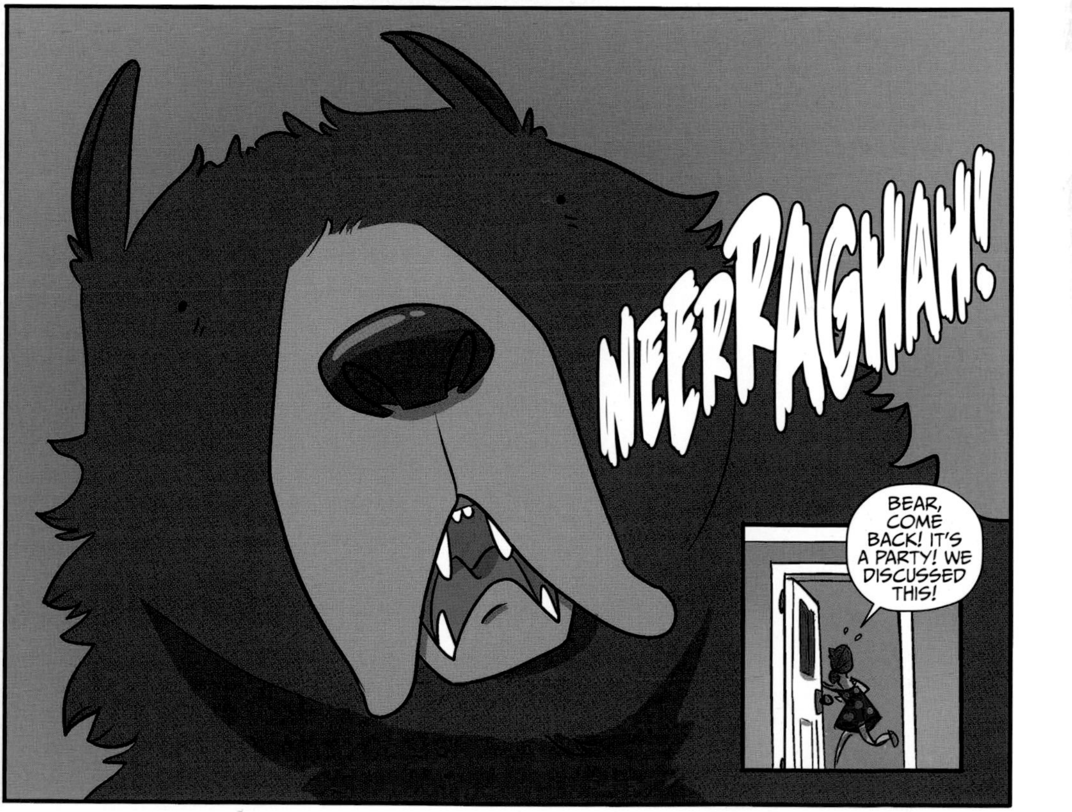
NEERRAGHAH!
BEAR, COME BACK! IT'S A PARTY! WE DISCUSSED THIS!

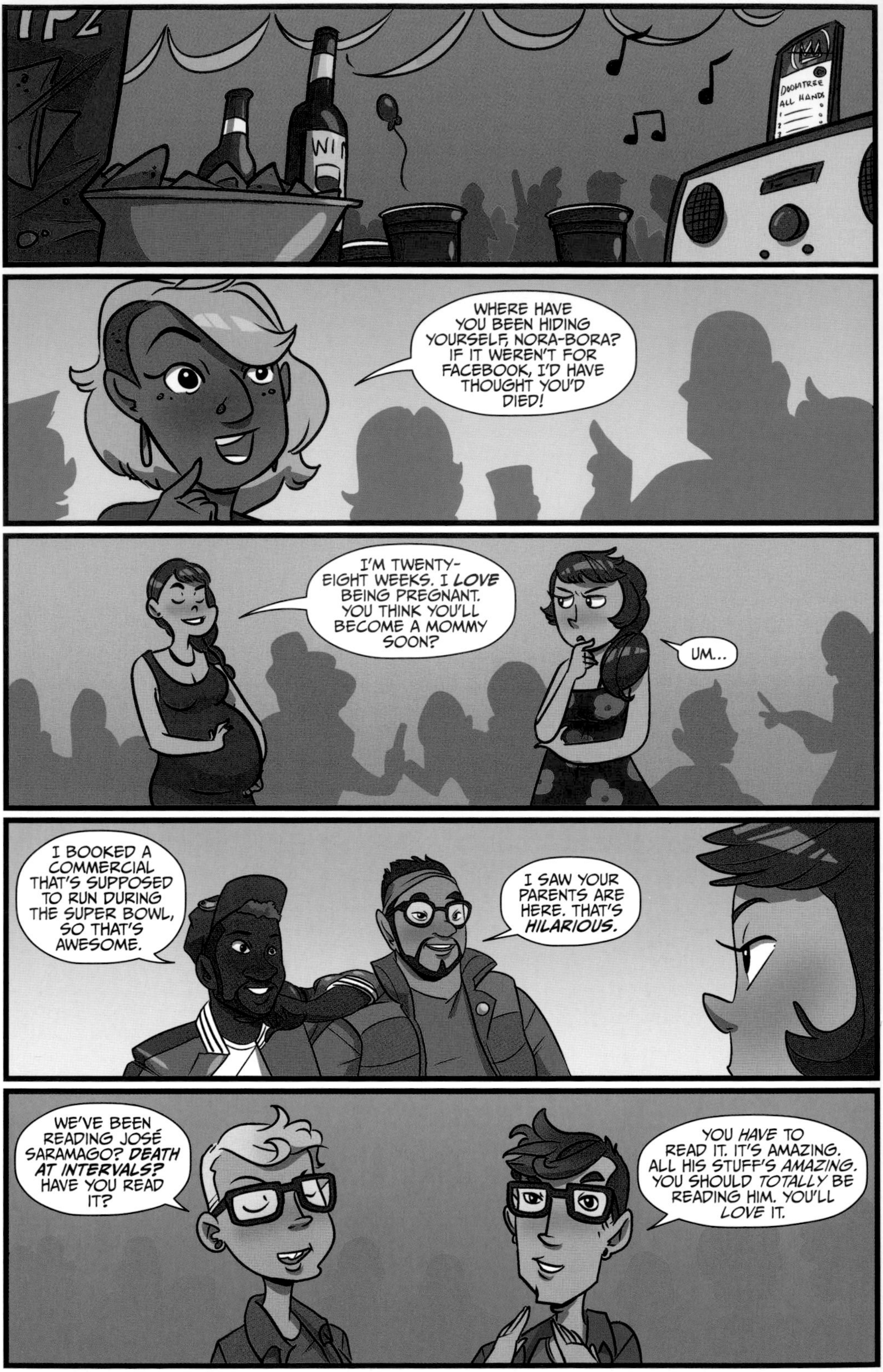
DOOMTREE ALL HANDS
WIN
WHERE HAVE YOU BEEN HIDING YOURSELF, NORA-BORA? IF IT WEREN'T FOR FACEBOOK, I'D HAVE THOUGHT YOU'D DIED!
I'M TWENTY-EIGHT WEEKS. I *LOVE* BEING PREGNANT. YOU THINK YOU'LL BECOME A MOMMY SOON?
UM...
I BOOKED A COMMERCIAL THAT'S SUPPOSED TO RUN DURING THE SUPER BOWL, SO THAT'S AWESOME.
I SAW YOUR PARENTS ARE HERE. THAT'S ***HILARIOUS.***
WE'VE BEEN READING JOSÉ SARAMAGO? ***DEATH AT INTERVALS?*** HAVE YOU READ IT?
YOU *HAVE* TO READ IT. IT'S AMAZING. ALL HIS STUFF'S *AMAZING.* YOU SHOULD *TOTALLY* BE READING HIM. YOU'LL *LOVE* IT.

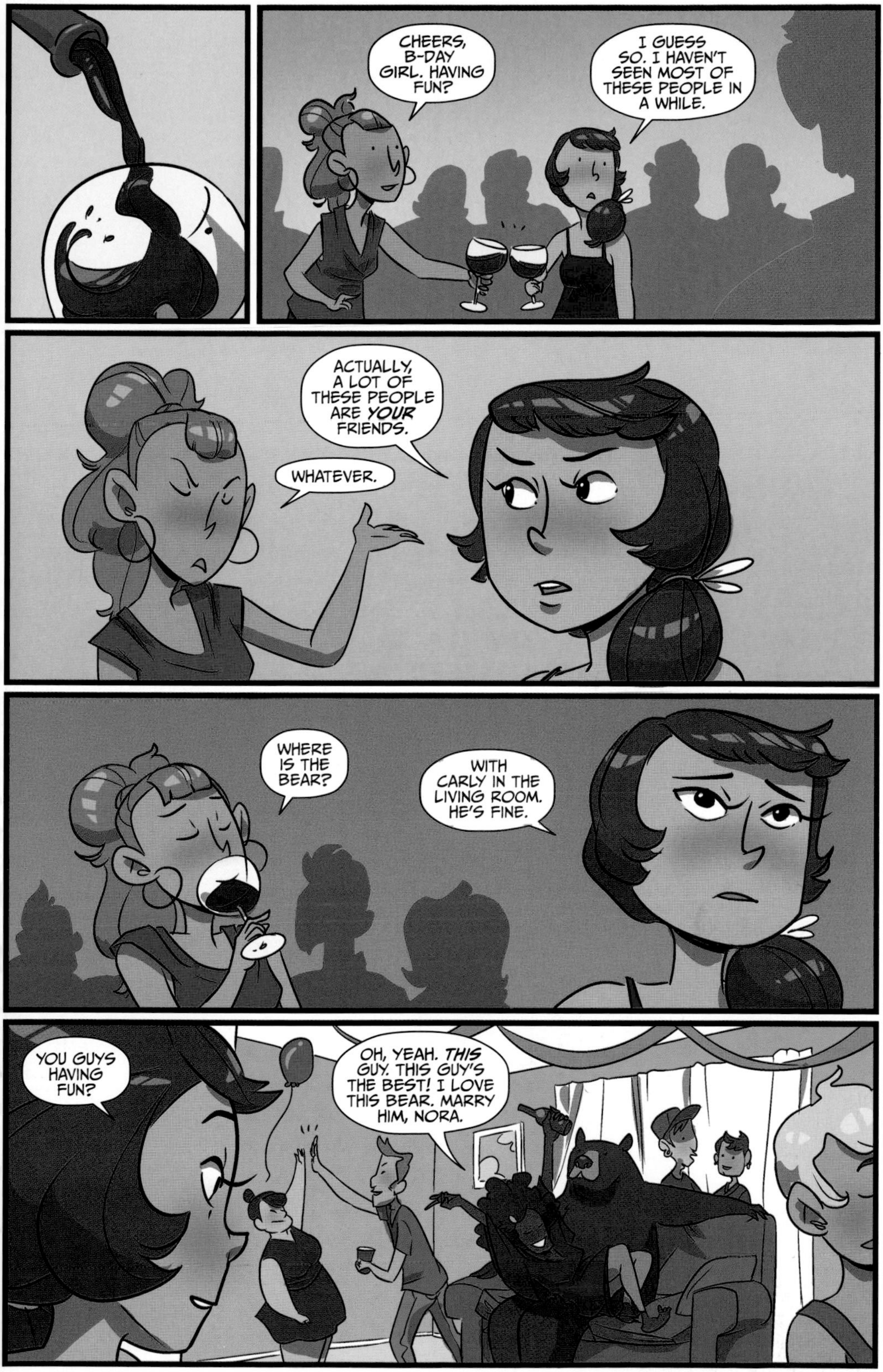
CHEERS, B-DAY GIRL. HAVING FUN?
I GUESS SO. I HAVEN'T SEEN MOST OF THESE PEOPLE IN A WHILE.
ACTUALLY, A LOT OF THESE PEOPLE ARE *YOUR* FRIENDS.
WHATEVER.
WHERE IS THE BEAR?
WITH CARLY IN THE LIVING ROOM. HE'S FINE.
YOU GUYS HAVING FUN?
OH, YEAH. *THIS* GUY. THIS GUY'S THE BEST! I LOVE THIS BEAR. MARRY HIM, NORA.

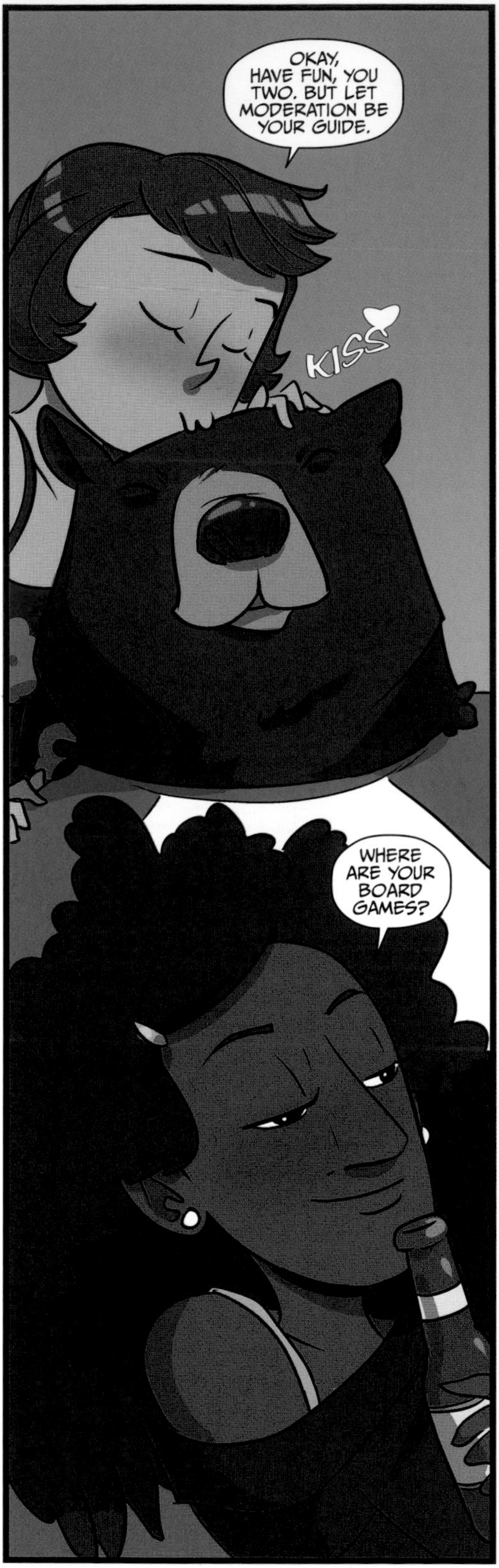
OKAY, HAVE FUN, YOU TWO. BUT LET MODERATION BE YOUR GUIDE.
KISS
WHERE ARE YOUR BOARD GAMES?

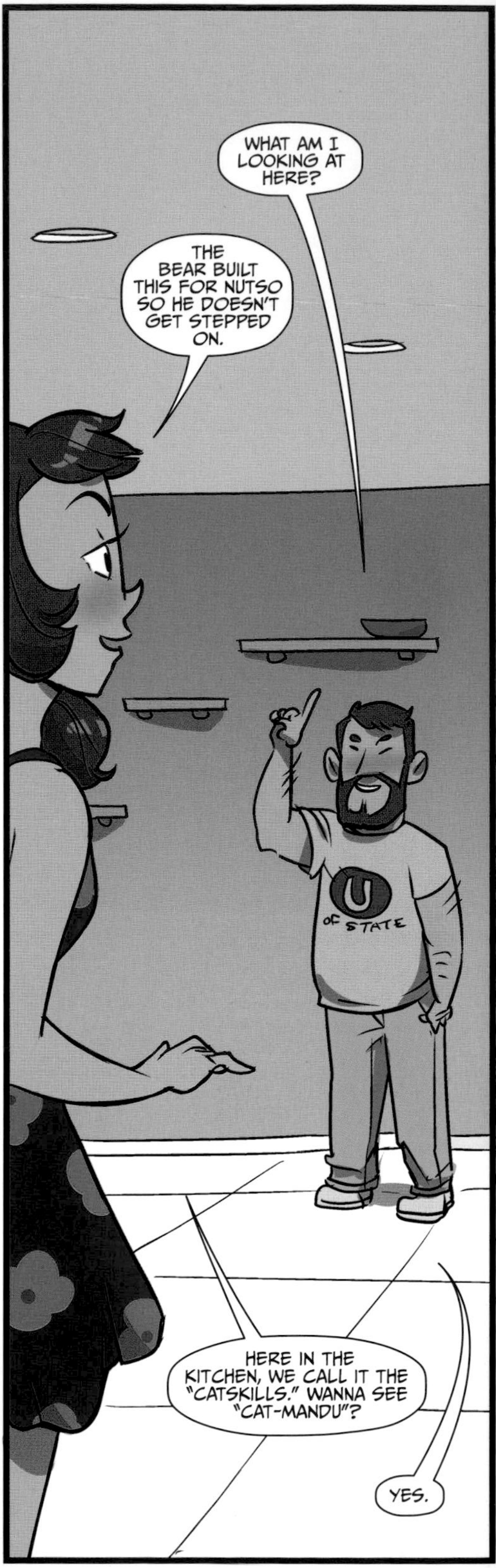
WHAT AM I LOOKING AT HERE?
THE BEAR BUILT THIS FOR NUTSO SO HE DOESN'T GET STEPPED ON.
U OF STATE
HERE IN THE KITCHEN, WE CALL IT THE "CATSKILLS." WANNA SEE "CAT-MANDU"?
YES.

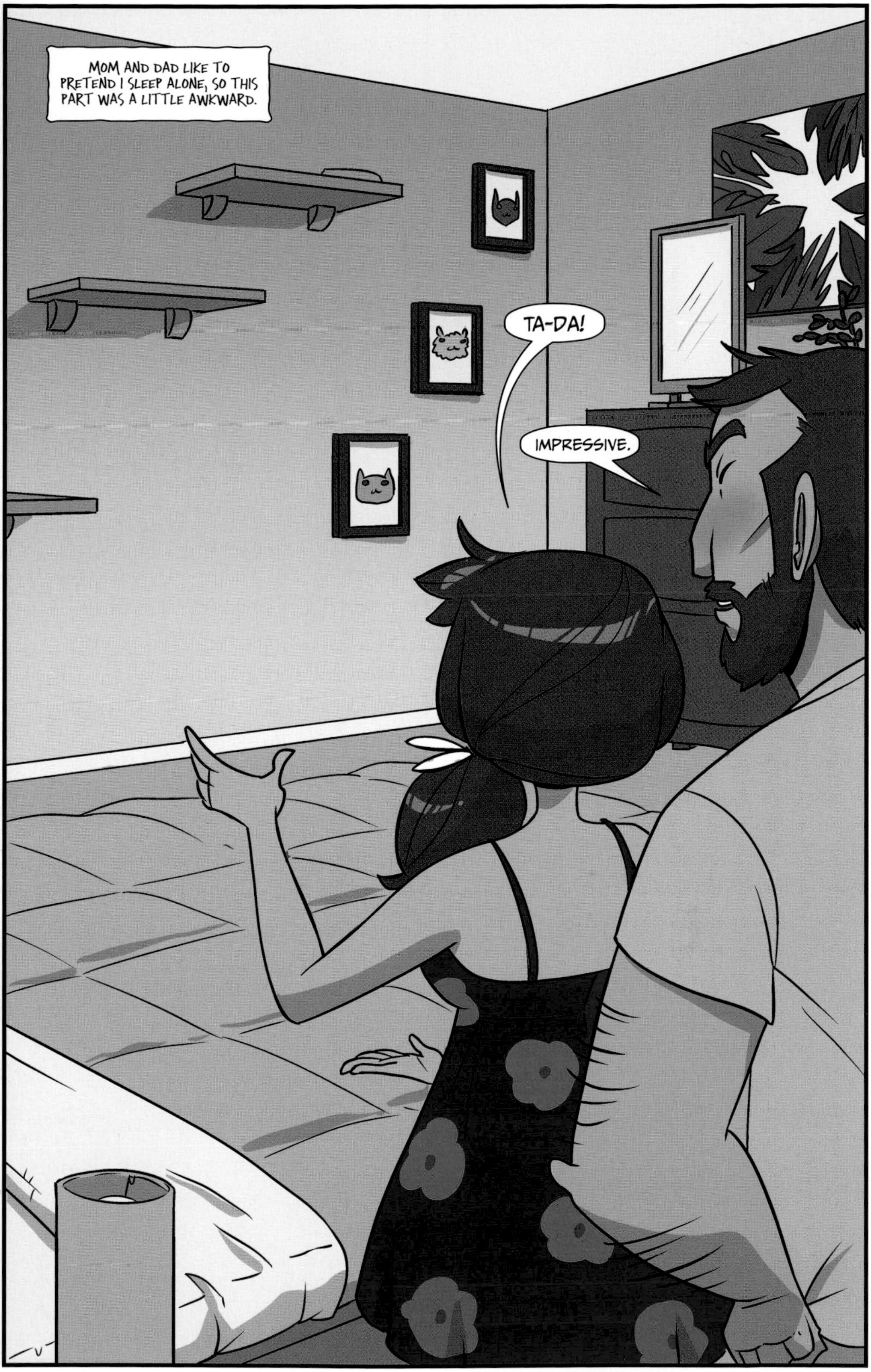
MOM AND DAD LIKE TO PRETEND I SLEEP ALONE, SO THIS PART WAS A LITTLE AWKWARD.
TA-DA!
IMPRESSIVE.

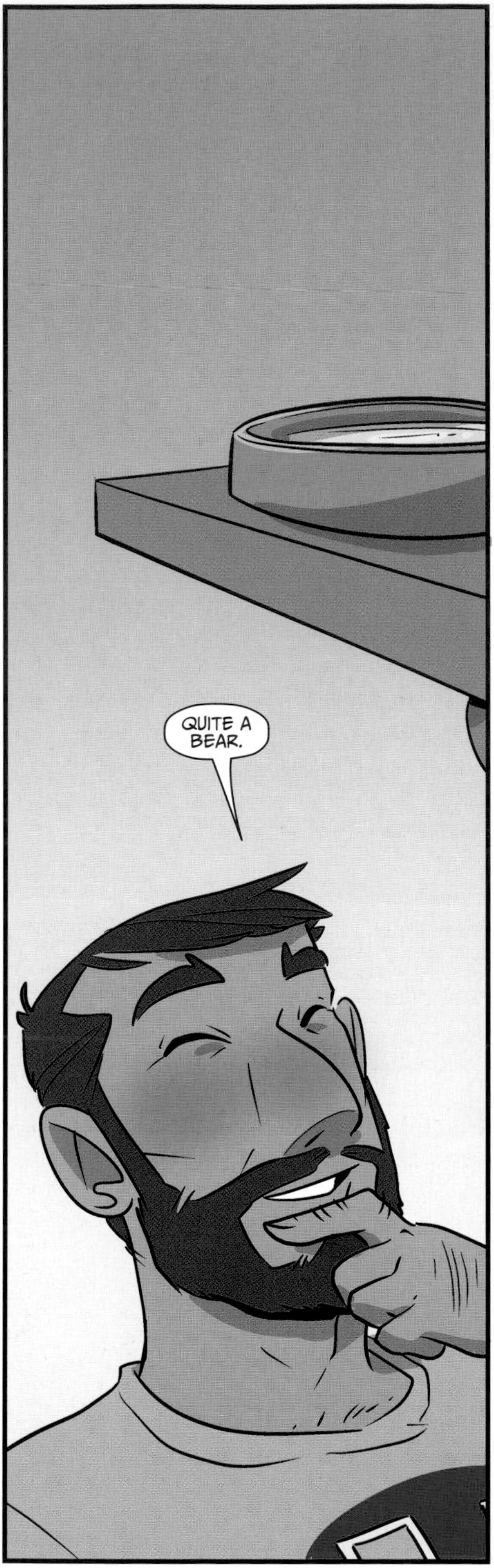
QUITE A BEAR.

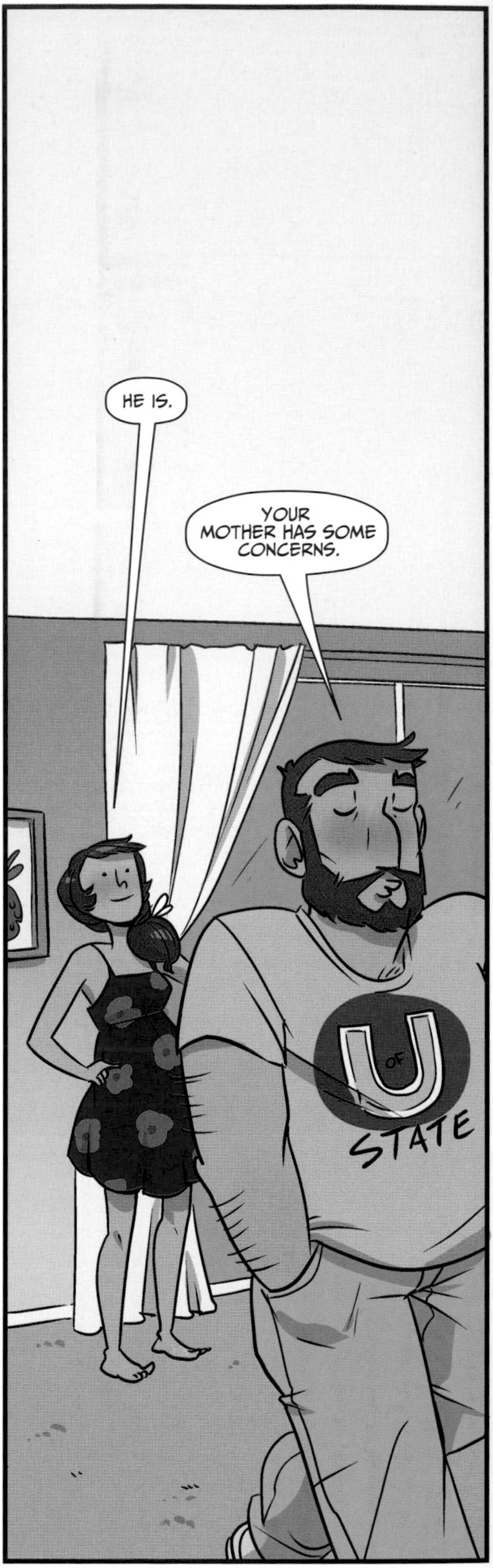
HE IS.
YOUR MOTHER HAS SOME CONCERNS.
U OF STATE

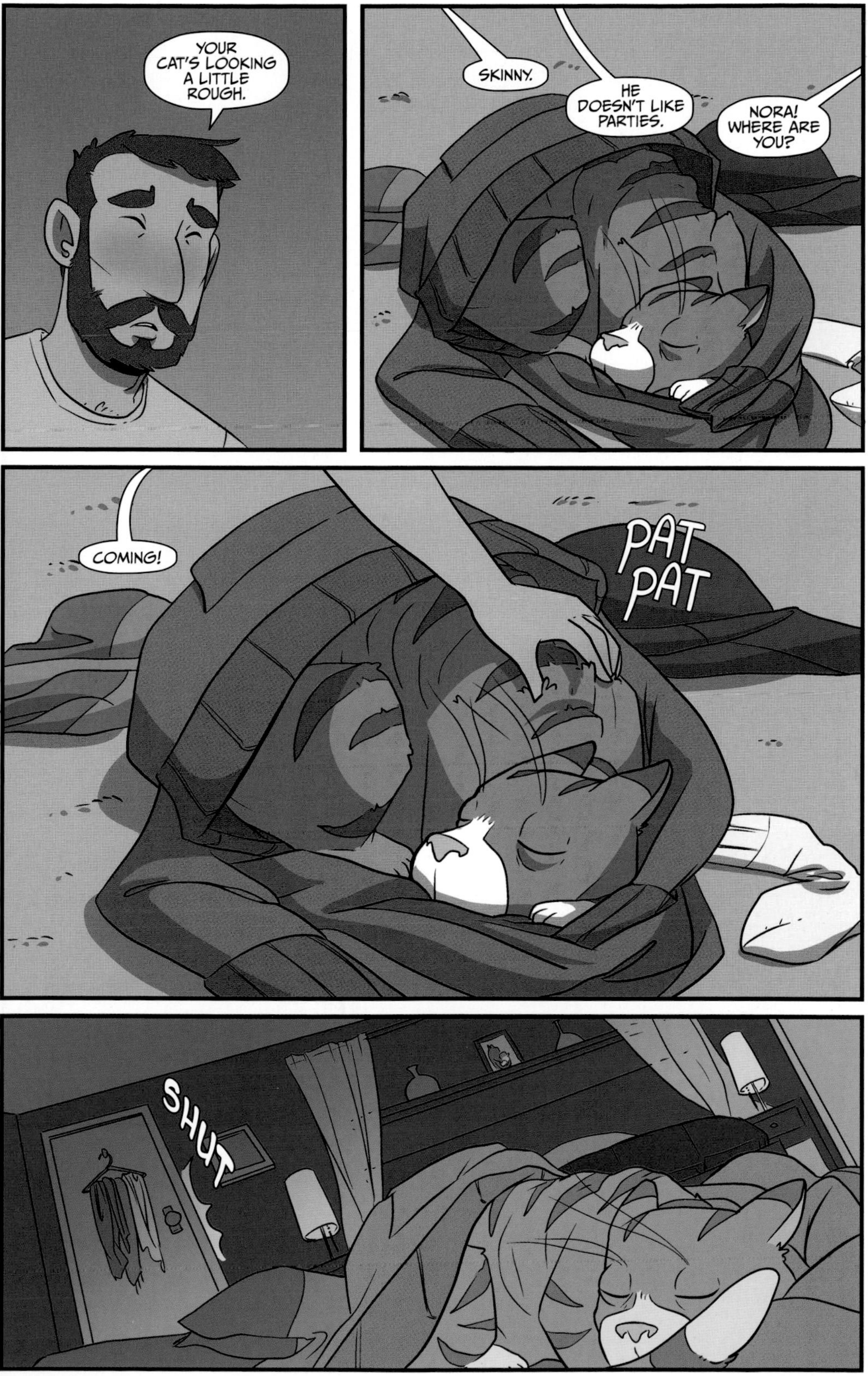
YOUR CAT'S LOOKING A LITTLE ROUGH.
SKINNY.
HE DOESN'T LIKE PARTIES.
NORA! WHERE ARE YOU?
COMING!
PAT PAT
SHUT

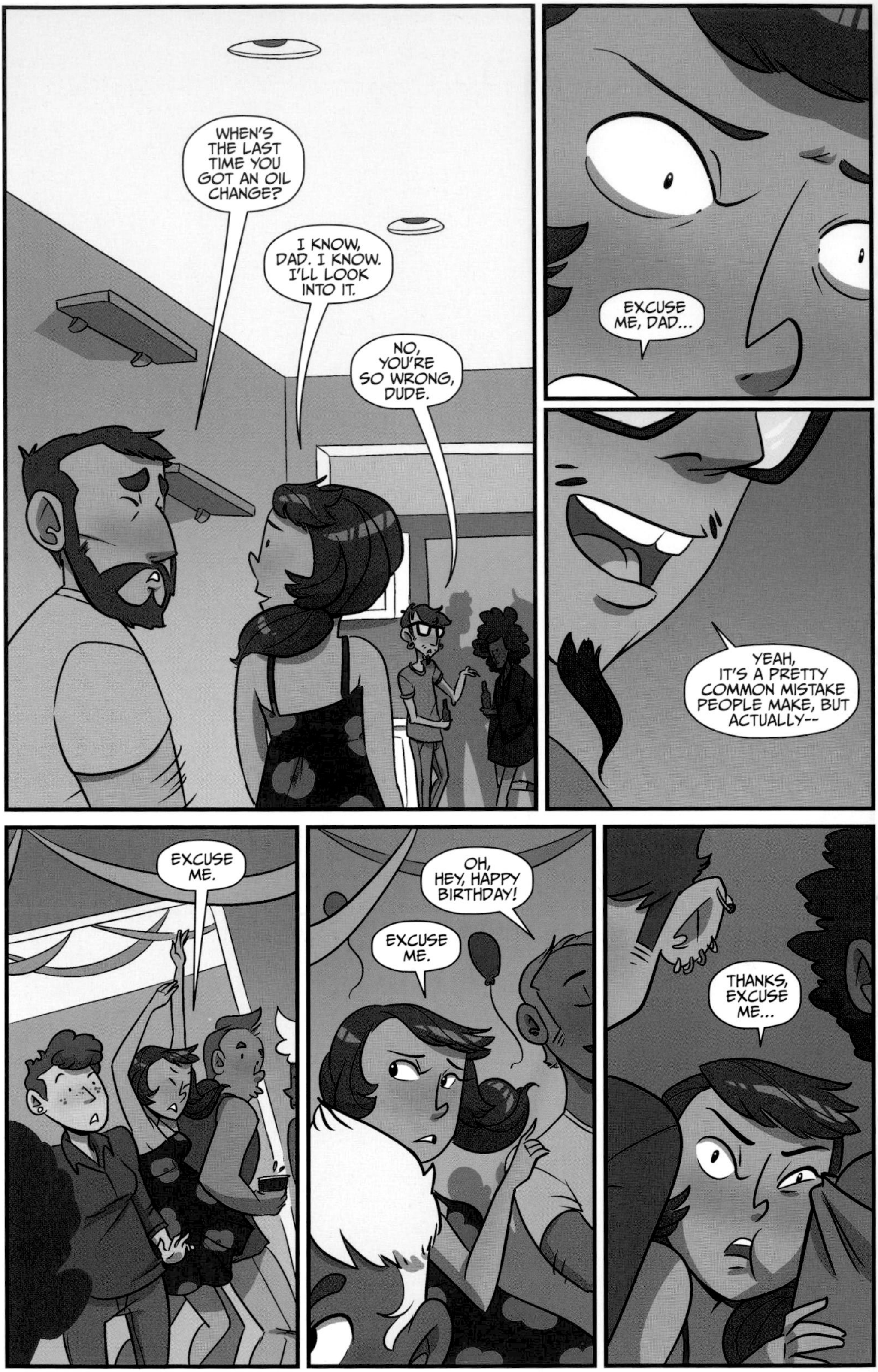
WHEN'S THE LAST TIME YOU GOT AN OIL CHANGE?
I KNOW, DAD. I KNOW. I'LL LOOK INTO IT.
NO, YOU'RE SO WRONG, DUDE.
EXCUSE ME, DAD...
YEAH, IT'S A PRETTY COMMON MISTAKE PEOPLE MAKE, BUT ACTUALLY--
EXCUSE ME.
OH, HEY, HAPPY BIRTHDAY!
EXCUSE ME.
THANKS, EXCUSE ME...

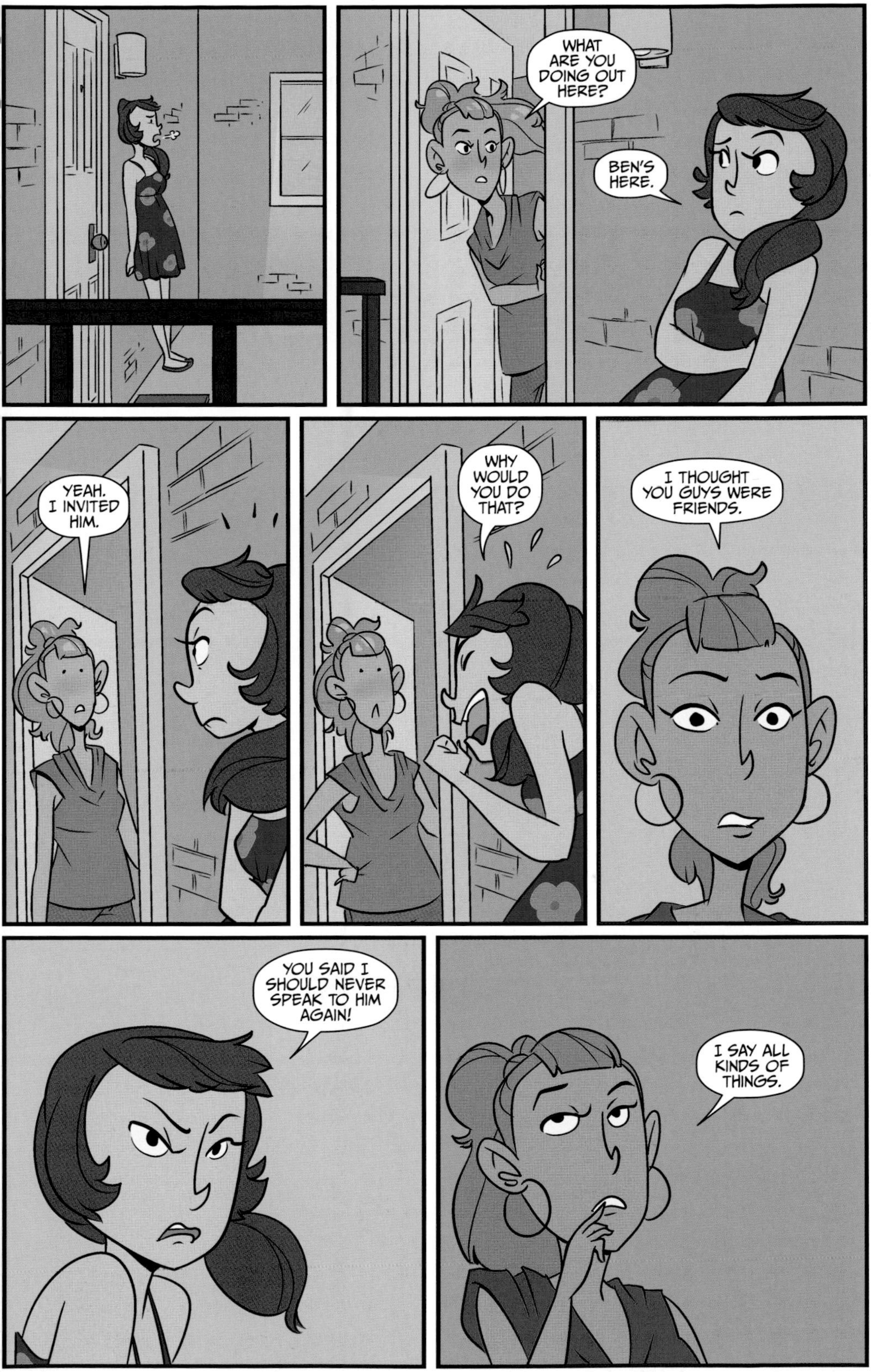
WHAT ARE YOU DOING OUT HERE?
BEN'S HERE.
YEAH. I INVITED HIM.
WHY WOULD YOU DO THAT?
I THOUGHT YOU GUYS WERE FRIENDS.
YOU SAID I SHOULD NEVER SPEAK TO HIM AGAIN!
I SAY ALL KINDS OF THINGS.

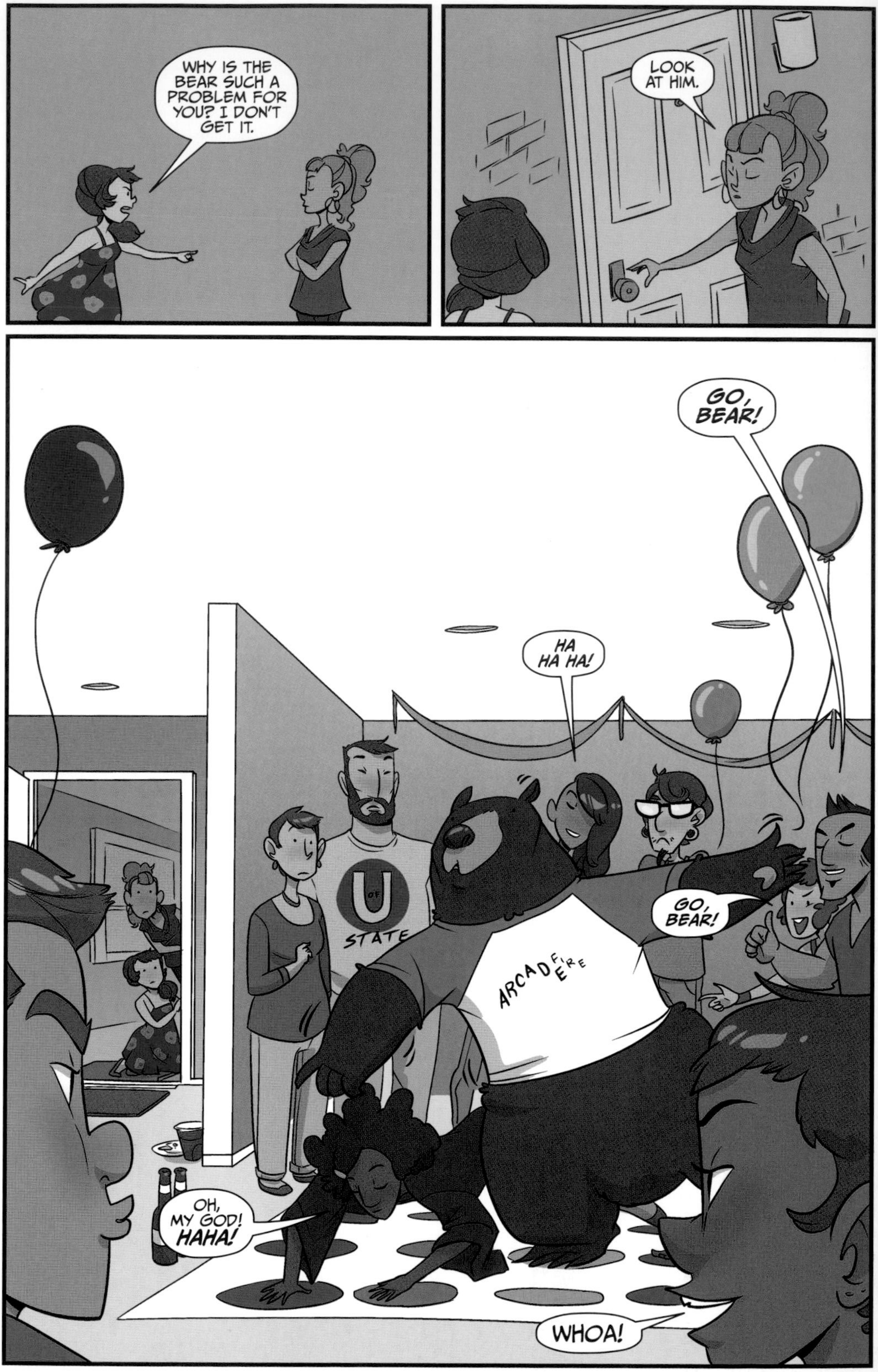
WHY IS THE BEAR SUCH A PROBLEM FOR YOU? I DON'T GET IT.
LOOK AT HIM.
GO, BEAR!
HA HA HA!
U OF STATE
GO, BEAR!
ARCADE FIRE
OH, MY GOD! HAHA!
WHOA!

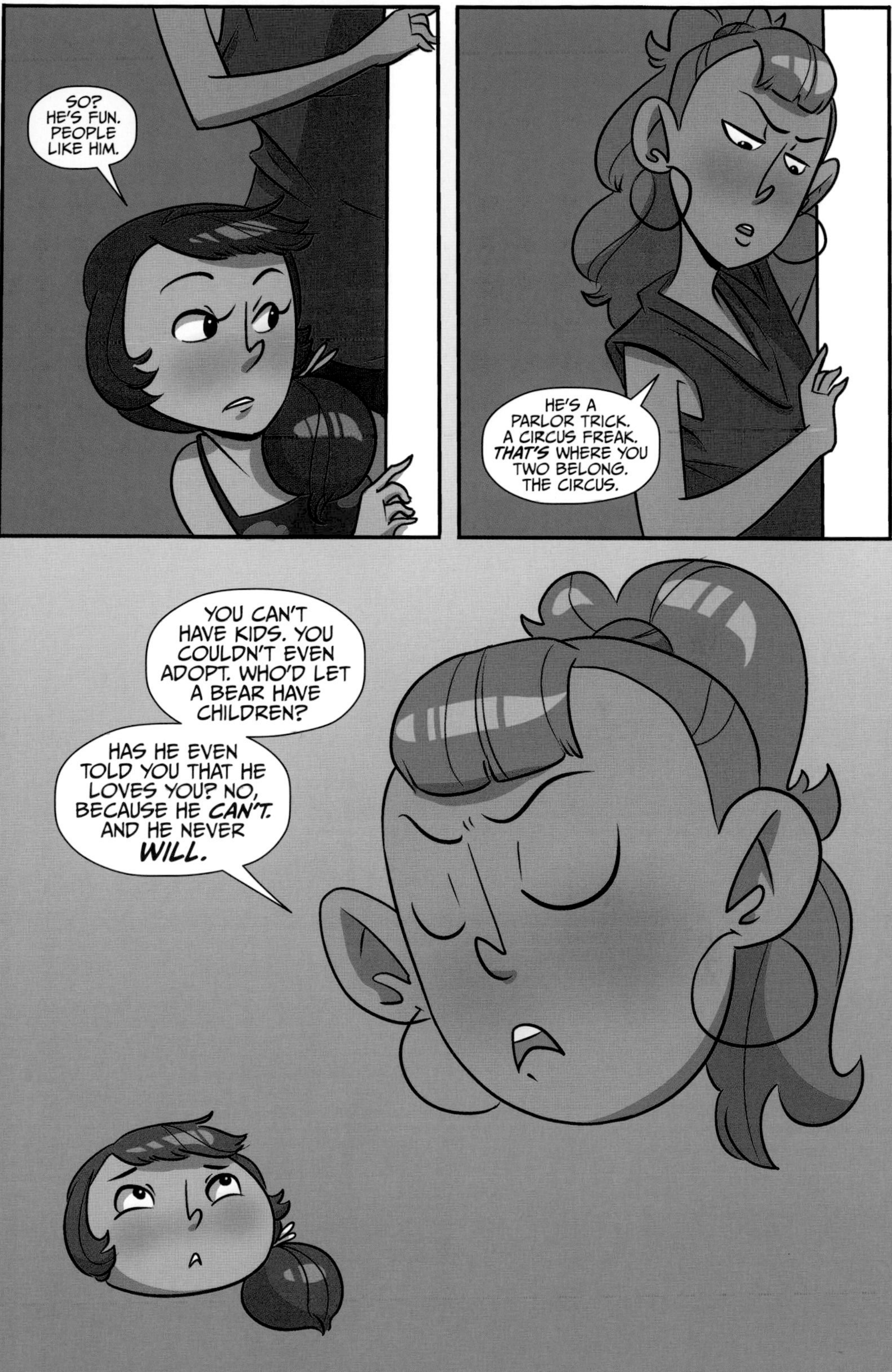
SO? HE'S FUN. PEOPLE LIKE HIM.
HE'S A PARLOR TRICK. A CIRCUS FREAK. THAT'S WHERE YOU TWO BELONG. THE CIRCUS.
YOU CAN'T HAVE KIDS. YOU COULDN'T EVEN ADOPT. WHO'D LET A BEAR HAVE CHILDREN?
HAS HE EVEN TOLD YOU THAT HE LOVES YOU? NO, BECAUSE HE CAN'T. AND HE NEVER WILL.

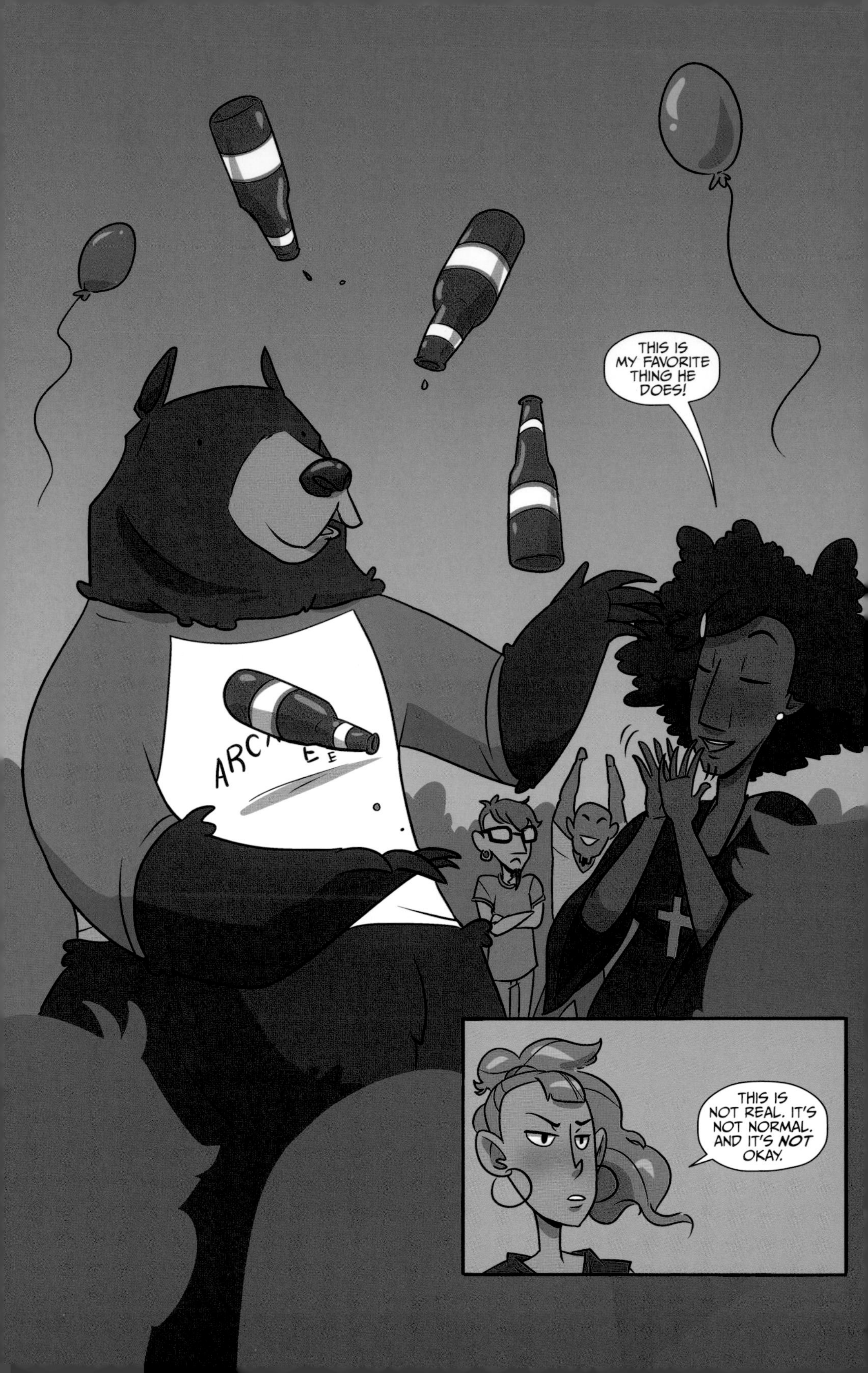
THIS IS MY FAVORITE THING HE DOES!
THIS IS NOT REAL. IT'S NOT NORMAL. AND IT'S ***NOT*** OKAY.

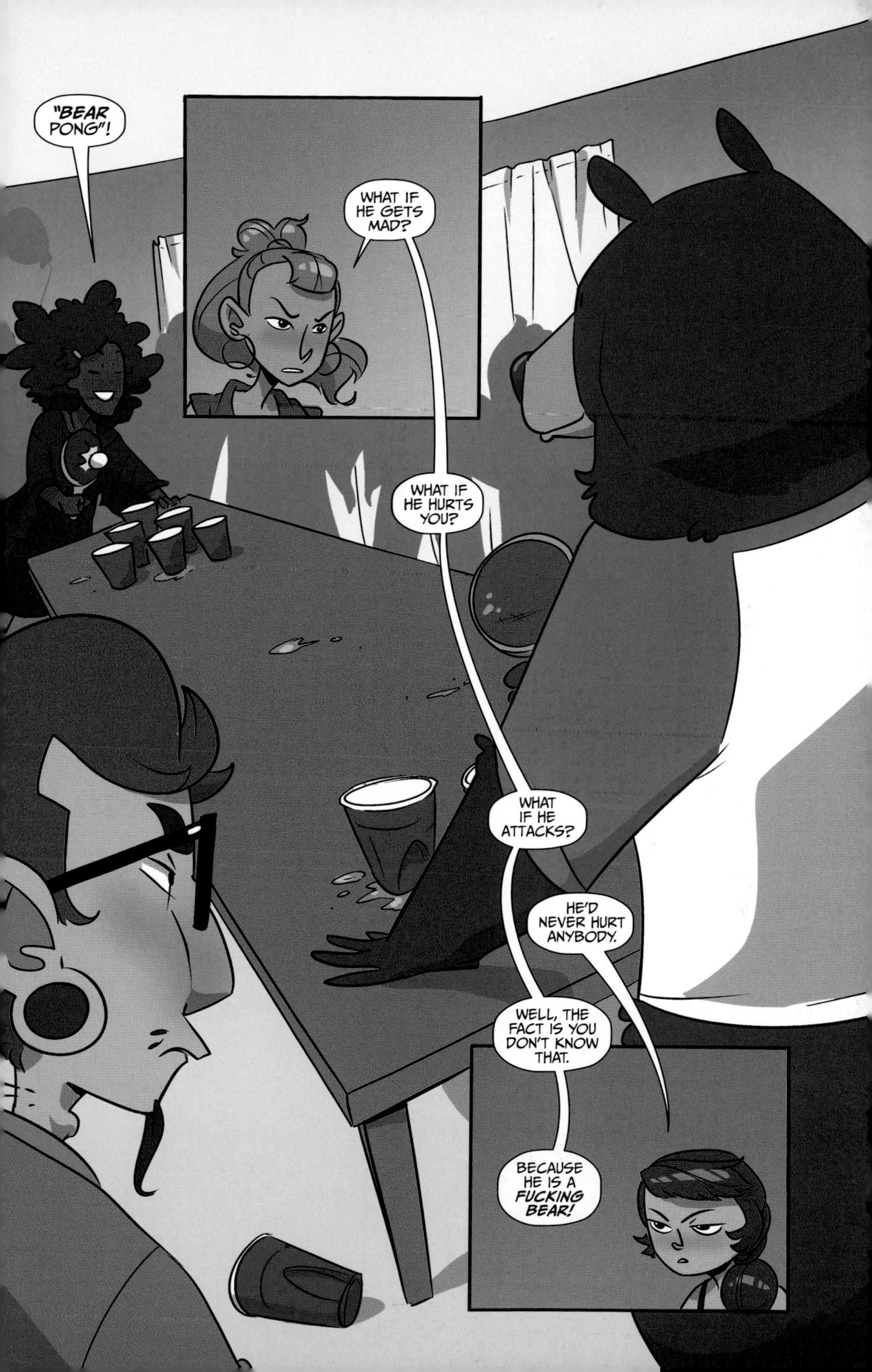
"BEAR PONG"!
WHAT IF HE GETS MAD?
WHAT IF HE HURTS YOU?
WHAT IF HE ATTACKS?
HE'D NEVER HURT ANYBODY.
WELL, THE FACT IS YOU DON'T KNOW THAT.
BECAUSE HE IS A *FUCKING BEAR!*

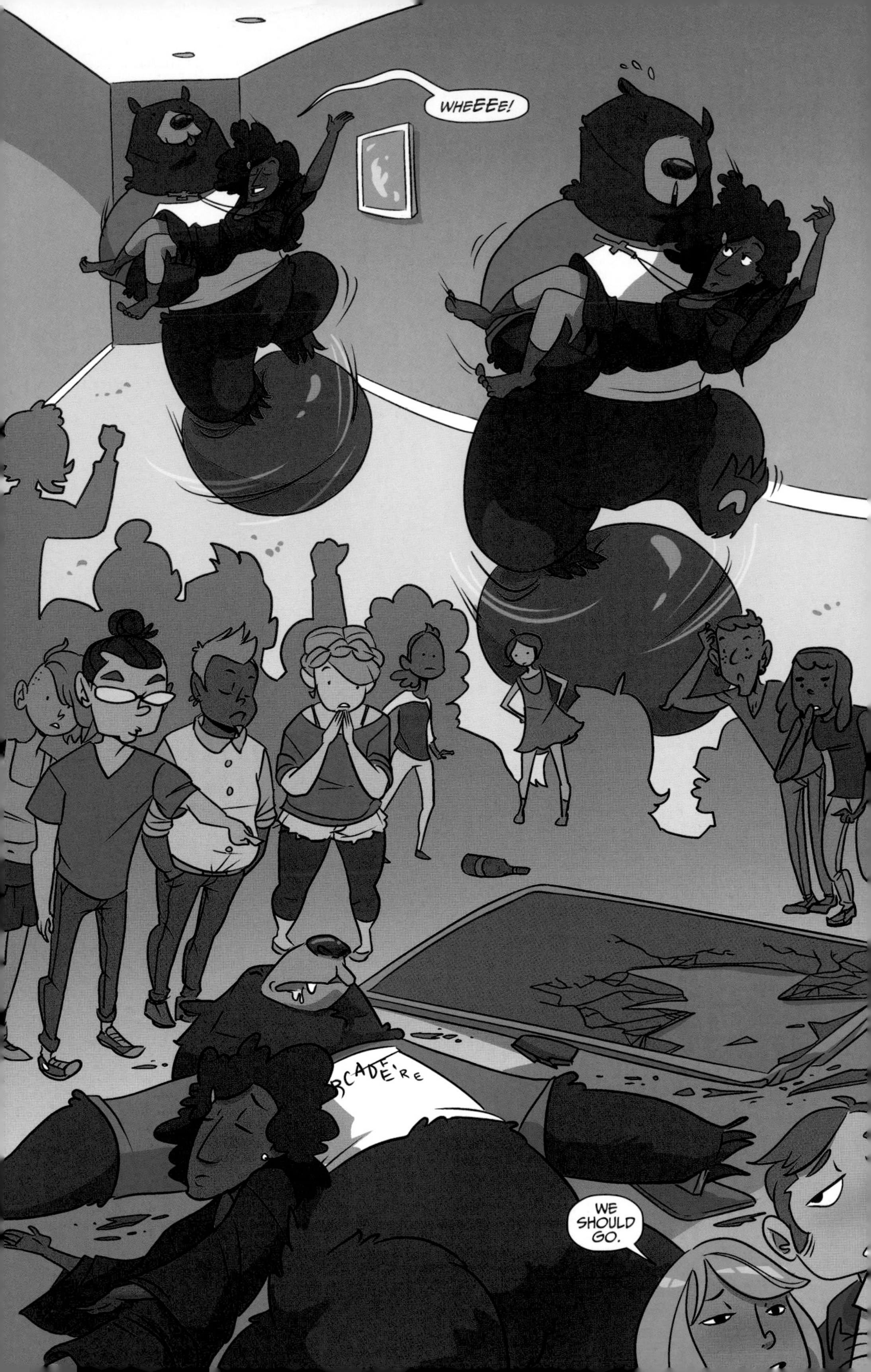
WHEEEe!
WE SHOULD GO.

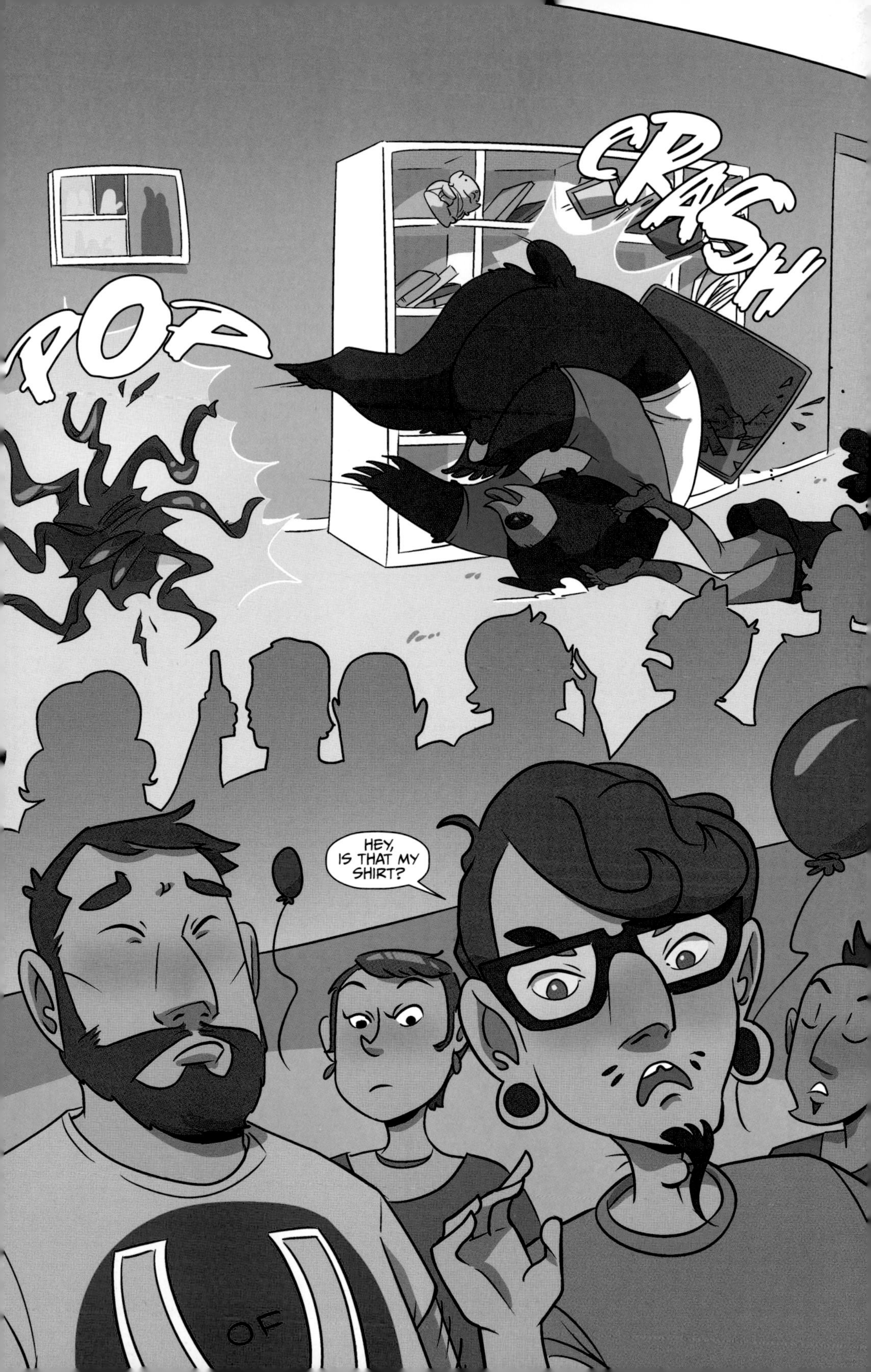
CRASH
POP
HEY, IS THAT MY SHIRT?
OF

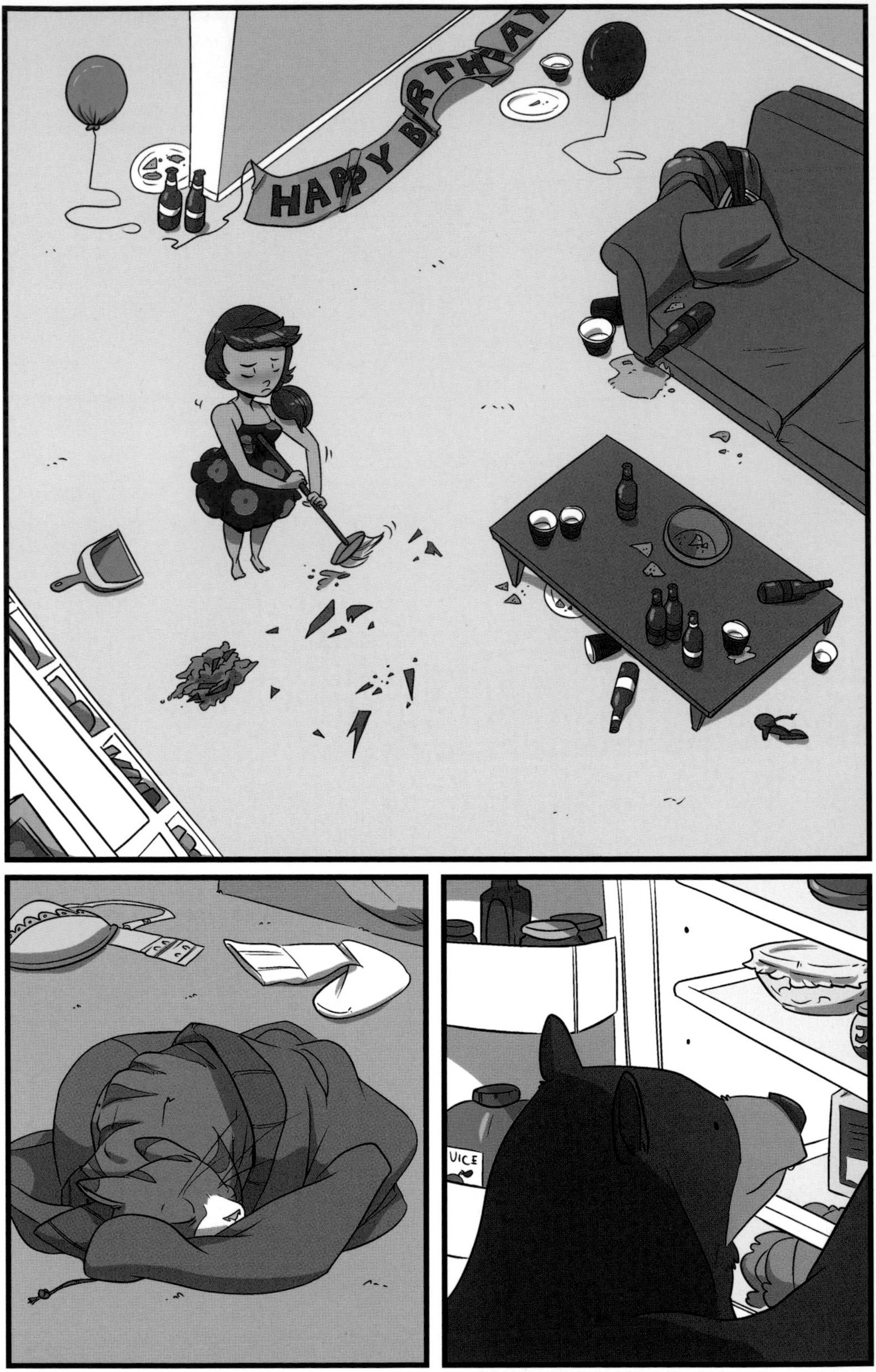
HAPPY

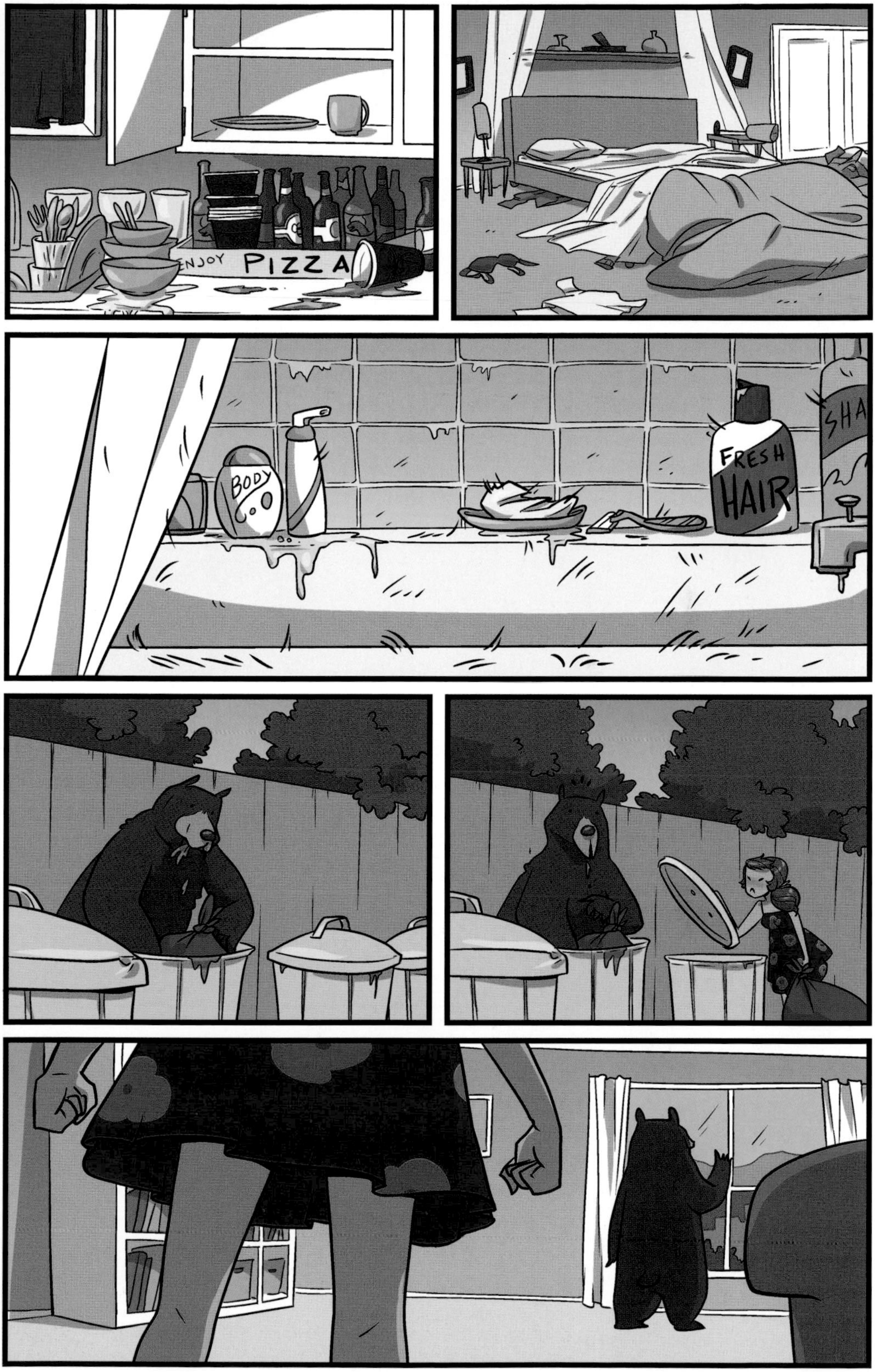
ENJOY PIZZA
BODY
FRESH HAIR
SHA

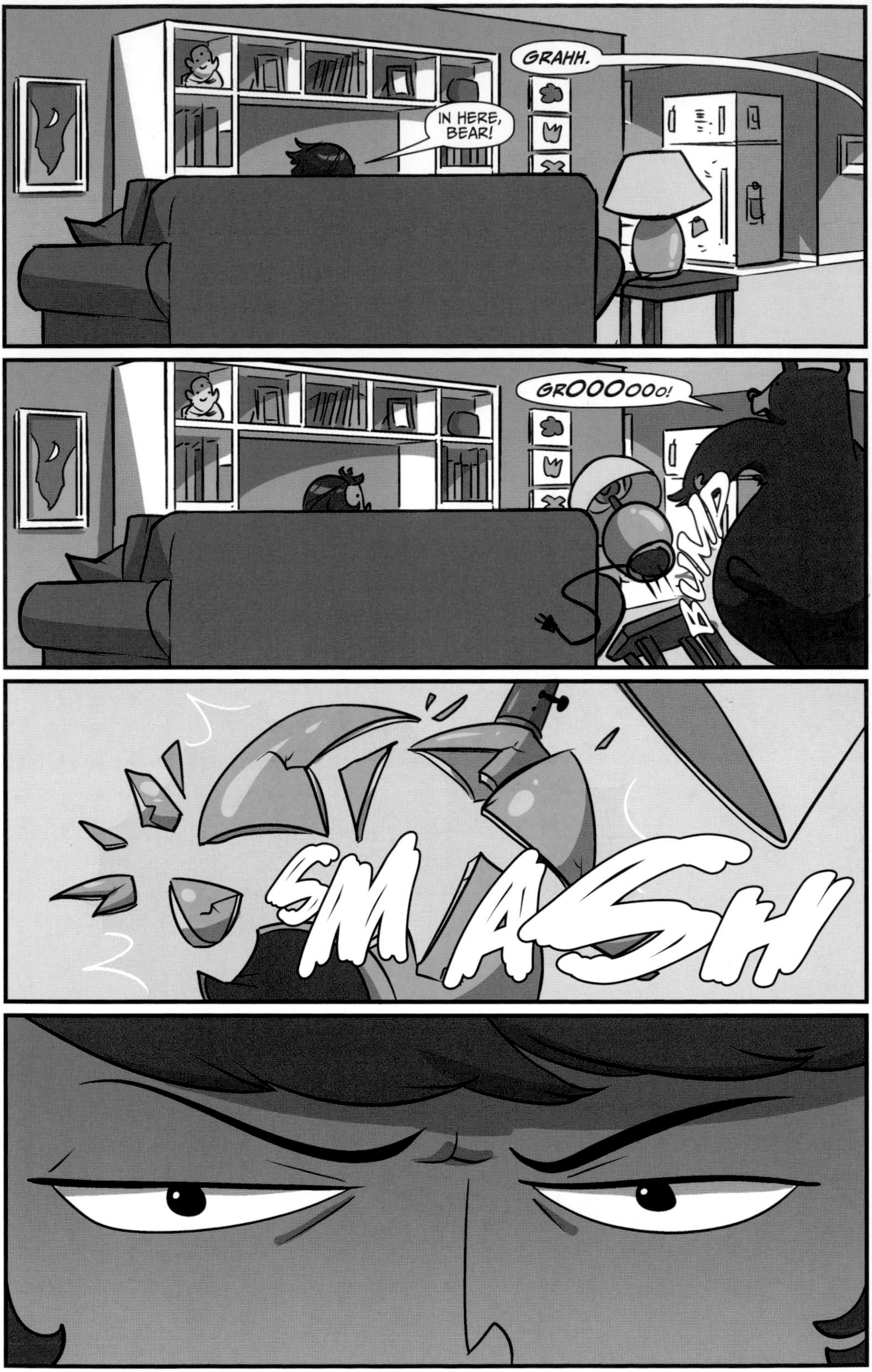
GRAHH.
IN HERE, BEAR!
GROOOOoo!
BUMP
SMASH

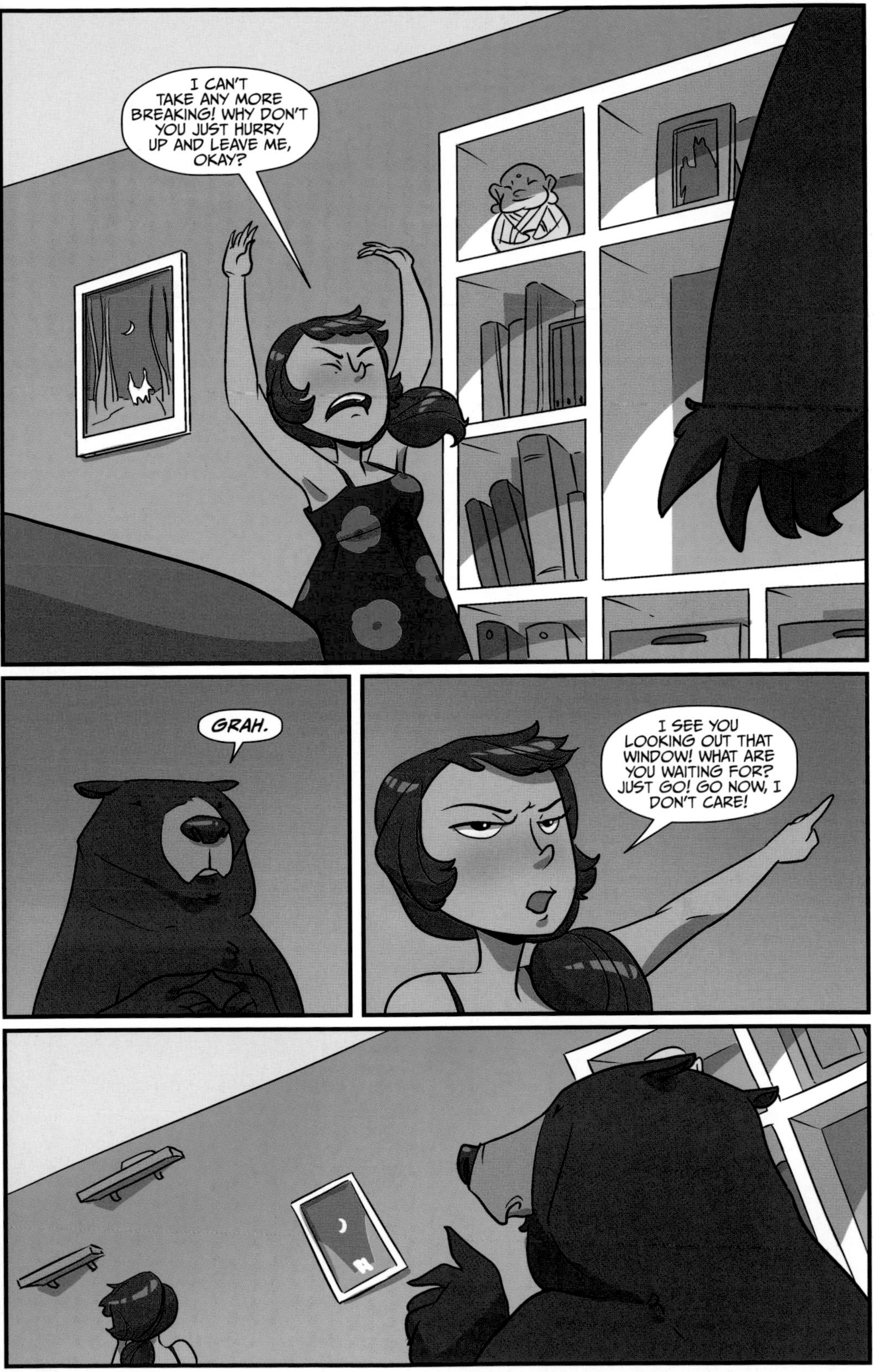
I CAN'T TAKE ANY MORE BREAKING! WHY DON'T YOU JUST HURRY UP AND LEAVE ME, OKAY?
GRAH.
I SEE YOU LOOKING OUT THAT WINDOW! WHAT ARE YOU WAITING FOR? JUST GO! GO NOW, I DON'T CARE!

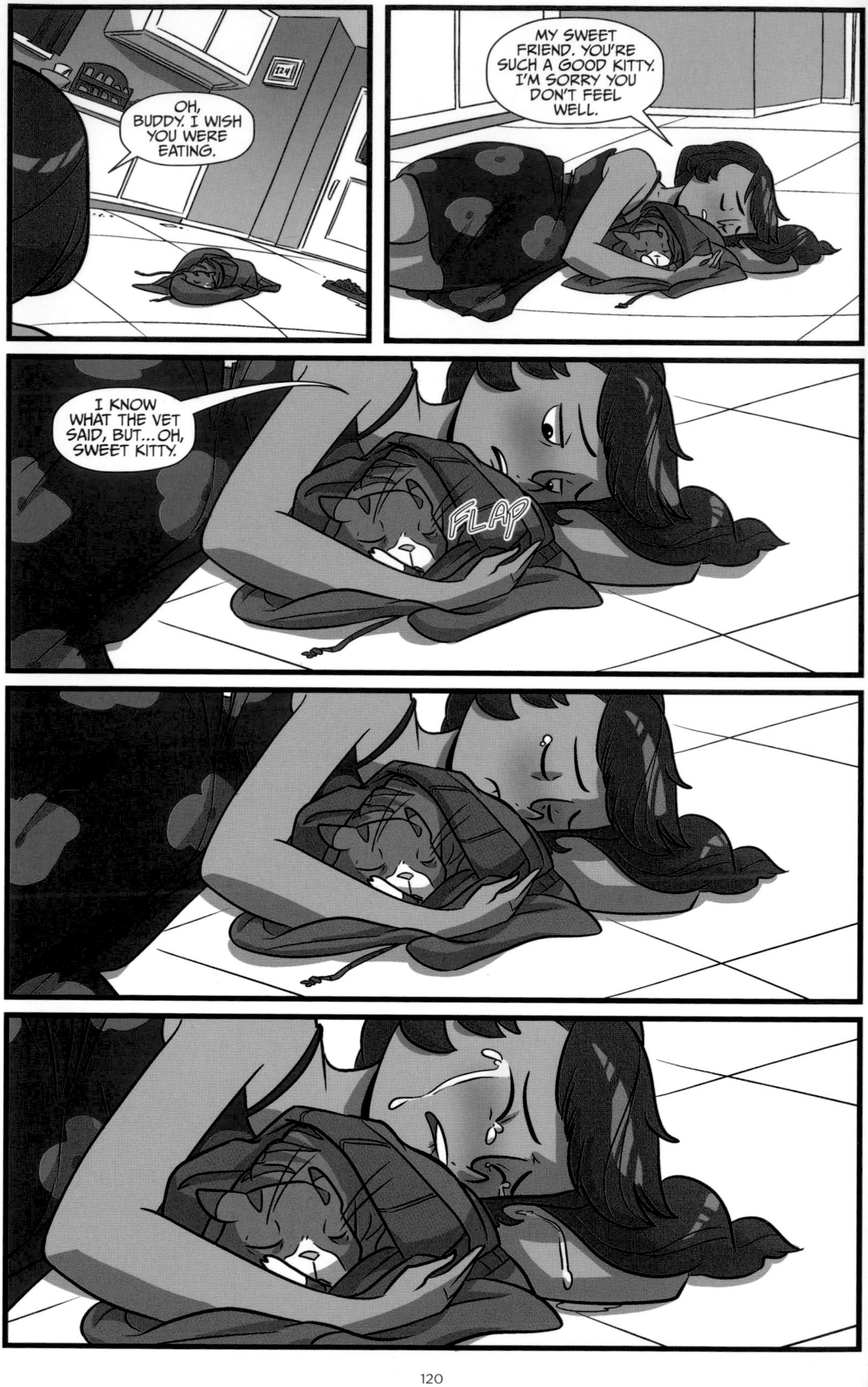
OH, BUDDY. I WISH YOU WERE EATING.
MY SWEET FRIEND. YOU'RE SUCH A GOOD KITTY. I'M SORRY YOU DON'T FEEL WELL.
I KNOW WHAT THE VET SAID, BUT...OH, SWEET KITTY.
FLAP

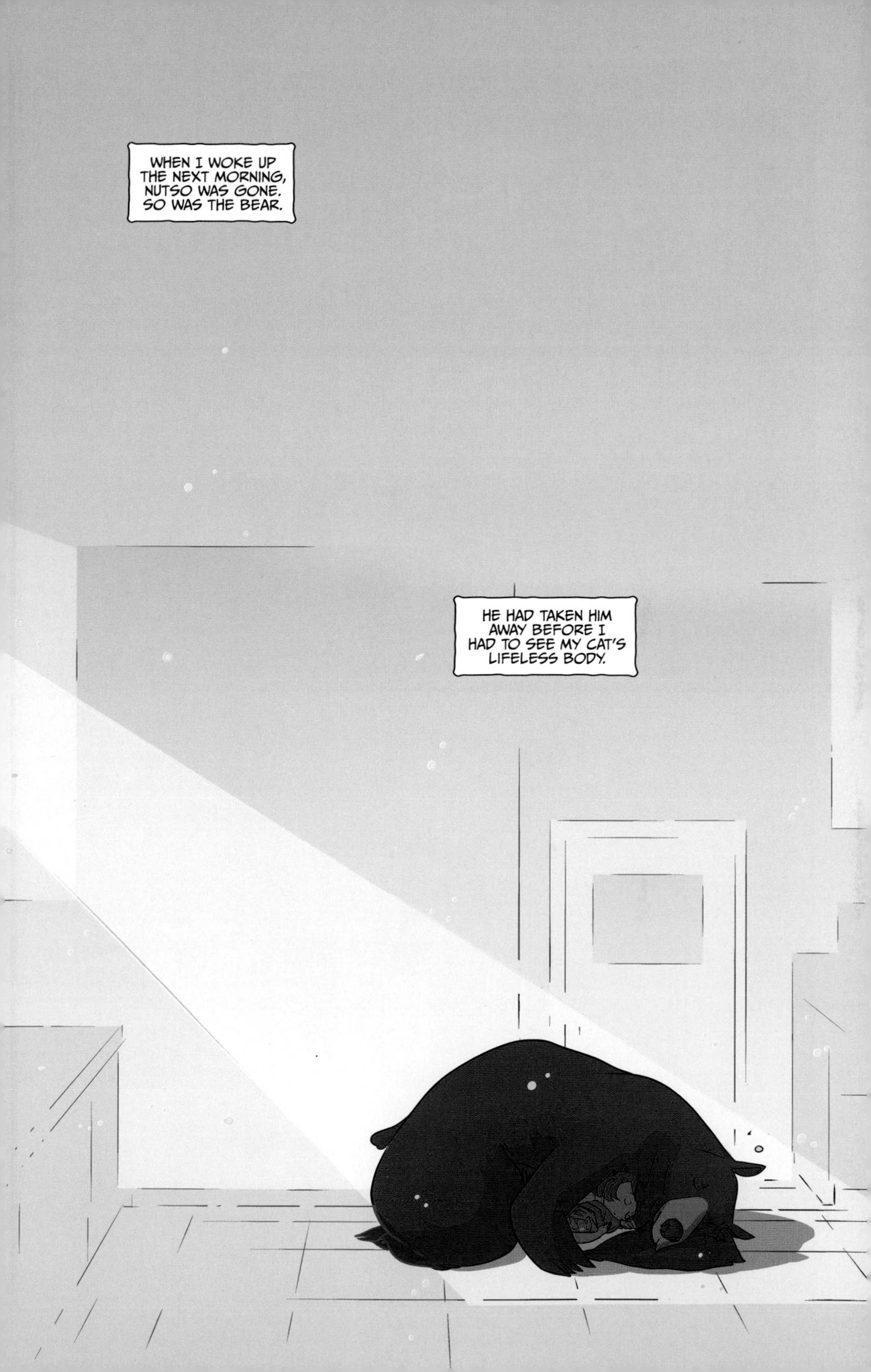
WHEN I WOKE UP THE NEXT MORNING, NUTSO WAS GONE. SO WAS THE BEAR.
HE HAD TAKEN HIM AWAY BEFORE I HAD TO SEE MY CAT'S LIFELESS BODY.

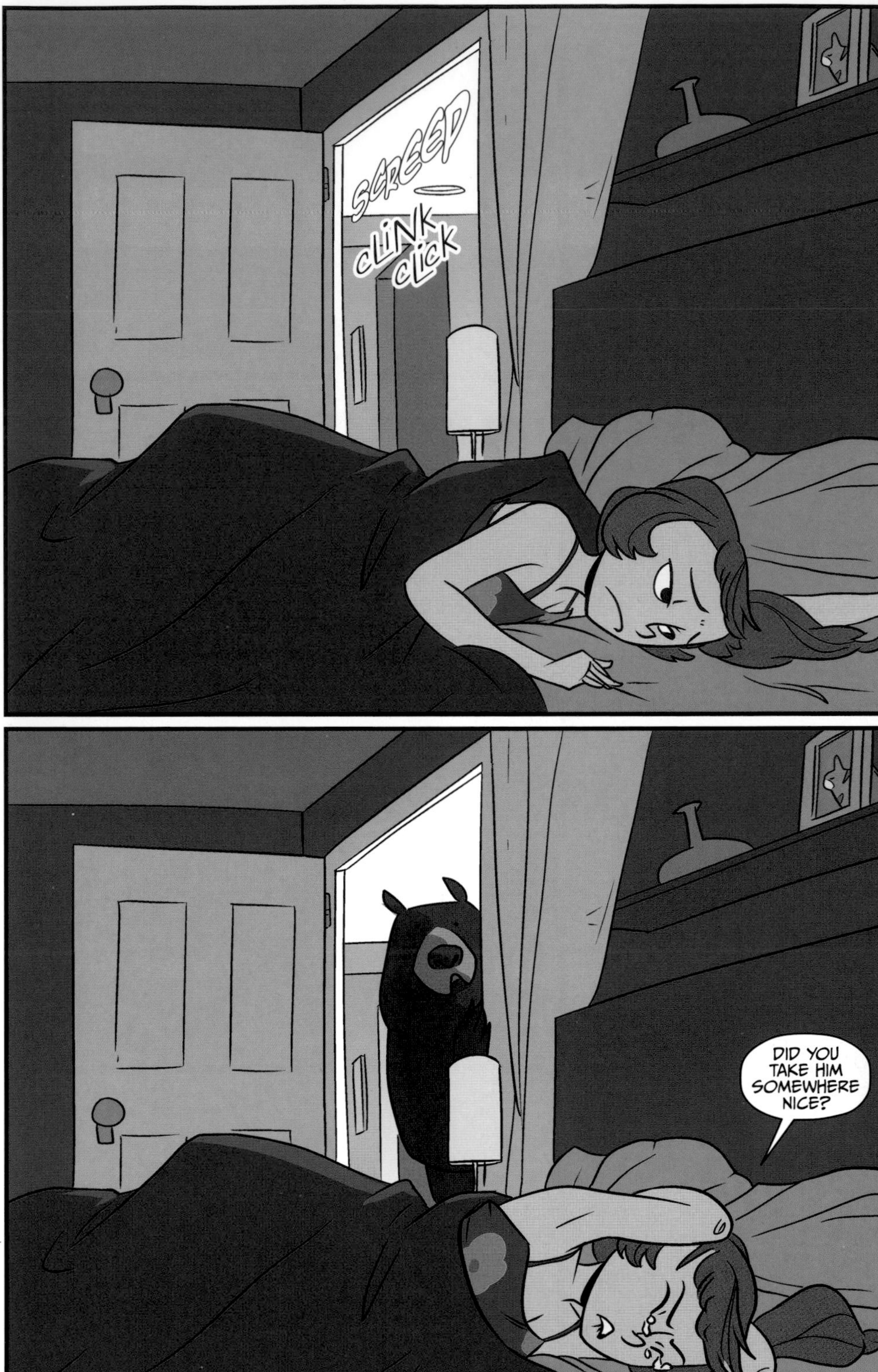
SCREED
CLINK
CLICK
DID YOU TAKE HIM SOMEWHERE NICE?

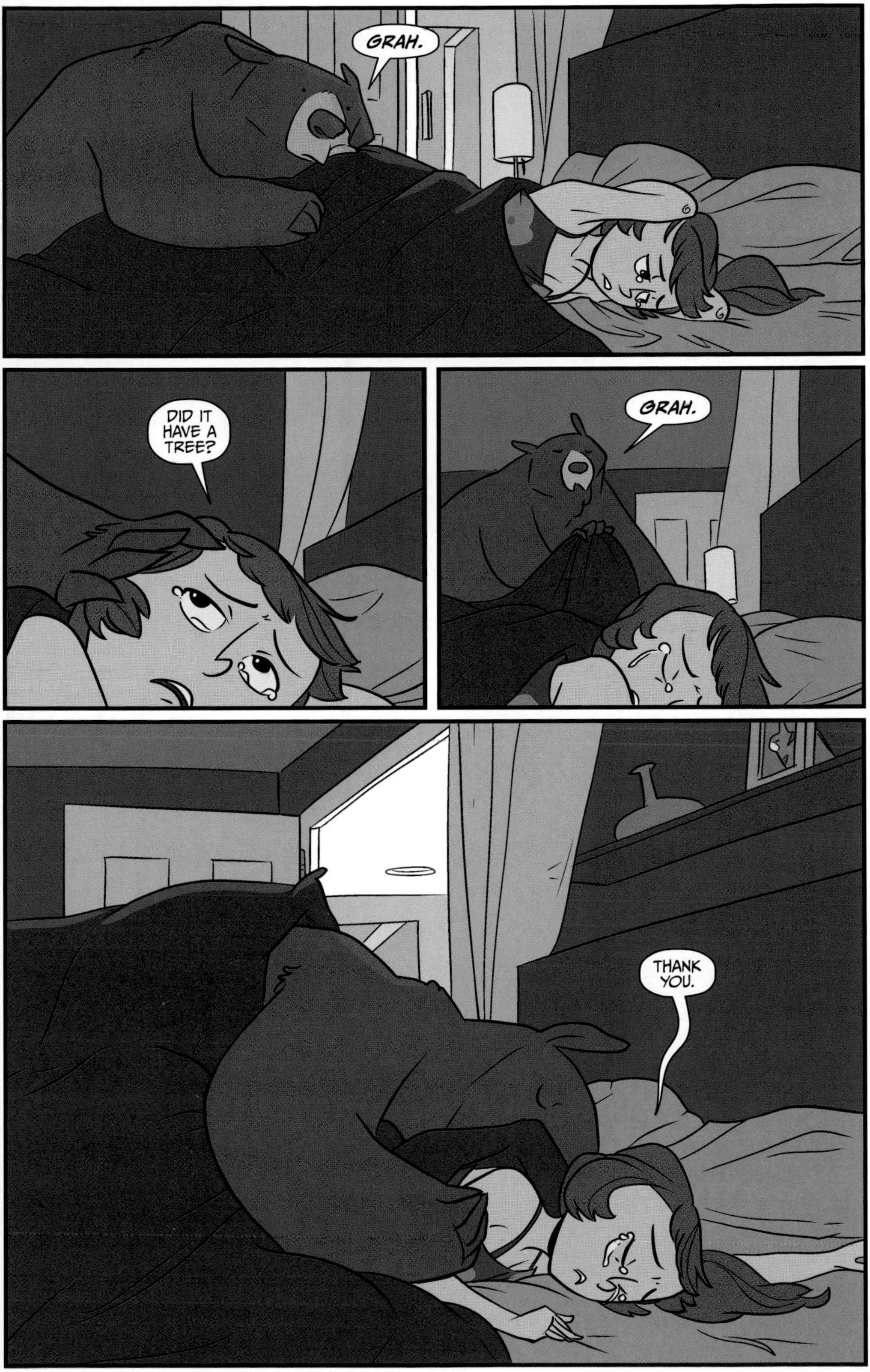
GRAH.
DID IT HAVE A TREE?
GRAH.
THANK YOU.

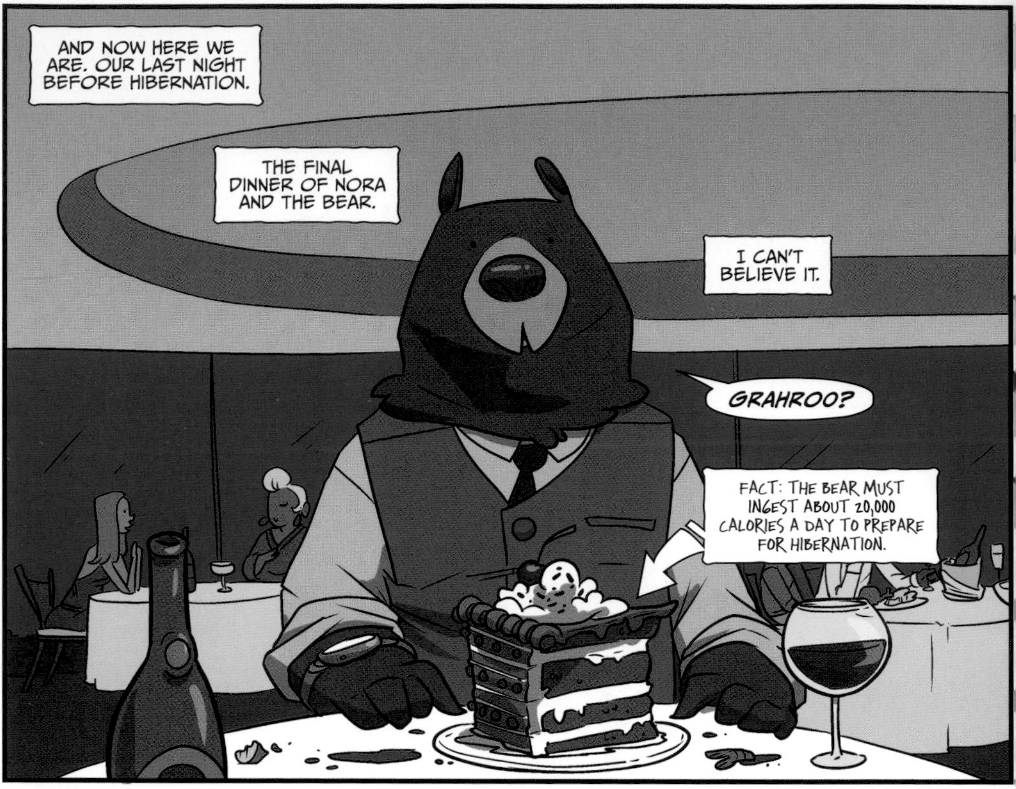
AND NOW HERE WE ARE. OUR LAST NIGHT BEFORE HIBERNATION.
THE FINAL DINNER OF NORA AND THE BEAR.
I CAN'T BELIEVE IT.
GRAHROO?
FACT: THE BEAR MUST INGEST ABOUT 20,000 CALORIES A DAY TO PREPARE FOR HIBERNATION.

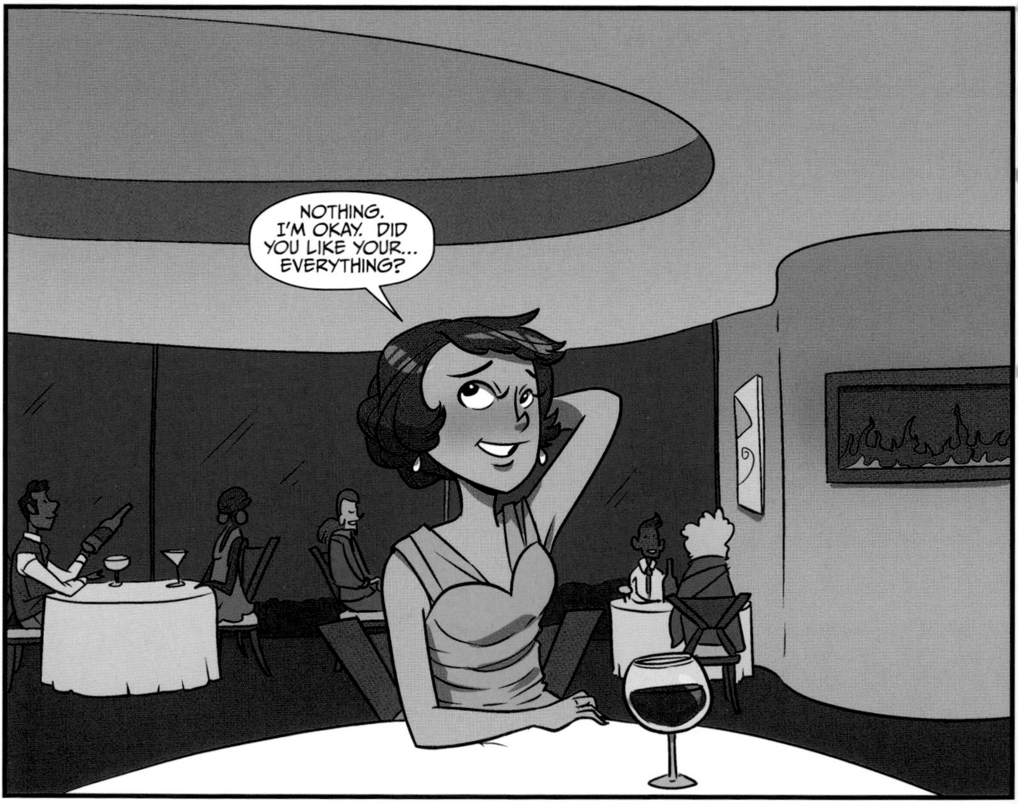
NOTHING. I'M OKAY. DID YOU LIKE YOUR... EVERYTHING?

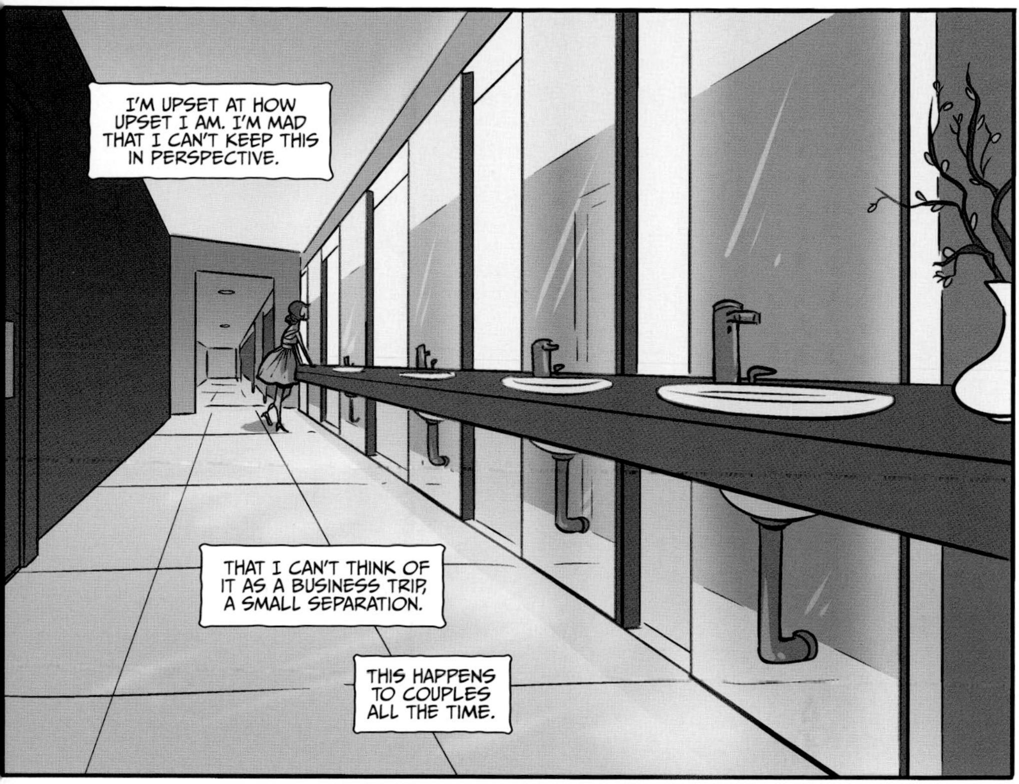
I'M UPSET AT HOW UPSET I AM. I'M MAD THAT I CAN'T KEEP THIS IN PERSPECTIVE.
THAT I CAN'T THINK OF IT AS A BUSINESS TRIP, A SMALL SEPARATION.
THIS HAPPENS TO COUPLES ALL THE TIME.

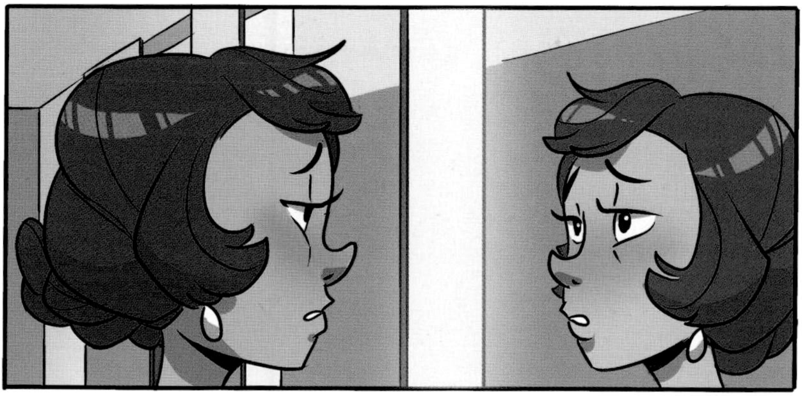

INSTEAD OF BITTERSWEET, TENDER PANGS OF LONGING, I'M FEELING SICK. I'VE RUN OUT OF TIME.

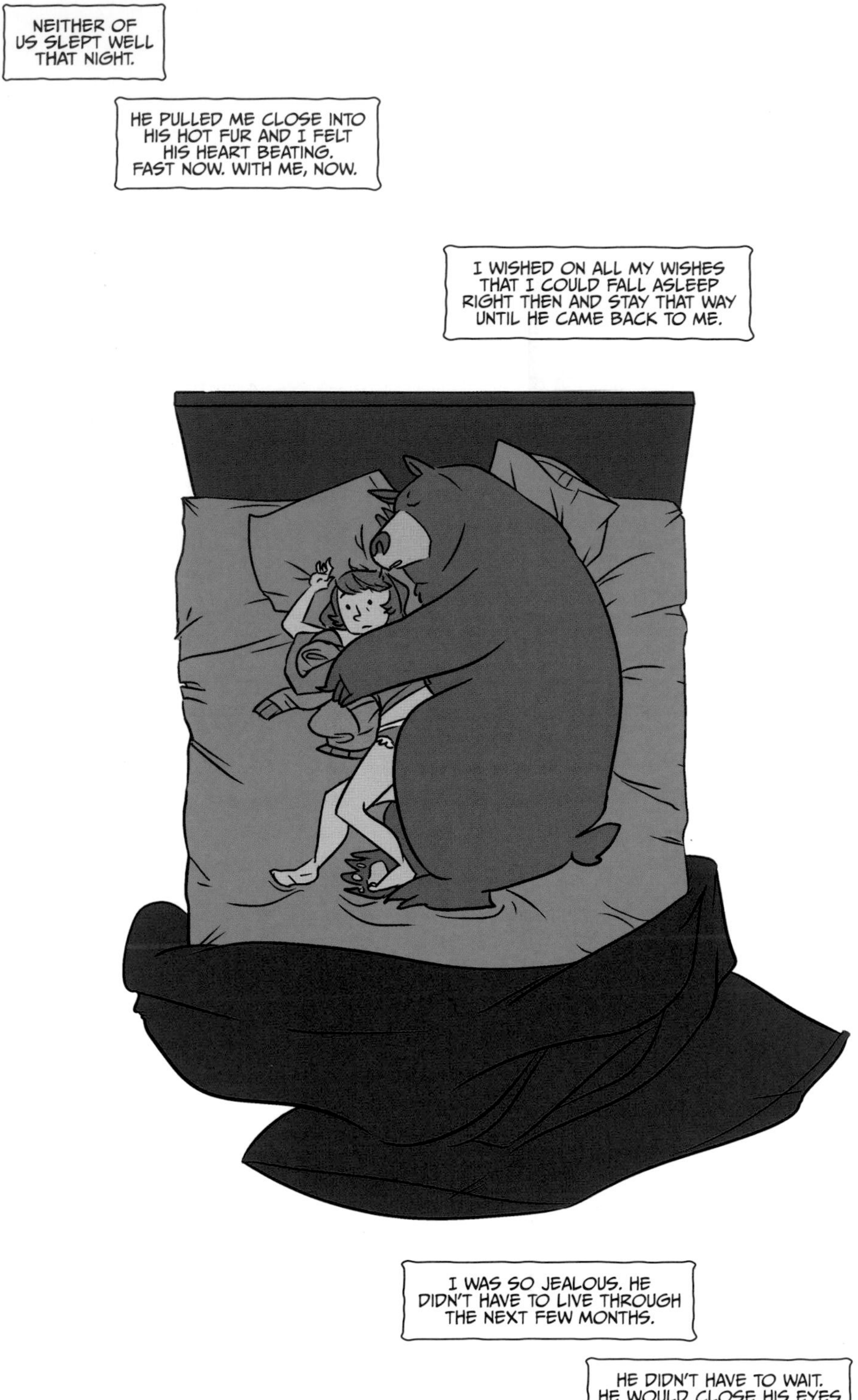
NEITHER OF US SLEPT WELL THAT NIGHT.
HE PULLED ME CLOSE INTO HIS HOT FUR AND I FELT HIS HEART BEATING. FAST NOW. WITH ME, NOW.
I WISHED ON ALL MY WISHES THAT I COULD FALL ASLEEP RIGHT THEN AND STAY THAT WAY UNTIL HE CAME BACK TO ME.
I WAS SO JEALOUS. HE DIDN'T HAVE TO LIVE THROUGH THE NEXT FEW MONTHS.
HE DIDN'T HAVE TO WAIT. HE WOULD CLOSE HIS EYES AND THEN IT'D BE OVER.

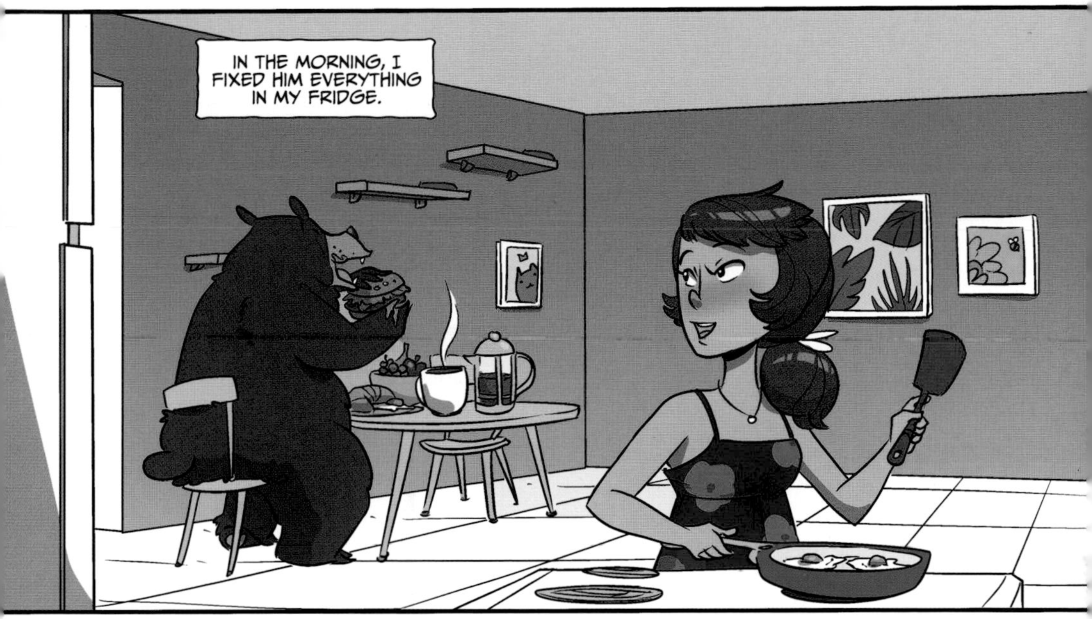
IN THE MORNING, I FIXED HIM EVERYTHING IN MY FRIDGE.

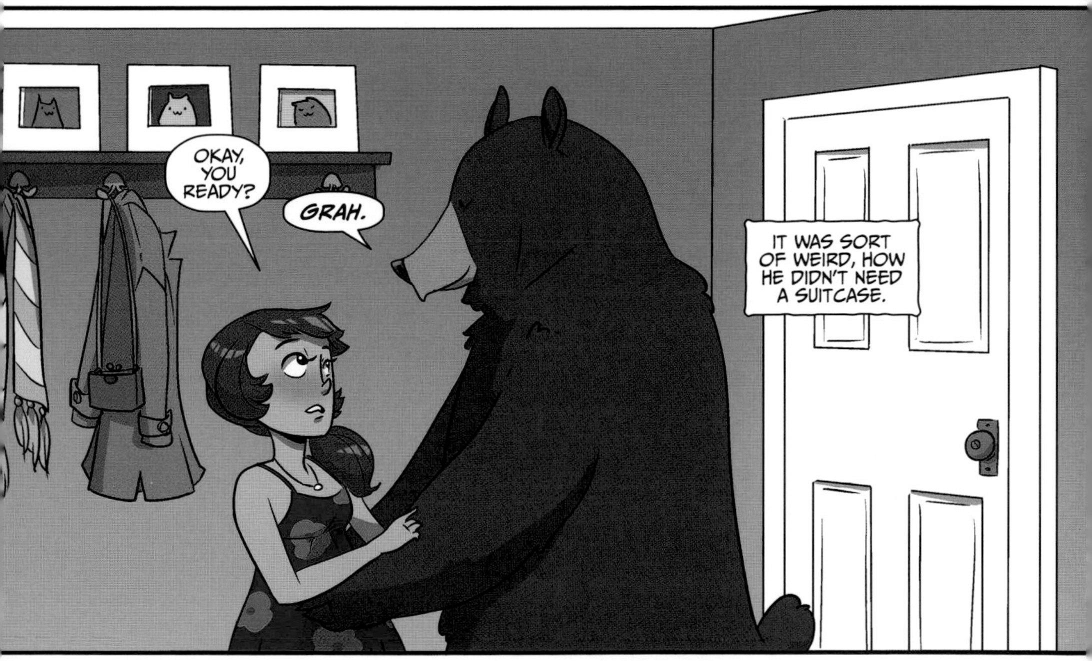
OKAY, YOU READY?
GRAH.
IT WAS SORT OF WEIRD, HOW HE DIDN'T NEED A SUITCASE.

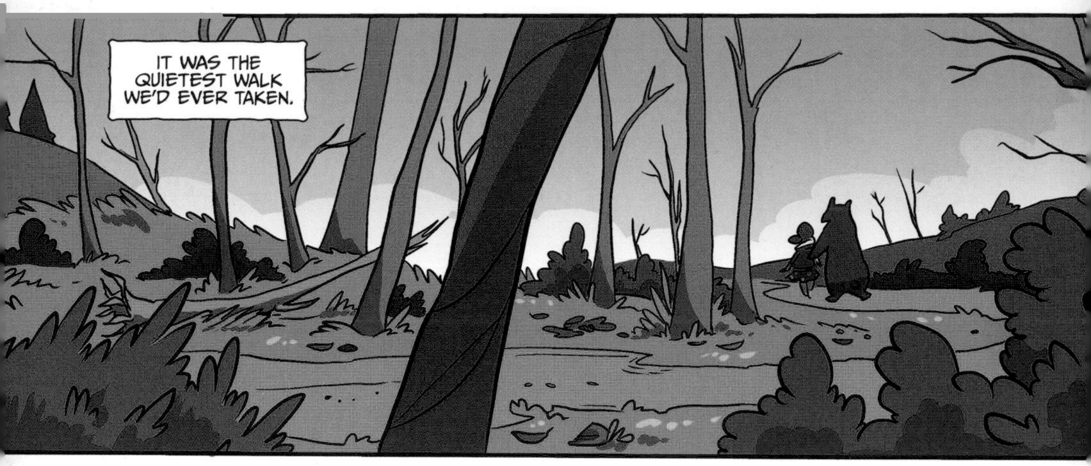
IT WAS THE QUIETEST WALK WE'D EVER TAKEN.

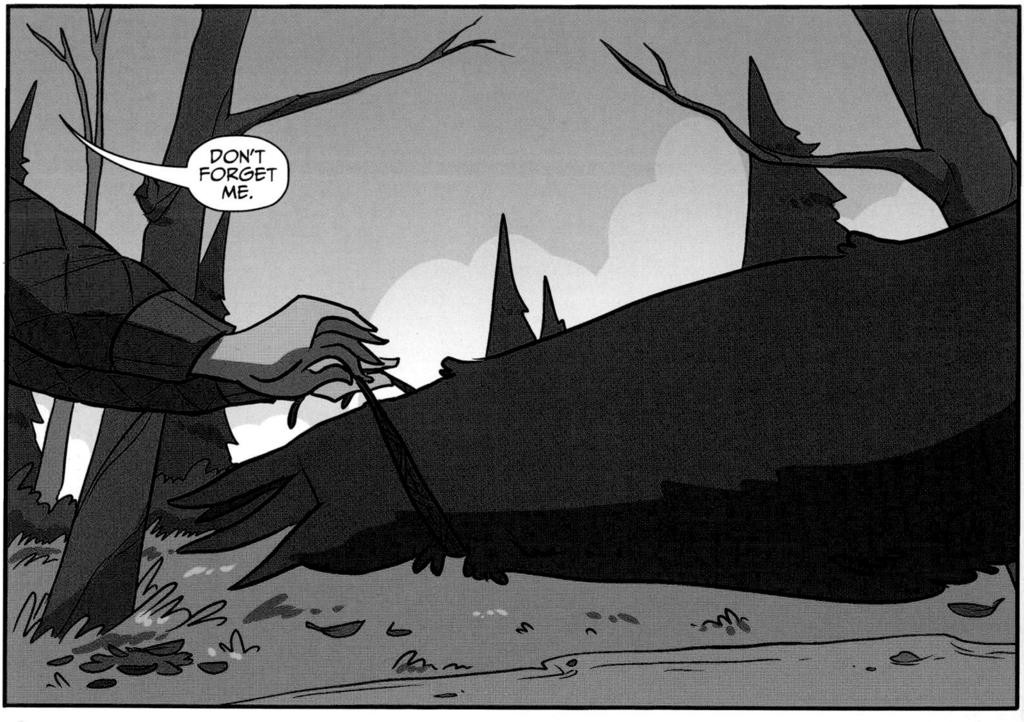
DON'T FORGET ME.

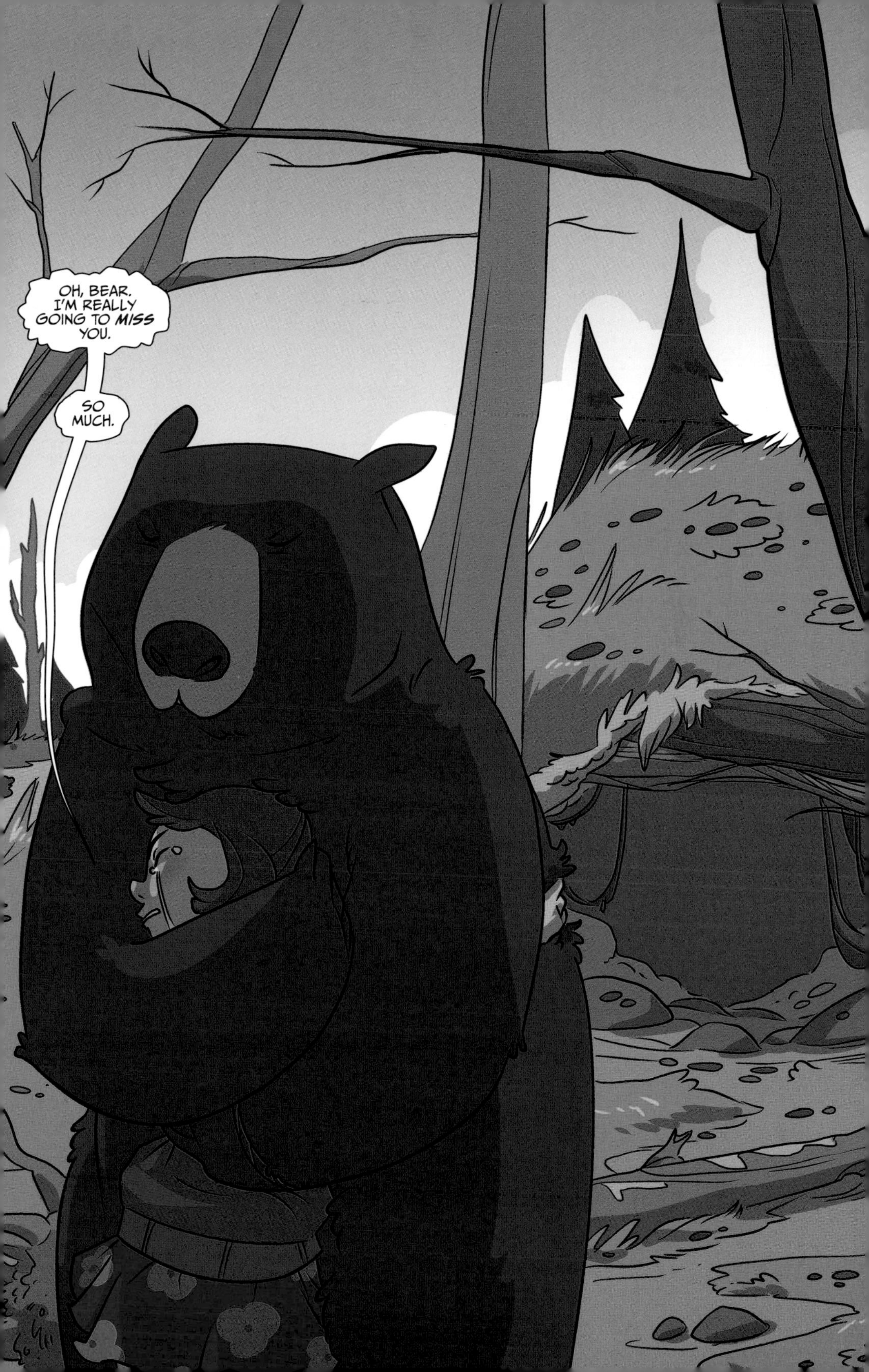
OH, BEAR. I'M REALLY GOING TO MISS YOU.
SO MUCH.

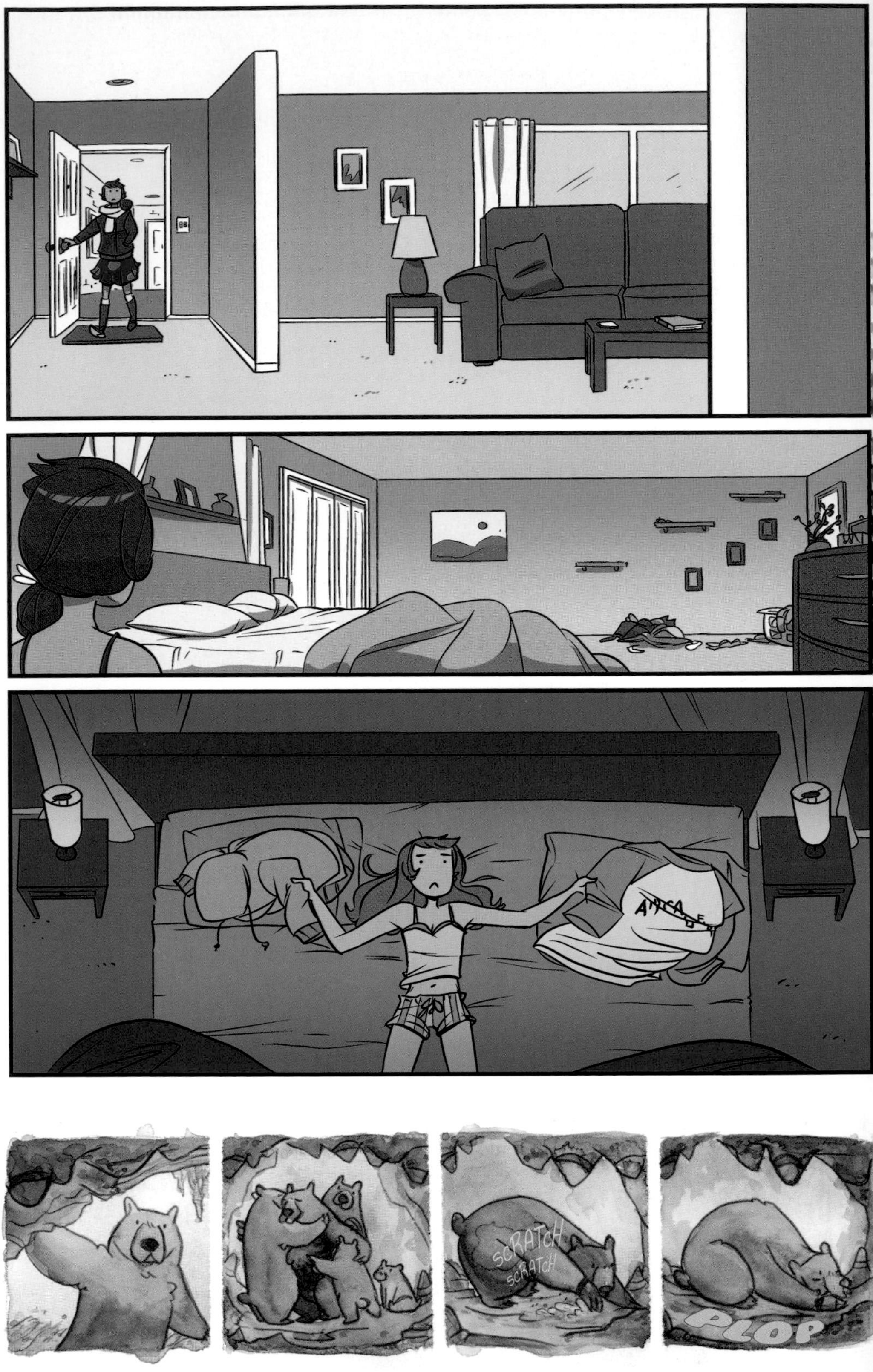
SCRATCH
SCRATCH
PLOP

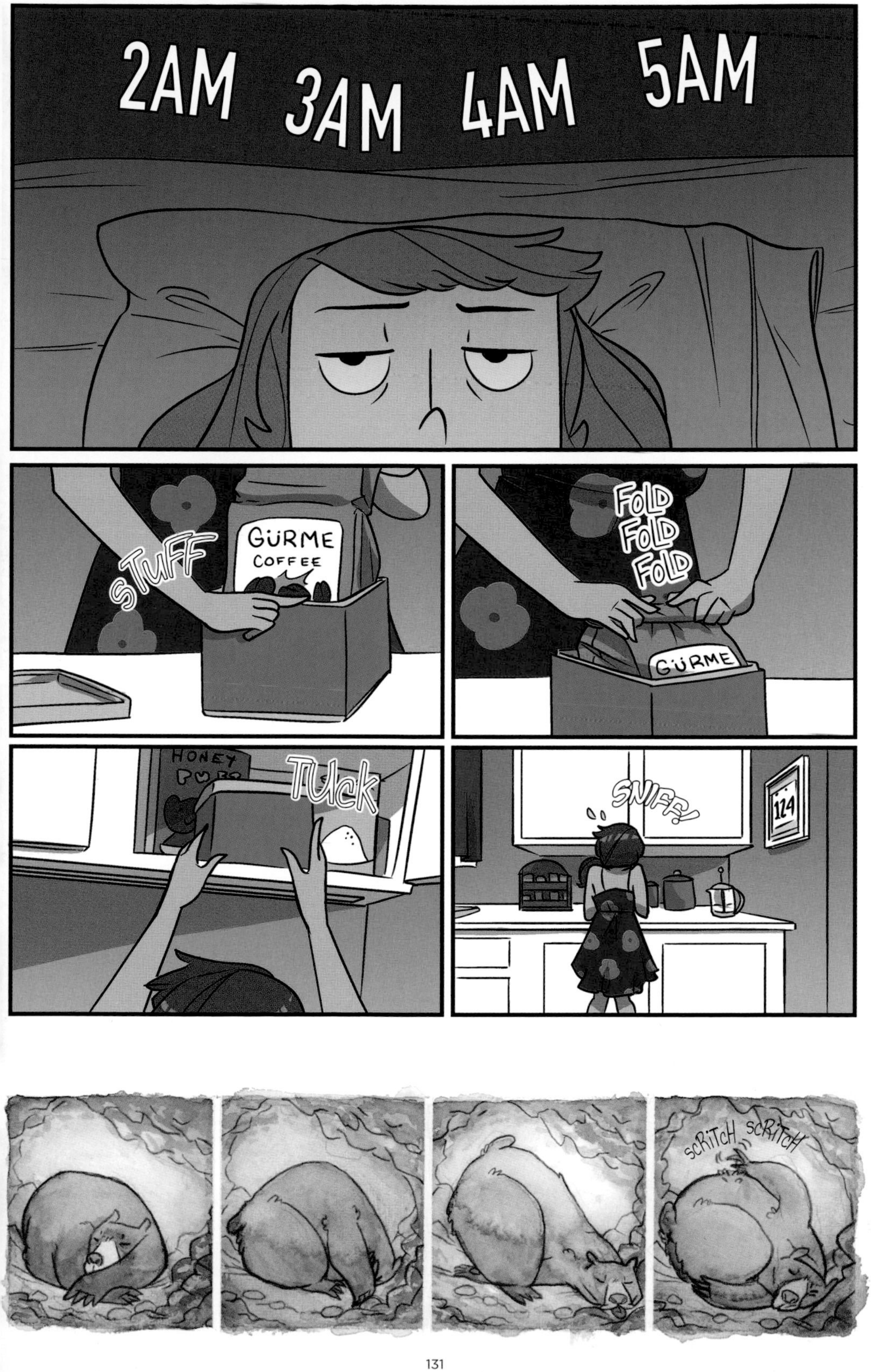
2AM 3AM 4AM 5AM
GÜRME COFFEE
STUFF
FOLD FOLD FOLD
GÜRME
HONEY PUBS
TUCK
SNIFF!
124
SCRITCH SCRITCH

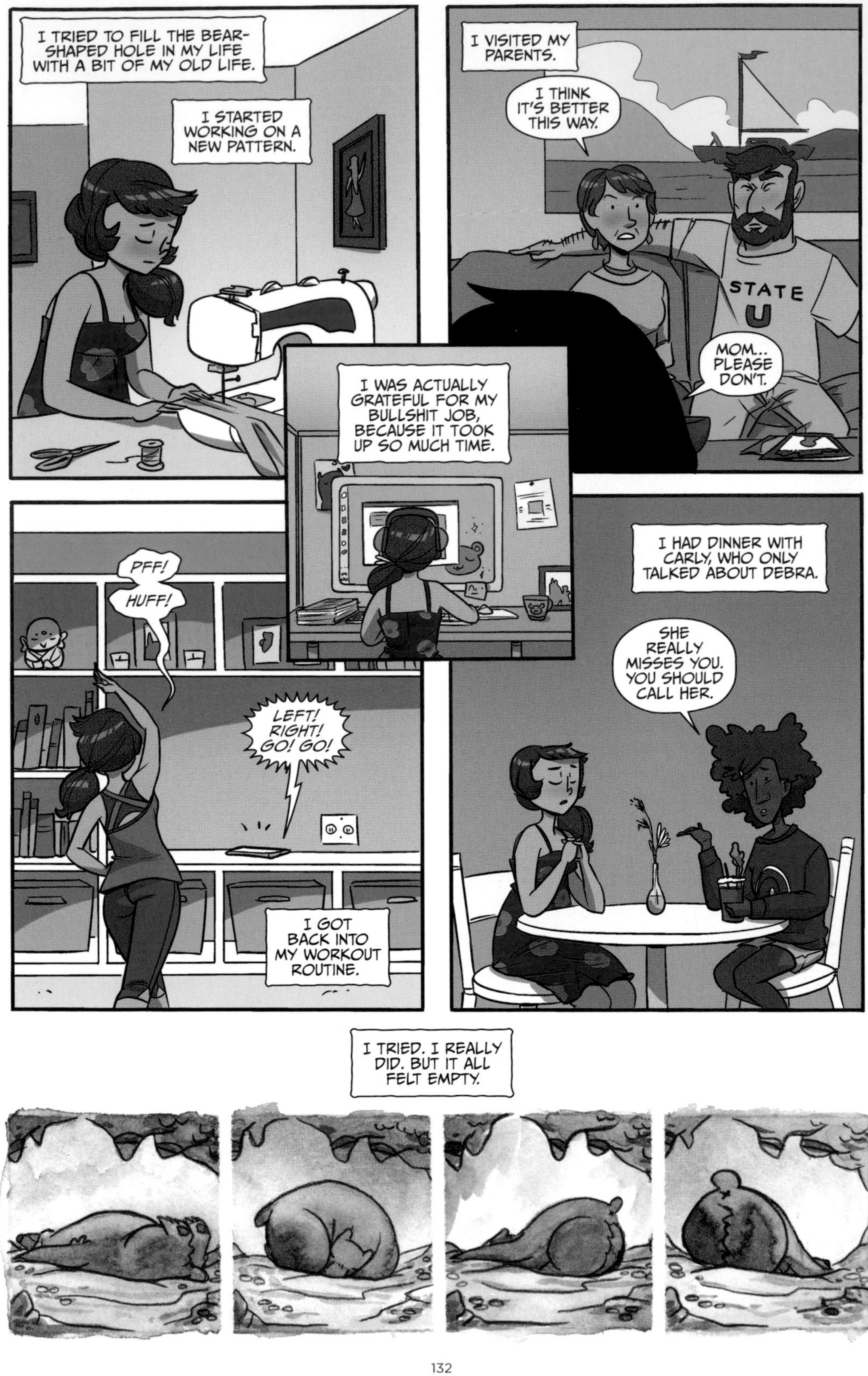
I TRIED TO FILL THE BEAR-SHAPED HOLE IN MY LIFE WITH A BIT OF MY OLD LIFE.
I STARTED WORKING ON A NEW PATTERN.
I VISITED MY PARENTS.
I THINK IT'S BETTER THIS WAY.
STATE U
MOM... PLEASE DON'T.
I WAS ACTUALLY GRATEFUL FOR MY BULLSHIT JOB, BECAUSE IT TOOK UP SO MUCH TIME.
PFF!
HUFF!
LEFT! RIGHT! GO! GO!
I GOT BACK INTO MY WORKOUT ROUTINE.
I HAD DINNER WITH CARLY, WHO ONLY TALKED ABOUT DEBRA.
SHE REALLY MISSES YOU. YOU SHOULD CALL HER.
I TRIED. I REALLY DID. BUT IT ALL FELT EMPTY.

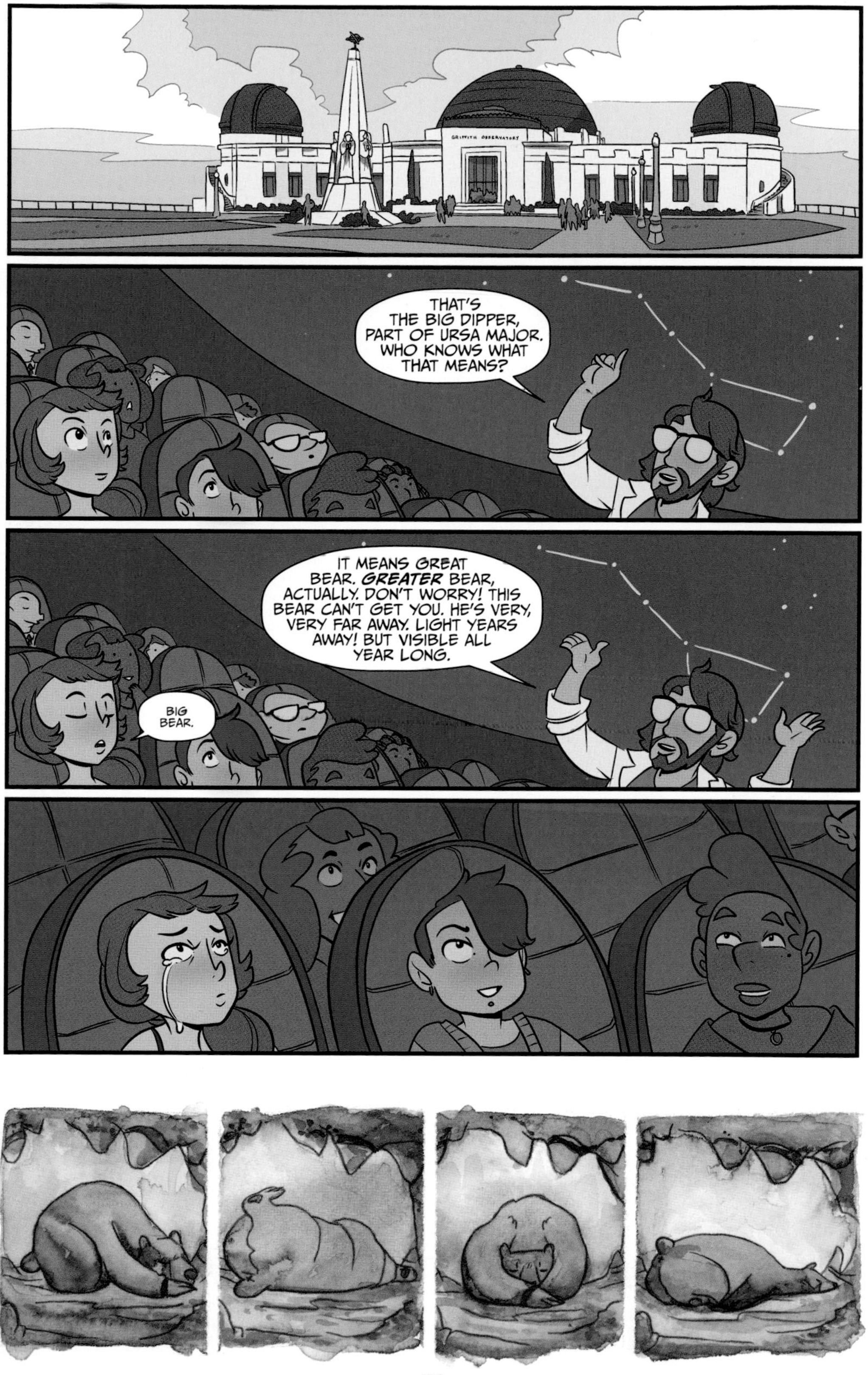
THAT'S THE BIG DIPPER, PART OF URSA MAJOR. WHO KNOWS WHAT THAT MEANS?
IT MEANS GREAT BEAR. ***GREATER*** BEAR, ACTUALLY. DON'T WORRY! THIS BEAR CAN'T GET YOU. HE'S VERY, VERY FAR AWAY. LIGHT YEARS AWAY! BUT VISIBLE ALL YEAR LONG.
BIG BEAR.

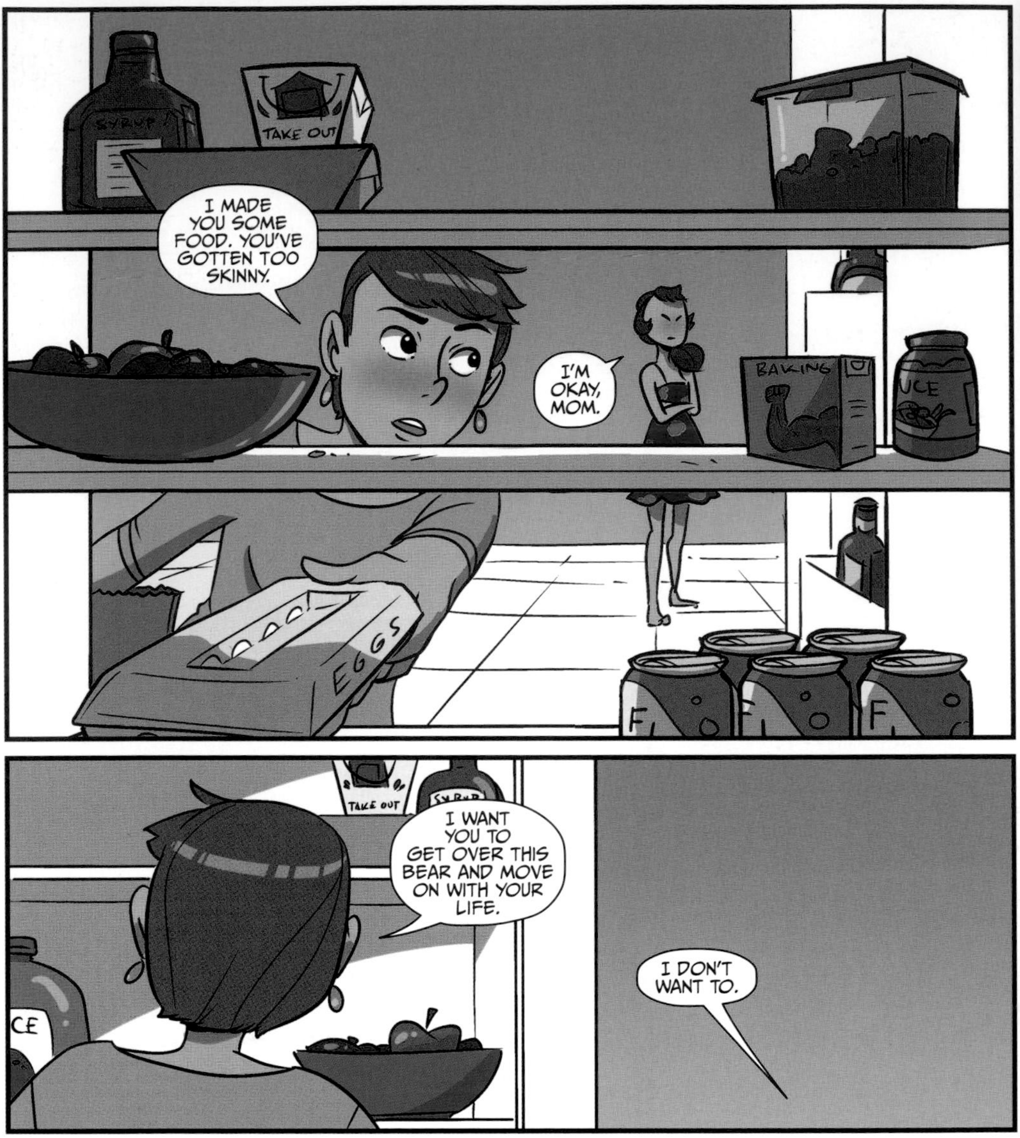
TAKE OUT
I MADE YOU SOME FOOD. YOU'VE GOTTEN TOO SKINNY.
I'M OKAY, MOM.
BAKING
EGGS
TAKE OUT
I WANT YOU TO GET OVER THIS BEAR AND MOVE ON WITH YOUR LIFE.
I DON'T WANT TO.

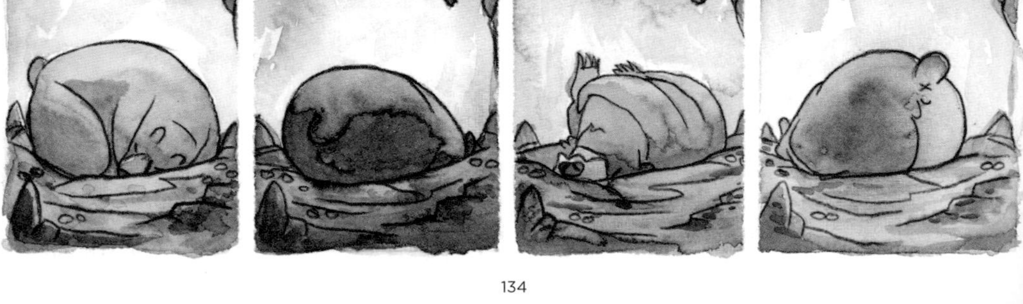

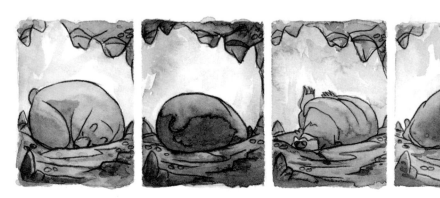

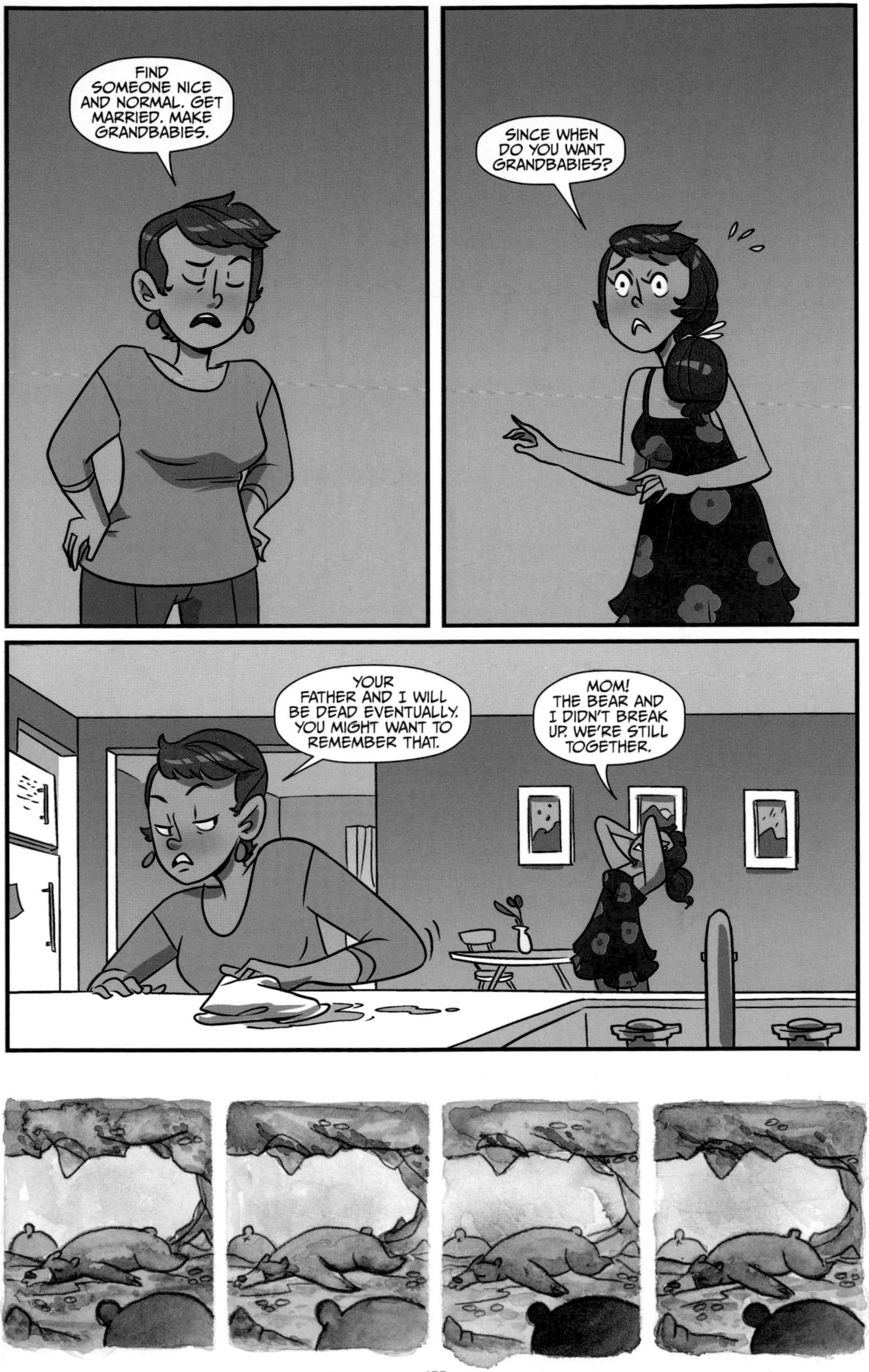
FIND SOMEONE NICE AND NORMAL. GET MARRIED. MAKE GRANDBABIES.
SINCE WHEN DO YOU WANT GRANDBABIES?
YOUR FATHER AND I WILL BE DEAD EVENTUALLY. YOU MIGHT WANT TO REMEMBER THAT.
MOM! THE BEAR AND I DIDN'T BREAK UP. WE'RE STILL TOGETHER.

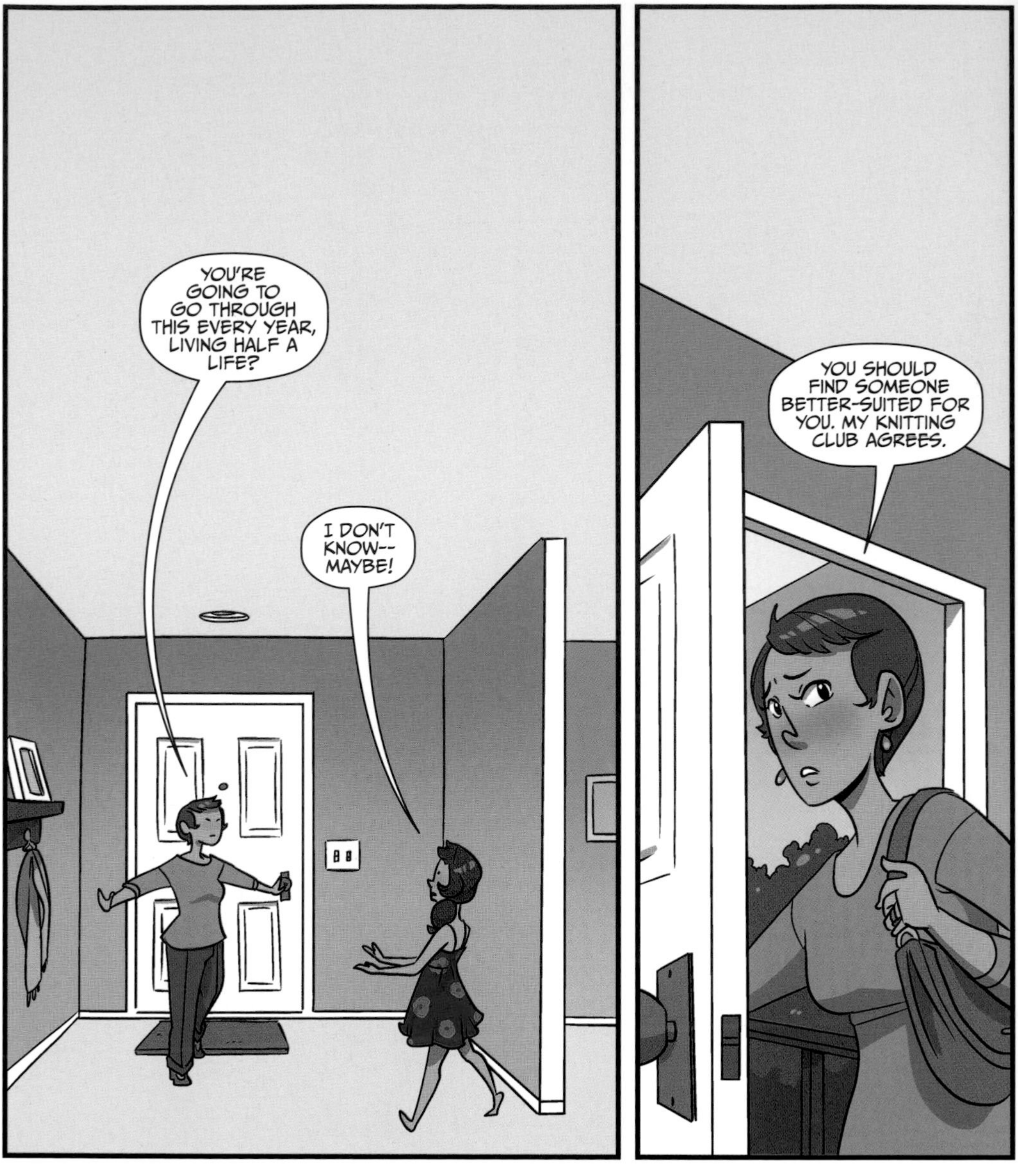
YOU'RE GOING TO GO THROUGH THIS EVERY YEAR, LIVING HALF A LIFE?
I DON'T KNOW-- MAYBE!
YOU SHOULD FIND SOMEONE BETTER-SUITED FOR YOU. MY KNITTING CLUB AGREES.

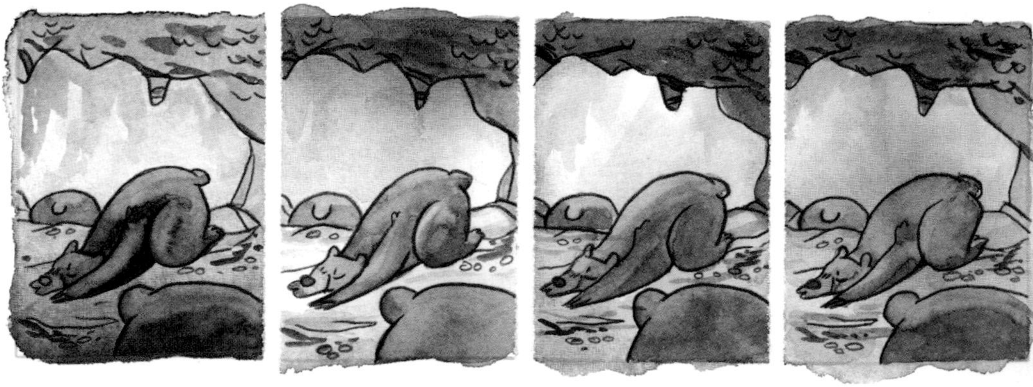

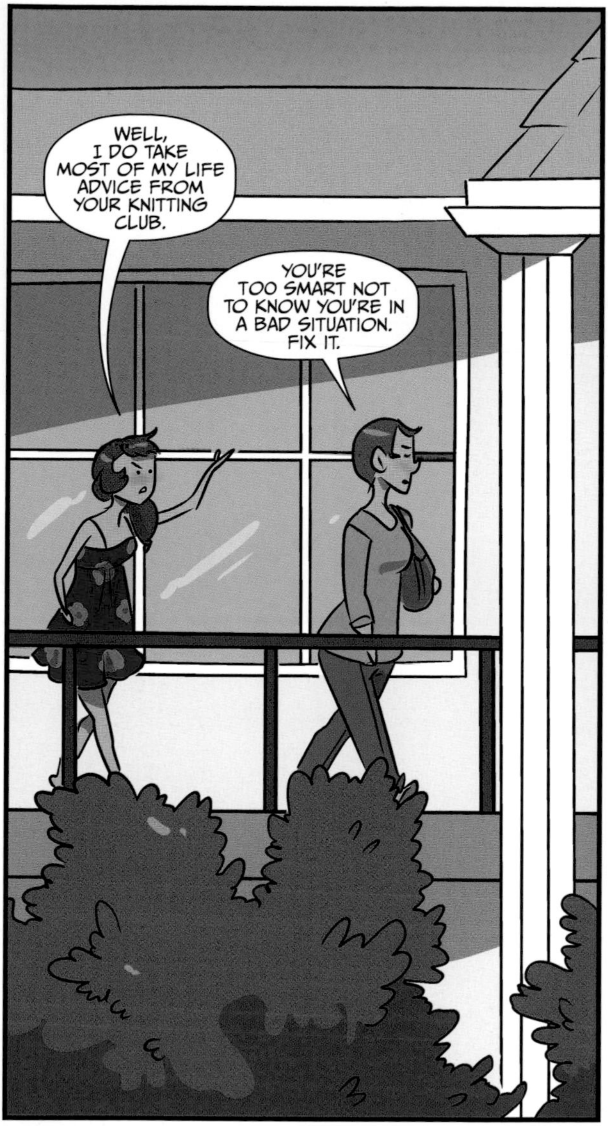
WELL, I DO TAKE MOST OF MY LIFE ADVICE FROM YOUR KNITTING CLUB.
YOU'RE TOO SMART NOT TO KNOW YOU'RE IN A BAD SITUATION. FIX IT.

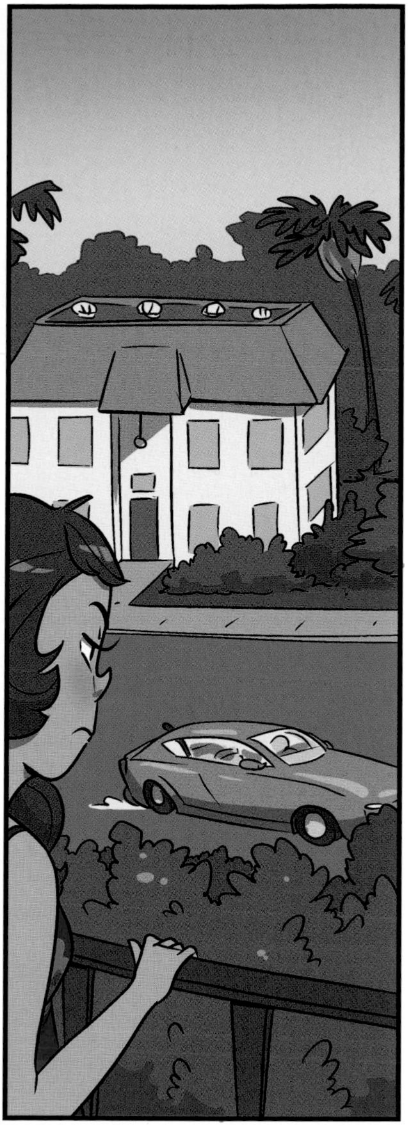

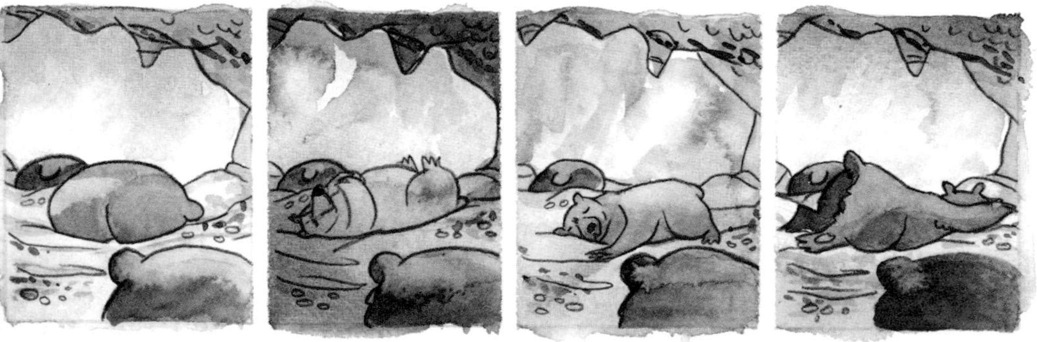

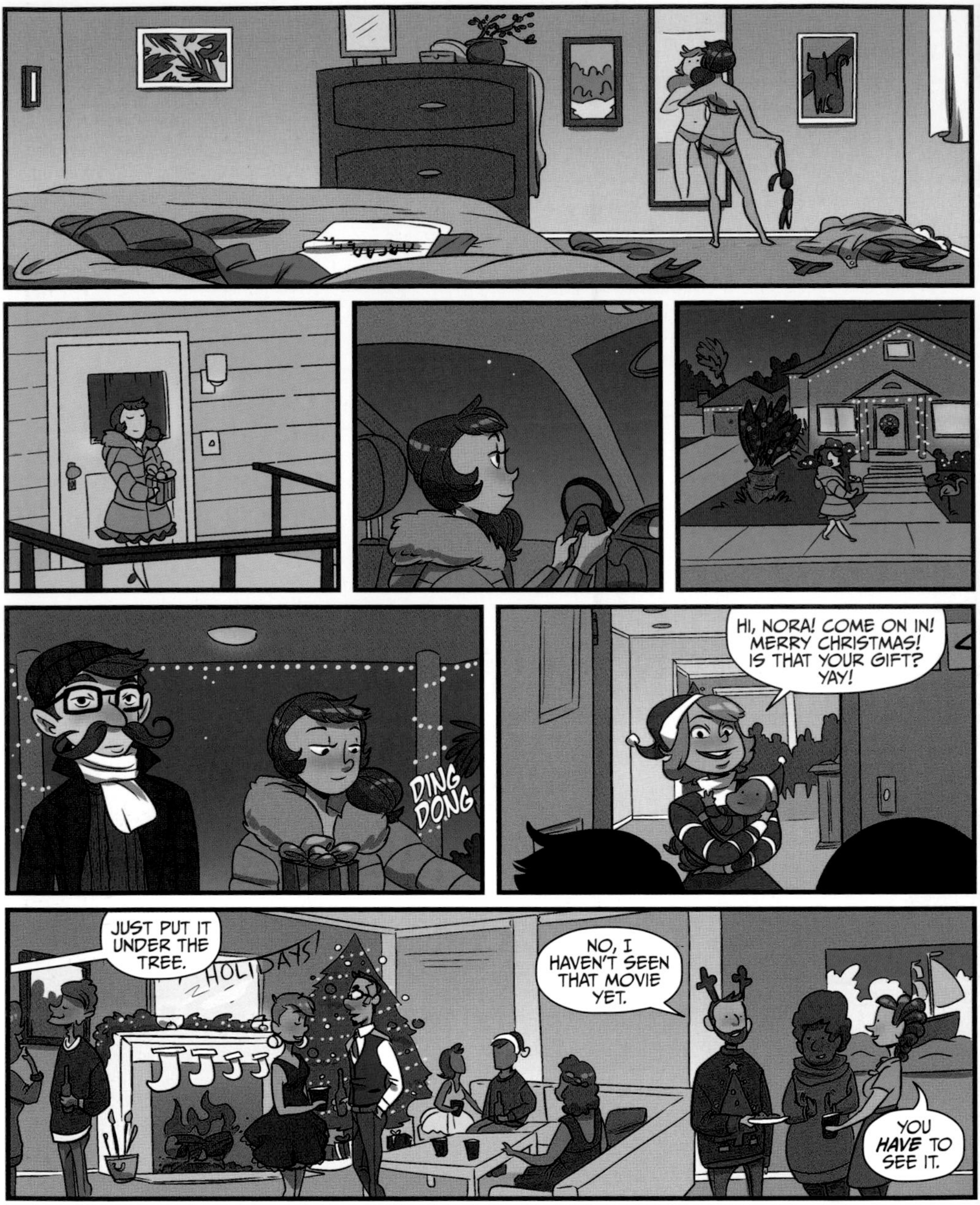
DING DONG
HI, NORA! COME ON IN! MERRY CHRISTMAS! IS THAT YOUR GIFT? YAY!
JUST PUT IT UNDER THE TREE.
HOLIDAYS!
NO, I HAVEN'T SEEN THAT MOVIE YET.
YOU *HAVE* TO SEE IT.

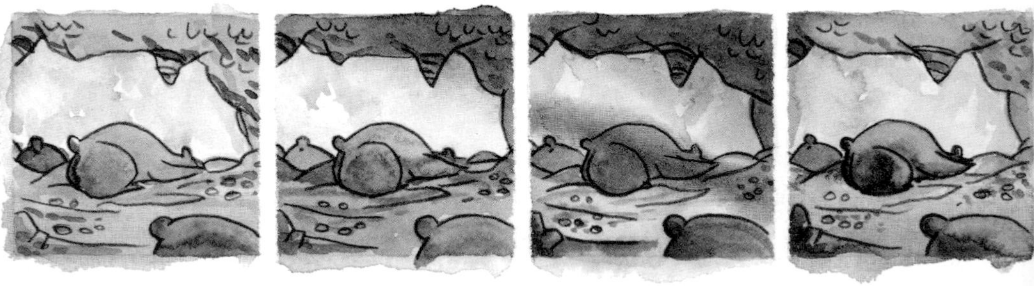

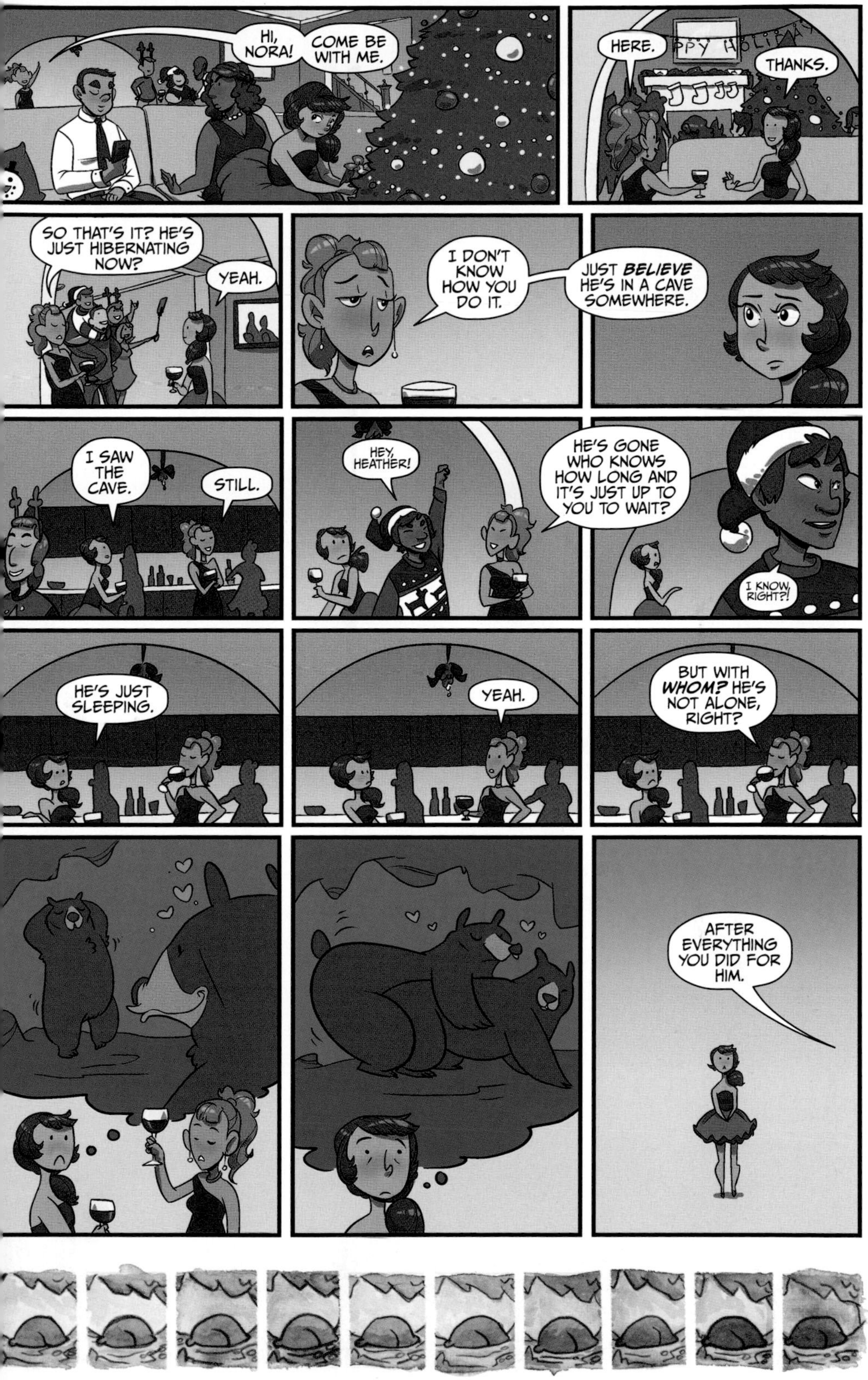
HI, NORA!
COME BE WITH ME.
HERE.
PPY HOLIDAY
THANKS.
SO THAT'S IT? HE'S JUST HIBERNATING NOW?
YEAH.
I DON'T KNOW HOW YOU DO IT.
JUST BELIEVE HE'S IN A CAVE SOMEWHERE.
I SAW THE CAVE.
STILL.
HEY, HEATHER!
HE'S GONE WHO KNOWS HOW LONG AND IT'S JUST UP TO YOU TO WAIT?
I KNOW, RIGHT?!
HE'S JUST SLEEPING.
YEAH.
BUT WITH WHOM? HE'S NOT ALONE, RIGHT?
AFTER EVERYTHING YOU DID FOR HIM.

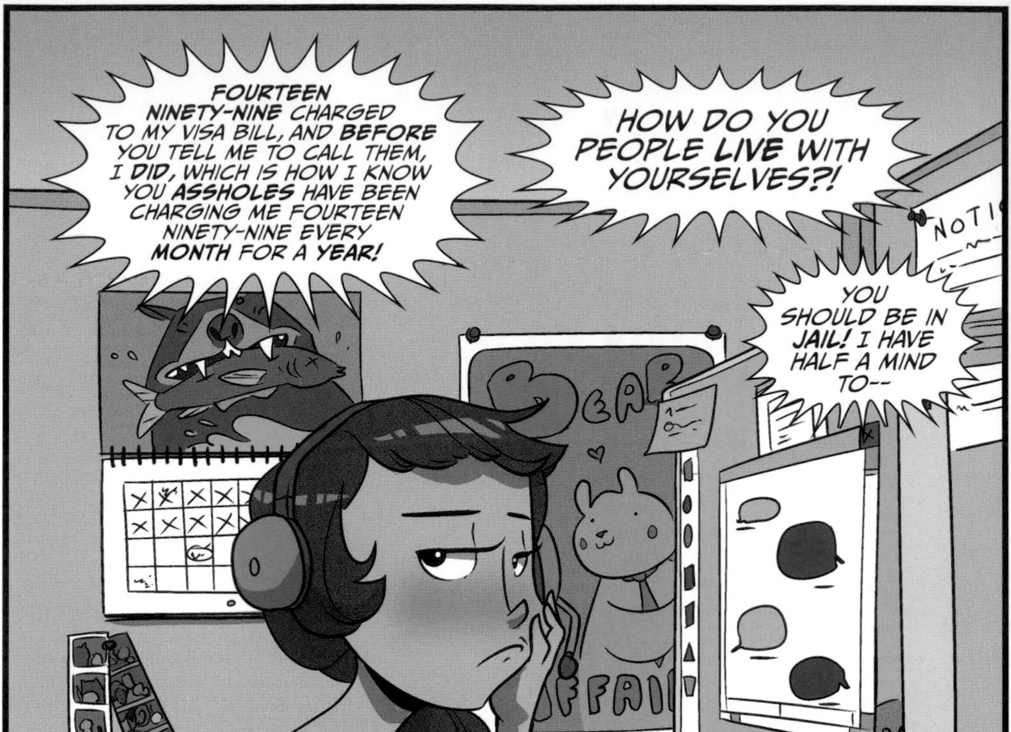
FOURTEEN NINETY-NINE CHARGED TO MY VISA BILL, AND BEFORE YOU TELL ME TO CALL THEM, I DID, WHICH IS HOW I KNOW YOU ASSHOLES HAVE BEEN CHARGING ME FOURTEEN NINETY-NINE EVERY MONTH FOR A YEAR!
HOW DO YOU PEOPLE LIVE WITH YOURSELVES?!
YOU SHOULD BE IN JAIL! I HAVE HALF A MIND TO--
WHAT IF DEBRA WAS, IN THE TINIEST WAY, JUST A LITTLE BIT RIGHT? WE NEVER TALKED ABOUT HIS LIFE IN THE CAVE.
WHAT IF HE HAD A BEAR GIRLFRIEND BEFORE HE MET ME? BEFORE HE HAD TO FLEE THE FIRES?

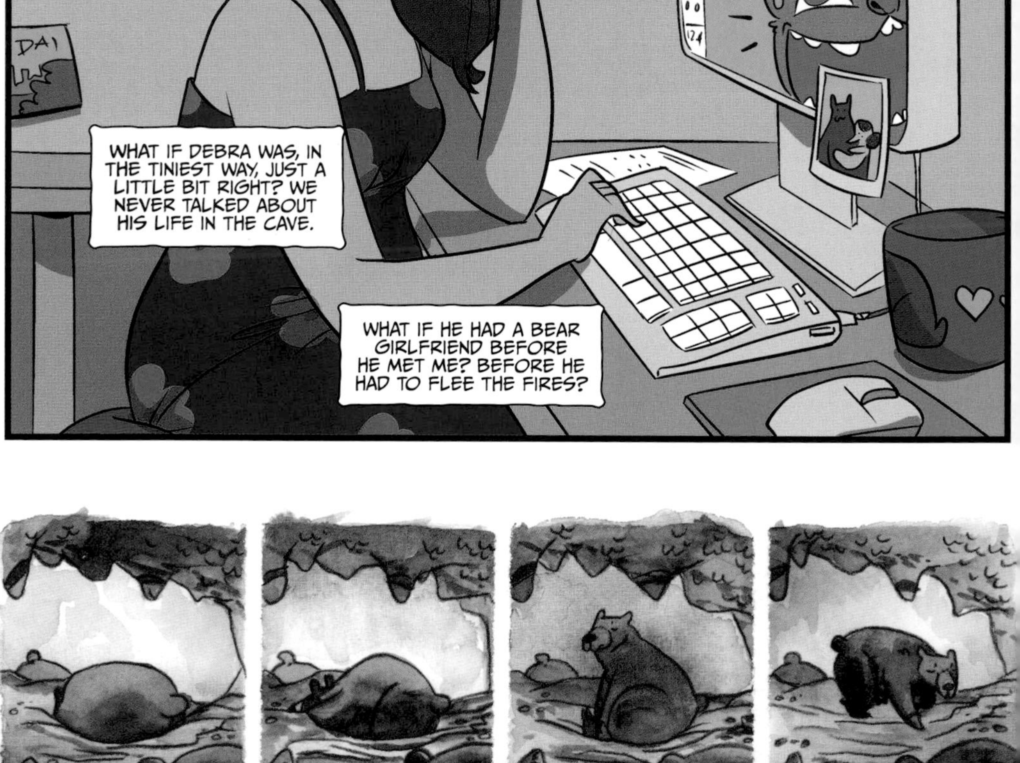

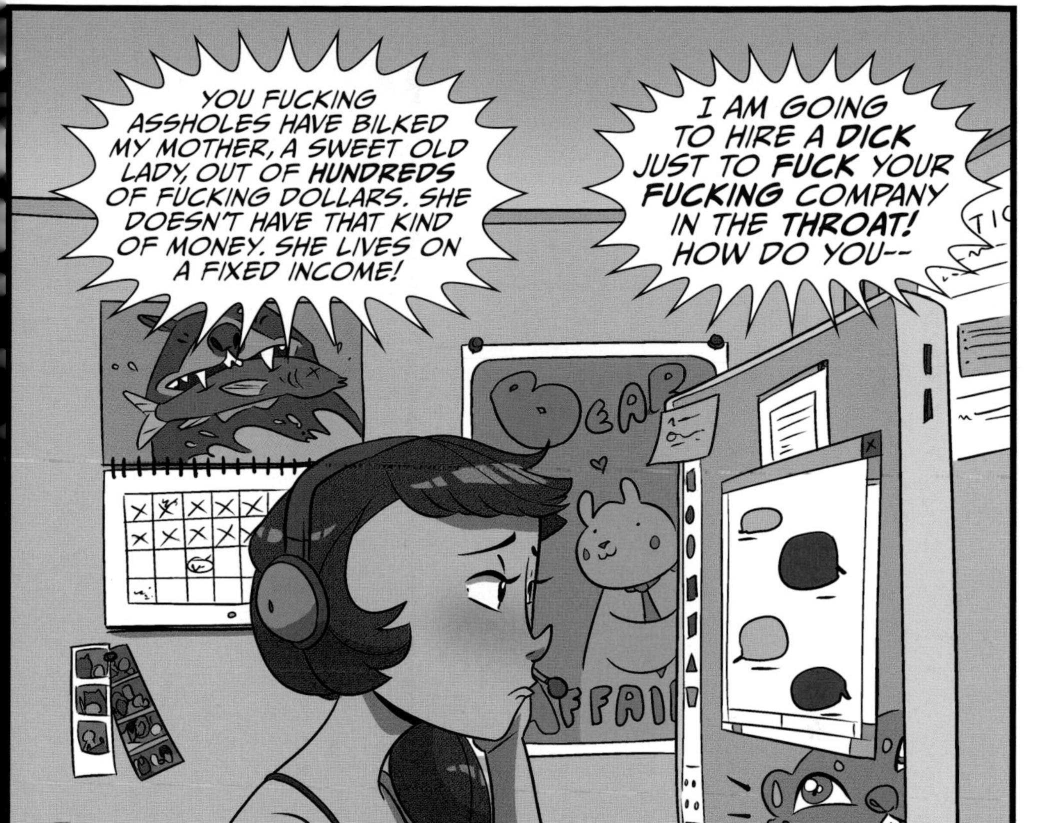
YOU FUCKING ASSHOLES HAVE BILKED MY MOTHER, A SWEET OLD LADY, OUT OF HUNDREDS OF FUCKING DOLLARS. SHE DOESN'T HAVE THAT KIND OF MONEY. SHE LIVES ON A FIXED INCOME!
I AM GOING TO HIRE A DICK JUST TO FUCK YOUR FUCKING COMPANY IN THE THROAT! HOW DO YOU--

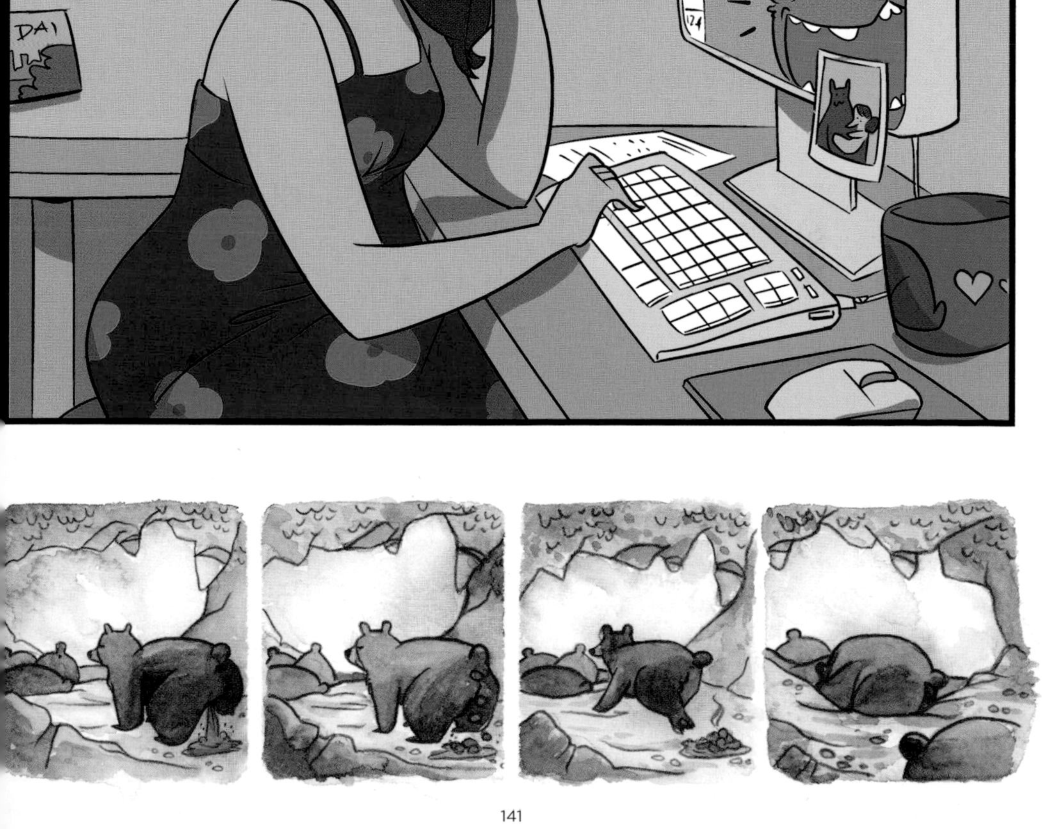

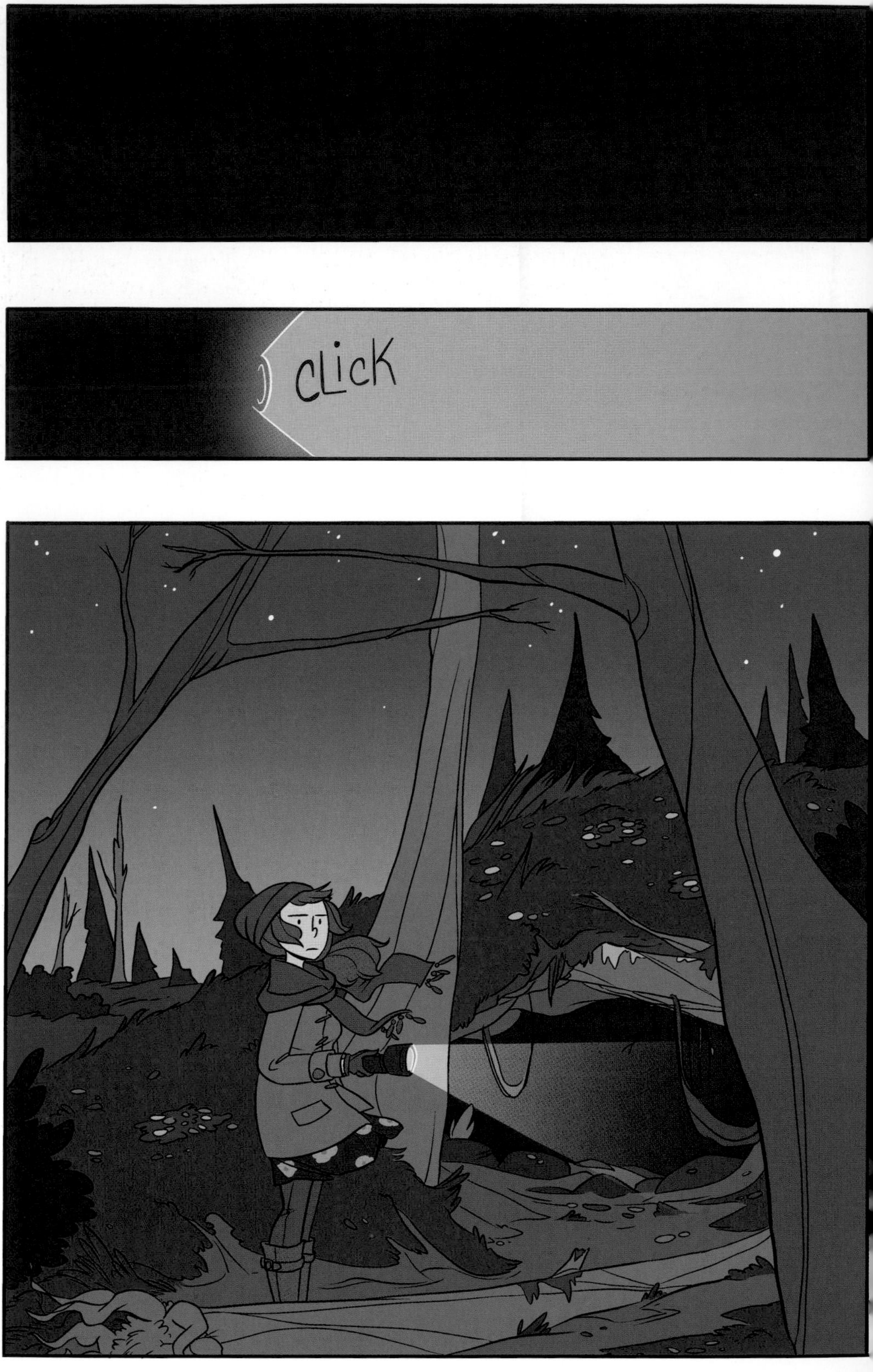
CLICK

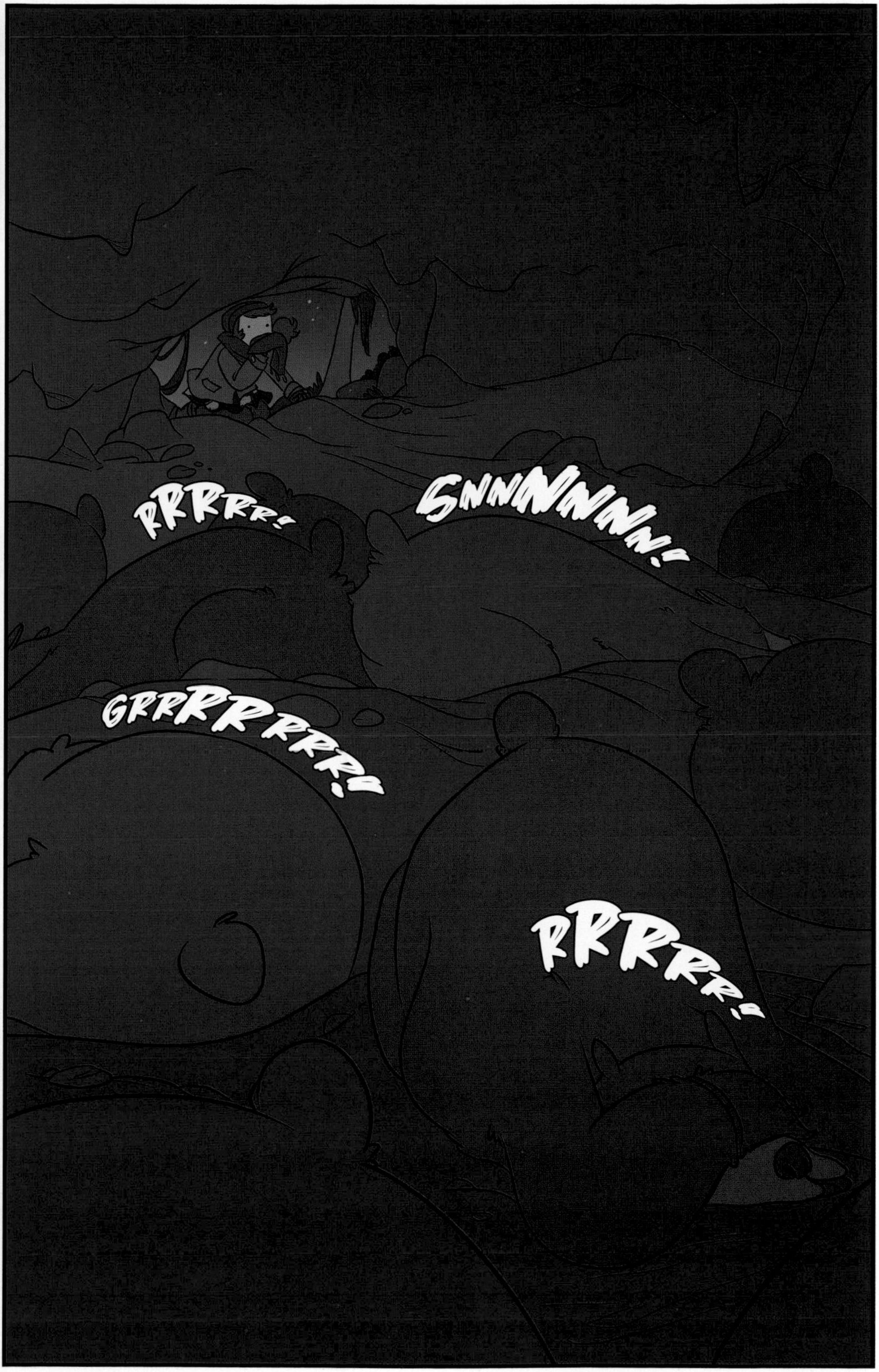
RRRRR!
SNNNNNNN!
GRRRRRRRR!
RRRRR!

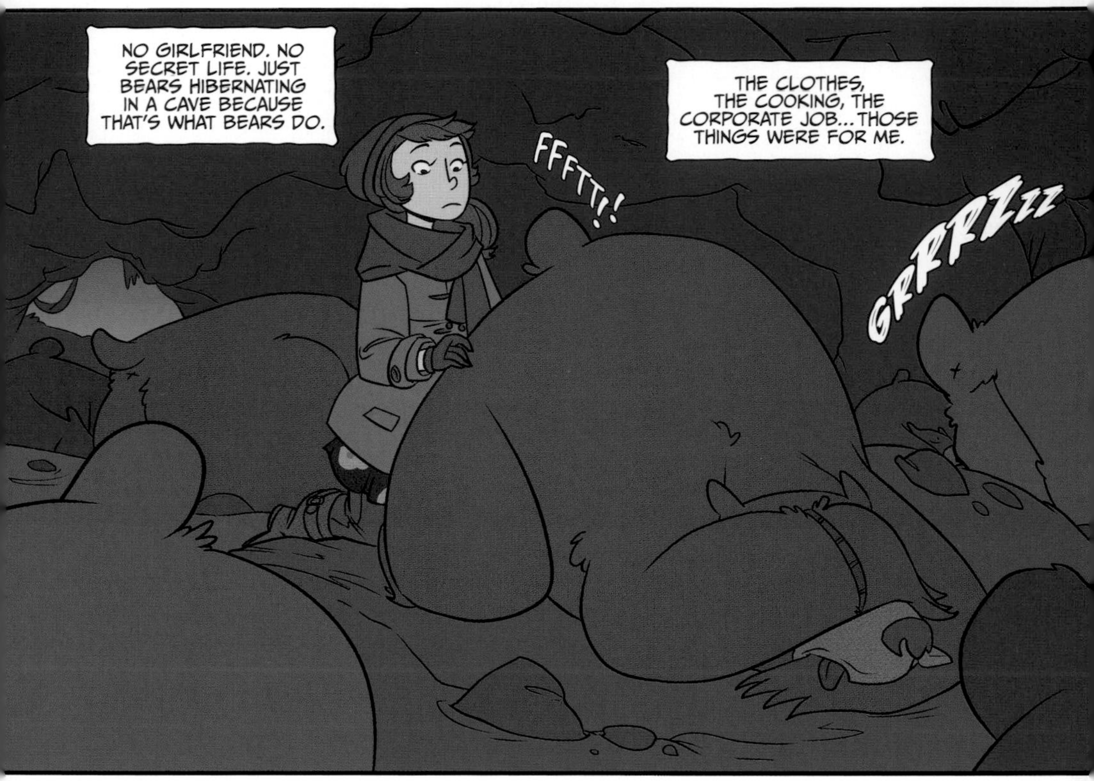
NO GIRLFRIEND. NO SECRET LIFE. JUST BEARS HIBERNATING IN A CAVE BECAUSE THAT'S WHAT BEARS DO.
FFFTT!!
THE CLOTHES, THE COOKING, THE CORPORATE JOB... THOSE THINGS WERE FOR ME.
GRRRZzz

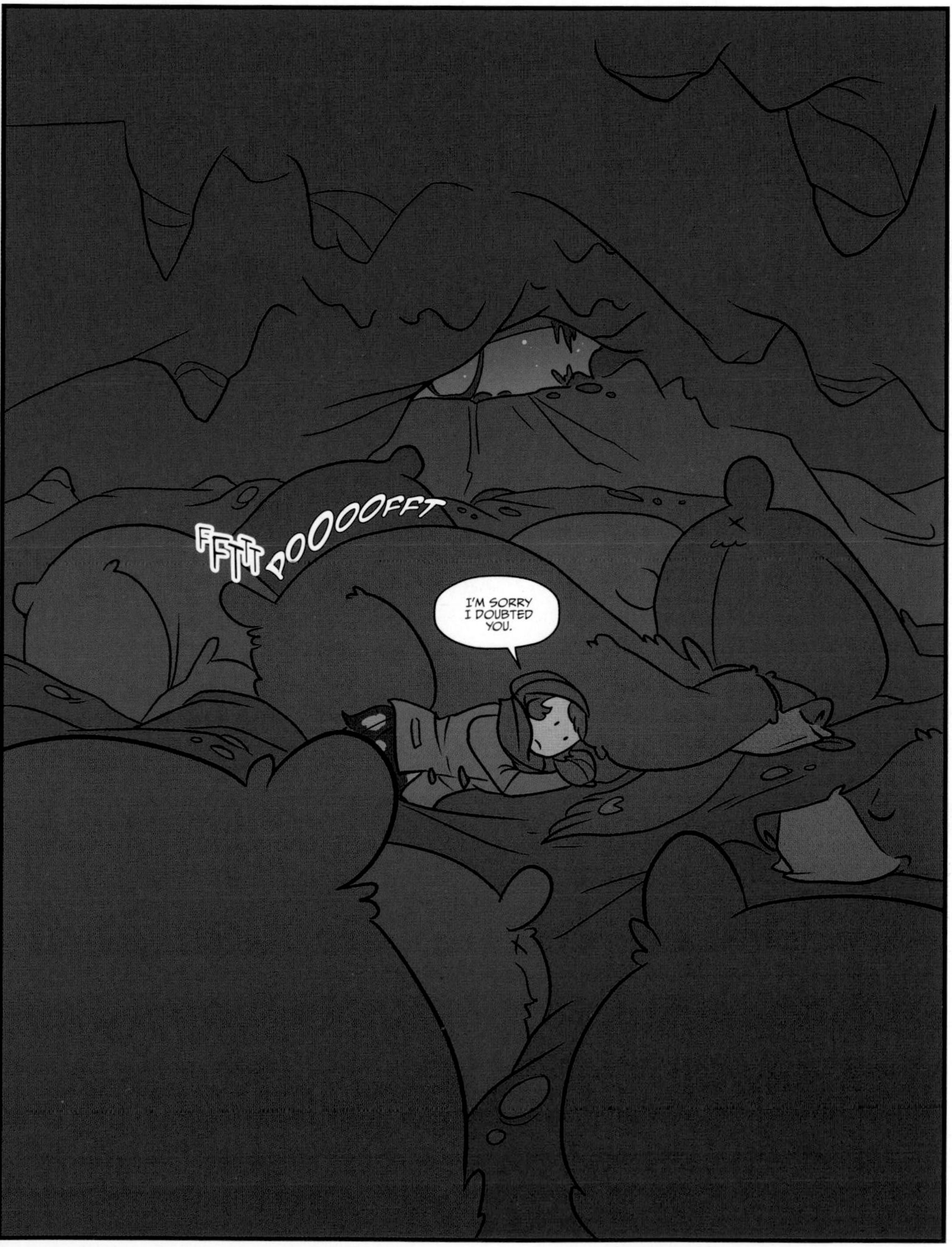
FFTTT POOOOOFFT
I'M SORRY I DOUBTED YOU.

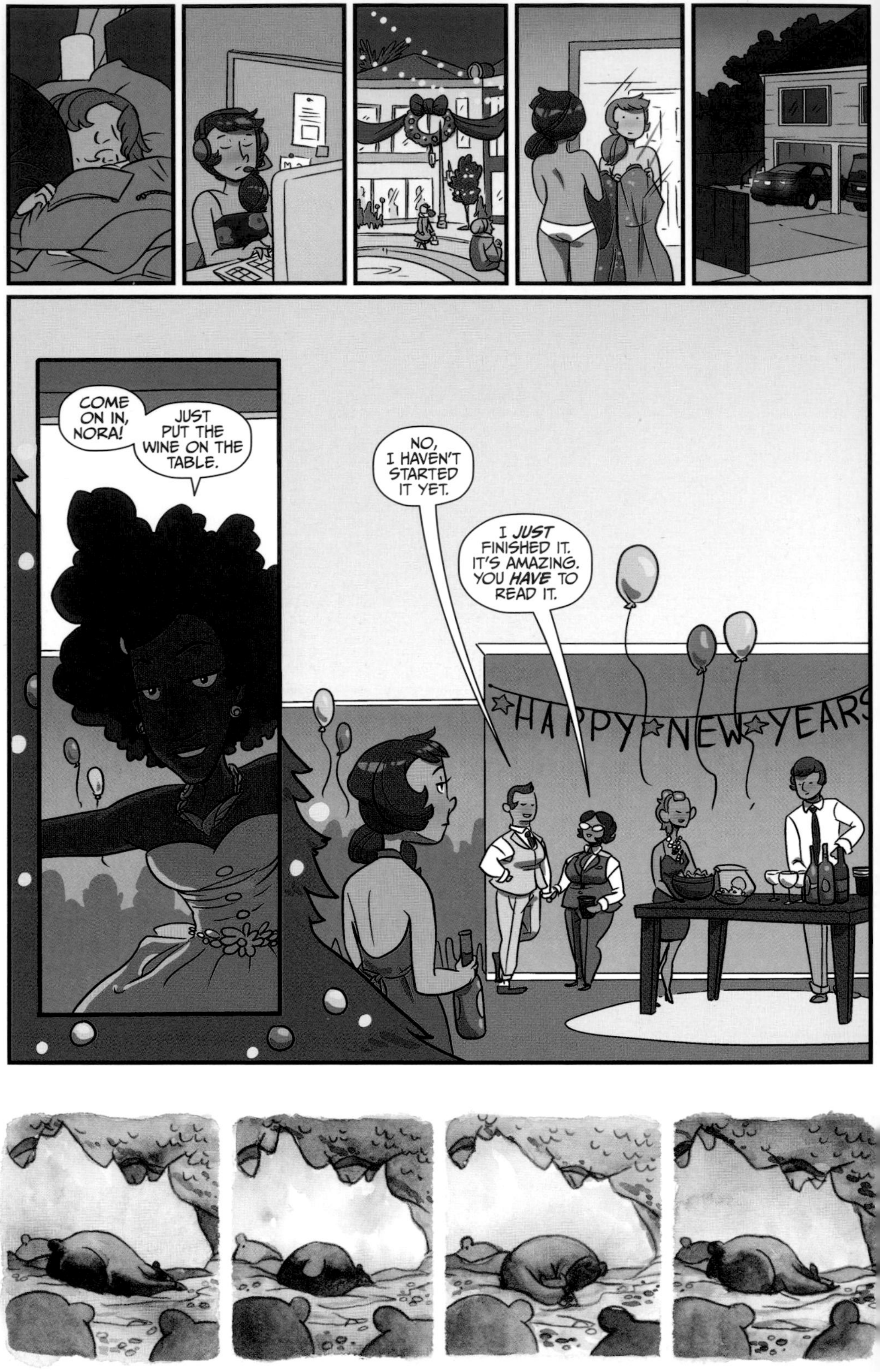
COME ON IN, NORA!
JUST PUT THE WINE ON THE TABLE.
NO, I HAVEN'T STARTED IT YET.
I *JUST* FINISHED IT. IT'S AMAZING. YOU *HAVE* TO READ IT.
HAPPY NEW YEARS

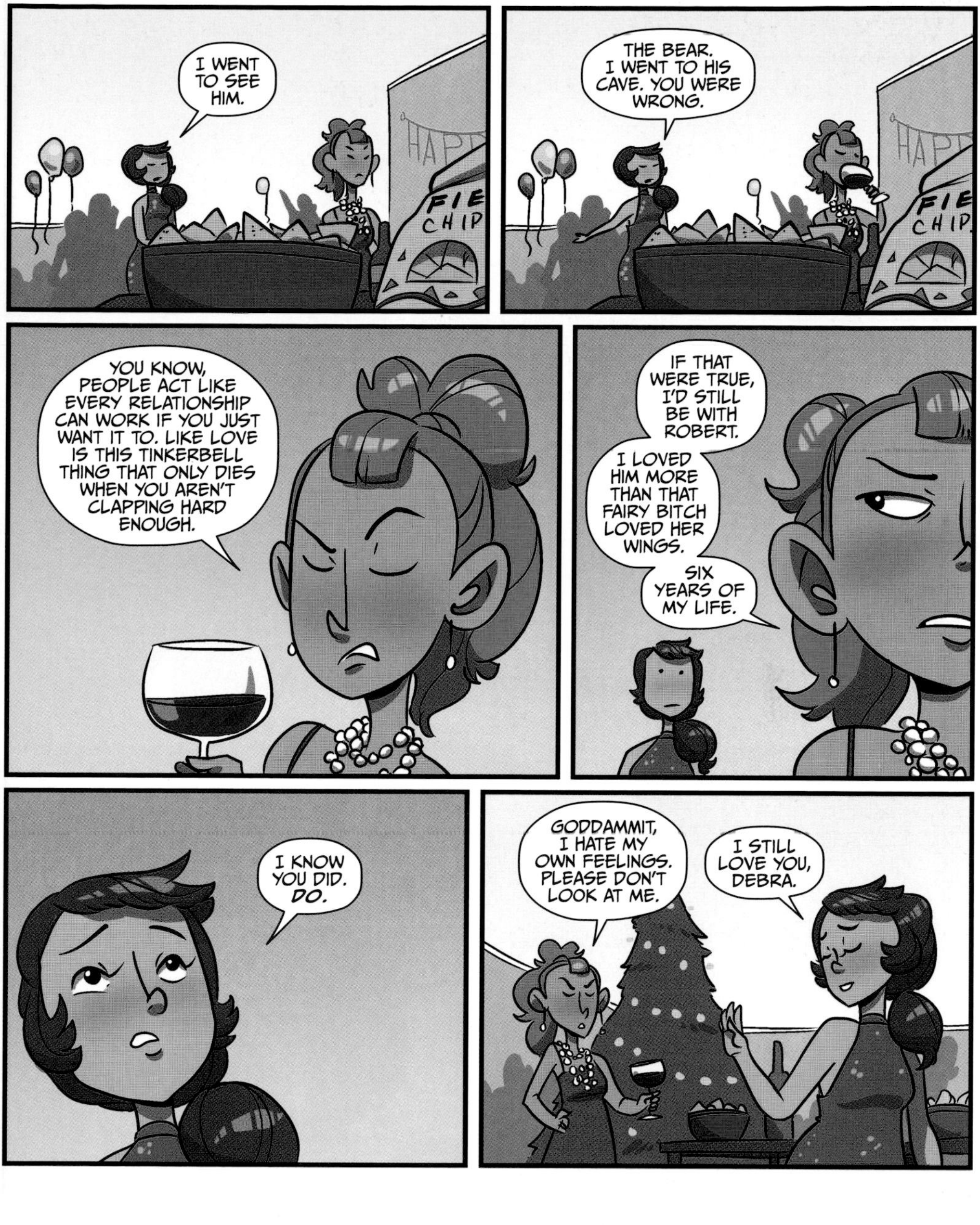
I WENT TO SEE HIM.
THE BEAR. I WENT TO HIS CAVE. YOU WERE WRONG.
YOU KNOW, PEOPLE ACT LIKE EVERY RELATIONSHIP CAN WORK IF YOU JUST WANT IT TO. LIKE LOVE IS THIS TINKERBELL THING THAT ONLY DIES WHEN YOU AREN'T CLAPPING HARD ENOUGH.
IF THAT WERE TRUE, I'D STILL BE WITH ROBERT.
I LOVED HIM MORE THAN THAT FAIRY BITCH LOVED HER WINGS.
SIX YEARS OF MY LIFE.
I KNOW YOU DID. *DO.*
GODDAMMIT, I HATE MY OWN FEELINGS. PLEASE DON'T LOOK AT ME.
I STILL LOVE YOU, DEBRA.

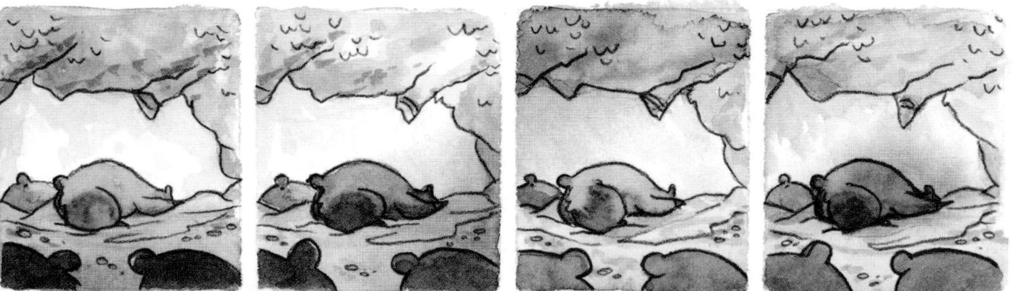

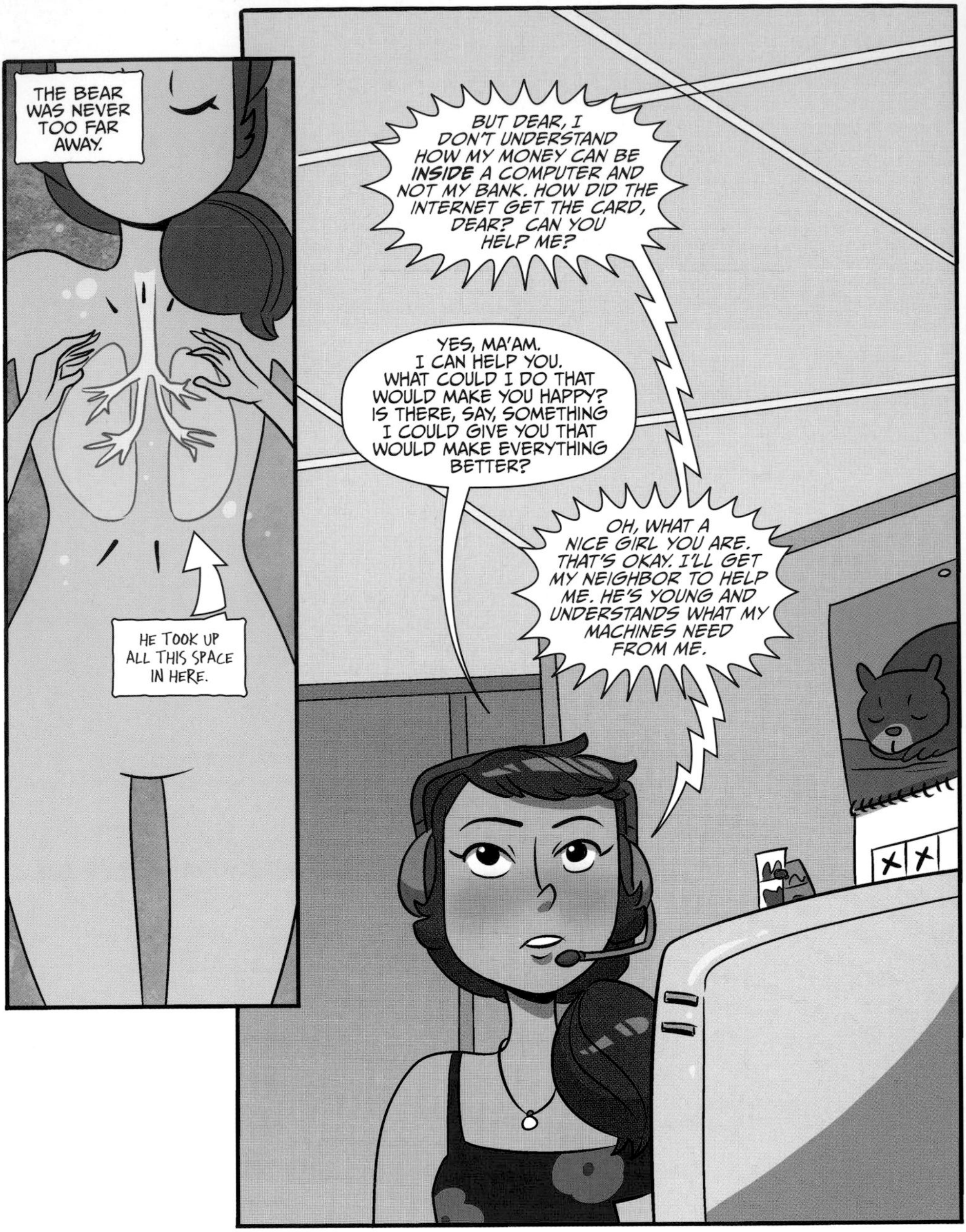
THE BEAR WAS NEVER TOO FAR AWAY.
HE TOOK UP ALL THIS SPACE IN HERE.
BUT DEAR, I DON'T UNDERSTAND HOW MY MONEY CAN BE INSIDE A COMPUTER AND NOT MY BANK. HOW DID THE INTERNET GET THE CARD, DEAR? CAN YOU HELP ME?
YES, MA'AM. I CAN HELP YOU. WHAT COULD I DO THAT WOULD MAKE YOU HAPPY? IS THERE, SAY, SOMETHING I COULD GIVE YOU THAT WOULD MAKE EVERYTHING BETTER?
OH, WHAT A NICE GIRL YOU ARE. THAT'S OKAY. I'LL GET MY NEIGHBOR TO HELP ME. HE'S YOUNG AND UNDERSTANDS WHAT MY MACHINES NEED FROM ME.

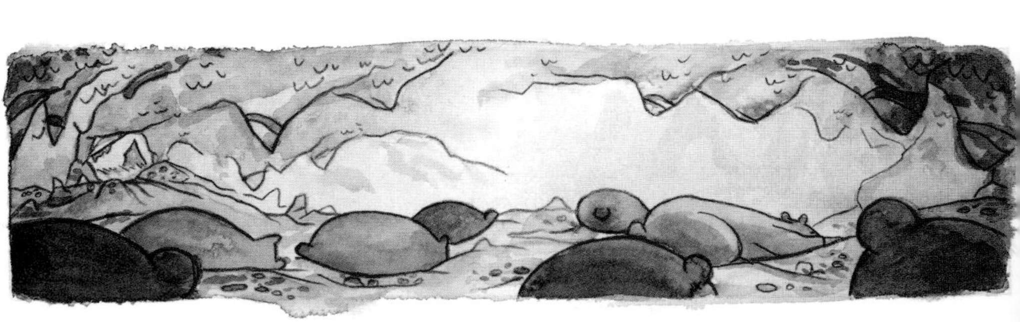

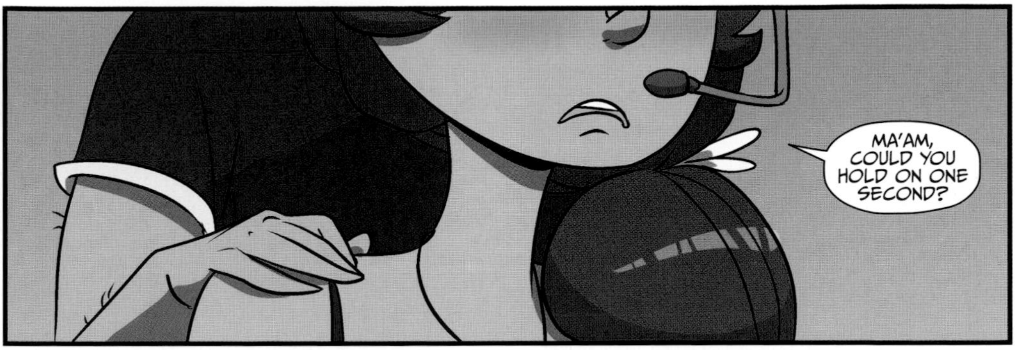
MA'AM, COULD YOU HOLD ON ONE SECOND?

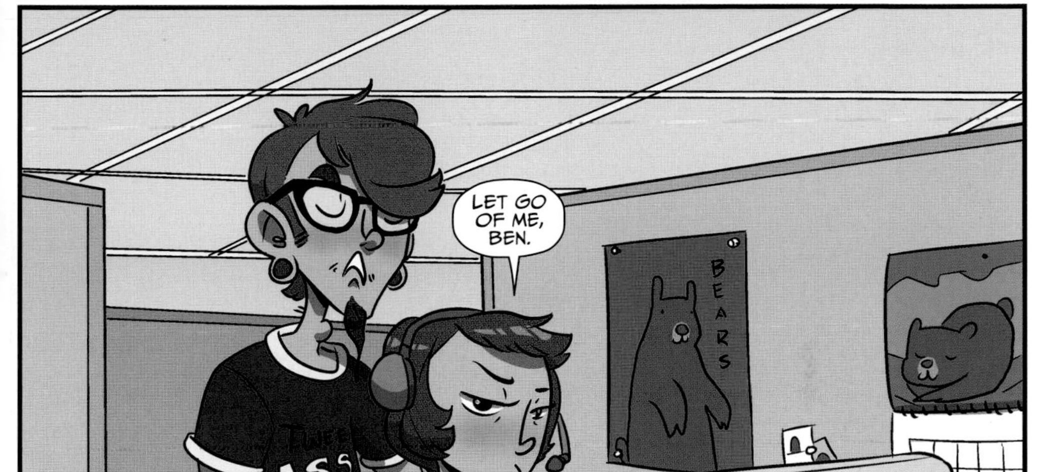
LET GO OF ME, BEN.
BEARS
IT'S JUST A BACKRUB, NORA.

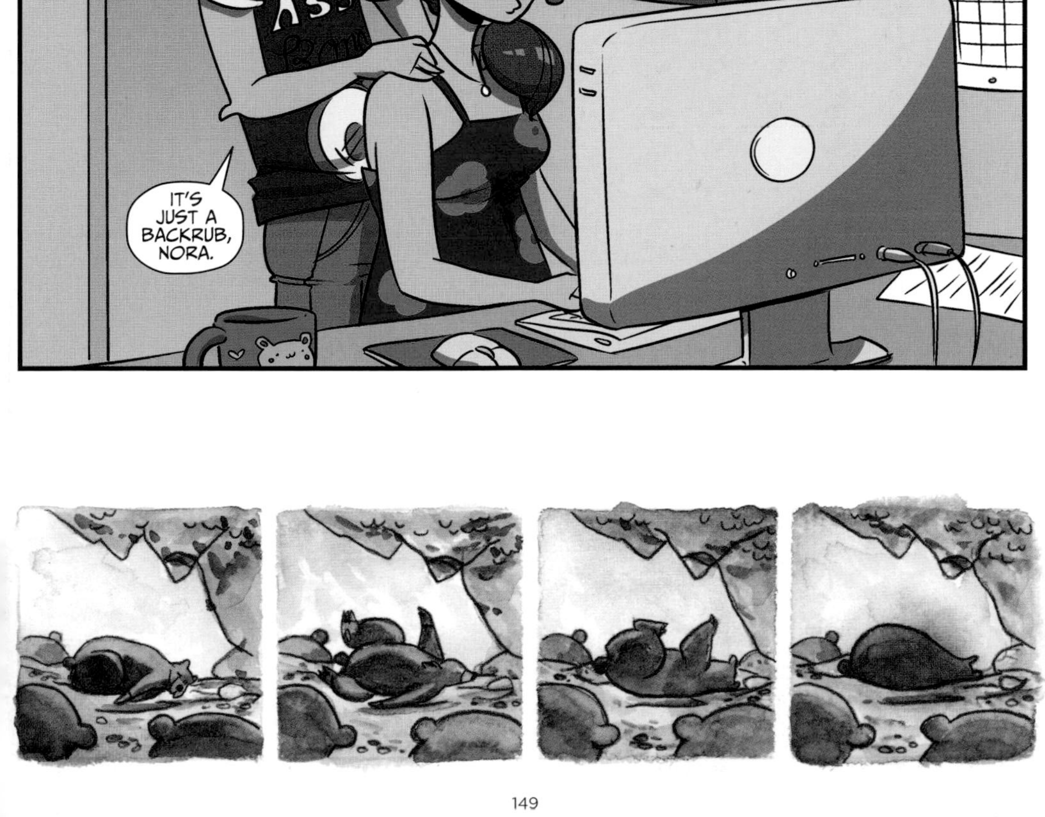

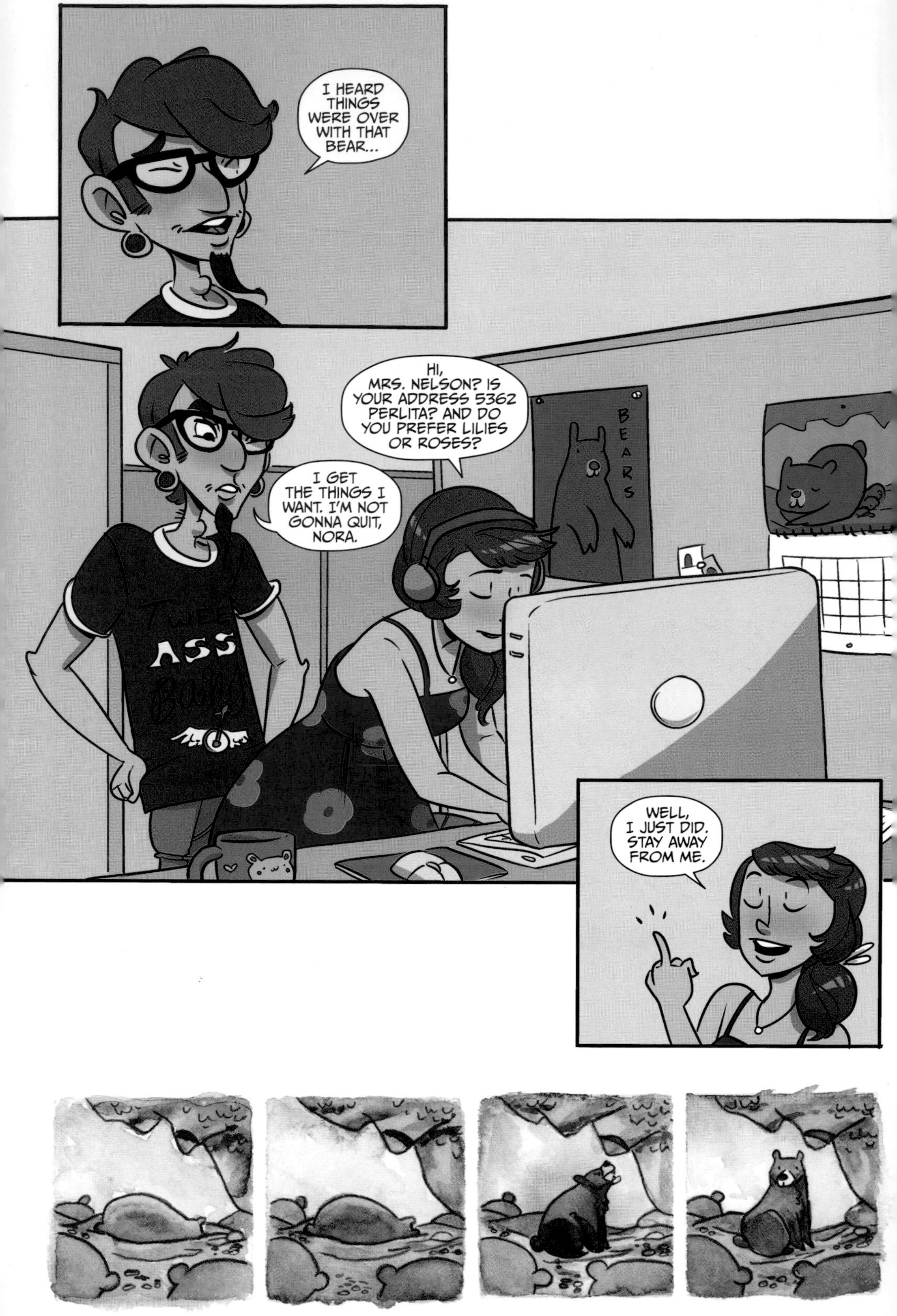

I HEARD THINGS WERE OVER WITH THAT BEAR...
HI, MRS. NELSON? IS YOUR ADDRESS 5362 PERLITA? AND DO YOU PREFER LILIES OR ROSES?
BEARS
I GET THE THINGS I WANT. I'M NOT GONNA QUIT, NORA.
WELL, I JUST DID. STAY AWAY FROM ME.

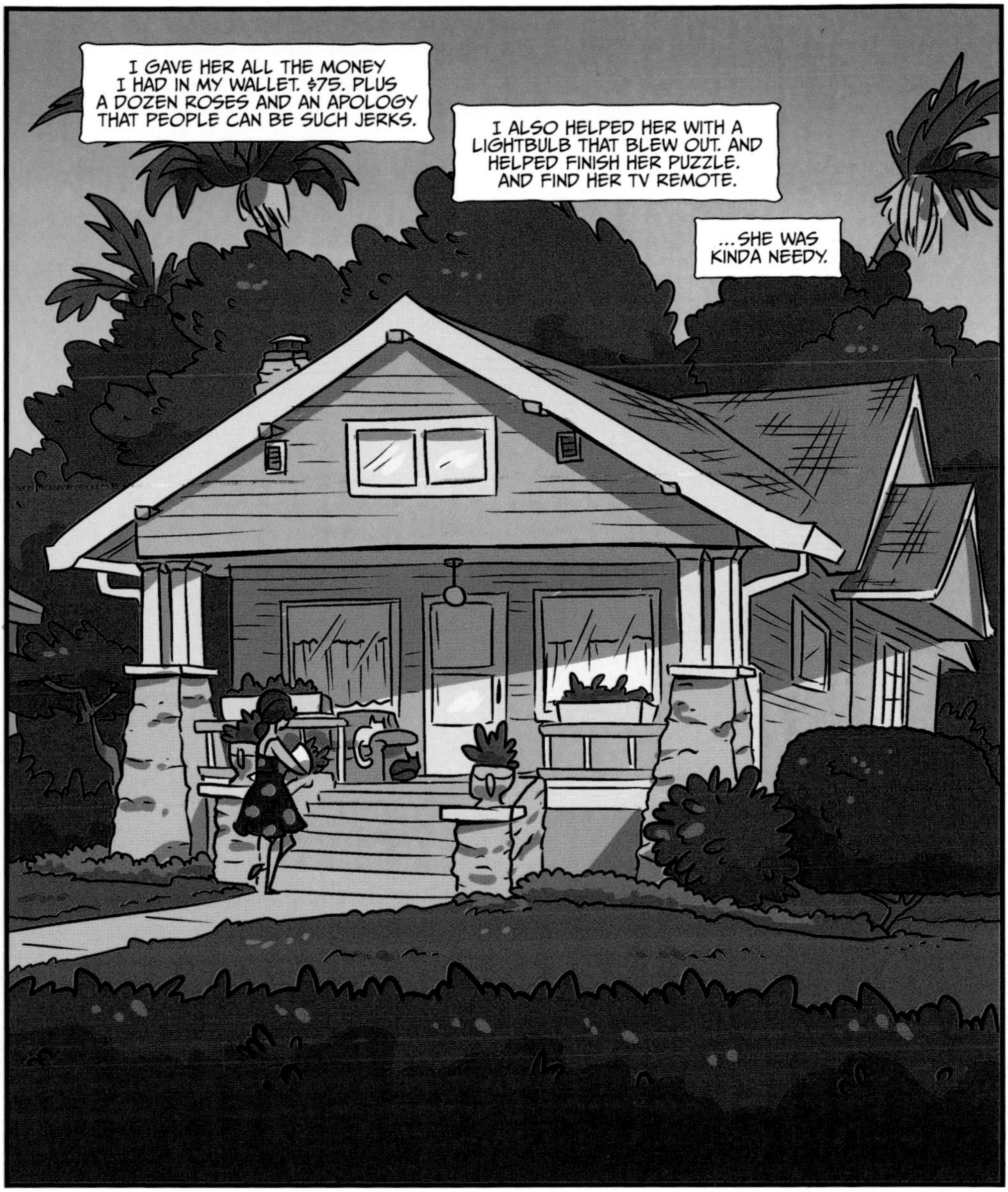
I GAVE HER ALL THE MONEY I HAD IN MY WALLET. $75. PLUS A DOZEN ROSES AND AN APOLOGY THAT PEOPLE CAN BE SUCH JERKS.
I ALSO HELPED HER WITH A LIGHTBULB THAT BLEW OUT. AND HELPED FINISH HER PUZZLE. AND FIND HER TV REMOTE.
...SHE WAS KINDA NEEDY.

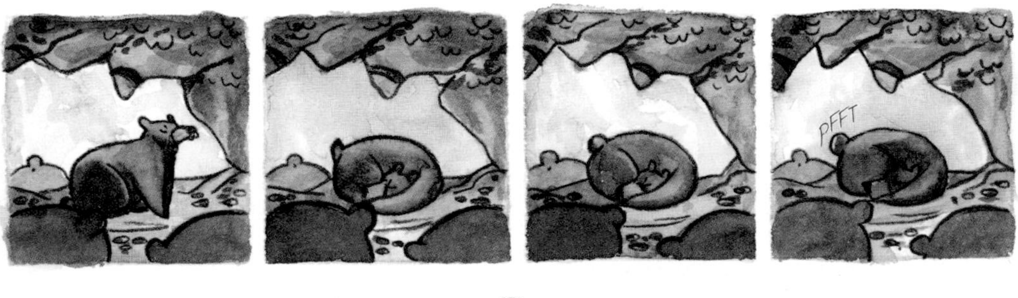
PFFT

EVERYTHING'S GREAT, MOM. I'M JUST BUSY.

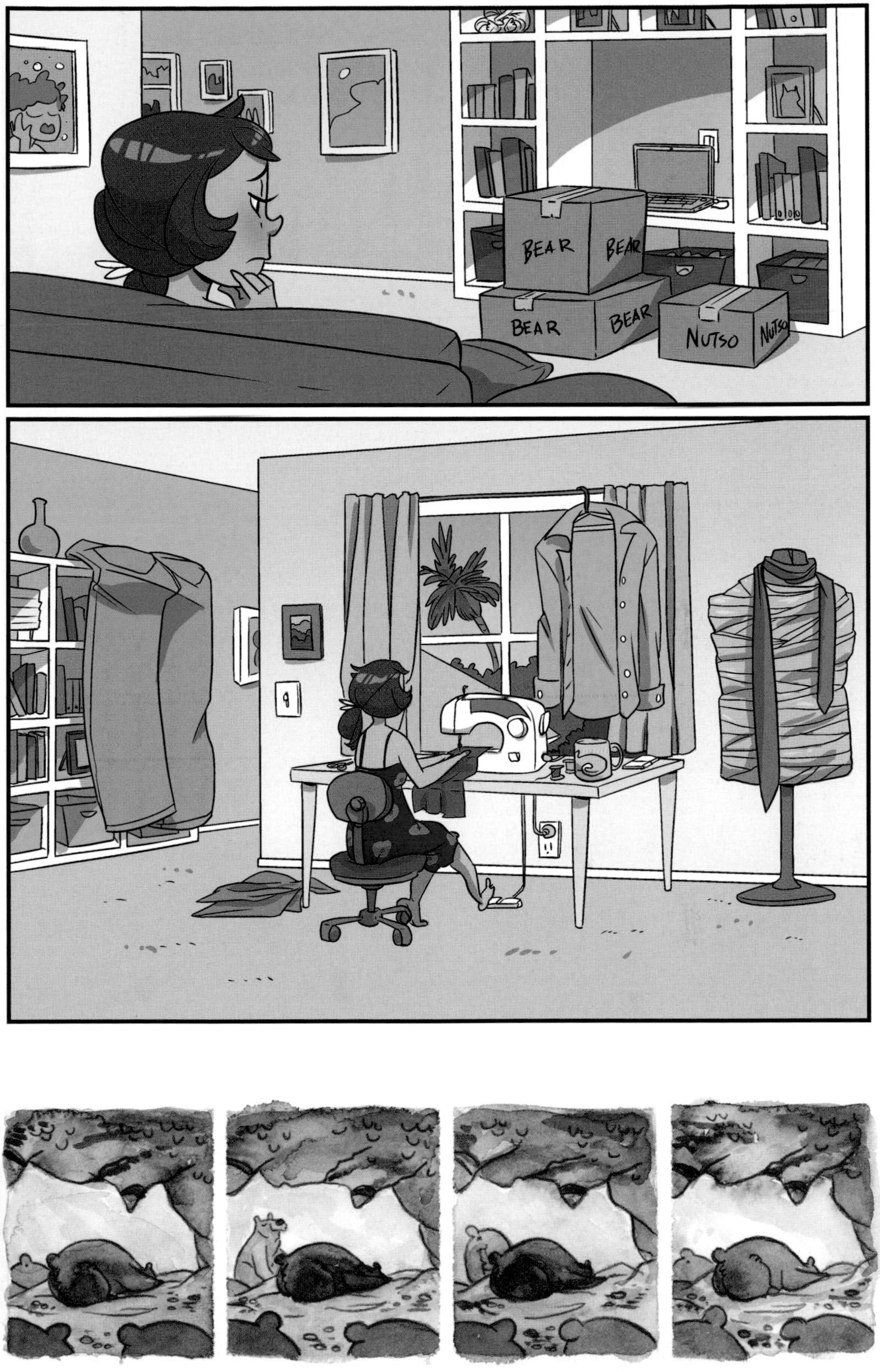
BEAR
BEAR
BEAR
BEAR
NUTSO
NUTSO

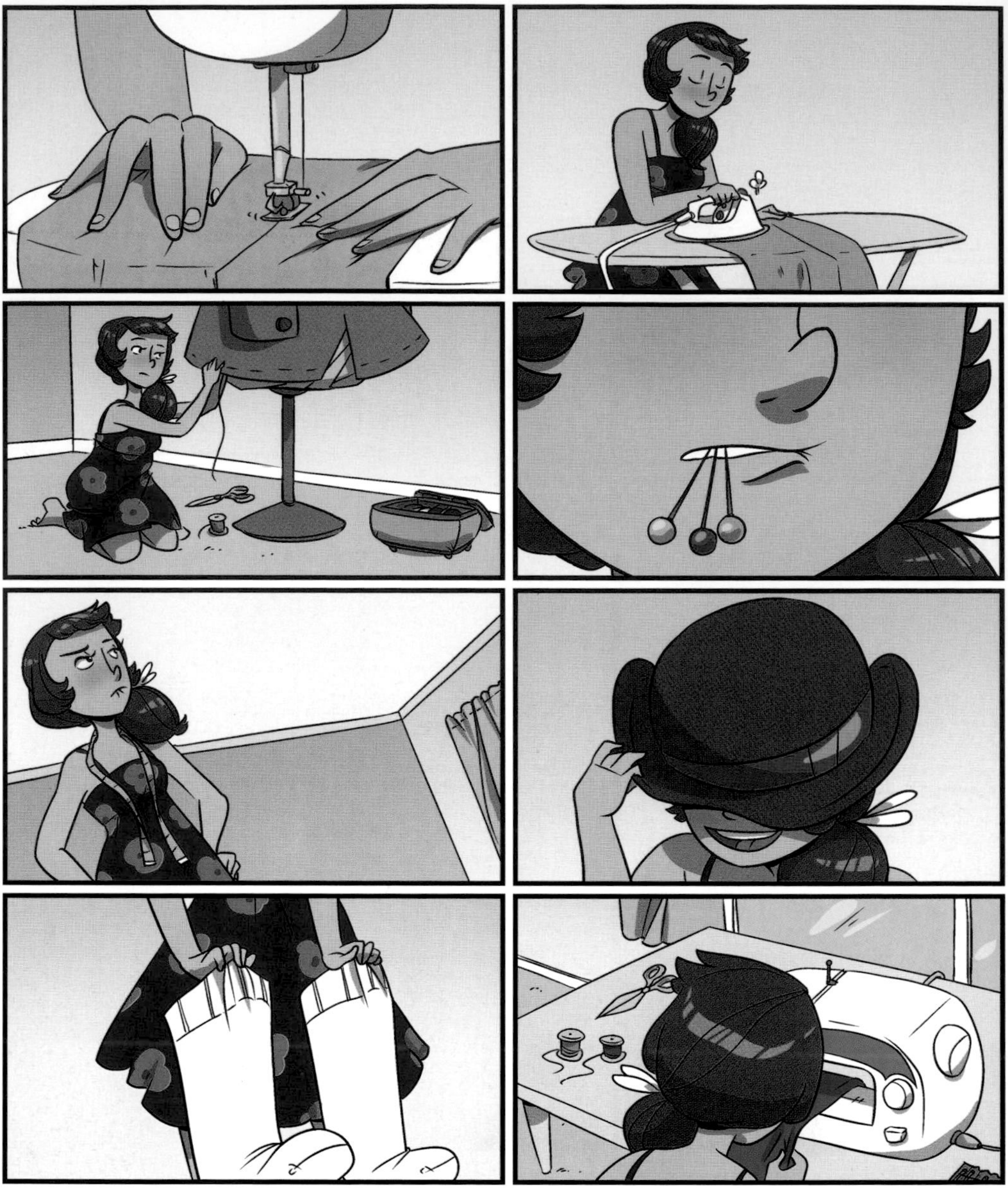

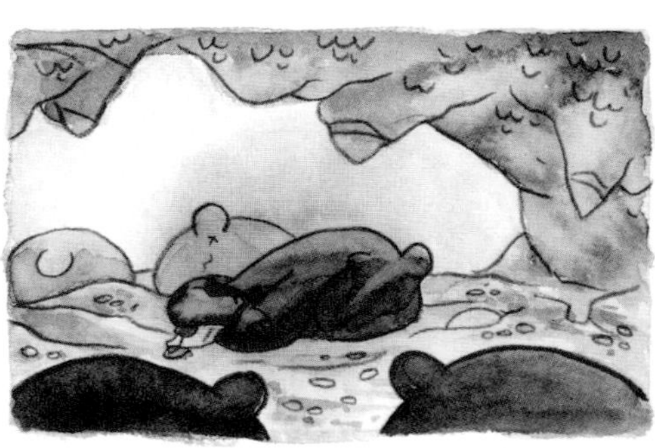

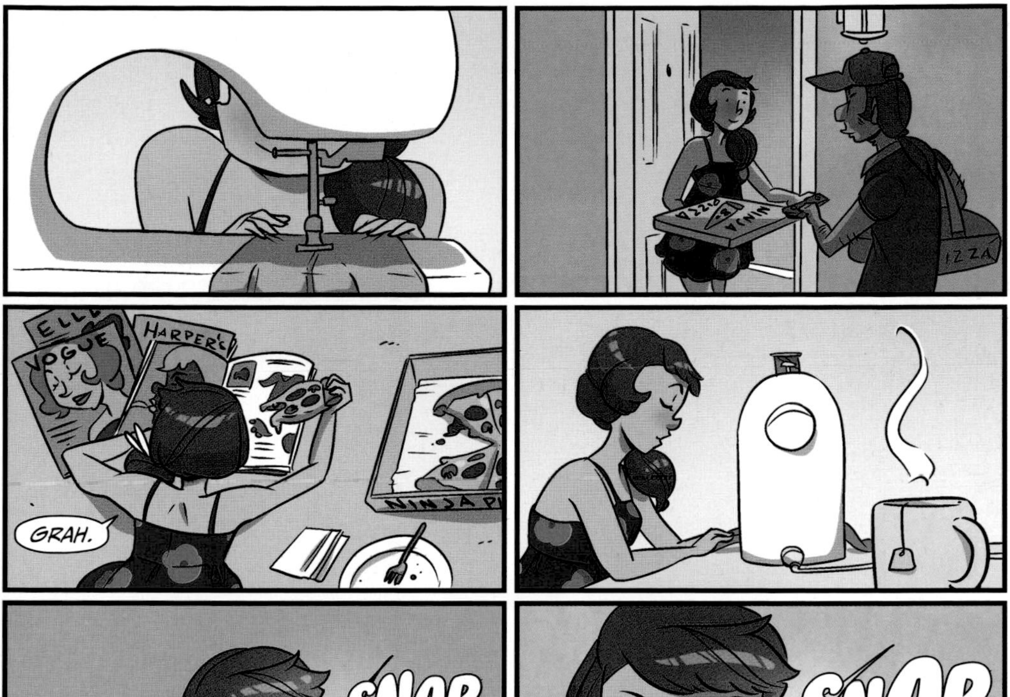
VOGUE
HARPER'S
GRAH.
SNAP
SNAP
SNAP

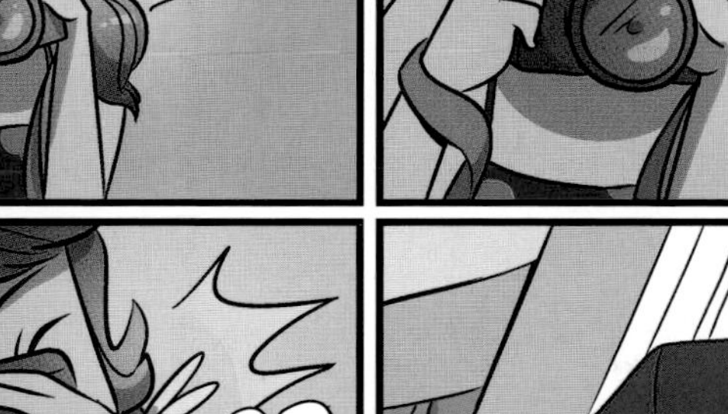

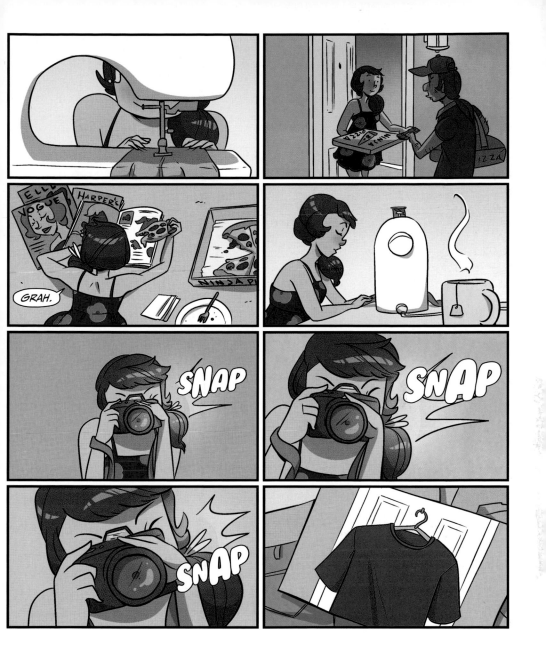

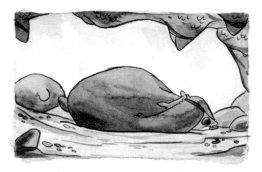

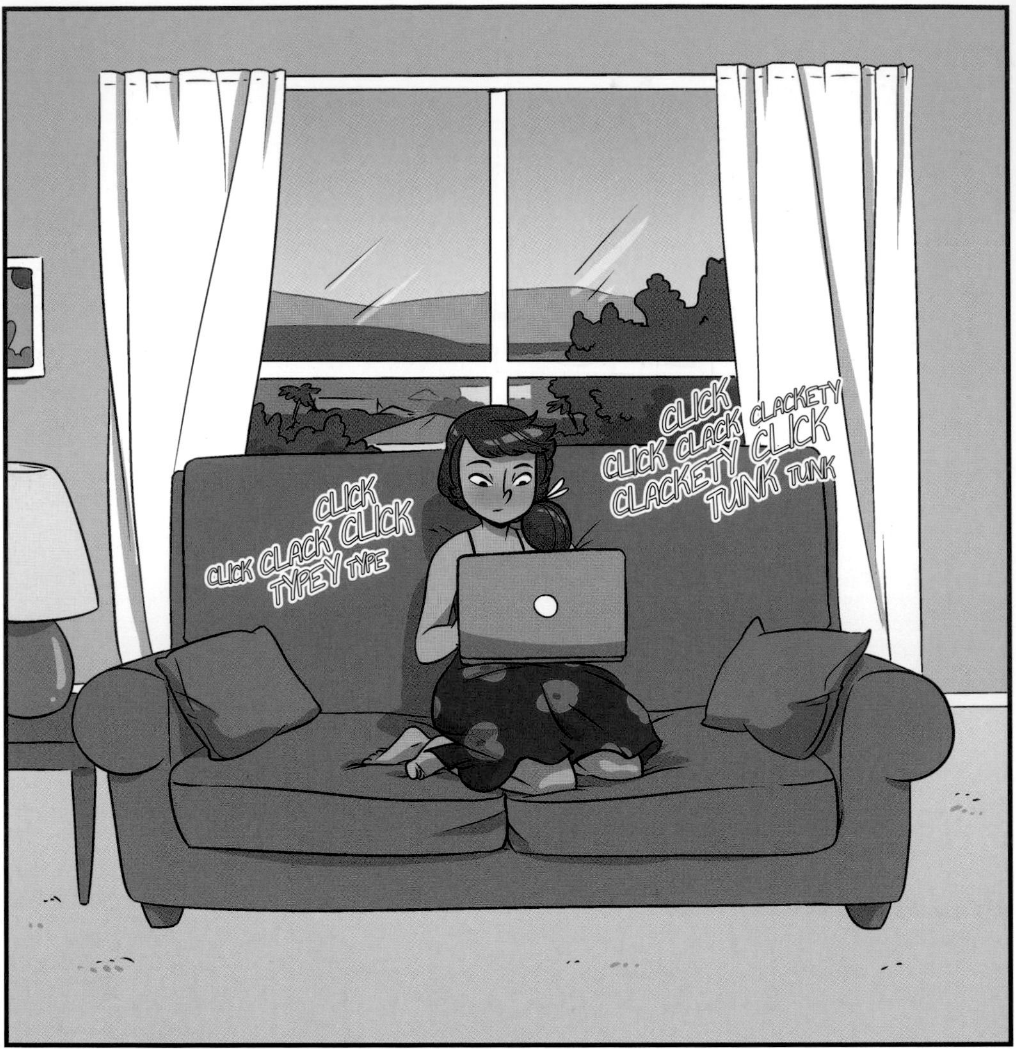
CLICK
CLICK CLACK CLICK
TYPEY TYPE
CLICK
CLICK CLACK CLACKETY
CLACKETY CLICK
TUNK TUNK

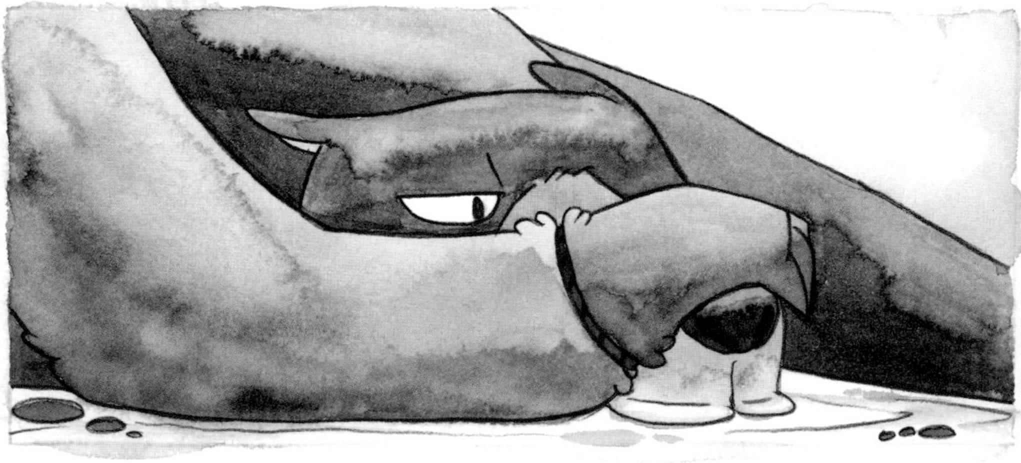

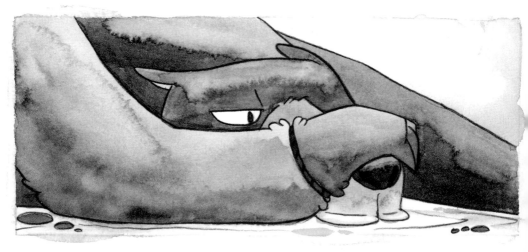

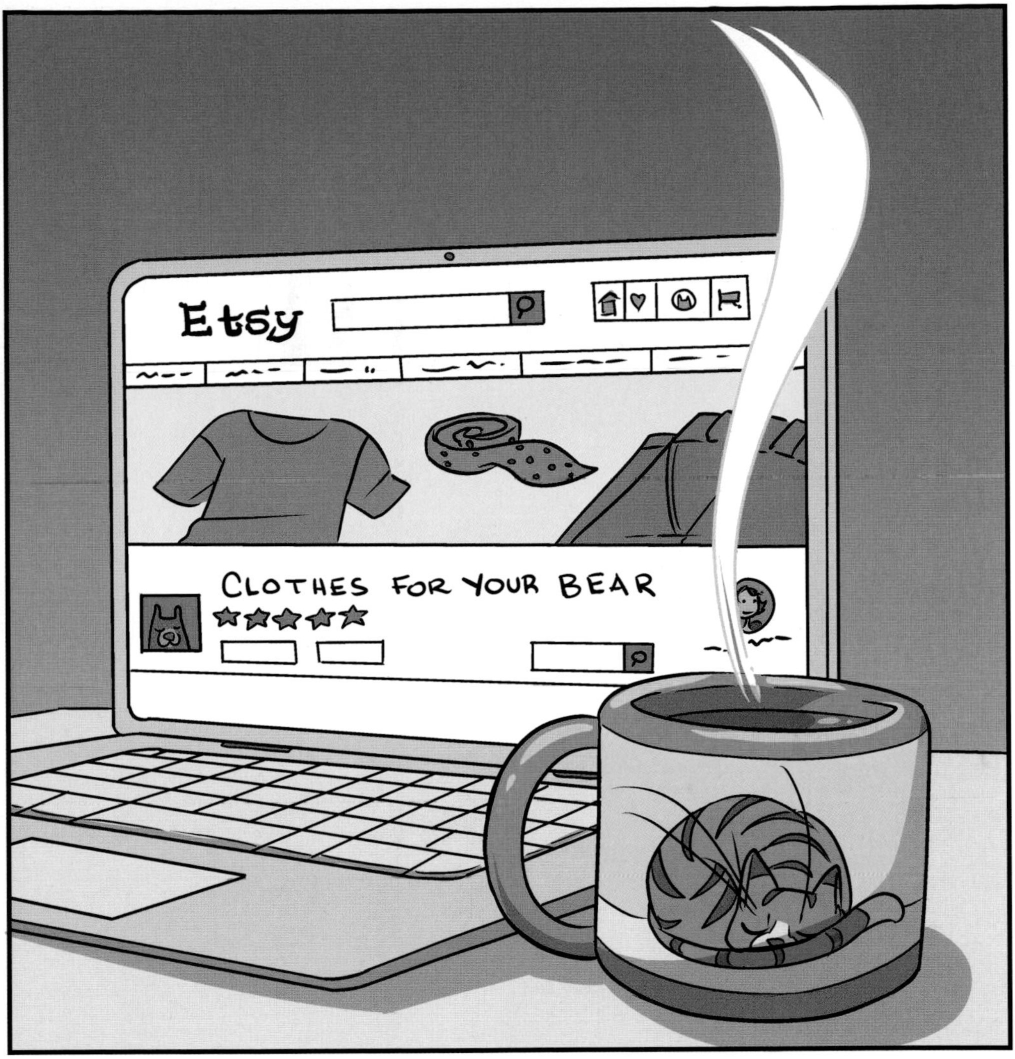
Etsy
CLOTHES FOR YOUR BEAR

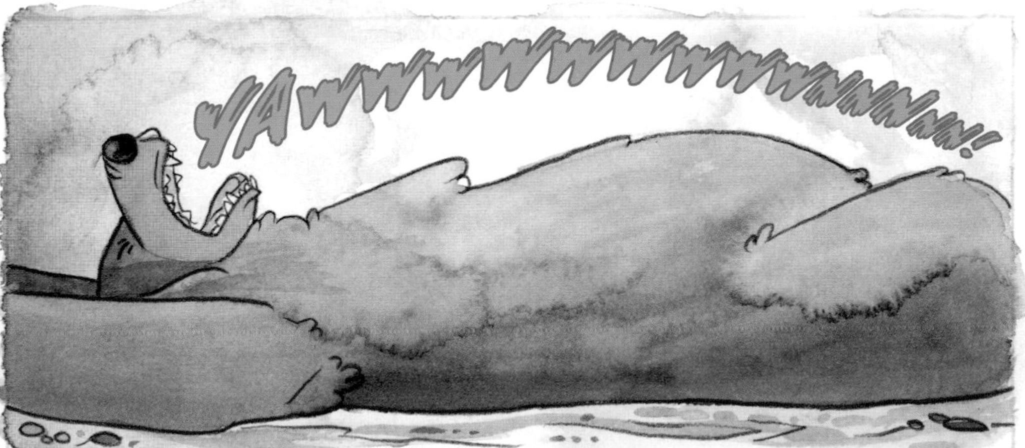
YAWWWWWWWWWWNNNN!!

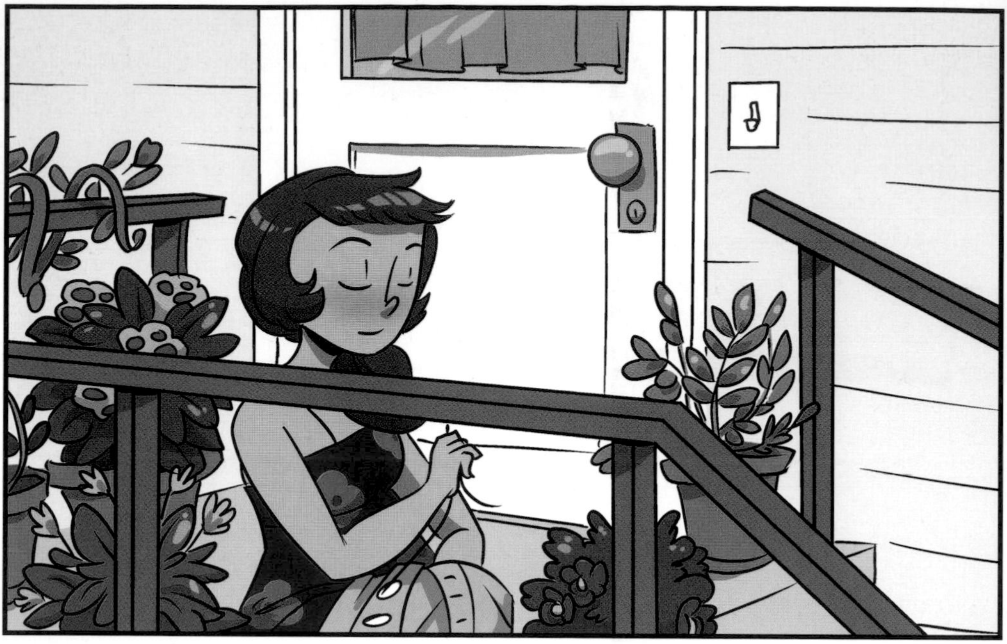

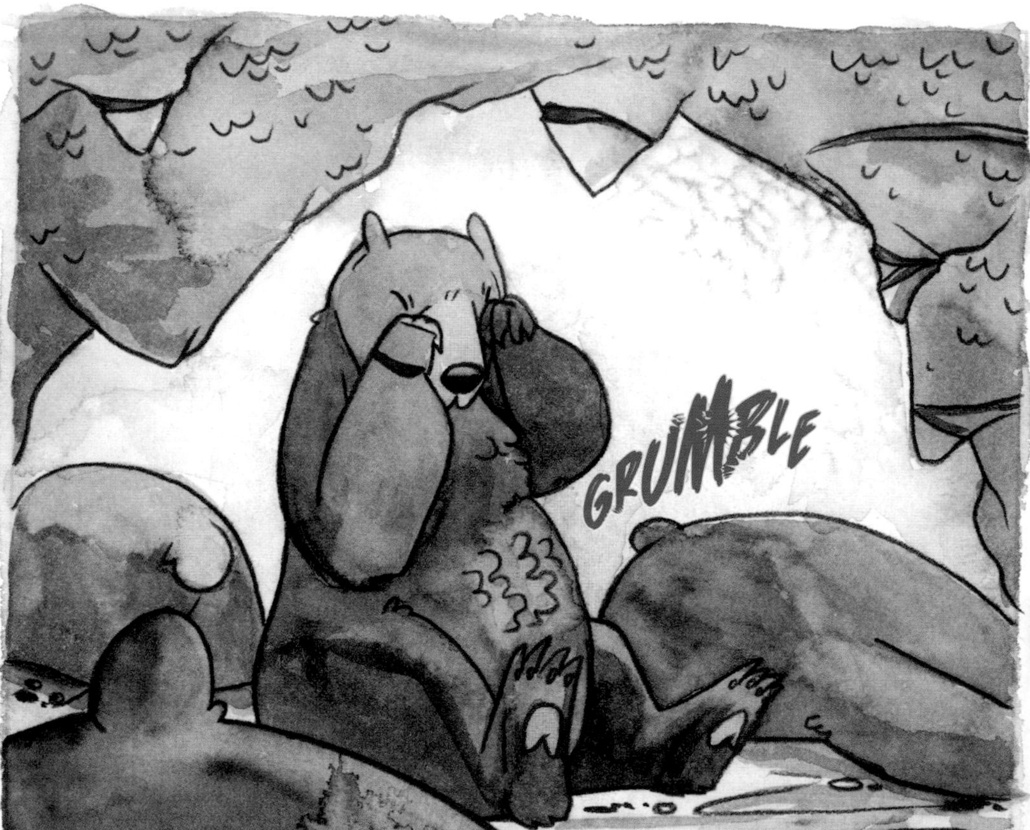
GRUMBLE

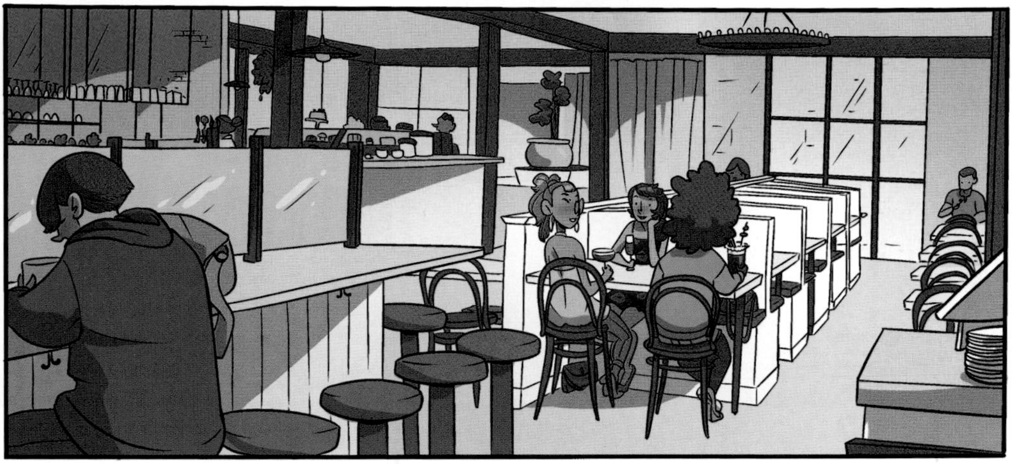

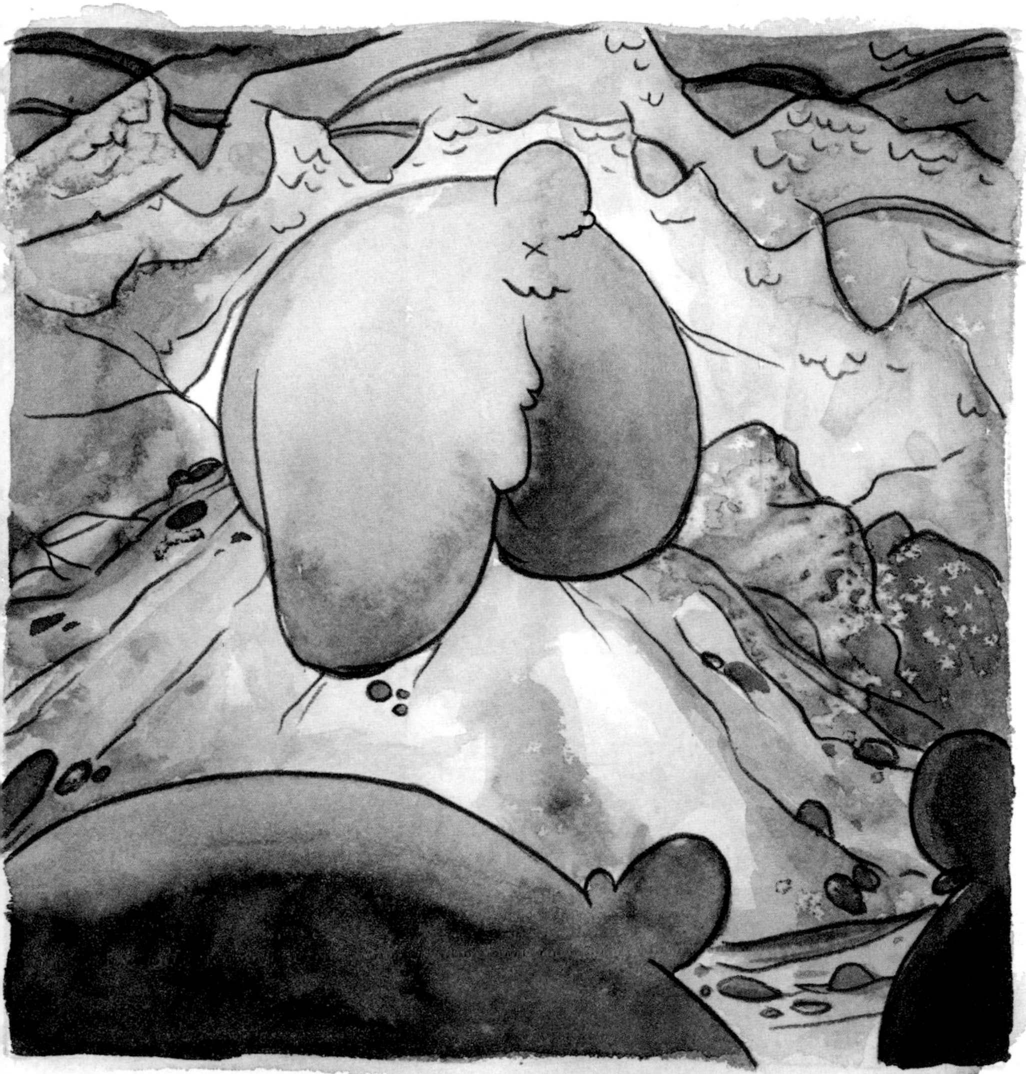

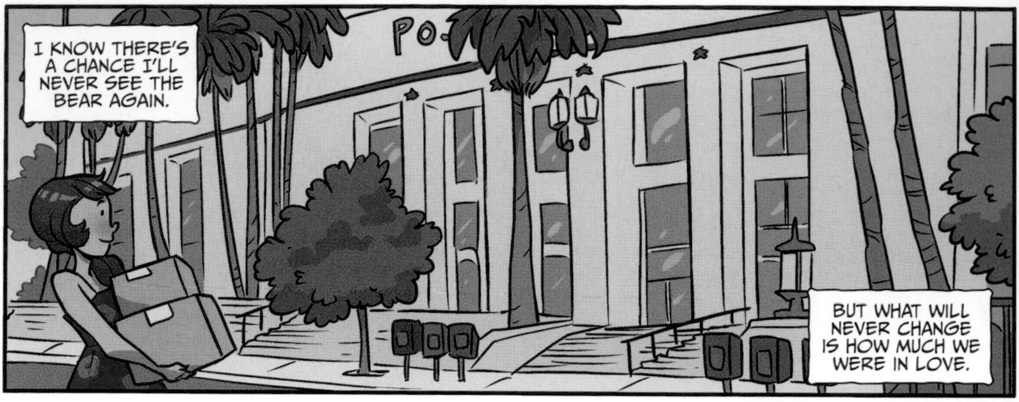
PO
I KNOW THERE'S A CHANCE I'LL NEVER SEE THE BEAR AGAIN.
BUT WHAT WILL NEVER CHANGE IS HOW MUCH WE WERE IN LOVE.

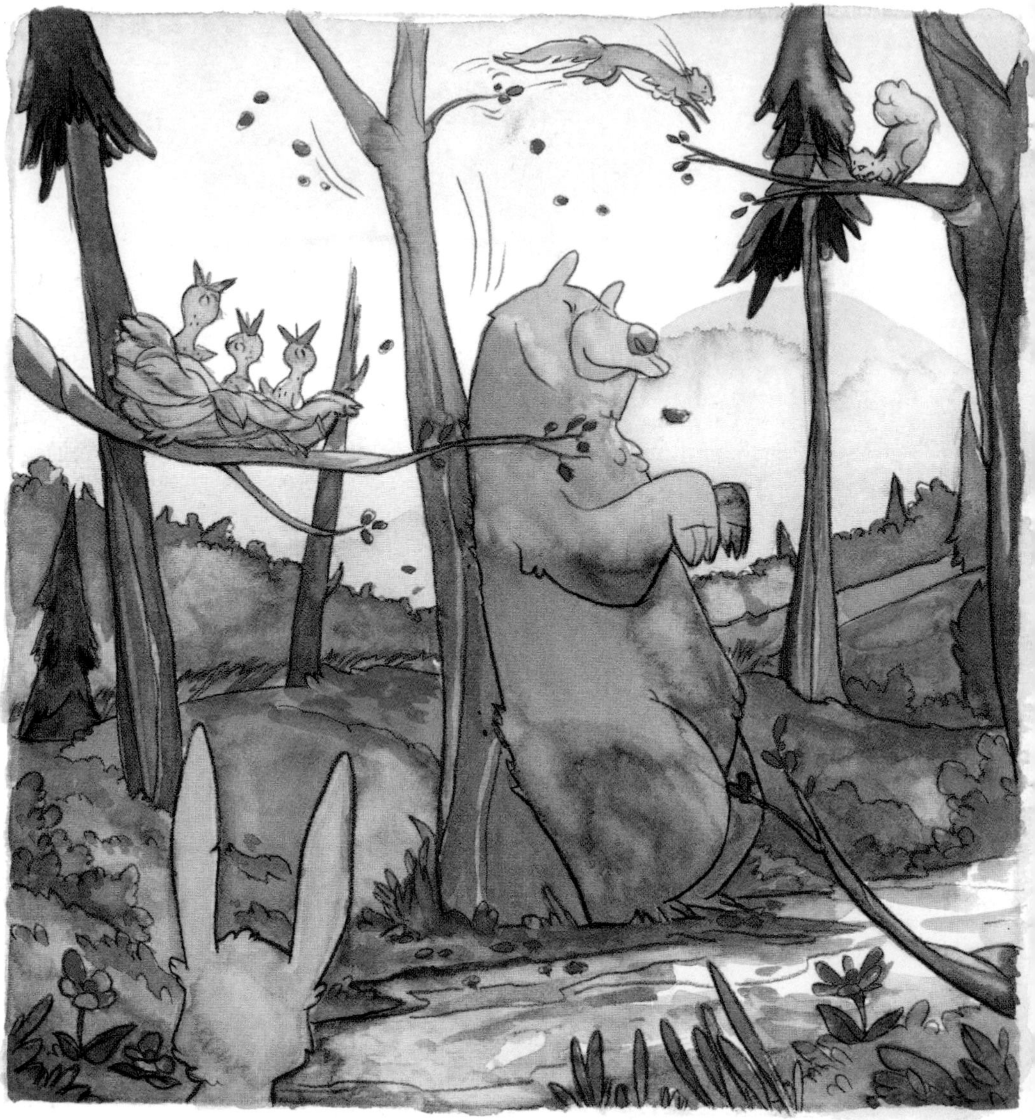

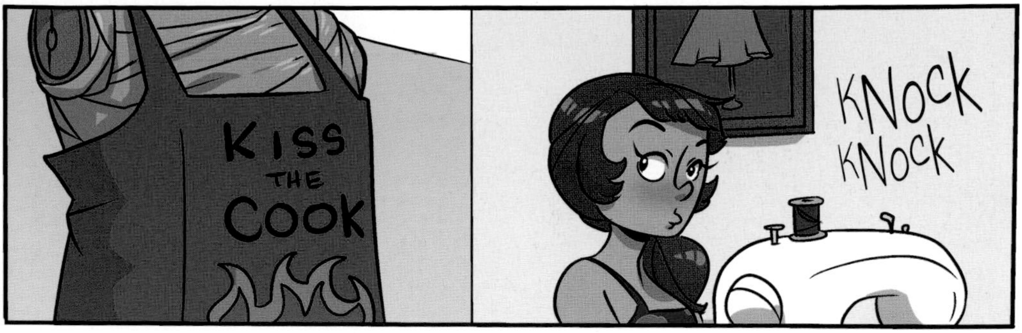
KISS THE COOK
KNOCK KNOCK

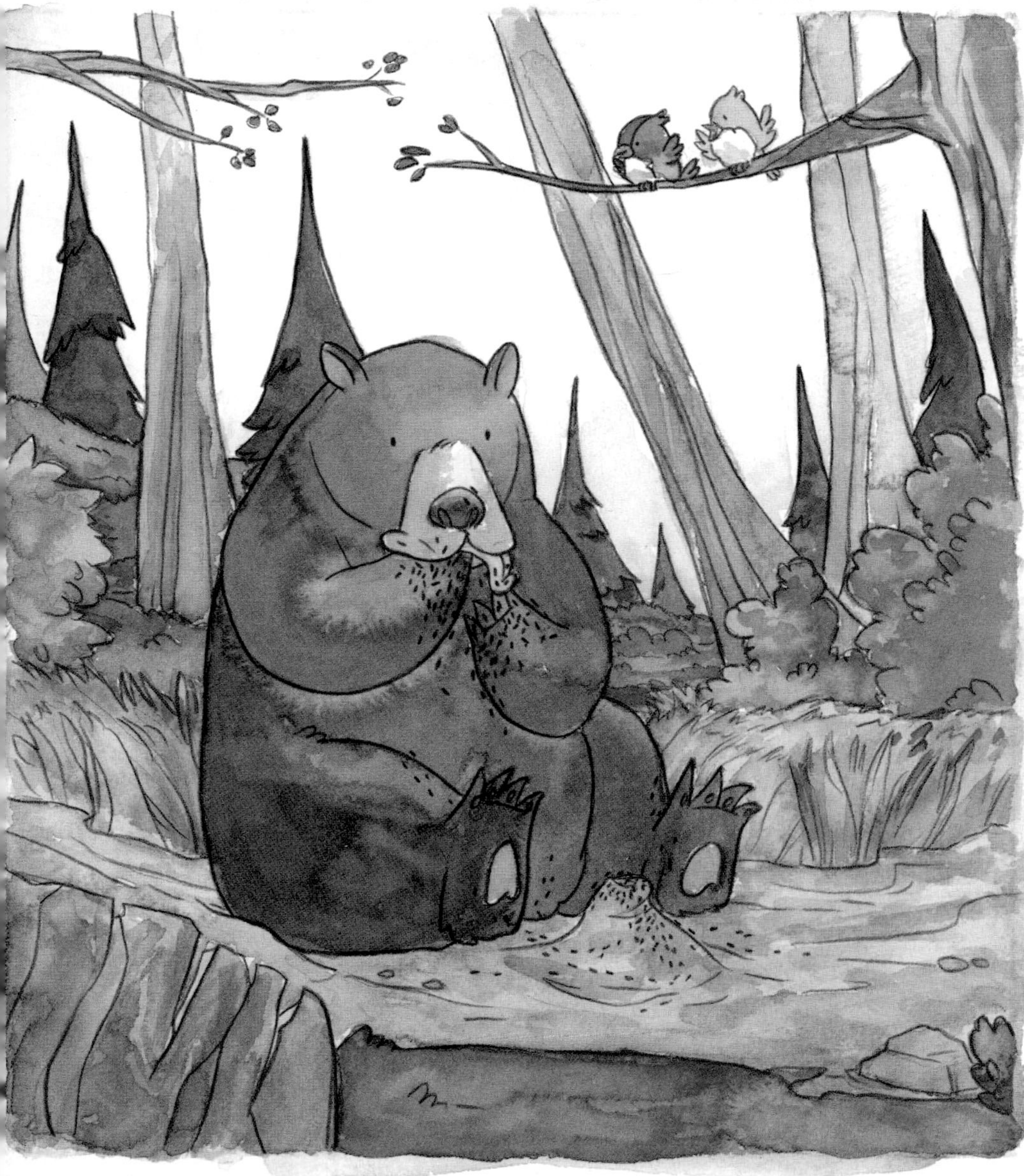

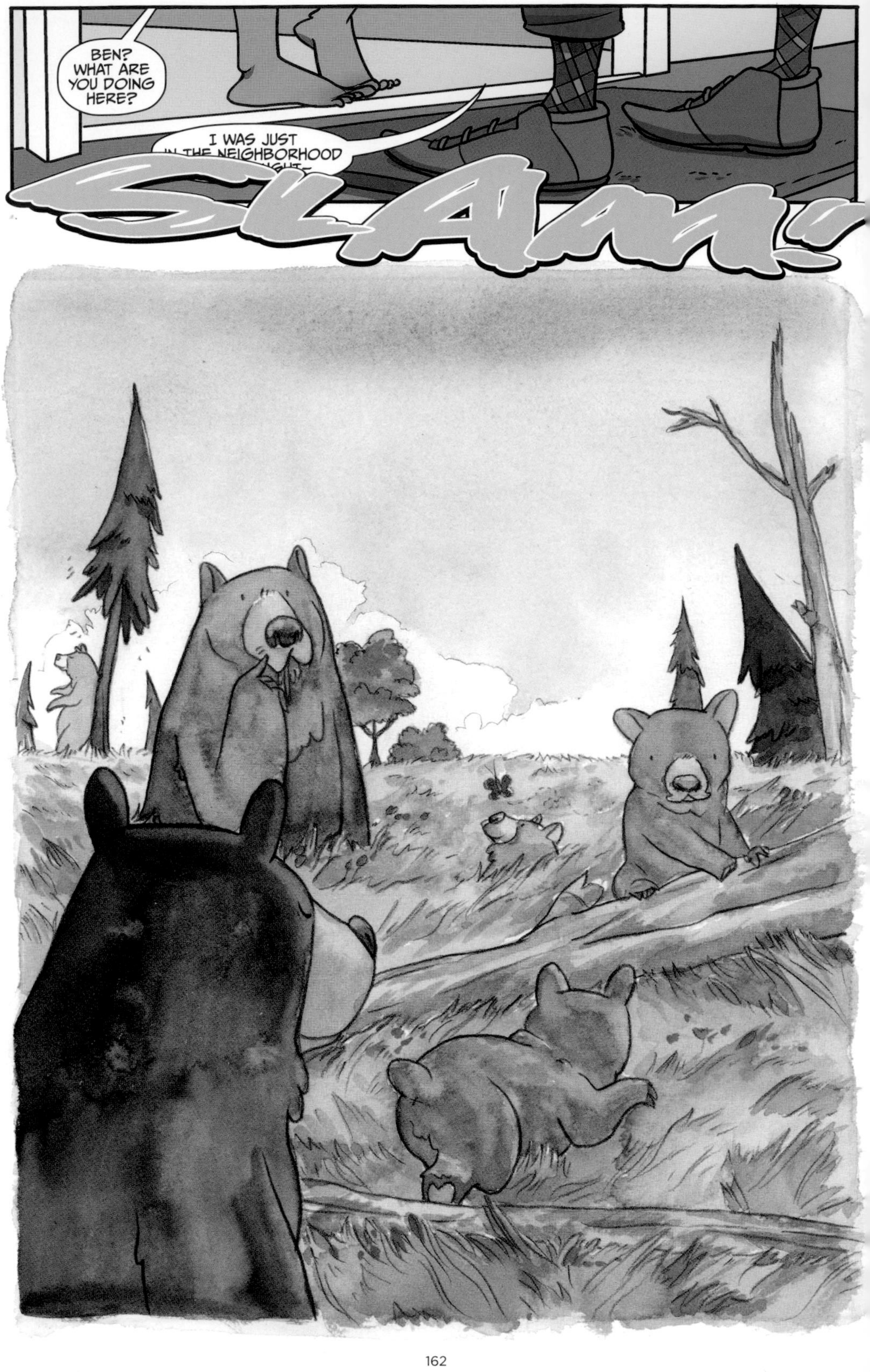

BEN? WHAT ARE YOU DOING HERE?
I WAS JUST IN THE NEIGHBORHOOD
SLAM!!

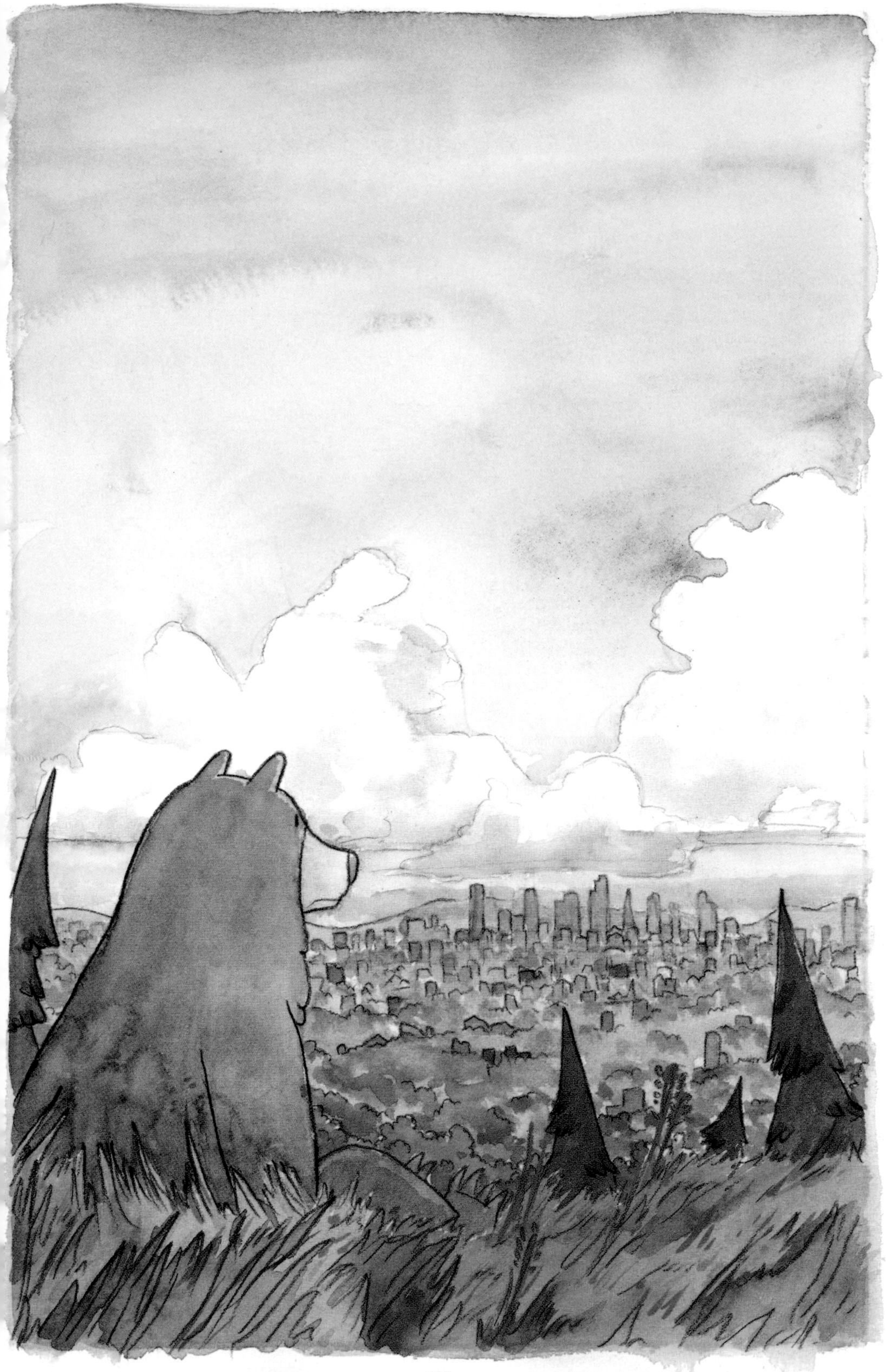

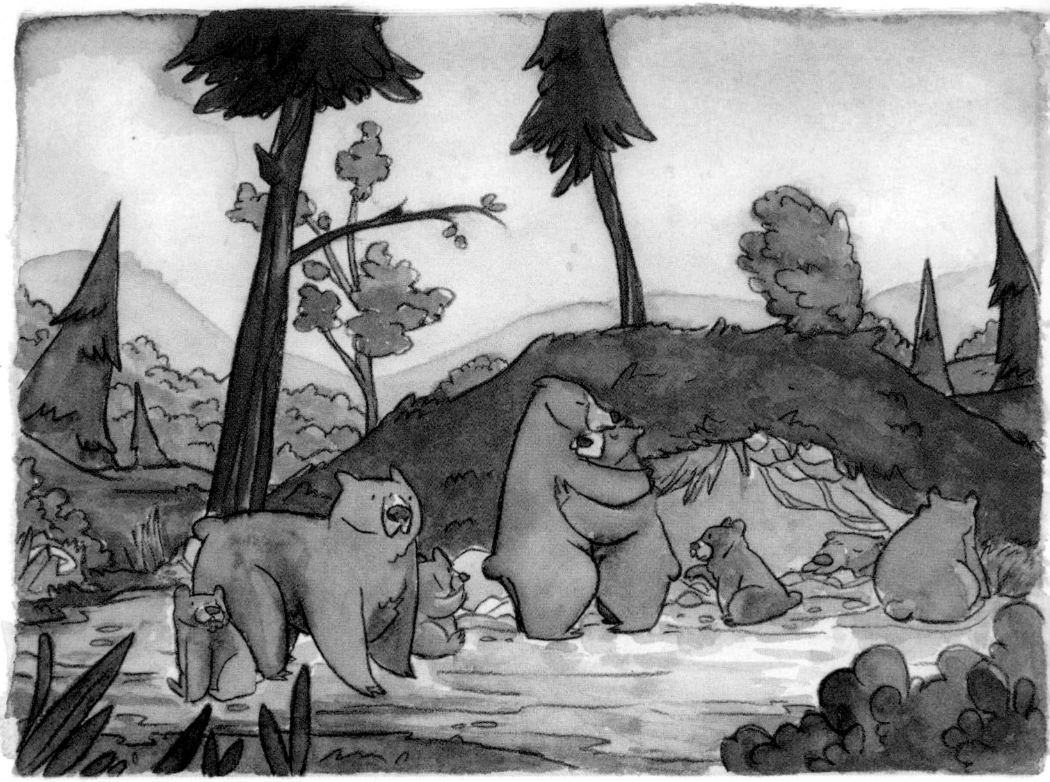

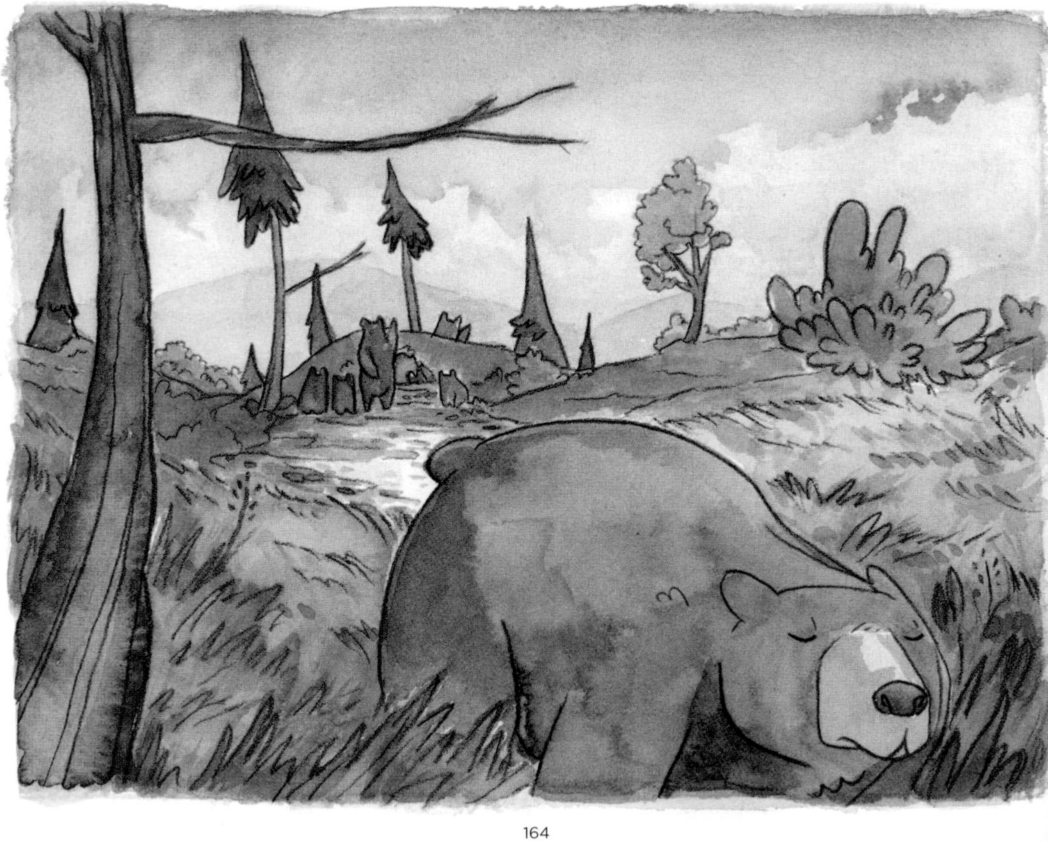

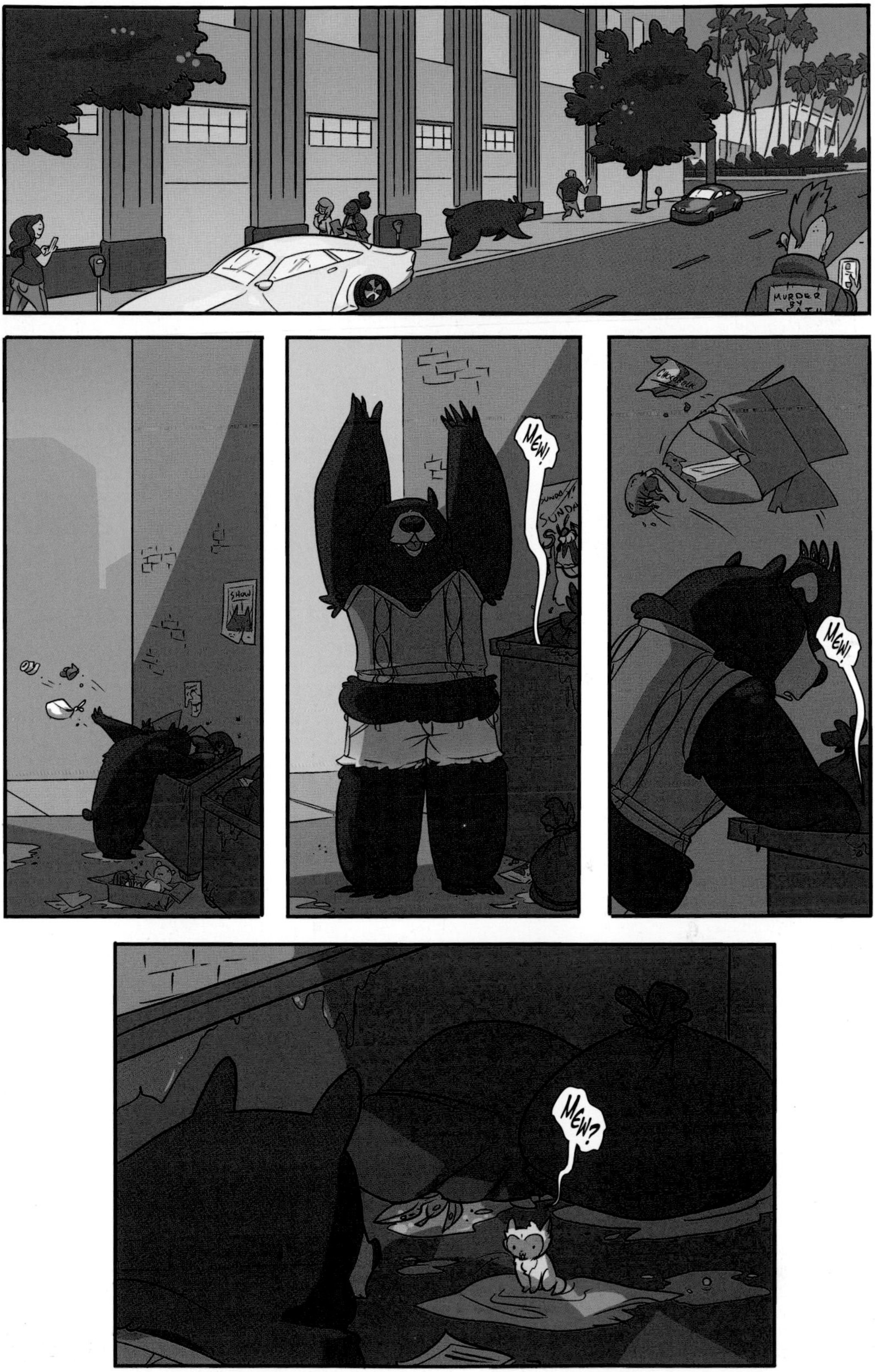
MURDER BY
MEW!
MEW!
MEW?

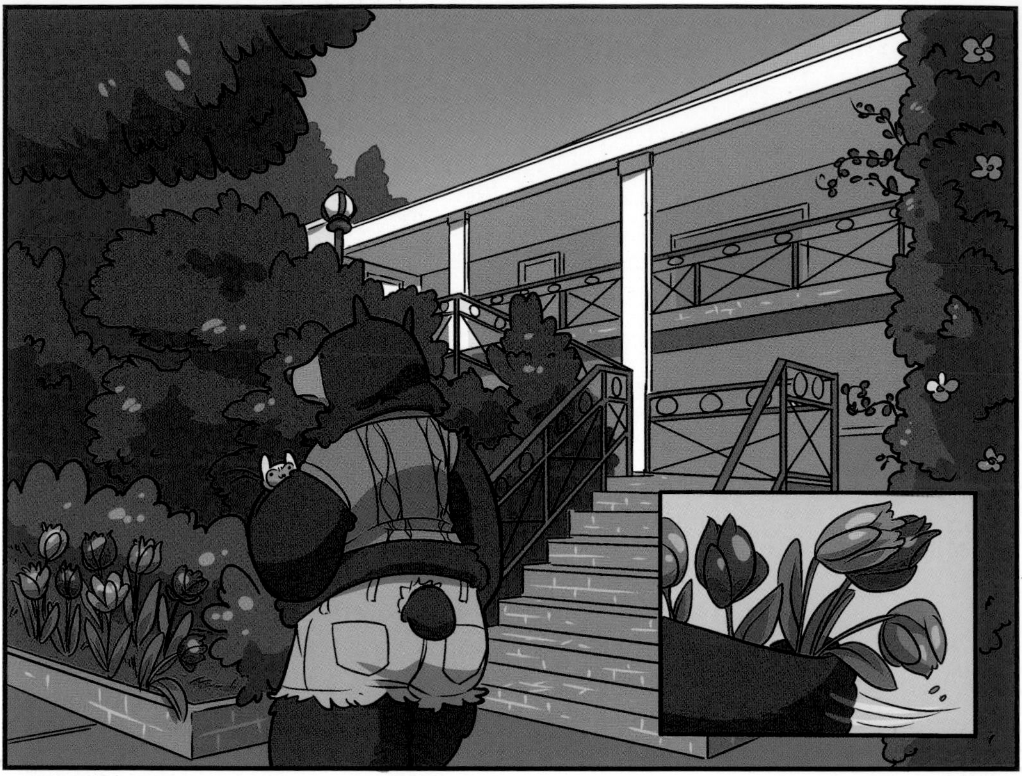

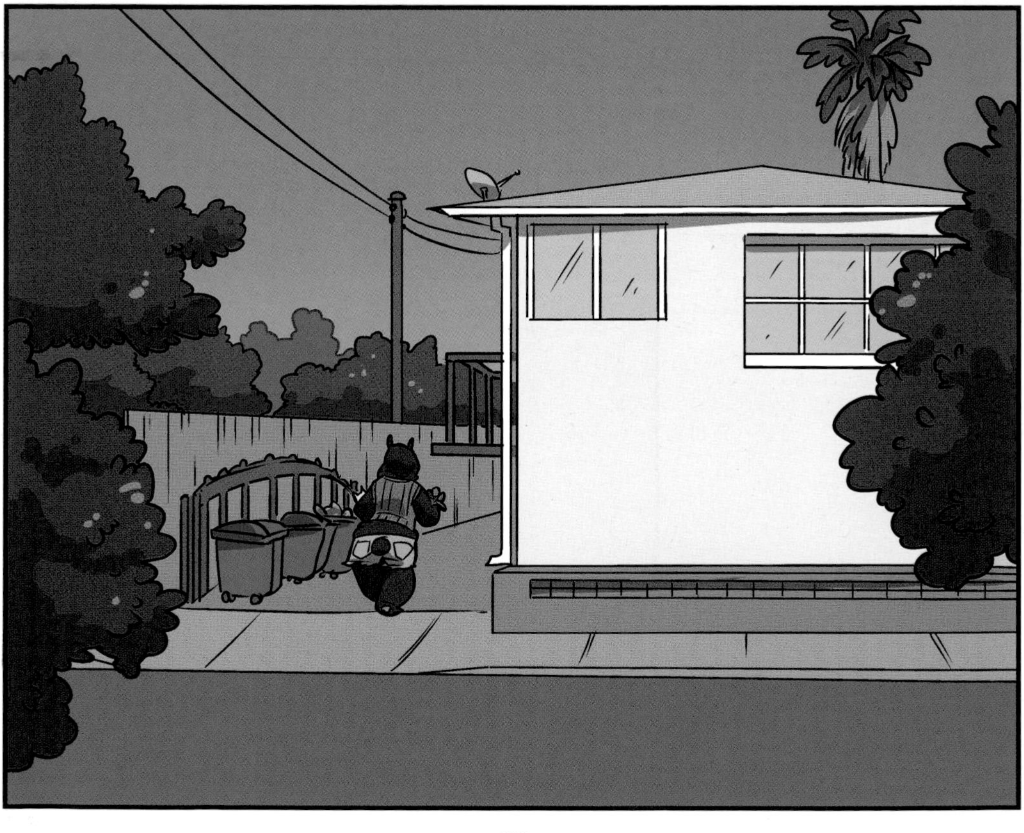

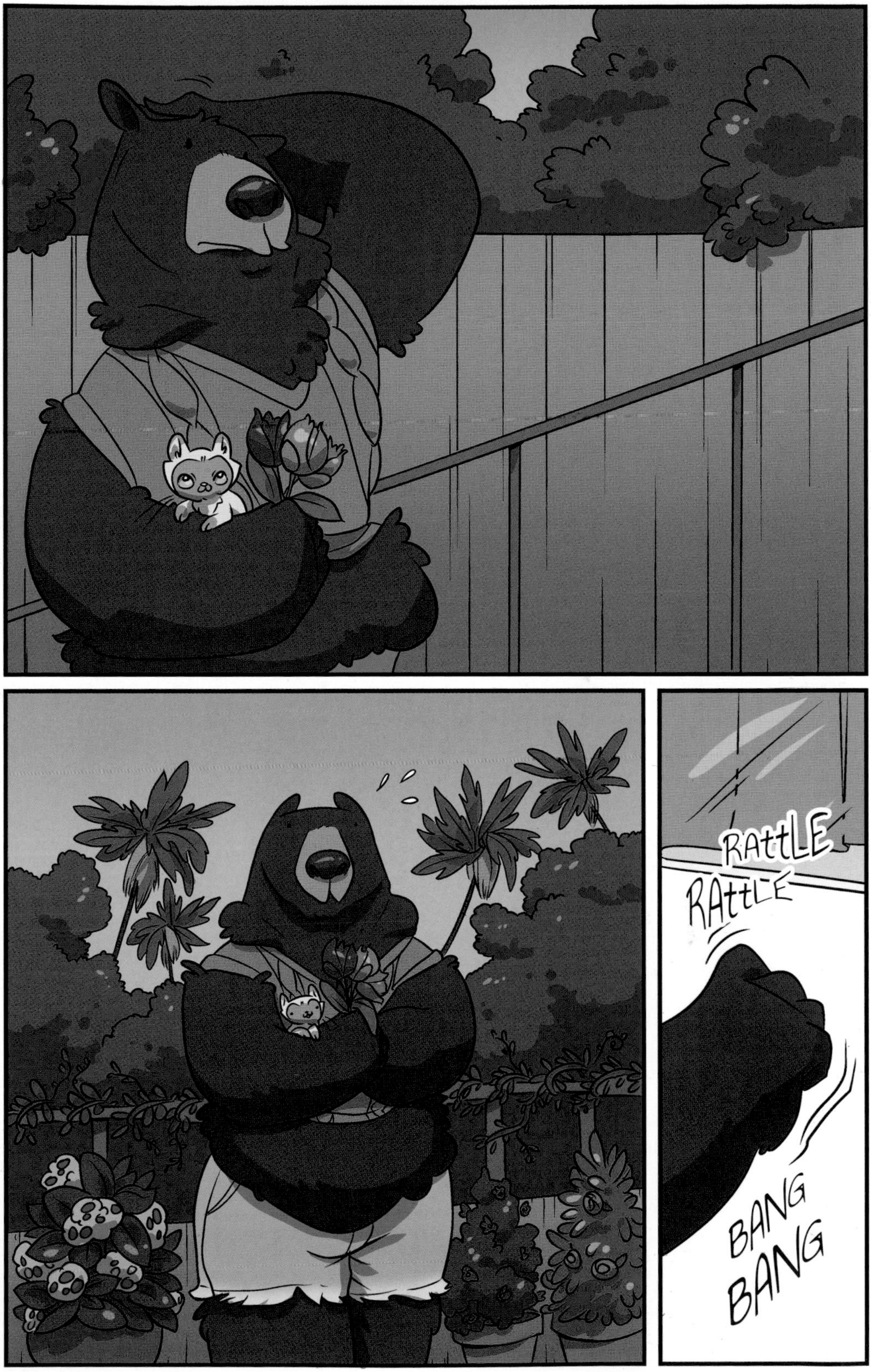
RATTLE
RATTLE
BANG
BANG

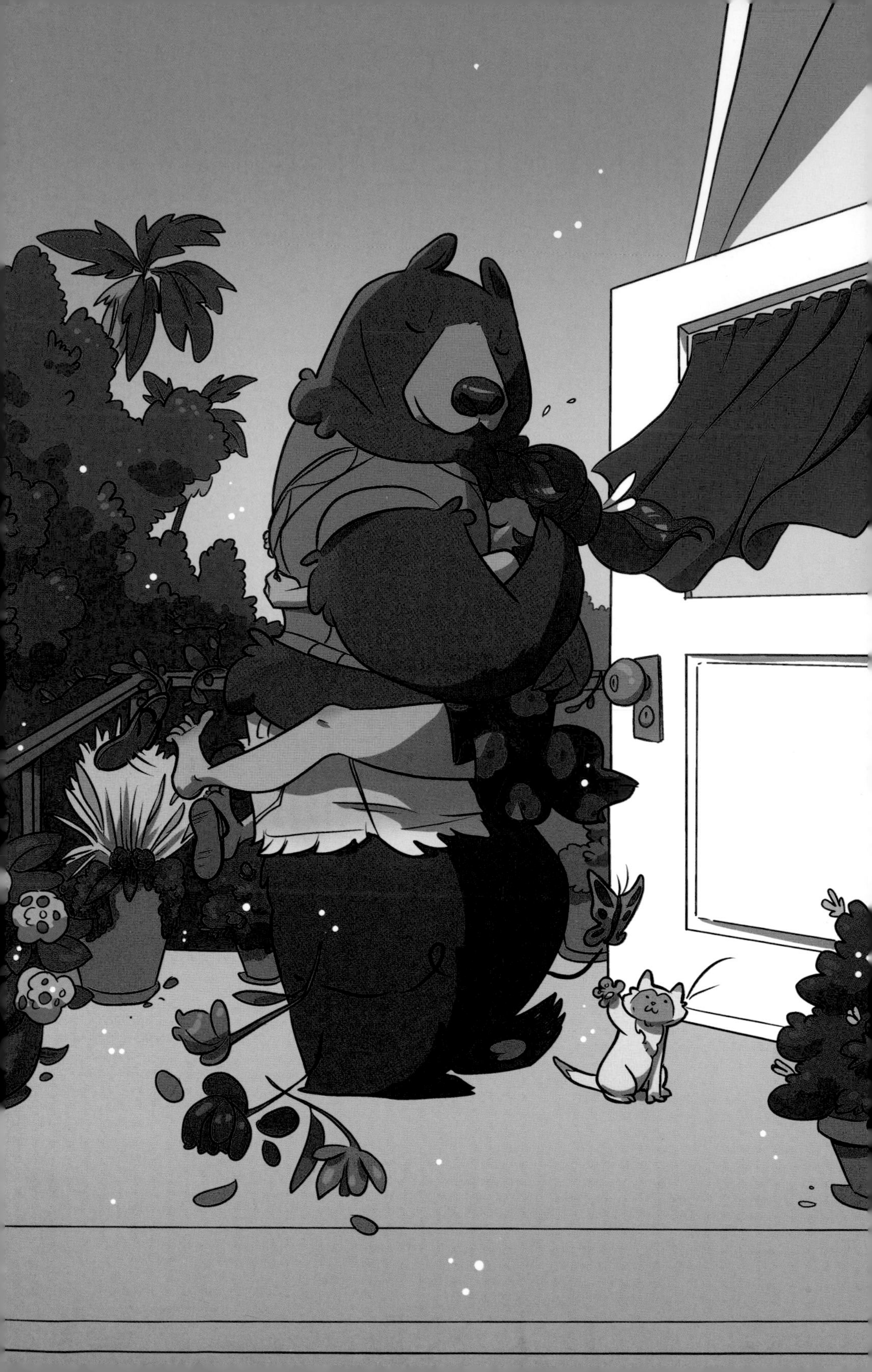

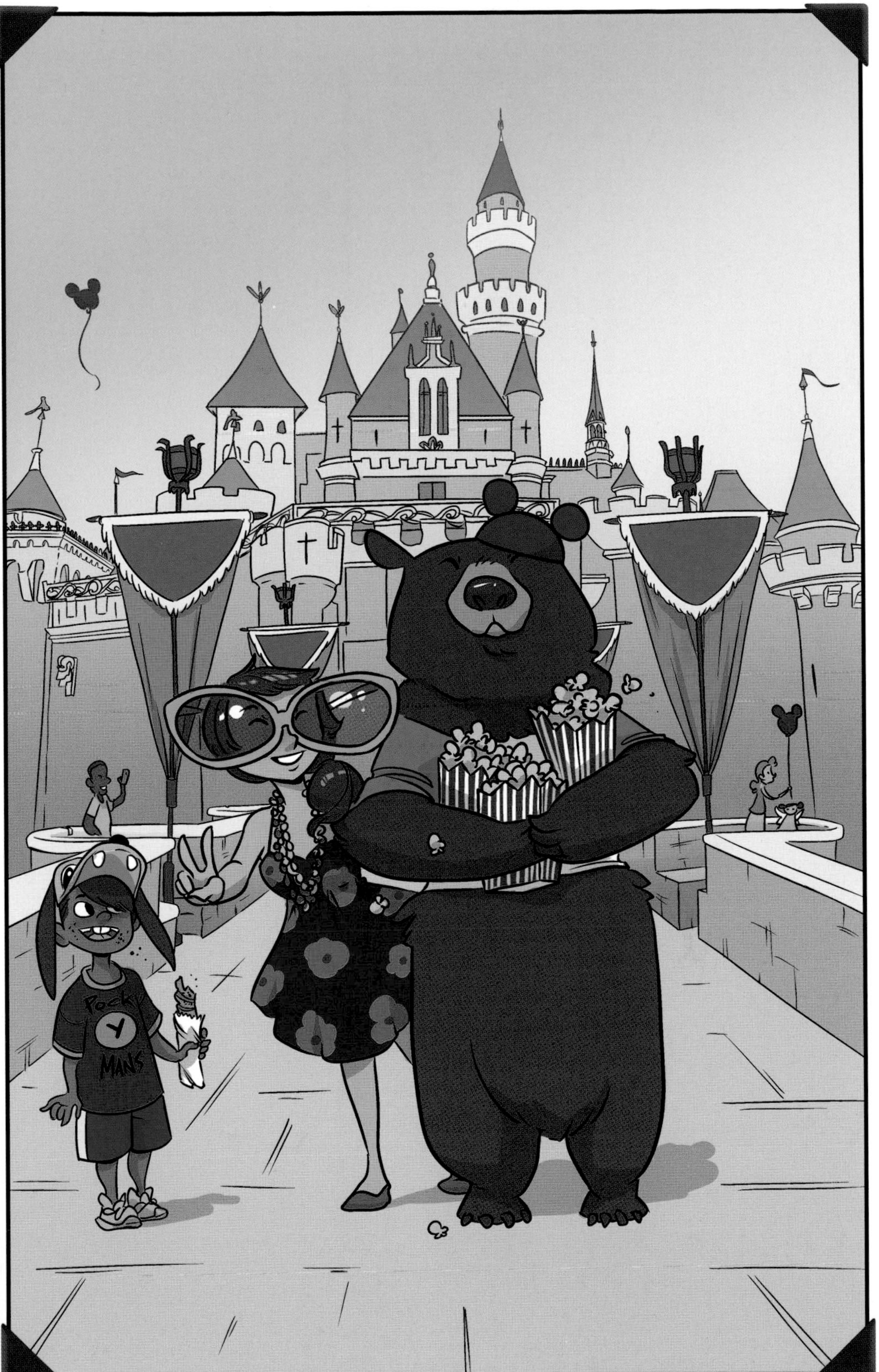
Pock
Y
MANS

Character Sketches

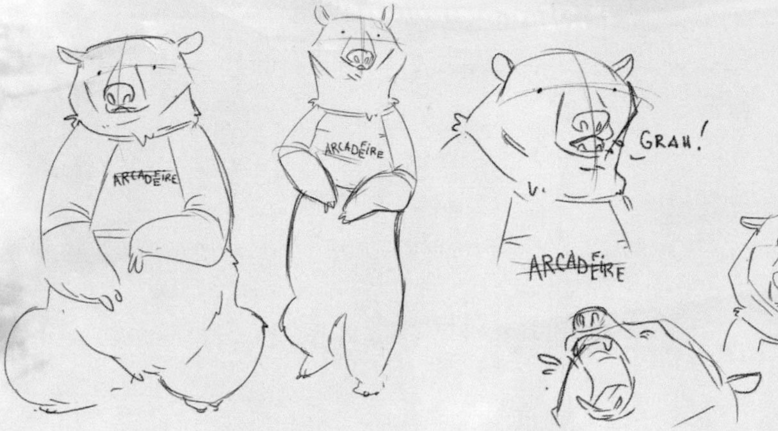

ARCADÉIRE
ARCADÉIRE
GRAH!
ARCADÉIRE
BEAR

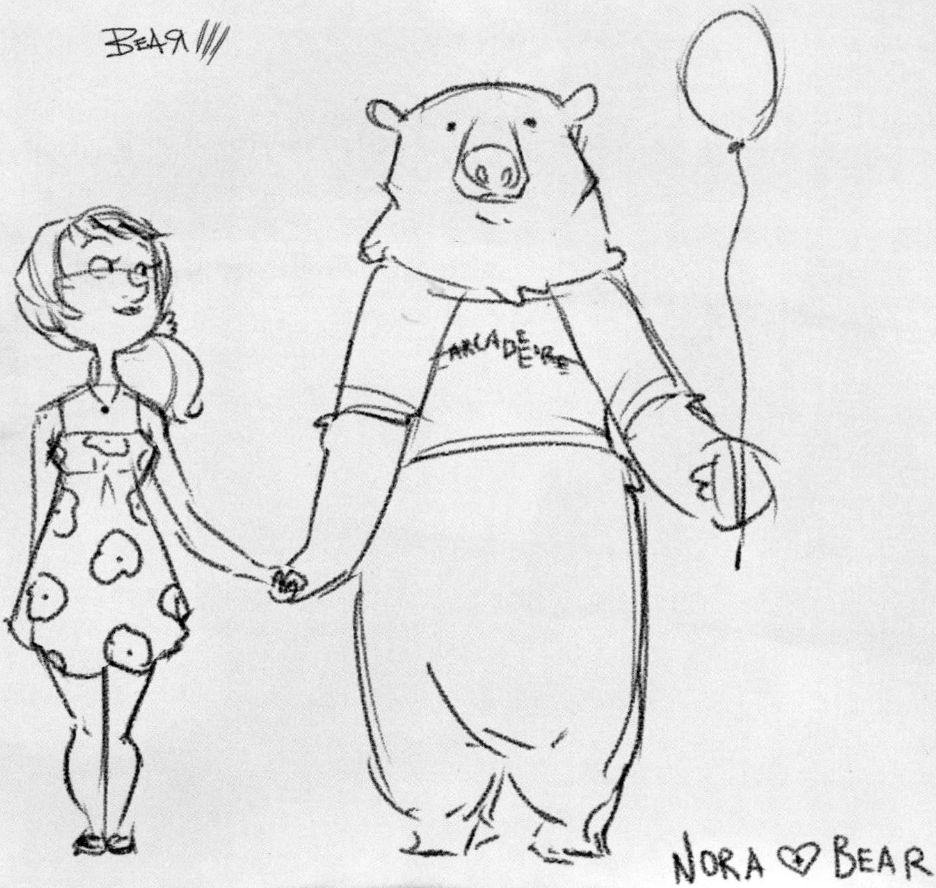

ARCADÉIRE
NORA ♡ BEAR

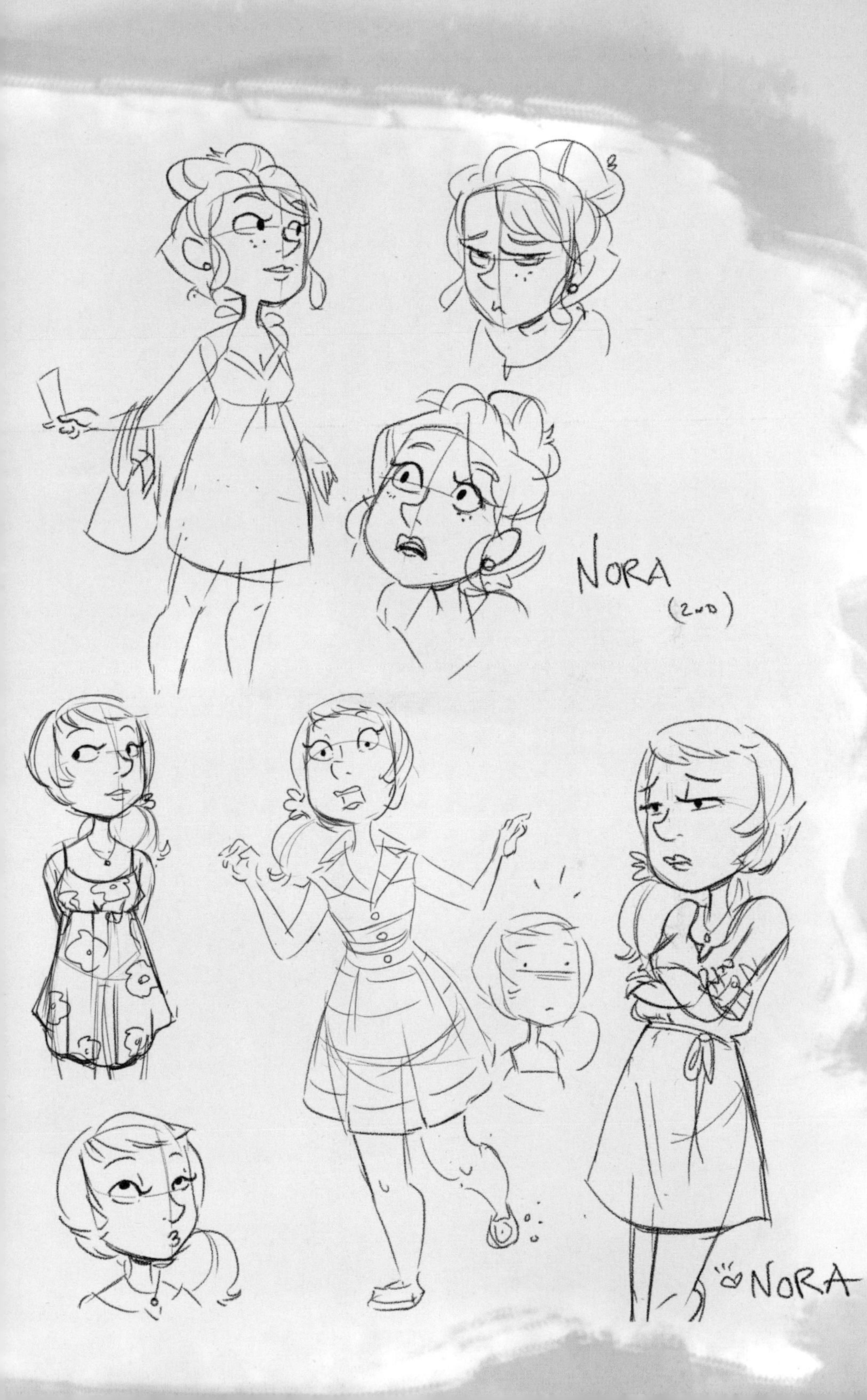
NORA
(2ND)
NORA

Cover Process

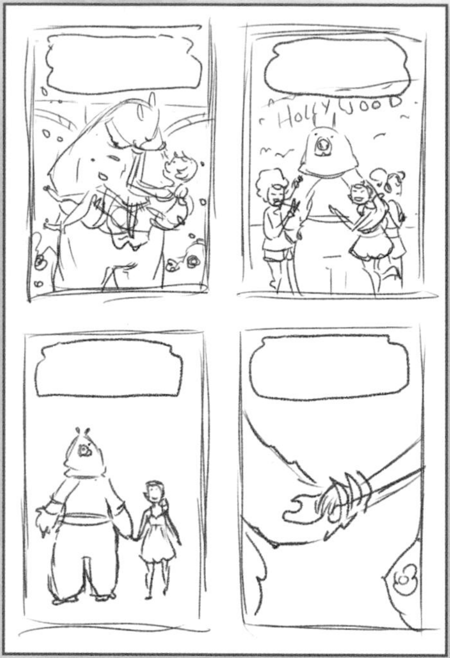
HOLLYWOOD

Thumbnail!

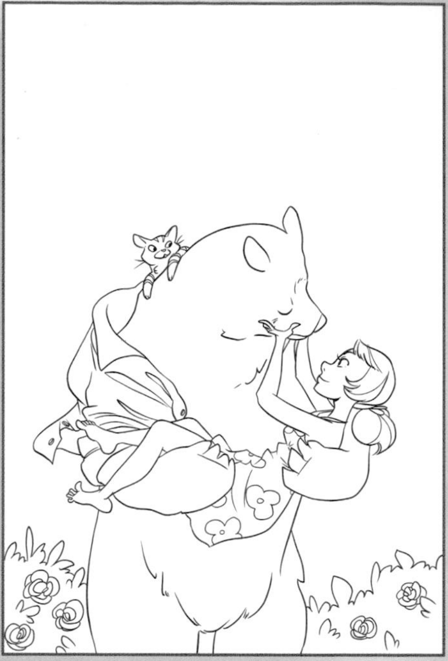

Inks!

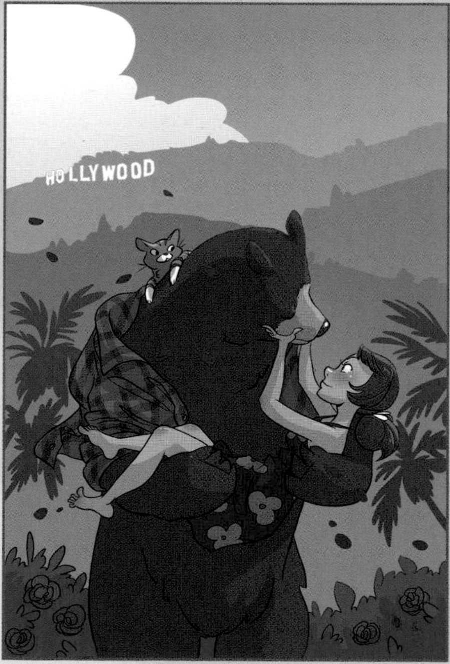
HOLLYWOOD

Colors!

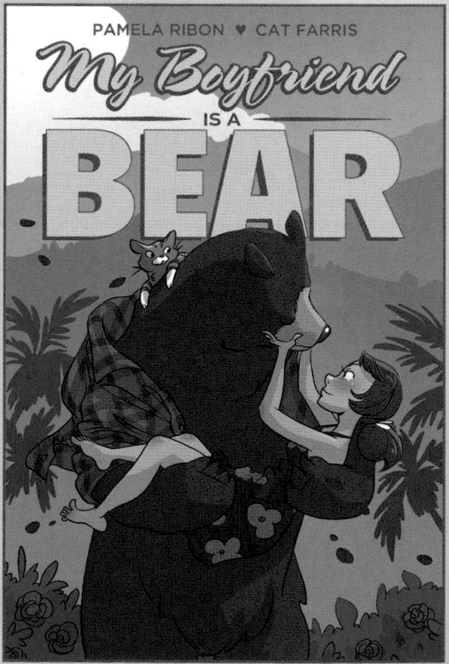
PAMELA RIBON ♥ CAT FARRIS
My Boyfriend
IS A
BEAR

Logo!

Pamela Ribon co-created and currently writes the roller derby comic *SLAM!*, and has penned guest issues of *Rick and Morty*™. Her screenwriting work includes *Moana* and *Ralph Breaks the Internet: Wreck-It Ralph 2*. She's a best-selling author, frequent troublemaker, and true fan of you.

Cat Farris is a native Portlander, an artist, and is pretty sure she's just making this up as she goes along. She is supported in this venture by the world's most beautiful husband, the laziest greyhound, and an all-star cast of Helioscope studiomates.

Saida Temofonte is originally from Italy. She letters comics for DC Comics, Lion Forge, Kymera Press, Oni Press and IDW, and calls Los Angeles her beloved home now.

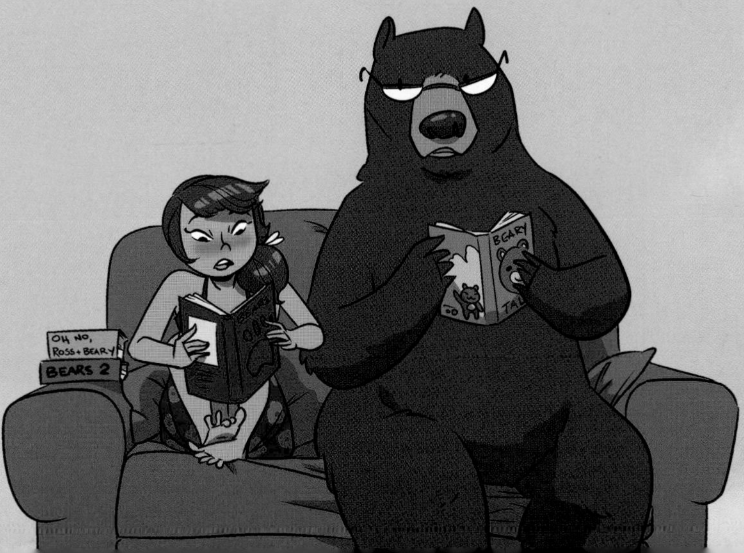
OH NO, ROSS+BEARY
BEARS 2
BEARY

More Oni Press Books you might enjoy...

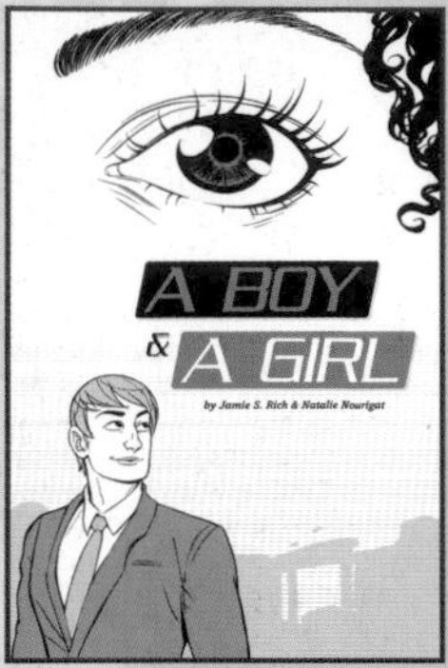
A BOY
& A GIRL
by Jamie S. Rich & Natalie Nourigat

A BOY AND A GIRL
By Jamie S. Rich
& Natalie Nourigat
ISBN 978-1-62010-089-9

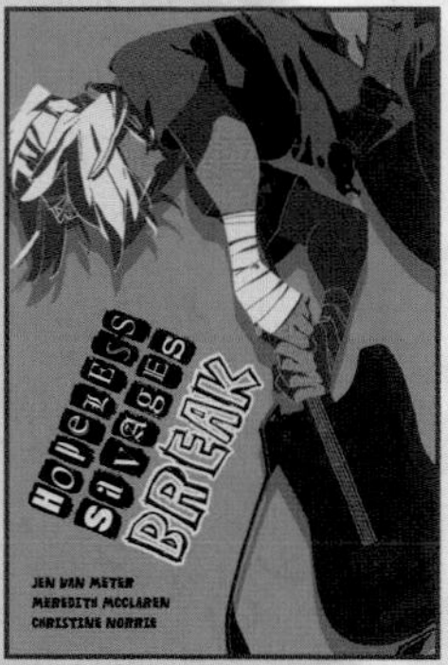
Hopeless Savages BREAK
JEN VAN METER
MEREDITH MCCLAREN
CHRISTINE NORRIE

HOPELESS SAVAGES: BREAK
By Jen Van Meter,
Meredith McClaren,
and Christine Norrie
ISBN 978-1-62010-252-7

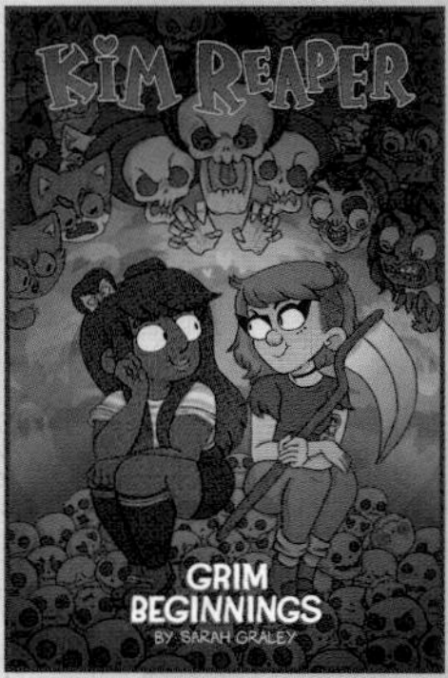
KIM REAPER
GRIM BEGINNINGS
BY SARAH GRALEY

KIM REAPER, VOL. 1: GRIM BEGINNINGS
By Sarah Graley
ISBN 978-1-62010-455-2

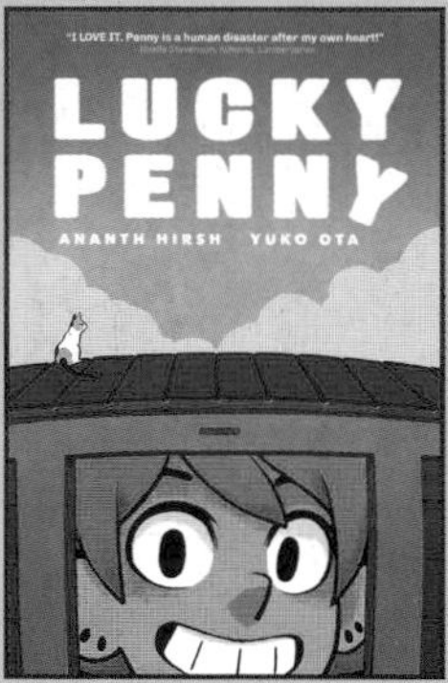
LUCKY PENNY
ANANTH HIRSH YUKO OTA

LUCKY PENNY
By Ananth Hirsh
& Yuko Ota
ISBN 978-1-62010-287-9

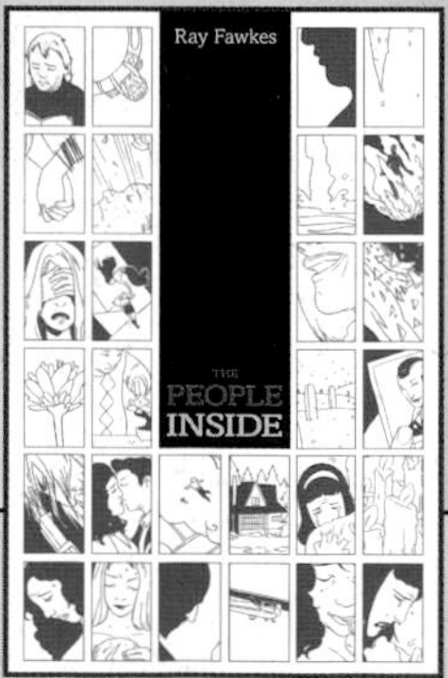
Ray Fawkes
THE PEOPLE INSIDE

THE PEOPLE INSIDE
By Ray Fawkes
ISBN 978-1-62010-168-1

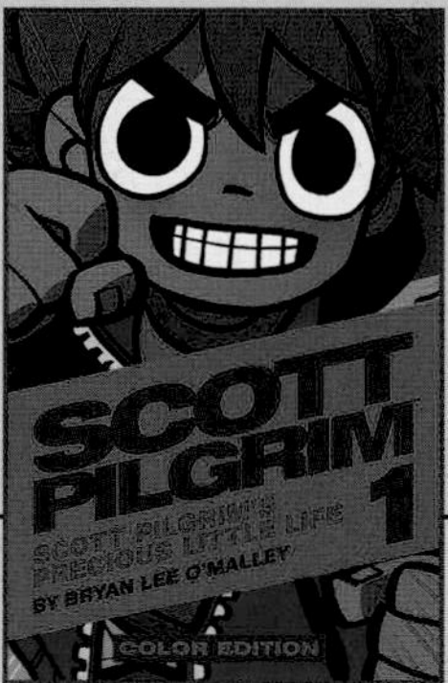
SCOTT PILGRIM 1
SCOTT PILGRIM'S PRECIOUS LITTLE LIFE
BY BRYAN LEE O'MALLEY
COLOR EDITION

SCOTT PILGRIM, VOL. 1: PRECIOUS LITTLE LIFE
By Bryan Lee O'Malley
ISBN 978-1-62010-000-4

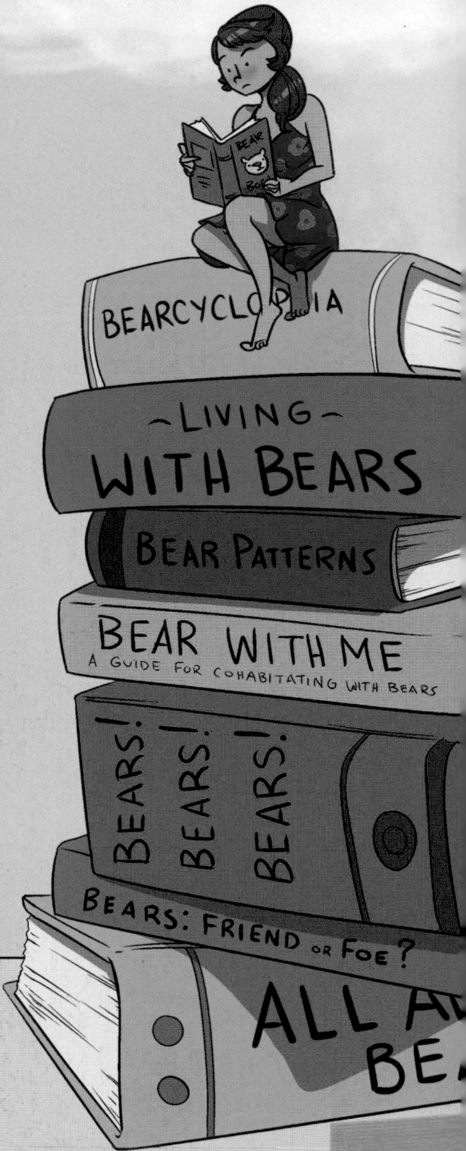
LIVING WITH BEARS
BEAR PATTERNS
BEAR WITH ME
A GUIDE FOR COHABITATING WITH BEARS
BEARS! BEARS! BEARS!
BEARS: FRIEND OR FOE?

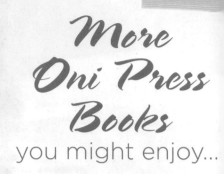